W9-BFR-289

# Private Pilot

## Test Prep

# 2004

**Study and Prepare for the Recreational and Private Airplane, Helicopter, Gyroplane, Glider, Balloon and Airship FAA Knowledge Tests**

- Effective June 2003, with Free Updates available online until June 2004
- All FAA Private and Recreational Questions included
- Organized by subject
- Answers, Explanations, References and additional Study Material included for each chapter
- Includes the official FAA Computerized Testing Supplement
- Plus . . . helpful tips and instructions for the FAA Knowledge Test

**Aviation Supplies & Academics, Inc.**
Newcastle, Washington

*Private Pilot Test Prep*
2004 Edition


Aviation Supplies & Academics, Inc.
7005 132nd Place SE
Newcastle, Washington 98059-3153
425.235.1500
www.asa2fly.com

FAA Questions herein are from United States government sources and contain current information as of: June 9, 2003.

None of the material in this publication supersedes any documents, procedures or regulations issued by the Federal Aviation Administration.

ASA assumes no responsibility for any errors or omissions. Neither is any liability assumed for damages resulting from the use of the information contained herein.

**Important:** This Test Prep should be sold with and used in conjunction with *Computerized Testing Supplement for Recreational Pilot and Private Pilot* (FAA-CT-8080-2D).

ASA reprints the FAA test figures and legends contained within this government document, and it is also sold separately and available from aviation retailers nationwide. Order #ASA-CT-8080-2D.


**ASA-TP-P-04**
ISBN 1-56027-489-1


Printed in the United States of America

04   03        5   4   3   2   1

## About the Contributors

### Charles L. Robertson
Assistant Professor, UND Aerospace
University of North Dakota

Charles Robertson as flight instructor, assistant professor and manager of training at UND Aerospace, contributes a vital and substantial combination of pilot and educator to ASA's reviewing team. After graduating with education degrees from Florida State University in 1967, and Ball State University in 1975, he began his twenty-year career in the United States Air Force as Chief of avionics branch, 58th Military Airlift Squadron, and went on to flight instruction, training for aircraft systems, and airport managing, while gaining many thousands of hours flying international passenger and cargo, aerial refueling and airlift missions. As Division Chief in 1988, Robertson directed the USAF Strategic Air Command's "Alpha Alert Force" and coordinated its daily flight training operations. He holds the CFI Airplane Land, Multi-Engine, Single-Engine and Instrument, the ATP Airplane Land and Multi-Engine, Commercial Pilot, Advanced and Instrument Ground Instructor licenses.

### Jackie Spanitz
Director of Curriculum Development
Aviation Supplies & Academics, Inc.

Jackie Spanitz earned a bachelor of science (B.S.) degree with Western Michigan University (WMU), in Aviation Technology and Operations—Pilot option. She completed her masters program with Embry-Riddle Aeronautical University, earning her degree in Aeronautical Science, specializing in Management. As Director of Curriculum Development for ASA, Jackie oversees new and existing product development, ranging from textbooks and flight computers to flight simulation software products, and integration of these products into new and existing curricula. She also provides technical support, research for product development, and project management. Jackie Spanitz holds the CFI Airplane, Land, Single-Engine and Instrument, Commercial Airplane, Land, Single-Engine, Multi-Engine and Instrument, and Advanced and Instrument Ground Instructor certificates; she is the author of *Guide to the Biennial Flight Review*, *Private Pilot Syllabus*, *Instrument Rating Syllabus*, and *Commercial Pilot Syllabus*, and is the technical editor for ASA's Test Prep series.

**About ASA:** Aviation Supplies & Academics, Inc. (ASA) is an industry leader in the development and sale of aviation supplies and publications for pilots, flight instructors, flight engineers, and aviation maintenance technicians. We manufacture and publish more than 200 products for the aviation industry. Aviators are invited to call 1-800-ASA-2-FLY for a free copy of our catalog. Visit ASA on the web: **www.asa2fly.com**

# Contents

# Preface

**W**elcome to ASA's Test Prep Series. ASA's test books have been helping pilots prepare for the FAA Knowledge Tests since 1984 with great success. We are confident that with proper use of this book, you will score very well on any of the private and recreational pilot certificate tests.

All of the questions in the FAA Private and Recreational Pilot test question bank are included here, and have been arranged into chapters based on subject matter. Topical study, in which similar material is covered under a common subject heading, promotes better understanding, aids recall, and thus provides a more efficient study guide. We suggest you begin by reading the book cover-to-cover. Then go back to the beginning and place emphasis on those questions most likely to be included in your test (identified by the aircraft category above each question). For example, a pilot preparing for the Private Airplane test would focus on the questions marked "ALL" and "AIR," and a pilot preparing for the Private Helicopter test would focus on the questions marked "ALL" and "RTC."

It is important to answer every question assigned on your FAA Knowledge Test. If in their ongoing review, the FAA authors decide a question has no correct answer, is no longer applicable, or is otherwise defective, your answer will be marked correct no matter which one you chose. However, you will not be given the automatic credit unless you have marked an answer. Unlike some other exams you may have taken, there is no penalty for "guessing" in this instance.

The FAA does not supply the correct answers to questions reproduced in this book, is not responsible for answers contained herein, and will not reveal what they consider the correct answers to be. The question and answer choices are duplicated from the FAA Question Bank; however, the FAA presents the questions in a different numerical sequence, they change the sequence of the A, B, C answer choices on the FAA website (http://afs600.faa.gov/Default.htm), and they include only samples of typical questions. They do this to discourage applicants from learning the test material by rote memory. The ASA test preps include a much wider sampling of the questions the FAA will issue at the test centers. A clear explanation is given directly below each question. Be careful to fully understand the intent of each question and corresponding answer while studying, rather than memorize the A, B, C answer. If your study leads you to question an answer choice, we recommend you seek the assistance of a local ground or flight instructor. If you still believe the answer needs review, please forward your questions, recommendations, or concerns to:

**Aviation Supplies & Academics, Inc.**

7005 132nd Place SE
Newcastle, WA 98059-3153

Voice 425.235.1500
Fax 425.235.0128
www.asa2fly.com

*Technical Editor:*
Jackie Spanitz, ASA

*Editor:*
Jennie Trerise, ASA

*Production Editor:*
Cynthia Wyckoff, ASA

# Update Information

## Free Test Updates for the One-Year Lifecycle of Test Prep Books

The FAA releases a new test database each spring, and makes amendments to this database approximately twice a year. However, a small number of questions may be withheld from the public for a period of time while the FAA gathers statistics and validates these questions. This means not all the questions are available to the public via the internet-posted databases, but they are being issued at the FAA testing centers. ASA combines years of experience with expertise in working with the tests to prepare the most comprehensive and accurate test preparation materials available in the industry.

You can feel confident that you will be prepared for your FAA Knowledge Exam by using the ASA test prep products. ASA publishes test books each July and stays abreast of all changes to the tests, as well as the new questions that have been validated, and posts these changes on the ASA website as a Test Update. Visit the ASA website before taking your test to be certain you have all the current information:

**www.asa2fly.com**

# Description of the Tests

All test questions are the objective, multiple-choice type, with three choices of answers. Each question can be answered by the selection of a single response. Each test question is independent of other questions, that is, a correct response to one does not depend upon or influence the correct response to another.

As stated in 14 CFR §61.63, an applicant need not take an additional knowledge test provided the applicant holds an airplane, rotorcraft, powered-lift, or airship rating at that pilot certificate level. For example, an applicant transitioning from gliders to airplanes or helicopters **will** need to take the test. An applicant transitioning from airplanes to gliders, or airplanes to helicopters, **will not** be required to take the test.

| Test Code | Test Name | Test Prep Study | Number of Questions | Min. Age | Allotted Time (hrs) |
|---|---|---|---|---|---|
| RPA | Recreational Pilot—Airplane | ALL, AIR, REC | 50 | 15 | 2.0 |
| RPH | Recreational Pilot—Helicopter | ALL, RTC, REC | 50 | 15 | 2.0 |
| RPG | Recreational Pilot—Gyroplane | ALL, RTC, REC | 50 | 15 | 2.0 |
| PAR | Private Pilot—Airplane | ALL, AIR | 60 | 15 | 2.5 |
| PRH | Private Pilot—Helicopter | ALL, RTC | 60 | 15 | 2.5 |
| PRG | Private Pilot—Gyroplane | ALL, RTC | 60 | 15 | 2.5 |
| PGL | Private Pilot—Glider | ALL, GLI | 60 | 14 | 2.5 |
| PBH | Private Pilot—Balloon–Hot Air | ALL, LTA | 60 | 14 | 2.5 |
| PBG | Private Pilot—Balloon–Gas | ALL, LTA | 60 | 14 | 2.5 |
| PLA | Private Pilot—Airship | ALL, LTA | 60 | 15 | 2.5 |
| PAT | Private Pilot Airplane/ Recreational Pilot—Transition | ALL, AIR | 30 | 15 | 1.5 |
| PGT | Private Pilot Gyroplane/ Recreational Pilot—Transition | ALL, RTC | 30 | 15 | 1.5 |
| PHT | Private Pilot Helicopter/ Recreational Pilot—Transition | ALL, RTC | 30 | 15 | 1.5 |

**A score of 70 percent must be attained to successfully pass each test.**

*Continued*

# Acceptable Forms of Authorization

1. Certificate of graduation or a statement of accomplishment certifying the satisfactory completion of the ground school portion of a course for the certificate or rating sought. The certificate or statement may be issued by a Federal Aviation Administration certified pilot school or an agency such as a high school, college, adult education program, Civil Air Patrol or Reserve Officers Training Corp (ROTC) flight training school.
2. Written statement or logbook endorsement from an authorized ground or flight instructor certifying that the applicant completed an applicable ground training or home study course and is prepared for the knowledge test.
3. Failed, passing or expired Airman Knowledge Test Report, provided the applicant still has the *original* test report in his/her possession. (*See* Retesting explanation.)

# Retesting Procedures

Applicants retesting *after failure* are required to submit the applicable score report indicating failure, along with an endorsement from an authorized instructor who gave the applicant the additional training, and certifying the applicant is competent to pass the test. The original failed test report presented as authorization shall be retained by the proctor and attached to the applicable sign-in/out log. The latest test taken will reflect the official score.

Applicants retesting *in an attempt to achieve a higher passing score* may retake the same test for a better grade after 30 days. The latest test taken will reflect the official score. Applicants are required to submit the *original* applicable score report indicating previous passing score to the testing center prior to testing. Testing center personnel must collect and destroy this report prior to issuing the new test report.

# Process for Taking a Knowledge Test

The Federal Aviation Administration (FAA) has available hundreds of computer testing centers worldwide. These testing centers offer the full range of airman knowledge tests including military competence, instrument foreign pilot, and pilot examiner predesignated tests. Refer to the list of computer testing designees (CTDs) at the end of this section.

The first step in taking a knowledge test is the registration process. You may either call the testing centers' 1-800 numbers or simply take the test on a walk-in basis. If you choose to use the 1-800 number to register, you will need to select a testing center, schedule a test date, and make financial arrangements for test payment. You may register for tests several weeks in advance, and you may cancel your appointment according to the CTD's cancellation policy. If you do not follow the CTD's cancellation policies, you could be subject to a cancellation fee.

The next step in taking a knowledge test is providing proper identification. You should determine what knowledge test prerequisites are necessary before going to the computer testing center. Your instructor or local Flight Standards District Office (FSDO) can assist you with what documentation to take to the testing facility. Testing center personnel will not begin the test until your identification is verified. A limited number of tests do not require authorization. Acceptable forms of authorization are:

• A certificate of graduation or a statement of accomplishment certifying the satisfactory completion of the ground school portion of a course from an FAA-certificated pilot school.

• A certificate of graduation or a statement of accomplishment certifying the satisfactory completion of the ground school portion of a course from an agency such as a high school, college, adult education program, U.S. Armed Force, ROTC Flight Training School, or Civil Air Patrol.

- A written statement or logbook endorsement from an authorized instructor certifying that you have accomplished a ground training or home study course required for the rating sought and you are prepared for the knowledge test.
- Failed Airman Test Report, passing Airman Test Report, or expired Airman Test Report (pass or fail), provided that you still have the original Airman Test Report in your possession.

Before you take the actual test, you will have the option to take a sample test. The actual test is time limited; however, you should have sufficient time to complete and review your test.

Upon completion of the knowledge test, you will receive your Airman Test Report, with the testing center's embossed seal, which reflects your score.

The Airman Test Report lists the subject matter knowledge codes for questions answered incorrectly. The total number of subject matter knowledge codes shown on the Airman Test Report is not necessarily an indication of the total number of questions answered incorrectly. Study these knowledge areas to improve your understanding of the subject matter. See the *Subject Matter Knowledge Code/Question Number Cross-Reference* in the back of this book for a complete list of which questions apply to each subject matter knowledge code.

Your instructor is required to provide instruction on each of the knowledge areas listed on your Airman Test Report and to complete an endorsement of this instruction. The Airman Test Report must be presented to the examiner prior to taking the practical test. During the oral portion of the practical test, the examiner is required to evaluate the noted areas of deficiency.

Should you require a duplicate Airman Test Report due to loss or destruction of the original, send a signed request accompanied by a check or money order for $1 payable to the FAA. Your request should be sent to the Federal Aviation Administration, Airmen Certification Branch, AFS-760, P.O. Box 25082, Oklahoma City, OK 73125.

## Computer Testing Designees

The following is a list of the computer testing designees authorized to give FAA knowledge tests. This list should be helpful in case you choose to register for a test or simply want more information. The latest listing of computer testing center locations may be obtained through the FAA website: http://afs600.faa.gov/Default.htm, then select AFS630, Airman Testing Standards, Computer Testing Sites.

### Computer Assisted Testing Service (CATS)

1849 Old Bayshore Highway
Burlingame, CA 94010
Applicant inquiry and test registration: 1-800-947-4228
From outside the U.S.: (650) 259-8550

### LaserGrade Computer Testing

16209 S.E. McGillivray, Suite L
Vancouver, WA 98683
Applicant inquiry and test registration: 1-800-211-2753 or 1-800-211-2754
From outside the U.S.: (360) 896-9111

International pilots who want to apply for an FAA certificate based on their ICAO foreign certificates should go to the nearest FAA Flight Standards District Office (FSDO). Phone numbers for these offices will be found in the blue pages of the local telephone book. This will allow you to fly a U.S.-registered aircraft while in the U.S. If you hold instrument privileges on your foreign license, you can take a 50-question knowledge test (Instrument Rating—Foreign Pilot), and if you pass it, have instrument privileges added to this FAA private pilot certificate.

If you are outside of the U.S., you will have to go in person to an FAA International Field Office (IFO) and apply for an FAA private pilot certificate. When outside of the U.S. you will only be authorized to fly a U.S.-registered aircraft.

### International Field Offices (IFO)

1. Brussels, Belgium (32-2) 508.2721
   FAA C/O American Embassy, PSC 82 Box 002, APO AE 09710

2. Frankfurt, Germany (49-69) 69.705.111
   FAA C/O IFO EA-33 Unit 7580, APO AE 09050

3. London, England (44-181) 754.88.19
   FAA C/O American Embassy, PSC 801 Box 63, FPO AE 09498-4063

4. Singapore (65) 543-1466
   FAA C/O American Embassy, PSC 470 AP 96507-0001

These special certificates will not allow you to fly for hire in the U.S. To qualify for a "clean" FAA commercial pilot certificate or higher, you must meet the full certification requirements of 14 CFR Part 61, for the level of certificate you are requesting. Your current, logged flying time will count towards the required experience. However, all required training, knowledge, and practical tests must be completed.

# Use of Test Aids and Materials

Airman knowledge tests require applicants to analyze the relationship between variables needed to solve aviation problems, in addition to testing for accuracy of a mathematical calculation. The intent is that all applicants are tested on concepts rather than rote calculation ability. It is permissible to use certain calculating devices when taking airman knowledge tests, provided they are used within the following guidelines. The term "calculating devices" is interchangeable with such items as calculators, computers, or any similar devices designed for aviation-related activities.

1. Guidelines for use of test aids and materials. The applicant may use test aids and materials within the guidelines listed below, if actual test questions or answers are not revealed.

   a. Applicants may use test aids, such as scales, straightedges, protractors, plotters, navigation computers, log sheets, and all models of aviation-oriented calculating devices that are directly related to the test. In addition, applicants may use any test materials provided with the test.

   b. Manufacturer's permanently inscribed instructions on the front and back of such aids listed in 1(a), e.g., formulas, conversions, regulations, signals, weather data, holding pattern diagrams, frequencies, weight and balance formulas, and air traffic control procedures are permissible.

   c. The test proctor may provide calculating devices to applicants and deny them use of their personal calculating devices if the applicant's device does not have a screen that indicates all memory has been erased. The test proctor must be able to determine the calculating device's erasure capability. The use of calculating devices incorporating permanent or continuous type memory circuits without erasure capability is prohibited.

d. The use of magnetic cards, magnetic tapes, modules, computer chips, or any other device upon which prewritten programs or information related to the test can be stored and retrieved is prohibited. Printouts of data will be surrendered at the completion of the test if the calculating device used incorporates this design feature.

e. The use of any booklet or manual containing instructions related to the use of the applicant's calculating device is not permitted.

f. Dictionaries are not allowed in the testing area.

g. The test proctor makes the final determination relating to test materials and personal possessions that the applicant may take into the testing area.

2. Guidelines for dyslexic applicant's use of test aids and materials. A dyslexic applicant may request approval from the local Flight Standards District Office (FSDO) to take an airman knowledge test using one of the three options listed in preferential order:

a. Option One. Use current testing facilities and procedures whenever possible.

b. Option Two. Applicants may use Franklin Speaking Wordmaster® to facilitate the testing process. The Wordmaster® is a self-contained electronic thesaurus that audibly pronounces typed in words and presents them on a display screen. It has a built-in headphone jack for private listening. The headphone feature will be used during testing to avoid disturbing others.

c. Option Three. Applicants who do not choose to use the first or second option may request a test proctor to assist in reading specific words or terms from the test questions and supplement material. In the interest of preventing compromise of the testing process, the test proctor should be someone who is non-aviation oriented. The test proctor will provide reading assistance only, with no explanation of words or terms. The Airman Testing Standards Branch, AFS-630, will assist in the selection of a test site and test proctor.

# Cheating or Other Unauthorized Conduct

Computer testing centers must follow strict security procedures to avoid test compromise. These procedures are established by the FAA and are covered in FAA Order 8080.6 Conduct of Airman Knowledge Tests. The FAA has directed testing centers to terminate a test at any time a test proctor suspects a cheating incident has occurred. An FAA investigation will then be conducted. If the investigation determines that cheating or unauthorized conduct has occurred, then any airman certificate or rating that you hold may be revoked, and you will be prohibited for 1 year from applying for or taking any test for a certificate or rating under 14 CFR Part 61.

# Validity of Airman Test Reports

Airman Test Reports are valid for the 24-calendar month period preceding the month you complete the practical test. If the Airman Test Report expires before completion of the practical test, you must retake the knowledge test.

# Eligibility Requirements for the Private Pilot Certificate

**A**lways check the current 14 CFR Part 61 for pilot certificate requirements. To be eligible for a private pilot certificate with an airplane, helicopter, or glider rating a person must:

1. Be at least 17 years old (16 for a glider or balloon rating).

2. Be able to read, speak, write, and understand English or have a limitation placed on the certificate.

3. Have at least a current third-class medical certificate. This medical certificate is usually, but not always, also the student pilot certificate. Glider and balloon applications need only certify they have no known medical deficiency that would prevent them from piloting a glider or balloon safely.

4. Score at least 70 percent on the required FAA Knowledge Test on the appropriate subjects.

5. Pass an oral exam and flight check on the subjects and maneuvers outlined in the Private Pilot Practical Test Standards (#ASA-8081-14AS, 8081-14AM, 8081-HD, or 8081-3).

6. For an airplane or helicopter rating, have a total of 40 hours of instruction (for Part 61 programs) and solo flight time which must include the following:

   a. 20 hours of flight instruction including at least—

      i. 3 hours cross-country,

      ii. 3 hours at night including 10 takeoffs and landings and one cross-country flight of over 100 NM total distance for airplanes (50 NM for helicopters),

      iii. 3 hours of instrument flight training in a single-engine airplane for the airplane rating, and

      iv. 3 hours in an airplane or helicopter within the last 60 days in preparation for the flight test.

   b. 10 hours of solo flight time including at least—

      i. 10 hours in airplanes or helicopters

      ii. 5 hours cross-country for airplanes, each flight with a landing more than 50 NM from the point of departure and one flight of at least 150 NM with 3 landings, one of which must be least 50 NM from the departure point. In helicopters, 3 hours of cross-country with landings at three points at least 25 miles from each other and one cross-country flight of at least 75 NM total distance, with landings at a minimum of three points, and one segment of the flight being a straight-line distance of at least 25 NM between the takeoff and landing locations; and

      iii. 3 takeoffs and landings to a full stop at an airport with an operating control tower, each landing separated by an enroute phase of flight and involving a flight in the traffic pattern in a helicopter.

7. For a glider rating, have at least one of the following:

    a. If the applicant has not logged at least 40 hours of flight time as a pilot in a heavier-than-air aircraft, at least 10 hours of flight training in a glider, and 20 training flights performed on the appropriate areas, including—

        i. 2 hours of solo flight in gliders in the areas of operation that apply to gliders, with not less than 10 launches and landings being performed; and

        ii. Three training flights in a glider in preparation for the practical test within the 60-day period preceding the practical test.

    b. If the applicant has logged at least 40 hours of flight time in heavier-than-air aircraft, at least 3 hours of flight training in a glider, and 10 training flights performed on the appropriate areas, including—

        i. 10 solo flights in gliders on the areas of operation that apply to gliders, and

        ii. Three training flights in preparation for the practical test within the 60-day waiting period preceding the test.

8. For a lighter-than-air rating, have at least one of the following:

    a. For an airship rating:

        i. 25 hours of flight training in airships, which consists of at least:

            • 3 hours of cross-country flight training in an airship;

            • 3 hours of night flight training in an airship that includes:

                — A cross-country flight of over 25 NM total distance; and

                — 5 takeoffs and 5 landings to a full stop (with each landing involving a flight in the traffice pattern) at an airport.

        ii. 3 hours of instrument flight training in an airship;

        iii. 3 hours of flight training in an airship in preparation for the practical test within the 60 days preceding the date of the test; and

        iv. 5 hours performing the duties of PIC in an airship with an authorized instructor.

    b. For a balloon rating. At least 10 hours of flight training that includes at least 6 training flights with an authorized instructor, that includes—

        i. If the training is in a gas balloon, at least 2 flights of 2 hours each that consists of—

            • At least one training flight with an authorized instructor within 60 days prior to application for the rating on the areas of operation for a gas balloon;

            • At least one flight performing the duties of pilot in command in a gas balloon with an authorized instructor; and

            • At least one flight involving a controlled ascent to 3,000 feet above the launch site.

        ii. If the training is in a balloon with an airborne heater, at least—

            • Two 1-hour flights within 60 days prior to application for the rating on the areas of operation appropriate to a balloon with an airborne heater;

            • One solo flight in a balloon with an airborne heater; and

            • At least one flight involving a controlled ascent to 2,000 feet above the launch site.

# Certificate and Logbook Endorsement

When you go to take your FAA Knowledge Test, you will be required to show proper identification and have certification of your preparation for the examination, signed by an authorized Flight or Ground Instructor. Ground Schools will have issued the endorsements as you complete the course. If you choose a home-study for your Knowledge Test, you can either get an endorsement from your instructor or submit your home-study materials to an FAA Office for review and approval prior to taking the test.

## Private and Recreational Endorsement

I certify that Mr./Ms. _____
has received the ground instruction or completed home-study required by 14 CFR §61.35, §61.103, and §61.105. I have determined he/she is prepared for the _____ knowledge test.


Signed _____     Date_____

CFI Number _____     Expires_____

# Test-Taking Tips

Follow these time-proven tips, which will help you develop a skillful, smooth approach to test-taking:

1. In order to maintain the integrity of each test, the FAA may rearrange the answer stems to appear in a different order on your test than you see in this book. For this reason, be careful to fully understand the intent of each question and corresponding answer while studying, rather than memorize the A, B, C answer choice.

2. Take with you to the testing center a sign-off from an instructor, photo I.D., the testing fee, calculator, flight computer (ASA's E6-B or CX-2 Pathfinder), plotter, magnifying glass, and a sharp pointer, such as a safety pin.

3. Your first action when you sit down should be to write on the scratch paper the weight and balance and any other formulas and information you can remember from your study. Remember, some of the formulas may be on your E6-B.

4. Answer each question in accordance with the latest regulations and guidance publications.

5. Read each question carefully before looking at the possible answers. You should clearly understand the problem before attempting to solve it.

6. After formulating an answer, determine which answer choice corresponds the closest with your answer. The answer chosen should completely resolve the problem.

7. From the answer choices given, it may appear that there is more than one possible answer. However, there is only one answer that is correct and complete. The other answers are either incomplete, erroneous, or represent popular misconceptions.

8. If a certain question is difficult for you, it is best to mark it for REVIEW and proceed to the other questions. After you answer the less difficult questions, return to those which you marked for review and answer them. Be sure to untag these questions once you have answered them. The review marking procedure will be explained to you prior to starting the test. Although the computer should alert you to unanswered questions, make sure every question has an answer recorded. This procedure will enable you to use the available time to the maximum advantage.

9. Perform each math calculation twice to confirm your answer. If adding or subtracting a column of numbers, reverse your direction the second time to reduce the possibility of error.

10. When solving a calculation problem, select the answer nearest to your solution. The problem has been checked with various types of calculators; therefore, if you have solved it correctly, your answer will be closer to the correct answer than any of the other choices.

11. Remember that information is provided in the FAA Legends and FAA Figures.

12. Remember to answer every question, even the ones with no completely correct answer, to ensure the FAA gives you credit for a bad question.

13. Take your time and be thorough but relaxed. Take a minute off every half-hour or so to relax the brain and the body. Get a drink of water halfway through the test.

# Suggested Materials for the Private Pilot Certificate

The following are some of the publications and products recommended for the Private and Recreational Pilot certificates. All are reprinted by ASA and available from authorized ASA dealers and distributors.

| | |
|---|---|
| ASA-ANA | *Aerodynamics for Naval Aviators* |
| ASA-AC00-6A | *Aviation Weather* |
| ASA-AC00-45E | *Aviation Weather Services* |
| ASA-8083-21 | *Rotorcraft Flying Handbook* |
| ASA-PPT | *The Complete Private Pilot* (textbook) by Bob Gardner |
| ASA-PPT-S | *The Complete Private Pilot Syllabus* |
| ASA-VFM-HI | *Visualized Flight Maneuvers Handbook–High-Wing Aircraft* |
| ASA-VFM-LO | *Visualized Flight Maneuvers Handbook–Low-Wing Aircraft* |
| ASA-FR-AM-BK | *Federal Aviation Regulations and Aeronautical Information Manual* (combined) |
| ASA-8083-3 | *Airplane Flying Handbook* |
| ASA-AC61-23C | *Pilot's Handbook of Aeronautical Knowledge* |
| ASA-8083-1 | *Aircraft Weight and Balance Handbook* |
| ASA-8081-14AS | *Private Pilot Practical Test Standards—Airplane (Single-Engine Land & Sea)* |
| ASA-8081-14AM | *Private Pilot Practical Test Standards—Airplane (Multi-Engine Land & Sea)* |
| ASA-8081-HD | *Private & Commercial Pilot Practical Test Standards—Rotorcraft/Helicopter* |
| ASA-8081-3 | *Private Pilot Practical Test Standards—Recreational Pilot* |
| ASA-PM-1A | *Flight School* (textbook) |
| ASA-PM-2 | *Private & Commercial* (textbook) |
| ASA-PM-S-P | *Private Pilot Syllabus* |
| ASA-CP-RLX | Ultimate Rotating Plotter |
| ASA-OEG-P | *Private Oral Exam Guide* by Michael Hayes |
| ASA-SP-30 | Pilot Logbook |
| ASA-CX-2 | CX-2 Pathfinder Electronic Flight Computer |
| ASA-E6B | E6-B Flight Computer |
| ASA-SFR-P2 | Private Student Flight Record |
| ASA-TW-PVT | Prepware Exam Software for Private Pilots |
| ASA-VTP-PVT | Private Pilot Virtual Test Prep (DVD Aviation Ground School) |

Visit the ASA website for more information on all these products: **www.asa2fly.com**

# ASA Test Prep Layout

**The FAA questions have been sorted into chapters according to subject matter.** Within each chapter, the questions have been further classified and all similar questions grouped together with a concise discussion of the material covered in each group. This discussion material of "Chapter text" is printed in a larger font and spans the entire width of the page. Immediately following the FAA Question is ASA's Explanation in *italics*. The last line of the Explanation contains the Subject Matter Knowledge Code and further reference (if applicable). *See* the EXAMPLE below.

**Figures referenced by the Chapter text only** are numbered with the appropriate chapter number, i.e., "Figure 1-1" is Chapter 1's first chapter-text figure.

**Some FAA Questions refer to Figures or Legends** immediately following the question number, i.e., "3201. (Refer to Figure 14.)." These are FAA Figures and Legends which can be found in the separate booklet: *Computerized Testing Supplement* (CT-8080-XX). This supplement is bundled with the Test Prep and is the exact material you will have access to when you take your computerized test. We provide it separately, so you will become accustomed to referring to the FAA Figures and Legends as you would during the test.

**Figures referenced by the Explanation** and pertinent to the understanding of that particular question are labeled by their corresponding Question number. For example: the caption "Questions 3245 and 3248" means the figure accompanies the Explanations for both Question 3245 and 3248.

**Answers** to each question are found at the bottom of each page, and in the Cross-Reference at the back of this book.

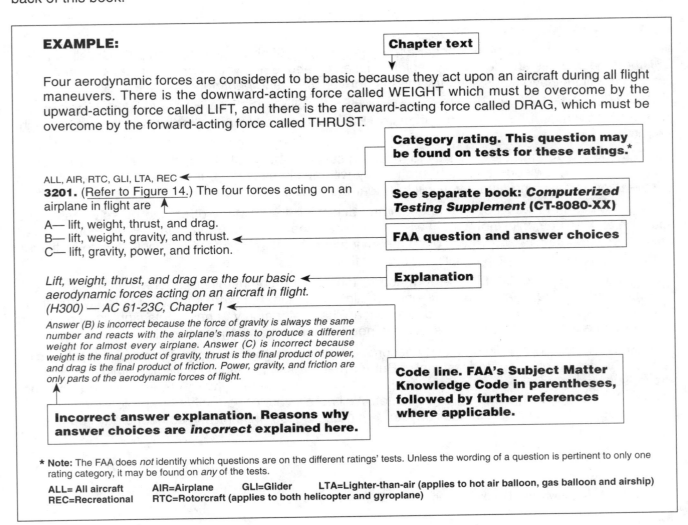

**EXAMPLE:**

Chapter text

Four aerodynamic forces are considered to be basic because they act upon an aircraft during all flight maneuvers. There is the downward-acting force called WEIGHT which must be overcome by the upward-acting force called LIFT, and there is the rearward-acting force called DRAG, which must be overcome by the forward-acting force called THRUST.

Category rating. This question may be found on tests for these ratings.*

ALL, AIR, RTC, GLI, LTA, REC
**3201.** (Refer to Figure 14.) The four forces acting on an airplane in flight are

See separate book: *Computerized Testing Supplement* (CT-8080-XX)

A— lift, weight, thrust, and drag.
B— lift, weight, gravity, and thrust.
C— lift, gravity, power, and friction.

FAA question and answer choices

*Lift, weight, thrust, and drag are the four basic aerodynamic forces acting on an aircraft in flight. (H300) — AC 61-23C, Chapter 1*

Explanation

*Answer (B) is incorrect because the force of gravity is always the same number and reacts with the airplane's mass to produce a different weight for almost every airplane. Answer (C) is incorrect because weight is the final product of gravity, thrust is the final product of power, and drag is the final product of friction. Power, gravity, and friction are only parts of the aerodynamic forces of flight.*

Code line. FAA's Subject Matter Knowledge Code in parentheses, followed by further references where applicable.

Incorrect answer explanation. Reasons why answer choices are *incorrect* explained here.

* **Note:** The FAA does *not* identify which questions are on the different ratings' tests. Unless the wording of a question is pertinent to only one rating category, it may be found on *any* of the tests.

**ALL**= All aircraft  **AIR**=Airplane  **GLI**=Glider  **LTA**=Lighter-than-air (applies to hot air balloon, gas balloon and airship)
**REC**=Recreational  **RTC**=Rotorcraft (applies to both helicopter and gyroplane)

# Opportunity Knocking: Become a Flight Instructor!

by Greg Brown, 2000 FAA/Industry Flight Instructor of the Year

*"Wanted—enthusiastic, knowledgeable pilots for part-time, full-time, or freelance professional flying. Lots of fun and adventure, highly respected position, and great learning experience. Age no factor. Travel as much (or as little) as you like. Get paid to fly!"*

Where do flight instructors come from? The most visible Certified Flight Instructors (CFIs) are often the aspiring airline pilots who populate flight schools on their way to a jet cockpit. Despite occasional concerns about "time-building," the vast majority of those folks do a super job.

But the current airline hiring boom is soaking up flight instructors faster than they can be replaced, and there's no end in sight. That means fewer CFIs to provide the quality instruction we need in both general and professional aviation.

Where can we find flight instructors with the commitment and long-term interest to meet the needs of general aviation? The answer is that more CFIs must sprout from the enthusiastic general aviation pilots we meet every day at the airport. You know, people like us, who find flying a 172, a Kitfox, or a Baron to be a blast. Pilots who delight in doing a professional job of piloting even while sustaining other full-time careers. Aviators who'd love a professional flying career, but who aren't interested in flying the "heavy iron."

## Me? An Instructor?

Many student and private pilots wonder about the feasibility of one day becoming a CFI. Well, with the CFI shortage upon us and deepening rapidly, that ad up above has *your name* on it! Let's consider why becoming a flight instructor is a worthy mission for you to pursue *right now*.

We've already touched upon some reasons for becoming a CFI; demand is high, and your experience and dedication can benefit the industry. But there are other great reasons to become a flight instructor.

First, the old adage, "the best way to master a subject is to teach it," is most definitely true. As an active CFI your knowledge and flight proficiency will rapidly exceed your greatest expectations as a Private Pilot. By teaching others you will truly learn to fly as a pro.

Next comes the reward of setting goals and achieving them. Many of us find ourselves sitting at home on a given day, thinking, "Gee, I wish there was a reason to go flying today." Well, there is! Start working toward that CFI and you've got a meaningful personal and professional objective to justify the time, effort, and investment in continuing regular flying.

Then there's the contribution to be made to the aviation community. Not only can you as a CFI personally impact the safety and proficiency of pilots you train, but there's also the critically important role CFIs serve in recruiting new blood to aviation. The vast majority of new pilots sign up through the direct or indirect efforts of active CFIs, and we need your help carrying the flag.

Best of all, here's your big chance to become an honest-to-goodness pro. Almost every active pilot harbors the dream of flying professionally. But for many reasons—age, family and lifestyle considerations, success in another occupation—only a certain percentage of pilots are in position to pursue, say, the captain's seat in a Boeing or a LearJet. Well here's your opportunity to fly professionally under schedule and conditions more or less of your own choosing, all while having someone pay you to do it.

## What Does It Take to Qualify?

"But hold on a minute," you say, "becoming a CFI takes years of full-time study, and many thousands of flight hours, right?"

Not at all! With dedication and concentrated effort one can become a CFI relatively quickly. After earning your Private Pilot certificate, it takes only three more steps to become a primary flight instructor: an Instrument rating, the Commercial Pilot certificate, and then the Flight Instructor certificate itself. That's certainly not a long path.

Recent regulations allow new Private Pilots to begin training for the instrument rating as soon as they like. (All CFI applicants must be instrument rated, even if they never plan to fly IFR.) The Instrument rating is roughly comparable in flight training hours to earning one's Private certificate, and is something many of us go on to earn anyway. As with the Private, FAA Knowledge (written) and Practical (oral and flight) Tests are required. But once earning your instrument rating the route to flight instructor status can be a quick one.

You'll need some flight experience to be eligible for your Commercial Pilot Certificate—190 to 250 hours total flight time are required by the time you complete your training. But earning the rating itself requires only a fraction of the effort required to earn a Private; it's entirely feasible to earn your Commercial in fifteen hours or less, if you set your mind to it. Again there are Knowledge and Practical tests to pass, and then you're ready to pursue your Flight Instructor Certificate.

There is no minimum training requirement for the Flight Instructor certificate itself, but it will probably take you some fifteen to twenty flight hours to earn, plus a good deal of ground instruction. Along with Knowledge and Practical Tests there is an additional FAA written addressing, "Fundamentals of Instruction."

The oral portion of the CFI Practical Test is notoriously challenging, but what's covered there is largely material you've seen before, so keep sharp on the Private and Commercial Pilot material you've learned, and you'll have little trouble mastering the CFI tests. Of course teaching technique is an important element of the test, too. If there's one certificate where you should seek out a truly outstanding instructor, the CFI is it.

As for flight physicals, CFIs fall into the most favorable regulatory status of almost any professional pilot. With recent regulation changes, one can instruct with a third-class medical certificate, so if you qualify medically for a student pilot certificate you can instruct. What's more, some instruction can even be conducted *without* a medical.

And other than the fact that you must be eighteen to earn your Commercial and therefore CFI Certificates, there are no age limits on instructing. This is one case where the experience and maturity of older pilots is desirable and unrestricted. You're a sixty-year-old student pilot? Cool! Move right along and earn your CFI.

## How Soon Can I Become an Instructor?

Before we get on with more privileges and benefits of instructing, here are a few tips to speed you along the path. First, many people don't realize that they can become certificated as Ground Instructors—teaching ground school and signing off applicants for their FAA Knowledge Exams—simply by passing several FAA written tests. That means you can start your instructing career almost immediately! Not only will ground instructing help pay for your flight training, but it's great preparation for flight instructing.

And for those who plan to knock off their Commercial and CFI certificates in short order, here's a little trick to accelerate your progress. Arrange with your CFI and pilot examiner to train for and take your Commercial Pilot Practical Test from the right seat. That way your right-seat flying skills will already be nailed when you dive into CFI training—doing it this way could save you five or even ten hours of training. Ask at your flight school about the details for your situation.

*Continued*

## What Are the Privileges and Benefits of Being a CFI?

Your initial Flight Instructor certificate will allow you to train Private and Commercial Pilot applicants through to their certificates, and also authorize you to perform flight reviews. (Imagine, *you* giving the flight review!) Additional instructor ratings, such as instrument, multiengine, and those for other aircraft categories such as glider and helicopter, are relatively easy to add if you have journeyman skills in the ratings sought.

The really great news is that given today's demand for flight instructors, you can be assured of employability in most locations the moment you earn your temporary CFI certificate, and you'll likely have your choice of whether to do it full-time or part-time, or in some cases, as a freelancer.

Okay, now lets talk about the "get paid to fly" part. In the past, earnings have often been pretty limited for full-time flight instructors, depending on location, employer, number of students and other factors. But with the developing CFI shortage, instructor pay and benefits are rapidly going up. If you want to pursue a full-time instructing career, excellent positions are now to be had around the country.

However, a great many CFIs choose to join the many part-timers and freelancers around the country who ply their trade in a professional manner, and contribute beyond their numbers to the well-being of general aviation. Many of those folks work other jobs, flying and non-flying, and instruct strictly for the fun and personal reward of it. When you look at instructing as a part-time activity that supports your flying and that of others, it's a pretty darned good deal.

First, instructing gets you up in the air on a regular basis at a price anyone can afford—free. Many part-time CFIs reinvest their instructing income into a fund for personal flying, yielding a good return in both professional and pleasure flying. Other not-so-obvious instructor benefits include discounts on aircraft rental, lower insurance premiums for aircraft owners, and broader insurability in the planes you fly.

Did you realize that as a CFI you get to log all the time flown by your students as PIC time? And as an instrument instructor the approaches flown by your students are often loggable for your own currency, too. What's more, each of those ratings you earn in the process of becoming a flight instructor—the IFR, the Commercial, and your CFI—count as flight reviews. That's the money-saving bureaucratic stuff. The important part is that you'll be sharp far beyond what flight reviews could do for you in themselves, and it all comes in the course of business without the need for lots of currency flights.

Instruct well and charge appropriately for your services, and you can generate some pretty good part-time income at this business. That also raises the possibility of deducting many flying expenses from your income taxes, including charts, headsets, recurrent training, your flight physical, and some or all flight training expenses. (Talk to your accountant for the official word on your situation.)

Now for the most important and rewarding reason to become a flight instructor—people. As a CFI you're going to meet many, many fine individuals from all walks of life who share your dream of flying. It will be you who introduces them to the special fraternity of aviators, you who delivers them the key to flight on their own, and you who conveys the skills and knowledge to help them fly safely and enjoyably with their thousands of future passengers. Your words will be riding with them many years in the future at times when they need you most.

Join the illustrious ranks of flight instructors. Whether you're eighteen, or beginning a new life after retirement; whether you're a schoolteacher with summers available, or looking to change careers altogether, we need you! No one cares whether you wear glasses or not, and the skies are yours to own in everything from ultralights to jets.

Just bring along your passion, your life experience, and some dedication. Here's your big chance to experience the ultimate thrill of flying, all from the seat with the world's greatest view—the spectacular high of opening doors of flight to yet another generation of pilots. Carpe diem! Become a CFI!

Portions of this material first appeared in *Flight Training* magazine.
Greg Brown is the author of *The Savvy Flight Instructor: Secrets of the Successful CFI*, published by ASA.

# Chapter 1
# Basic Aerodynamics

# Aerodynamic Terms

An **airfoil** is a structure or body which produces a useful reaction to air movement. Airplane wings, helicopter rotor blades, and propellers are airfoils. *See* Figure 1-1.

The **chord line** is an imaginary straight line from the leading edge to the trailing edge of an airfoil. *See* Figure 1-2. Changing the shape of an airfoil (by lowering flaps, for example) will change the chord line. *See* Figure 1-3.

In aerodynamics, **relative wind** is the wind felt by an airfoil. It is created by the movement of air past an airfoil, by the motion of an airfoil through the air, or by a combination of the two. Relative wind is parallel and in the opposite direction to the flight path of the airfoil. *See* Figure 1-4.

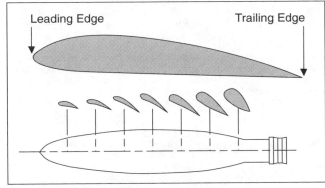

**Figure 1-1.** A typical airfoil cross-section

**Figure 1-2.** Chord line

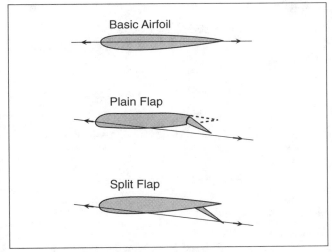

**Figure 1-3.** Changing shape of wing changes the chord line

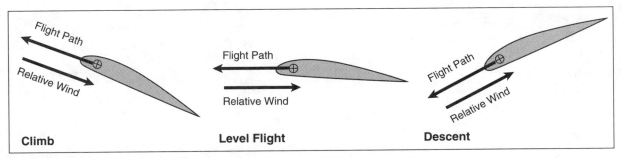

**Figure 1-4.** Relative wind

The **angle of attack** is the angle between the chord line of the airfoil and the relative wind. By manipulating the aircraft controls, the pilot can vary the angle of attack. *See* Figure 1-5.

The **angle of incidence** is the angle at which a wing is attached to the aircraft fuselage. The pilot has no control over the angle of incidence. *See* Figure 1-6.

**Figure 1-5.** Angle of attack

**Figure 1-6.** Angle of incidence

ALL
**3203.** (Refer to Figure 1.) The acute angle A is the angle of

A—incidence.
B—attack.
C—dihedral.

*The angle of attack is the acute angle between the relative wind and the chord line of the wing. (H300) — AC 61-23C, Chapter 1*

Answer (A) is incorrect because the angle of incidence is the angle formed by the longitudinal axis of the airplane and the chord line. Answer (C) is incorrect because the dihedral is the upward angle of the airplane's wings with respect to the horizontal.

ALL
**3204.** The term "angle of attack" is defined as the angle

A—between the wing chord line and the relative wind.
B—between the airplane's climb angle and the horizon.
C—formed by the longitudinal axis of the airplane and the chord line of the wing.

*The angle of attack is the acute angle between the relative wind and the chord line of the wing. (H300) — AC 61-23C, Chapter 1*

Answer (B) is incorrect because there is no specific aviation term for this. Answer (C) is incorrect because this is the definition of the angle of incidence.

RTC
**3317.** Angle of attack is defined as the angle between the chord line of an airfoil and the

A—direction of the relative wind.
B—pitch angle of an airfoil.
C—rotor plane of rotation.

*The angle of attack is the angle between the chord line of the airfoil and the direction of the relative wind. (H702) — FAA-H-8083-21, Chapter 2*

---

**Answers**

3203    [B]          3204    [A]          3317    [A]

# Axes of Rotation and the Four Forces Acting in Flight

An airplane has three axes of rotation: the lateral axis, longitudinal axis, and the vertical axis. *See* Figure 1-7.

The **lateral axis** is an imaginary line from wing tip to wing tip. The rotation around this axis is called **pitch**. Pitch is controlled by the elevators, and this rotation is referred to as **longitudinal control** or **longitudinal stability**. *See* Figure 1-8.

The **longitudinal axis** is an imaginary line from the nose to the tail. Rotation around the longitudinal axis is called **roll**. Roll is controlled by the ailerons, and this rotation is referred to as **lateral control** or **lateral stability**. *See* Figure 1-9.

The **vertical axis** is an imaginary line extending vertically through the intersection of the lateral and longitudinal axes. Rotation about the vertical axis is called **yaw**. Yaw is controlled by the rudder, and this rotation is referred to as **directional control** or **directional stability**. *See* Figure 1-10.

**Figure 1-7.** Axes of rotation

**Figure 1-9.** Effect of ailerons

**Figure 1-8.** Effect of elevators

**Figure 1-10.** Effect of rudder

The **center of gravity** (the imaginary point where all the weight is concentrated) is the point at which an airplane would balance if it were suspended at that point. The three axes intersect at the center of gravity.

Four aerodynamic forces are considered to be basic because they act upon an aircraft during all flight maneuvers: there is the downward-acting force called **weight** which must be overcome by the upward-acting force called **lift**; and there is the rearward-acting force called **drag**, which must be overcome by the forward-acting force called **thrust**. *See* Figure 1-11.

## Lift

Air is a gas which can be compressed or expanded. When compressed, more air can occupy a given volume and air density is increased. When allowed to expand, air occupies a greater space and density is decreased. Temperature, atmospheric pressure, and humidity all affect air density. Air density has significant effects on an aircraft's performance.

As the velocity of a fluid (gas or liquid) increases, its pressure decreases. This is known as **Bernoulli's Principle**. *See* Figure 1-12.

Lift is the result of a pressure difference between the top and the bottom of the wing. A wing is designed to accelerate air over the top camber of the wing, thereby decreasing the pressure on the top and producing lift. *See* Figure 1-13.

Several factors are involved in the creation of lift: angle of attack, wing area and shape (planform), air velocity, and air density. All of these factors have an effect on the amount of lift produced at any given moment. The pilot can actively control the angle of attack and the airspeed, and increasing either of these will result in an increase in lift.

**Figure 1-11.** Relationship of forces in flight

**Figure 1-12.** Flow of air through a constriction

**Figure 1-13.** Development of lift

## Weight
Weight is the force with which gravity attracts all bodies vertically toward the center of the earth.

## Thrust
Thrust is the forward force which is produced by the propeller acting as an airfoil to displace a large mass of air to the rear.

## Drag
Drag is a rearward-acting force which resists the forward movement of an airplane through the air. Drag may be classified into two main types: parasite drag and induced drag.

**Parasite drag** is the resistance of the air produced by any part of an airplane that does not produce lift (antennae, landing gear, etc.). Parasite drag will increase as airspeed increases.

**Induced drag** is a by-product of lift. In other words, drag is induced as the wing develops lift. The high-pressure air beneath the wing, which is trying to flow around and over the wing tips into the area of low pressure, causes a vortex behind the wing tip. This vortex induces a spanwise flow and creates vortices all along the trailing edge of the wing. As the angle of attack is increased (up to the critical angle), lift will increase and so will the vortices and downwash. This downwash redirects the lift vector rearward, causing a rearward component of lift (induced drag). Induced drag will increase as airspeed decreases. *See* Figure 1-14.

During unaccelerated (straight-and-level) flight, the four aerodynamic forces which act on an airplane are said to be in equilibrium, or:

Lift = Weight and Thrust = Drag

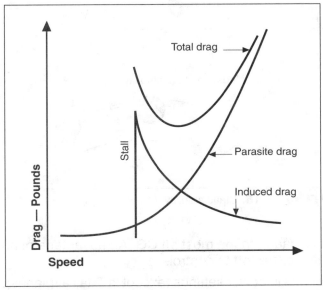

**Figure 1-14.** Drag curve diagram

AIR
**3213.** What is the purpose of the rudder on an airplane?

A—To control yaw.
B—To control overbanking tendency.
C—To control roll.

*The purpose of the rudder is to control yaw. (H302) — AC 61-23C, Chapter 1*

Answer (B) is incorrect because the ailerons control overbanking. Answer (C) is incorrect because roll is controlled by the ailerons.

ALL
**3201.** The four forces acting on an airplane in flight are

A—lift, weight, thrust, and drag.
B—lift, weight, gravity, and thrust.
C—lift, gravity, power, and friction.

*Lift, weight, thrust, and drag are the four basic aerodynamic forces acting on an aircraft in flight. (H300) — AC 61-23C, Chapter 1*

**Answers**
3213 [A]      3201 [A]

AIR, GLI

**3202.** When are the four forces that act on an airplane in equilibrium?

A—During unaccelerated flight.
B—When the aircraft is accelerating.
C—When the aircraft is at rest on the ground.

*In unaccelerated (steady state) flight the opposing forces are in equilibrium. (H300) — AC 61-23C, Chapter 1*

Answer (B) is incorrect because thrust must exceed drag in order for the airplane to accelerate. Answer (C) is incorrect because when the airplane is at rest on the ground, the only aerodynamic force acting on it is weight.

AIR

**3205.** What is the relationship of lift, drag, thrust, and weight when the airplane is in straight-and-level flight?

A—Lift equals weight and thrust equals drag.
B—Lift, drag, and weight equal thrust.
C—Lift and weight equal thrust and drag.

*Lift and thrust are considered positive forces, while weight and drag are considered negative forces and the sum of the opposing forces is zero. That is, lift = weight and thrust = drag. (H300) — AC 61-23C, Chapter 1*

# Stability

**Stability** is the inherent ability of an airplane to return, or not return, to its original flight condition after being disturbed by an outside force, such as rough air.

**Positive static stability** is the initial tendency of an aircraft to return or not return to its original position. *See* Figure 1-15.

**Positive dynamic stability** is the tendency of an oscillating airplane (with positive static stability) to return to its original position relative to time. *See* Figure 1-16 on the next page.

Aircraft design normally ensures that the aircraft will be stable in pitch. The pilot can adversely affect this longitudinal stability by allowing the center of gravity (CG) to move forward or aft of specified CG limits through improper loading procedures. One undesirable flight characteristic a pilot might experience in an airplane loaded with the CG located aft of the aft CG limit would be the inability to recover from a stalled condition.

The location of the CG with respect to the center of lift (CL) will determine the longitudinal stability of an airplane. *See* Figure 1-17 on the next page.

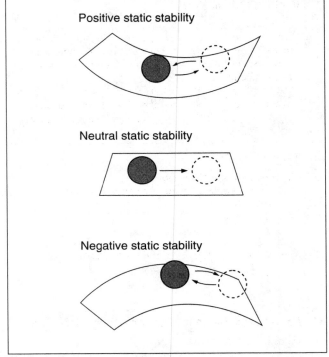

**Figure 1-15.** Static stability

An airplane will be less stable at all airspeeds if it is loaded to the most aft CG. An advantage of an airplane said to be inherently stable is that it will require less effort to control.

Changes in pitch can also be experienced with changes in power settings (except in T-tail airplanes). When power is reduced, there is a corresponding reduction in downwash on the tail, which results in the nose "pitching" down.

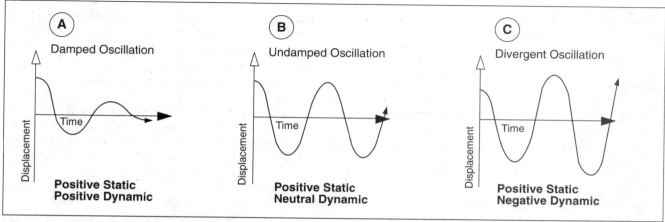

**Figure 1-16.** Positive static stability relative to dynamic stability

---

### Effects of Forward CG

1. Increased longitudinal stability.
2. Lower cruise speed. The wing flies at a higher angle of attack to create more lift to counter the added downward forces produced by the tail, therefore the wing also produces more induced drag.
3. Higher stall speed. The wing flies at a higher angle of attack to create more lift to counter the added downward forces produced by the tail, therefore the wing also produces more induced drag.

### Effects of Aft CG

1. Decreased longitudinal stability.
2. Higher cruise speed (for just the opposite reason listed above).
3. Lower stall speed.
4. Poor stall/spin recovery.

**Figure 1-17.** Effect of CG on aircraft stability

AIR, GLI

**3210.** An airplane said to be inherently stable will

A—be difficult to stall.
B—require less effort to control.
C—not spin.

*A stable airplane will tend to return to the original condition of flight if disturbed by a force such as turbulent air. This means that a stable airplane is easy to fly. (H302) — AC 61-23C, Chapter 1*

Answer (A) is incorrect because stability of an airplane has an effect on its stall recovery, not the difficulty of stall entry. Answer (C) is incorrect because an inherently stable aircraft can still spin.

AIR, GLI

**3211.** What determines the longitudinal stability of an airplane?

A—The location of the CG with respect to the center of lift.
B—The effectiveness of the horizontal stabilizer, rudder, and rudder trim tab.
C—The relationship of thrust and lift to weight and drag.

*The location of the center of gravity with respect to the center of lift determines to a great extent the longitudinal stability of an airplane. Center of gravity aft of the center of lift will result in an undesirable pitch-up moment during flight. An airplane with the center of gravity forward of the center of lift will pitch down when power is reduced. This will increase the airspeed and the downward force on the elevators. This increased downward force on the elevators will bring the nose up, providing positive stability. The farther forward the CG is, the more stable the airplane. (H302) — AC 61-23C, Chapter 1*

Answer (B) is incorrect because the rudder and rudder trim tab control the yaw. Answer (C) is incorrect because the relationship of thrust and lift to weight and drag affects speed and altitude.

---

**Answers**

3210  [B]          3211  [A]

AIR, GLI

**3212.** What causes an airplane (except a T-tail) to pitch nosedown when power is reduced and controls are not adjusted?

A—The CG shifts forward when thrust and drag are reduced.

B—The downwash on the elevators from the propeller slipstream is reduced and elevator effectiveness is reduced.

C—When thrust is reduced to less than weight, lift is also reduced and the wings can no longer support the weight.

*The location of the center of gravity with respect to the center of lift determines to a great extent the longitudinal stability of an airplane. Center of gravity aft of the center of lift will result in an undesirable pitch-up moment during flight. An airplane with the center of gravity forward of the center of lift will pitch down when power is reduced. This will increase the airspeed and the downward force on the elevators. This increased downward force on the elevators will bring the nose up, providing positive stability. The farther forward the CG is, the more stable the airplane. (H302) — AC 61-23C, Chapter 1*

Answer (A) is incorrect because the CG is not affected by changes in thrust or drag. Answer (C) is incorrect because thrust and weight have a small relationship to each other, unless thrust is opposite weight, as in the case of jet fighters and space shuttles.

AIR, GLI

**3287.** An airplane has been loaded in such a manner that the CG is located aft of the aft CG limit. One undesirable flight characteristic a pilot might experience with this airplane would be

A—a longer takeoff run.

B—difficulty in recovering from a stalled condition.

C—stalling at higher-than-normal airspeed.

*Loading in a tail-heavy condition can reduce the airplane's ability to recover from stalls and spins. Tail-heavy loading also produces very light stick forces, making it easy for the pilot to inadvertently overstress the airplane. (H315) — AC 61-23C, Chapter 4*

Answer (A) is incorrect because an airplane with an aft CG has less drag from a reduction in horizontal stabilizer lift, resulting in a short takeoff run. Answer (C) is incorrect because an airplane with an aft CG flies at a lower angle of attack, resulting in a lower stall speed.

AIR, GLI

**3288.** Loading an airplane to the most aft CG will cause the airplane to be

A—less stable at all speeds.

B—less stable at slow speeds, but more stable at high speeds.

C—less stable at high speeds, but more stable at low speeds.

*Loading in a tail-heavy condition can reduce the airplane's ability to recover from stalls and spins. Tail-heavy loading also produces very light stick forces at all speeds, making it easy for the pilot to inadvertently overstress the airplane. (H315) — AC 61-23C, Chapter 4*

Answers (B) and (C) are incorrect because an aft CG location causes an aircraft to be less stable at all airspeeds, due to less elevator effectiveness.

# Turns, Loads, and Load Factors

When an airplane is banked into a turn, a portion of the vertical lift being developed is diverted into a **horizontal lift component**. It is this horizontal (sideward) force that forces the airplane from straight-and-level flight and causes it to turn. The reduced **vertical lift component** results in a loss of altitude unless total lift is increased by increasing angle of attack, increasing airspeed, or increasing both.

In aerodynamics, **load** is the force (imposed stress) that must be supported by an airplane structure in flight. The loads imposed on the wings in flight are stated in terms of load factor.

In straight-and-level flight, the wings of an airplane support a load equal to the sum of the weight of the airplane plus its contents. This particular load factor is equal to "One G," where "**G**" refers to the pull of gravity.

However, a force called **centrifugal force** is generated which acts toward the outside of the curve any time an airplane is flying a curved path (turns, climbs, or descents).

**Answers**

| | | |
|---|---|---|
| 3212 [B] | 3287 [B] | 3288 [A] |

Whenever the airplane is flying in a curved flight path with a positive load, the load that the wings must support will be equal to the weight of the airplane plus the load imposed by centrifugal force; therefore, it can be said that turns increase the load factor on an airplane.

As the angle of bank of a turn increases, the load factor increases, as is shown in Figure 1-18.

**Figure 1-18.** Increase in load on wings as angle of bank increases

The amount of excess load that can be imposed on the wing of an airplane depends on the speed of the airplane. An example of this would be a change in direction made at high speed with forceful control movement, which results in a high load factor being imposed.

An increased **load factor** (weight) will cause an airplane to stall at a higher airspeed, as shown in Figure 1-19.

Some conditions that increase the weight (load) of an aircraft are: overloading the airplane, too steep an angle of bank, turbulence and abrupt movement of the controls.

Because different types of operations require different maneuvers (and therefore varying bank angles and load factors), aircraft are separated into categories determined by the loads that their wing structures can support:

| Category | Positive Limit Load |
|---|---|
| *Normal*.................................... (nonacrobatic) (N) | 3.8 times gross wt. |
| *Utility* ..................................... (normal operations and limited acrobatic maneuvers) | 4.4 times gross wt. |
| *Acrobatic* ............................... (A) | 6.0 times gross wt. |

The limit loads should not be exceeded in actual operation, even though a safety factor of 50% above limit loads is incorporated in the strength of the airplane.

**Figure 1-19.** Effect of angle of bank on stall speed

AIR
**3214.** (Refer to Figure 2.) If an airplane weighs 2,300 pounds, what approximate weight would the airplane structure be required to support during a 60° banked turn while maintaining altitude?

A—2,300 pounds.
B—3,400 pounds.
C—4,600 pounds.

*Referencing FAA Figure 2, use the following steps:*

1. *Enter the chart at a 60° angle of bank and proceed upward to the curved reference line. From the point of intersection, move to the left side of the chart and read a load factor of 2 Gs.*

2. *Multiply the aircraft weight by the load factor:*

    *2,300 x 2 = 4,600 lbs*

*Or, working from the table:*

   *2,300 x 2.0 (load factor) = 4,600 lbs*

*(H303) — AC 61-23C, Chapter 1*

AIR
**3215.** (Refer to Figure 2.) If an airplane weighs 3,300 pounds, what approximate weight would the airplane structure be required to support during a 30° banked turn while maintaining altitude?

A—1,200 pounds.
B—3,100 pounds.
C—3,960 pounds.

*Referencing FAA Figure 2, use the following steps:*

1. *Enter the chart at a 30° angle of bank and proceed upward to the curved reference line. From the point of intersection, move to the left side of the chart and read an approximate load factor of 1.2 Gs.*

2. *Multiply the aircraft weight by the load factor:*

    *3,300 x 1.2 = 3,960 lbs*

*Or, working from the table:*

   *3,300 x 1.154 (load factor) = 3,808 lbs*

*Answer C is the closest.*

*(H303) — AC 61-23C, Chapter 1*

Answers (A) and (B) are incorrect because they are less than 3,300 pounds; load factor increases with bank for level flight.

AIR
**3216.** (Refer to Figure 2.) If an airplane weighs 4,500 pounds, what approximate weight would the airplane structure be required to support during a 45° banked turn while maintaining altitude?

A—4,500 pounds.
B—6,750 pounds.
C—7,200 pounds.

*Referencing FAA Figure 2, use the following steps:*

1. *Enter the chart at a 45° angle of bank and proceed upward to the curved reference line. From the point of intersection, move to the left side of the chart and read a load factor of 1.5 Gs.*

2. *Multiply the aircraft weight by the load factor.*

    *4,500 x 1.5 = 6,750 lbs*

*Or, working from the table:*

   *4,500 x 1.414 (load factor) = 6,363 lbs*

*Answer B is the closest.*

*(H303) — AC 61-23C, Chapter 1*

AIR
**3217.** The amount of excess load that can be imposed on the wing of an airplane depends upon the

A—position of the CG.
B—speed of the airplane.
C—abruptness at which the load is applied.

*At slow speeds, the maximum available lifting force of the wing is only slightly greater than the amount necessary to support the weight of the airplane. However, at high speeds, the capacity of the elevator controls, or a strong gust, may increase the load factor beyond safe limits. (H303) — AC 61-23C, Chapter 1*

Answer (A) is incorrect because the position of the CG affects the stability of the airplane, but not the total load the wings can support. Answer (C) is incorrect because abrupt control inputs do not limit load.

AIR, GLI
**3301.** What force makes an airplane turn?

A—The horizontal component of lift.
B—The vertical component of lift.
C—Centrifugal force.

*As the airplane is banked, lift acts horizontally as well as vertically and the airplane is pulled around the turn. (H534) — FAA-H-8083-3, Chapter 4*

Answer (B) is incorrect because the vertical component of lift has no horizontal force to make the airplane turn. Answer (C) is incorrect because the centrifugal force acts against the horizontal component of lift.

**Answers**

| 3214 [C] | 3215 [C] | 3216 [B] | 3217 [B] | 3301 [A] |

AIR

**3218.** Which basic flight maneuver increases the load factor on an airplane as compared to straight-and-level flight?

A—Climbs.
B—Turns.
C—Stalls.

*A change in speed during straight flight will not produce any appreciable change in load, but when a change is made in the airplane's flight path, an additional load is imposed upon the airplane structure. This is particularly true if a change in direction is made at high speeds with rapid, forceful control movements. (H303) — AC 61-23C, Chapter 1*

*Answer (A) is incorrect because the load increases only as the angle of attack is changed, momentarily. Once the climb attitude has been set, the wings only carry the load produced by the weight of the aircraft. Answer (C) is incorrect because in a stall, the wings are not producing lift.*

AIR, GLI

**3316.** During an approach to a stall, an increased load factor will cause the airplane to

A—stall at a higher airspeed.
B—have a tendency to spin.
C—be more difficult to control.

*Stall speed increases in proportion to the square root of the load factor. Thus, with a load factor of 4, an aircraft will stall at a speed which is double the normal stall speed. (H303) — AC 61-23C, Chapter 1*

*Answer (B) is incorrect because an airplane's tendency to spin does not relate to an increase in load factors. Answer (C) is incorrect because an airplane's stability determines its controllability.*

## Stalls and Spins

As the angle of attack is increased (to increase lift), the air will no longer flow smoothly over the upper wing surface but instead will become turbulent or "burble" near the trailing edge. A further increase in the angle of attack will cause the turbulent area to expand forward. At an angle of attack of approximately 18° to 20° (for most wings), turbulence over the upper wing surface decreases lift so drastically that flight can not be sustained and the wing **stalls**. *See* Figure 1-20.

The angle at which a stall occurs is called the **critical angle of attack**. An airplane can stall at any airspeed or any attitude, but will always stall at the same critical angle of attack. The indicated airspeed at which a given airplane will stall in a particular configuration, however, will remain the same regardless of altitude. Because air density decreases with an increase in altitude, the airplane has to be flown faster at higher altitudes to cause the same pressure difference between pitot impact pressure and static pressure.

**Figure 1-20.** Flow of air over wing at various angles of attack

An aircraft will **spin** only after it has stalled, and will continue to spin as long as the outside wing continues to provide more lift than the inside wing and the aircraft remains stalled.

**Answers**

3218 [B]          3316 [A]

AIR, GLI

**3263.** As altitude increases, the indicated airspeed at which a given airplane stalls in a particular configuration will

A—decrease as the true airspeed decreases.
B—decrease as the true airspeed increases.
C—remain the same regardless of altitude.

*An increase in altitude has no effect on the indicated airspeed at which an airplane stalls at altitudes normally used by general aviation aircraft. This means that the same indicated airspeed should be maintained during the landing approach regardless of the elevation or the density altitude at the airport of landing. (H312) — AC 61-23C, Chapter 3*

Answer (A) is incorrect because true airspeed does not decrease with increased altitude, and indicated airspeed at which an airplane stalls does not change. Answer (B) is incorrect because the indicated airspeed of the stall does not decrease with increased altitude.

AIR, GLI

**3309.** In what flight condition must an aircraft be placed in order to spin?

A—Partially stalled with one wing low.
B—In a steep diving spiral.
C—Stalled.

*A spin results when a sufficient degree of rolling or yawing control input is imposed on an airplane in the stalled condition. If the wing is not stalled, a spin cannot occur. (H540) — FAA-H-8083-3, Chapter 5*

Answer (A) is incorrect because the aircraft must be at a full stall in order to spin. Answer (B) is incorrect because an airplane is not necessarily stalled when in a steep diving spiral.

AIR, GLI

**3310.** During a spin to the left, which wing(s) is/are stalled?

A—Both wings are stalled.
B—Neither wing is stalled.
C—Only the left wing is stalled.

*One wing is less stalled than the other, but both wings are stalled in a spin. (H540) — FAA-H-8083-3, Chapter 5*

Answer (B) is incorrect because both wings must be stalled through the spin. Answer (C) is incorrect because both wings are stalled; but the right wing is less fully stalled than the left.

AIR, GLI

**3311.** The angle of attack at which an airplane wing stalls will

A—increase if the CG is moved forward.
B—change with an increase in gross weight.
C—remain the same regardless of gross weight.

*When the angle of attack is increased to between 18° and 20° (critical angle of attack) on most airfoils, the airstream can no longer follow the upper curvature of the wing because of the excessive change in direction. The airplane will stall if the critical angle of attack is exceeded. The indicated airspeed at which stall occurs will be determined by weight and load factor, but the stall angle of attack is the same. (H303) — AC 61-23C, Chapter 1*

Answers (A) and (B) are incorrect because an airplane will always stall at the same angle of attack, regardless of the CG position or gross weight.

# Flaps

Extending the flaps increases the wing camber and the angle of attack of a wing. This increases wing lift and also increases induced drag. *See* Figure 1-21.

The increased drag enables the pilot to make steeper approaches to a landing, without an increase in airspeed. VFR approaches to a landing at night should be made the same as during the daytime.

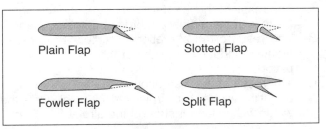

**Figure 1-21.** Use of flaps increases lift and drag

AIR, GLI

**3219.** One of the main functions of flaps during approach and landing is to

A—decrease the angle of descent without increasing the airspeed.
B—permit a touchdown at a higher indicated airspeed.
C—increase the angle of descent without increasing the airspeed.

*Flaps increase drag, allowing the pilot to make steeper approaches without increasing airspeed. (H305) — AC 61-23C, Chapter 2*

Answer (A) is incorrect because extending the flaps increases drag, which enables the pilot to increase the angle of descent without increasing the airspeed. Answer (B) is incorrect because flaps increase lift at slow airspeed, which permits touchdown at a lower indicated airspeed.

AIR, GLI

**3220.** What is one purpose of wing flaps?

A—To enable the pilot to make steeper approaches to a landing without increasing the airspeed.
B—To relieve the pilot of maintaining continuous pressure on the controls.
C—To decrease wing area to vary the lift.

*Flaps increase drag, allowing the pilot to make steeper approaches without increasing airspeed. (H305) — AC 61-23C, Chapter 2*

Answer (B) is incorrect because trim tabs help relieve control pressures. Answer (C) is incorrect because wing area usually remains the same, except for certain specialized flaps which increase the wing area.

# Ground Effect

**Ground effect** occurs when flying within one wingspan or less above the surface. The airflow around the wing and wing tips is modified and the resulting pattern reduces the downwash and the induced drag. These changes can result in an aircraft becoming airborne before reaching recommended takeoff speed or floating during an approach to land. *See* Figure 1-22.

An airplane leaving ground effect after takeoff will require an increase in angle of attack to maintain the same lift coefficient, which in turn will cause an increase in induced drag and therefore, require increased thrust.

**Figure 1-22.** Ground effect phenomenon

**Answers**

3219   [C]          3220   [A]

AIR, GLI, RTC
**3312.** What is ground effect?

A—The result of the interference of the surface of the Earth with the airflow patterns about an airplane.

B—The result of an alteration in airflow patterns increasing induced drag about the wings of an airplane.

C—The result of the disruption of the airflow patterns about the wings of an airplane to the point where the wings will no longer support the airplane in flight.

*Ground effect is the result of the interference of the surface of the Earth with the airflow patterns about an airplane. (H317) — AC 61-23C, Chapter 4*

Answer (B) is incorrect because induced drag is decreased. Answer (C) is incorrect because the disruption of wing-tip vortices increases lift.

AIR, GLI, RTC
**3313.** Floating caused by the phenomenon of ground effect will be most realized during an approach to land when at

A—less than the length of the wingspan above the surface.

B—twice the length of the wingspan above the surface.

C—a higher-than-normal angle of attack.

*When the wing is at a height equal to its span, the reduction in induced drag is only 1.4%. However, when the wing is at a height equal to one-fourth its span, the reduction in induced drag is 23.5% and when the wing is at a height equal to one-tenth its span, the reduction in induced drag is 47.6%. (H317) — AC 61-23C, Chapter 4*

Answer (B) is incorrect because ground effect extends up to one wingspan length. Answer (C) is incorrect because floating will result from higher-than-normal angle of attack.

AIR, GLI, RTC
**3314.** What must a pilot be aware of as a result of ground effect?

A—Wingtip vortices increase creating wake turbulence problems for arriving and departing aircraft.

B—Induced drag decreases; therefore, any excess speed at the point of flare may cause considerable floating.

C—A full stall landing will require less up elevator deflection than would a full stall when done free of ground effect.

*The reduction of the wing-tip vortices, due to ground effect, alters the spanwise lift distribution and reduces the induced angle of attack, and induced drag causing floating. (H317) — AC 61-23C, Chapter 4*

Answer (A) is incorrect because wing-tip vortices are decreased. Answer (C) is incorrect because a full stall landing will require more up-elevator deflection, due to the increased lift in ground effect.

ALL
**3315.** Ground effect is most likely to result in which problem?

A—Settling to the surface abruptly during landing.

B—Becoming airborne before reaching recommended takeoff speed.

C—Inability to get airborne even though airspeed is sufficient for normal takeoff needs.

*Due to the reduced drag in ground effect, the airplane may seem capable of takeoff well below the recommended speed. It is important that no attempt be made to force the airplane to become airborne with a deficiency of speed. The recommended takeoff speed is necessary to provide adequate initial climb performance. (H317) — AC 61-23C, Chapter 4*

Answer (A) is incorrect because the airplane gains lift from a reduction in induced drag while entering ground effect; therefore, it does not cause the airplane to settle abruptly. Answer (C) is incorrect because ground effect helps the airplane become airborne before the airspeed is sufficient for a normal takeoff.

RTC
**3324.** Which is a result of the phenomenon of ground effect?

A—The induced angle of attack of each rotor blade is increased.

B—The lift vector becomes more horizontal.

C—The angle of attack generating lift is increased.

*In ground effect, as downwash velocity is reduced, the induced angle of attack is reduced and the lift vector becomes more vertical. Simultaneously, a reduction in induced drag occurs. In addition, as the induced angle of attack is reduced, the angle of attack generating lift is increased. The net result of these actions is a beneficial increase in lift and a lower power requirement to support a given weight. (H703) — FAA-H-8083-21, Chapter 3*

---

**Answers**

| 3312 [A] | 3313 [A] | 3314 [B] | 3315 [B] | 3324 [C] |

RTC
**3735.** (Refer to Figure 47.) The airspeed range to avoid while flying in ground effect is

A—25 – 40 MPH.
B—25 – 57 MPH.
C—40 MPH and above.

*Use the following steps:*

1. *Locate the ground effect unsafe area on FAA Figure 47.*

2. *Note that the ground effect altitude in the forward flight region is 40 feet.*

3. *The diagram depicts that a pilot should avoid flight of 40 MPH or greater at altitudes lower than 40 feet.*

*(H747) — FAA-H-8083-21, Chapter 11*

# Wake Turbulence

All aircraft leave two types of **wake turbulence**: Prop or jet blast, and wing-tip vortices.

The prop or jet blast could be hazardous to light aircraft on the ground behind large aircraft which are either taxiing or running-up their engines. In the air, jet or prop blast dissipates rapidly.

**Wing-tip vortices** are a by-product of lift. When a wing is flown at a positive angle of attack, a pressure differential is created between the upper and lower wing surfaces, and the pressure above the wing will be lower than the pressure below the wing. In attempting to equalize the pressure, air moves outward, upward, and around the wing tip, setting up a **vortex** which trails behind each wing. *See* Figure 1-23.

The strength of a vortex is governed by the weight, speed, and the shape of the wing of the generating aircraft. Maximum vortex strength occurs when the generating aircraft is heavy, clean, and slow.

Vortices generated by large aircraft in flight tend to sink below the flight path of the generating aircraft. A pilot should fly at or above the larger aircraft's flight path in order to avoid the wake turbulence created by the wing-tip vortices. *See* Figure 1-24.

Close to the ground, vortices tend to move laterally. A crosswind will tend to hold the upwind vortex over the landing runway, while a tailwind may move the vortices of a preceding aircraft forward into the touchdown zone.

**Figure 1-23.** Wing-tip vortices

**Figure 1-24.** Vortices in cruise flight

**Answers**
3735   [C]

To avoid wake turbulence when landing, a pilot should note the point where a preceding large aircraft touched down and then land past that point. *See* Figure 1-25.

On takeoff, lift off should be accomplished prior to reaching the rotation point of a preceding large aircraft; the flight path should then remain upwind and above the preceding aircraft's flight path. *See* Figure 1-26.

**Figure 1-25.** Touchdown and wake end

**Figure 1-26.** Rotation and wake beginning

AIR, GLI, RTC

**3824.** Wingtip vortices are created only when an aircraft is

A—operating at high airspeeds.
B—heavily loaded.
C—developing lift.

*Lift is generated by the creation of a pressure differential over the wing surface. The lowest pressure occurs over the wing surface and the highest pressure occurs under the wing. This pressure differential triggers the roll up of the airflow aft of the wing, resulting in wing-tip vortices. Vortices are generated from the moment an aircraft leaves the ground, since trailing vortices are a by-product of wing lift. (J27) — AIM ¶7-3-2*

Answer (A) is incorrect because the greatest turbulence is produced from an airplane developing lift at a slow airspeed. Answer (B) is incorrect because even though a heavily loaded airplane may produce greater turbulence, an airplane does not have to be heavily loaded in order to produce wing-tip vortices.

AIR, GLI, RTC

**3825.** The greatest vortex strength occurs when the generating aircraft is

A—light, dirty, and fast.
B—heavy, dirty, and fast.
C—heavy, clean, and slow.

*The strength of the vortex is governed by the weight, speed, and shape of the wing of the generating aircraft. The greatest vortex strength occurs when the generating aircraft is heavy, clean and slow. (J27) — AIM ¶7-3-3*

Answer (A) is incorrect because light aircraft produce less vortex turbulence than heavy aircraft. Answer (B) is incorrect because in order to be fast, the wing tip must be at a lower angle of attack, thus producing less lift than during climbout. Also, being dirty presents less of a danger than when clean and/or slow.

AIR, GLI, RTC

**3826.** Wingtip vortices created by large aircraft tend to

A—sink below the aircraft generating turbulence.
B—rise into the traffic pattern.
C—rise into the takeoff or landing path of a crossing runway.

*Flight tests have shown that the vortices from large aircraft sink at a rate of about 400 to 500 feet per minute. They tend to level off at a distance about 900 feet below the path of the generating aircraft. (J27) — AIM ¶7-3-4*

Answers (B) and (C) are incorrect because wing-tip vortices sink toward the ground; however, they may move horizontally depending on crosswind conditions.

**Answers**

3824    [C]          3825    [C]          3826    [A]

AIR

**3827.** When taking off or landing at an airport where heavy aircraft are operating, one should be particularly alert to the hazards of wingtip vortices because this turbulence tends to

A—rise from a crossing runway into the takeoff or landing path.
B—rise into the traffic pattern area surrounding the airport.
C—sink into the flightpath of aircraft operating below the aircraft generating the turbulence.

*Flight tests have shown that the vortices from large aircraft sink at a rate of about 400 to 500 feet per minute. They tend to level off at a distance about 900 feet below the path of the generating aircraft. (J27) — AIM ¶7-3-5*

Answer (A) is incorrect because wing-tip vortices always trail behind an airplane and descend toward the ground; they will also drift with the wind. Answer (B) is incorrect because wing-tip vortices descend.

AIR, GLI, RTC

**3828.** The wind condition that requires maximum caution when avoiding wake turbulence on landing is a

A—light, quartering headwind.
B—light, quartering tailwind.
C—strong headwind.

*A tailwind condition can move the vortices of a preceding aircraft forward into the touchdown zone. A light quartering tailwind requires maximum caution. Pilots should be alert to large aircraft upwind from their approach and takeoff flight paths. (J27) — AIM ¶7-3-6*

Answer (A) is incorrect because headwinds push the vortices out of the touchdown zone when landing beyond the touchdown point of the preceding aircraft. Answer (C) is incorrect because strong winds help diffuse wake turbulence vortices.

AIR, GLI, RTC

**3829.** When landing behind a large aircraft, the pilot should avoid wake turbulence by staying

A—above the large aircraft's final approach path and landing beyond the large aircraft's touchdown point.
B—below the large aircraft's final approach path and landing before the large aircraft's touchdown point.
C—above the large aircraft's final approach path and landing before the large aircraft's touchdown point.

*When landing behind a large aircraft stay at or above the large aircraft's final approach path. Note its touchdown point and land beyond it. (J27) — AIM ¶7-3-6*

Answer (B) is incorrect because below the flight path, you will fly into the sinking vortices generated by the large aircraft. Answer (C) is incorrect because by landing before the large aircraft's touchdown point, you will have to fly below the preceding aircraft's flight path, and into the vortices.

AIR, GLI, RTC

**3830.** When departing behind a heavy aircraft, the pilot should avoid wake turbulence by maneuvering the aircraft

A—below and downwind from the heavy aircraft.
B—above and upwind from the heavy aircraft.
C—below and upwind from the heavy aircraft.

*When departing behind a large aircraft, note the large aircraft's rotation point, rotate prior to it, continue to climb above it, and request permission to deviate upwind of the large aircraft's climb path until turning clear of the aircraft's wake. (J27) — AIM ¶7-3-6*

**Answers**

3827 [C]    3828 [B]    3829 [A]    3830 [B]

# Chapter 2
# Aircraft Systems

# Reciprocating Engines

Most small airplanes are powered by **reciprocating** ("recip") **engines** made up, in part, of cylinders, pistons, connecting rods and a crankshaft. The pistons move back and forth within the cylinders. Connecting rods connect the pistons to the crankshaft, which converts the back and forth movements of the pistons to a rotary motion. It is this rotary motion which drives the propeller.

One cycle of the engine consists of two revolutions of the crankshaft. These two crankshaft revolutions require four strokes of the piston; namely, the **intake**, **compression**, **power**, and **exhaust** strokes.

The top end of the cylinder houses an intake valve, an exhaust valve, and two spark plugs.

During the intake stroke, the intake valve is open and the piston moves away from the top of the cylinder and draws in an air/fuel mixture (Figure 2-1A).

At the completion of the intake stroke, the intake valve closes and the piston returns to the top of the cylinder and compresses the air/fuel mixture (Figure 2-1B).

When the piston reaches a precise point near the top of its stroke, the spark plugs ignite the compressed mixture and the rapid expansion of the burning mixture forces the piston downward (Figure 2-1C).

As the piston completes the downward movement of the power stroke, the exhaust valve opens and the piston rises to the top of the cylinder. This exhaust stroke forces out the burned gases and completes one cycle of the engine (Figure 2-1D).

Because of the many moving parts in a reciprocating engine, as soon as the engine is started, power should be set to the RPM recommended for engine warm-up and the engine gauges checked for the desired indications.

Should it be necessary to start the engine by "**hand propping**," it is extremely important that a competent pilot be at the controls in the cockpit. In addition, the person turning the propeller should be thoroughly familiar with the procedure.

Fuel Mixture **IN**

Burned Gases **OUT**

**A.** Intake　　**B.** Compression　　**C.** Power　　**D.** Exhaust

**Figure 2-1.** Four strokes of an internal combustion engine

AIR, RTC

**3656.** What should be the first action after starting an aircraft engine?

A—Adjust for proper RPM and check for desired indications on the engine gauges.
B—Place the magneto or ignition switch momentarily in the OFF position to check for proper grounding.
C—Test each brake and the parking brake.

*As soon as the engine starts, check for unintentional movement of the aircraft and set power to the recommended warm-up RPM. The oil pressure should then be checked to determine that the oil system is functioning properly with pressure at recommended levels within the manufacturer's time limit. (H309) — AC 61-23C, Chapter 2*

Answer (B) is incorrect because this is usually done at the end of the flight. Answer (C) is incorrect because brakes are checked when beginning to taxi.

AIR

**3657.** Should it become necessary to handprop an airplane engine, it is extremely important that a competent pilot

A—call "contact" before touching the propeller.
B—be at the controls in the cockpit.
C—be in the cockpit and call out all commands.

*Because of the hazards involved in hand-starting airplane engines, it is extremely important that a competent pilot be at the controls in the cockpit and that all communications and procedures be agreed upon and rehearsed beforehand. (H309) — AC 61-23C, Chapter 2*

Answer (A) is incorrect because the person propping the engine is not required to be a pilot, and calling "contact" is not required. Answer (C) is incorrect because a pilot must be in control of the aircraft, not only in the cockpit. Also, the person propping the engine calls out the commands.

# Ignition Systems

Most reciprocating engines that are used to power small aircraft incorporate two separate magneto ignition systems.

A **magneto** ("mag") is a self-contained source of electrical energy, so even if an aircraft loses total electrical power, the engine will continue to run.

When checking for magneto operation prior to flight, the engine should run smoothly when operating with the magneto selector set on "BOTH," and should experience a slight drop in revolutions per minute (RPM) when running on only one or the other magneto.

The main advantages of the dual ignition system are increased safety and improved engine performance.

AIR

**3223.** One purpose of the dual ignition system on an aircraft engine is to provide for

A—improved engine performance.
B—uniform heat distribution.
C—balanced cylinder head pressure.

*The dual ignition system has two magnetos to supply the electrical current to two spark plugs for each combustion chamber. This provides both a redundancy of ignition and an improvement of engine performance. (H307) — AC 61-23C, Chapter 2*

Answer (B) is incorrect because heat distribution is not affected by the ignition system. Answer (C) is incorrect because cylinder head pressure in not affected by the ignition system.

**Answers**

3656 [A]          3657 [B]          3223 [A]

# Fuel Induction Systems

Most light airplane engines use either a carburetor or a fuel injection system to deliver an **air/fuel mixture** to the cylinders.

In a **carburetor induction system**, the float-type carburetor takes in air that flows through a restriction (venturi), which creates a low-pressure area. The pressure difference between the low-pressure area and outside air forces fuel into the airstream where it is mixed with the flowing air, drawn through an intake manifold, and delivered to the combustion chambers and ignited.

Carburetors are normally set to deliver the correct air/fuel mixture at sea level. Since air density decreases with altitude, a mixture control allows the pilot to decrease the fuel flow as altitude increases and thus maintain the correct mixture. Otherwise the mixture may become too "rich" at high altitudes.

When descending, air density increases. Unless fuel flow is increased, the mixture may become excessively "lean," i.e., the amount of fuel is too small for the amount of air reaching the cylinders.

In a **fuel injection system** the fuel and air are mixed just prior to entering the combustion chamber. No carburetor is used.

AIR, RTC
**3225.** The operating principle of float-type carburetors is based on the

A—automatic metering of air at the venturi as the aircraft gains altitude.
B—difference in air pressure at the venturi throat and the air inlet.
C—increase in air velocity in the throat of a venturi causing an increase in air pressure.

*In a carburetor system, outside air flows into the carburetor and through a venturi (a narrow throat in the carburetor). When air flows rapidly through the venturi, a low pressure area is created. This low pressure allows the fuel to flow through the main fuel jet (located within the throat) and into the airstream where it mixes with the flowing air. (H307) — AC 61-23C, Chapter 2*

Answer (A) is incorrect because fuel, rather than air, is metered manually with the mixture control. Answer (C) is incorrect because there is a decrease in air pressure.

AIR, RTC
**3226.** The basic purpose of adjusting the fuel/air mixture at altitude is to

A—decrease the amount of fuel in the mixture in order to compensate for increased air density.
B—decrease the fuel flow in order to compensate for decreased air density.
C—increase the amount of fuel in the mixture to compensate for the decrease in pressure and density of the air.

*The mixture becomes richer as the airplane gains altitude, because the carburetor meters the same amount of fuel as at sea level. Leaning the mixture control prevents this by decreasing the rate of fuel discharge to compensate for the decrease in air density. (H307) — AC 61-23C, Chapter 2*

Answer (A) is incorrect because the pilot would increase the amount of fuel to compensate for increased air density. Answer (C) is incorrect because the pilot would decrease the amount of fuel to compensate for decreased air density.

AIR, RTC
**3228.** While cruising at 9,500 feet MSL, the fuel/air mixture is properly adjusted. What will occur if a descent to 4,500 feet MSL is made without readjusting the mixture?

A—The fuel/air mixture may become excessively lean.
B—There will be more fuel in the cylinders than is needed for normal combustion, and the excess fuel will absorb heat and cool the engine.
C—The excessively rich mixture will create higher cylinder head temperatures and may cause detonation.

*Air density increases in the descent, but the amount of fuel drawn into the carburetor remains the same. To reestablish a balanced fuel/air mixture in a descent, the mixture control must be adjusted toward "rich." (H307) — AC 61-23C, Chapter 2*

Answer (B) is incorrect because the mixture will become too lean and the engine temperature will increase. Answer (C) is incorrect because an excessively lean mixture will result.

**Answers**

3225  [B]          3226  [B]          3228  [A]

# Carburetor Ice

As air flows through a carburetor it expands rapidly. At the same time, fuel forced into the airstream is vaporized. Expansion of the air and vaporization of the fuel causes a sudden cooling of the mixture which may cause ice to form inside the carburetor. The possibility of icing should always be considered when operating in conditions where the temperature is between 20°F and 70°F, and the relative humidity is high.

**Carburetor heat** preheats the air before it enters the carburetor and either prevents carburetor ice from forming or melts any ice which may have formed. When carburetor heat is applied, the heated air that enters the carburetor is less dense. This causes the fuel/air mixture to become enriched, and this in turn decreases engine output and increases engine operating temperatures.

During engine runup prior to departure from a high-altitude airport, the pilot may notice a slight engine roughness which is not affected by the magneto check, but grows worse during the carburetor heat check. In this case, the air/fuel mixture may be too rich due to the lower air density at the high altitude, and applying carburetor heat decreases the air density even more. A leaner setting of the mixture control may correct this problem.

In an airplane with a fixed-pitch propeller, the first indication of carburetor ice would likely be a decrease in RPM as the air supply is choked off. Application of carburetor heat will decrease air density, causing the RPM to drop even lower. Then, as the carburetor ice melts, the RPM will rise gradually.

Fuel injection systems do not utilize a carburetor and are generally considered to be less susceptible to icing than carburetor systems are.

AIR

**3227.** During the run-up at a high-elevation airport, a pilot notes a slight engine roughness that is not affected by the magneto check but grows worse during the carburetor heat check. Under these circumstances, what would be the most logical initial action?

A—Check the results obtained with a leaner setting of the mixture.
B—Taxi back to the flight line for a maintenance check.
C—Reduce manifold pressure to control detonation.

*When carburetor heat is applied, the air/fuel mixture of an engine will be enriched because any given volume of hot air is less dense than cold air of the same volume. This condition would be aggravated at high altitude where, because of decreased air density, the mixture is already richer than at sea level. (H307) — AC 61-23C, Chapter 2*

*Answer (B) is incorrect because the pilot should taxi back only if positive results were not obtained by leaning the mixture. Answer (C) is incorrect because detonation would not occur if the mixture was too rich, and a rich fuel mixture was the condition described in the question.*

AIR, RTC

**3229.** Which condition is most favorable to the development of carburetor icing?

A—Any temperature below freezing and a relative humidity of less than 50 percent.
B—Temperature between 32 and 50°F and low humidity.
C—Temperature between 20 and 70°F and high humidity.

*If the temperature is between -7°C (20°F) and 21°C (70°F) with visible moisture or high humidity, the pilot should be constantly on the alert for carburetor ice. (H307) — AC 61-23C, Chapter 2*

*Answers (A) and (B) are incorrect because carburetor icing is more likely with high humidity.*

**Answers**

3227 [A]        3229 [C]

AIR, RTC

**3230.** The possibility of carburetor icing exists even when the ambient air temperature is as

A—high as 70°F and the relative humidity is high.
B—high as 95°F and there is visible moisture.
C—low as 0°F and the relative humidity is high.

*If the temperature is between -7°C (20°F) and 21°C (70°F) with visible moisture or high humidity, the pilot should be constantly on the alert for carburetor ice. (H307) — AC 61-23C, Chapter 2*

Answer (B) is incorrect because icing is less likely to occur above 70°F. Answer (C) is incorrect because icing is less likely to occur below 20°F.

AIR

**3231.** If an aircraft is equipped with a fixed-pitch propeller and a float-type carburetor, the first indication of carburetor ice would most likely be

A—a drop in oil temperature and cylinder head temperature.
B—engine roughness.
C—loss of RPM.

*For airplanes with a fixed-pitch propeller, the first indication of carburetor ice is loss of RPM. (H307) — AC 61-23C, Chapter 2*

Answers (A) and (B) are incorrect because these symptoms may develop, but only after a loss of RPM.

AIR, RTC

**3232.** Applying carburetor heat will

A—result in more air going through the carburetor.
B—enrich the fuel/air mixture.
C—not affect the fuel/air mixture.

*Carburetors are normally calibrated at sea level pressure to meter the correct fuel/air mixture. As altitude increases, air density decreases and the amount of fuel is too great for the amount of air — the mixture is "too rich." This same result may be brought about by the application of carburetor heat. The heated air entering the carburetor has less density than unheated air and the fuel/air mixture is enriched. (H307) — AC 61-23C, Chapter 2*

Answer (A) is incorrect because applying carburetor heat decreases the density of air but does not affect the air going through the carburetor. Answer (C) is incorrect because the mixture is enriched by applying carburetor heat.

AIR, RTC

**3233.** What change occurs in the fuel/air mixture when carburetor heat is applied?

A—A decrease in RPM results from the lean mixture.
B—The fuel/air mixture becomes richer.
C—The fuel/air mixture becomes leaner.

*Carburetors are normally calibrated at sea level pressure to meter the correct fuel/air mixture. As altitude increases, air density decreases and the amount of fuel is too great for the amount of air—the mixture is "too rich." This same result may be brought about by the application of carburetor heat. The heated air entering the carburetor has less density than unheated air and the fuel/air mixture is enriched. (H307) — AC 61-23C, Chapter 2*

Answers (A) and (C) are incorrect because the fuel/air mixture becomes richer.

AIR, RTC

**3234.** Generally speaking, the use of carburetor heat tends to

A—decrease engine performance.
B—increase engine performance.
C—have no effect on engine performance.

*Use of carburetor heat tends to reduce the output of the engine and also to increase the operating temperature. (H307) — AC 61-23C, Chapter 2*

AIR

**3235.** The presence of carburetor ice in an aircraft equipped with a fixed-pitch propeller can be verified by applying carburetor heat and noting

A—an increase in RPM and then a gradual decrease in RPM.
B—a decrease in RPM and then a constant RPM indication.
C—a decrease in RPM and then a gradual increase in RPM.

*When heat is applied there will be a drop in RPM in airplanes equipped with fixed-pitch propellers. If carburetor ice is present, there will normally be a rise in RPM after the initial drop. Then, when the carburetor heat is turned off, the RPM will rise to a setting greater than that before application of the heat. The engine should also run more smoothly after the ice has been removed. (H307) — AC 61-23C, Chapter 2*

Answer (A) is incorrect because the warm air decreases engine RPM; melting ice also decreases RPM. Once the ice is gone, the RPM increases. Answer (B) is incorrect because this would only happen if there was no carburetor ice to begin with.

**Answers**

| 3230 | [A] | 3231 | [C] | 3232 | [B] | 3233 | [B] | 3234 | [A] | 3235 | [C] |

AIR, RTC
**3236.** With regard to carburetor ice, float-type carburetor systems in comparison to fuel injection systems are generally considered to be

A— more susceptible to icing.
B— equally susceptible to icing.
C— susceptible to icing only when visible moisture is present.

*Fuel injection systems are less susceptible to icing than carburetor systems because of the lack of the temperature drop caused by the venturi in a carburetor. Be aware that one can acquire carburetor ice even without easily visible moisture and, in the right circumstances, even at full power. (H307) — AC 61-23C, Chapter 2*

*Answer (B) is incorrect because the venturi throat of carburetors makes them more susceptible to icing than fuel injection systems. Answer (C) is incorrect because visible moisture is not necessary if the humidity is high.*

# Aviation Fuel

Fuel does two things for the engine; it acts both as an agent for combustion and as an agent for cooling (based on the mixture setting of the engine).

Aviation fuel is available in several grades. The proper grade for a specific engine will be listed in the aircraft flight manual. If the proper grade of fuel is not available, it is possible to use the next higher grade. A lower grade of fuel should never be used.

The use of low-grade fuel or an air/fuel mixture which is too lean may cause **detonation**, which is the uncontrolled spontaneous explosion of the mixture in the cylinder. Detonation produces extreme heat.

**Preignition** is the premature burning of the air/fuel mixture. It is caused by an incandescent area (such as a carbon or lead deposit heated to a red hot glow) which serves as an ignitor in advance of normal ignition.

Fuel can be contaminated by water and/or dirt. The air inside the aircraft fuel tanks can cool at night, and this cooling forms water droplets (through condensation) on the insides of the fuel tanks. These droplets then fall into the fuel. To avoid this problem, always fill the tanks completely when parking overnight.

Thoroughly drain all of the aircraft's sumps, drains, and strainers before a flight to get rid of all the water that might have collected.

Dirt can get into the fuel if refueling equipment is poorly maintained or if the refueling operation is sloppy. Use care when refueling an aircraft.

Two fuel pump systems are used on most airplanes. The main pump system is engine driven and an auxiliary electric driven pump is provided for use in the event the engine pump fails. The auxiliary pump, commonly known as the "boost pump," provides added reliability to the fuel system, and is also used as an aid in engine starting. The electric auxiliary pump is controlled by a switch in the cockpit.

AIR, RTC
**3237.** If the grade of fuel used in an aircraft engine is lower than specified for the engine, it will most likely cause

A— a mixture of fuel and air that is not uniform in all cylinders.
B— lower cylinder head temperatures.
C— detonation.

*Using aviation fuel of a lower rating is harmful under any circumstances because it may cause loss of power, excessive heat, burned spark plugs, burned and sticky valves, high oil consumption, and detonation. (H307) — AC 61-23C, Chapter 2*

*Answer (A) is incorrect because the carburetor will meter the lower-grade fuel the same as the proper fuel. Answer (B) is incorrect because lower-grade fuel raises cylinder head temperatures.*

**Answers**

3236  [A]       3237  [C]

AIR, RTC

**3238.** Detonation occurs in a reciprocating aircraft engine when

A—the spark plugs are fouled or shorted out or the wiring is defective.
B—hot spots in the combustion chamber ignite the fuel/air mixture in advance of normal ignition.
C—the unburned charge in the cylinders explodes instead of burning normally.

*Using low-grade fuel or too lean a mixture can cause detonation. Detonation is a sudden explosion or shock to a small area of the piston top, similar to striking it with a hammer. (H307) — AC 61-23C, Chapter 2*

*Answer (A) is incorrect because these conditions would cause the engine to run rough, or not at all. Answer (B) is incorrect because these conditions describe preignition.*

AIR, RTC

**3240.** The uncontrolled firing of the fuel/air charge in advance of normal spark ignition is known as

A—combustion.
B—pre-ignition.
C—detonation.

*Preignition is defined as ignition of the fuel prior to normal ignition. (H307) — AC 61-23C, Chapter 2*

*Answer (A) is incorrect because combustion is the normal engine process. Answer (C) is incorrect because detonation is the exploding of the fuel/air mixture.*

AIR, RTC

**3242.** What type fuel can be substituted for an aircraft if the recommended octane is not available?

A—The next higher octane aviation gas.
B—The next lower octane aviation gas.
C—Unleaded automotive gas of the same octane rating.

*If the proper grade of fuel is not available, it is possible (but not desirable), to use the next higher (aviation) grade as a substitute. (H307) — AC 61-23C, Chapter 2*

*Answer (B) is incorrect because burning lower octane fuel causes excessive engine temperatures. Answer (C) is incorrect because only aviation fuel should be used, except under special circumstances.*

AIR, RTC

**3243.** Filling the fuel tanks after the last flight of the day is considered a good operating procedure because this will

A—force any existing water to the top of the tank away from the fuel lines to the engine.
B—prevent expansion of the fuel by eliminating airspace in the tanks.
C—prevent moisture condensation by eliminating airspace in the tanks.

*Water in the fuel system is dangerous and the pilot must prevent contamination. The fuel tanks should be filled after each flight, or at least after the last flight of the day. This will prevent moisture condensation within the tank, since no air space will be left inside. (H307) — AC 61-23C, Chapter 2*

*Answer (A) is incorrect because water will settle to the bottom of a gas tank. Answer (B) is incorrect because fuel is allowed to expand by the fuel vent, whether the tanks are full or not.*

AIR

**3224.** On aircraft equipped with fuel pumps, when is the auxiliary electric driven pump used?

A—All the time to aid the engine-driven fuel pump.
B—In the event engine-driven fuel pump fails.
C—Constantly except in starting the engine.

*Two fuel pump systems are used on most airplanes. The main pump system is engine driven and an auxiliary electric driven pump is provided for use in the event the engine pump fails. The auxiliary pump, commonly known as the "boost pump," provides added reliability to the fuel system, and is also used as an aid in engine starting. The electric auxiliary pump is controlled by a switch in the cockpit. (H307) — AC 61-23C, Chapter 2*

**Answers**

3238 [C]     3240 [B]     3242 [A]     3243 [C]     3224 [B]

# Engine Temperatures

Engine lubricating **oil** not only prevents direct metal-to-metal contact of moving parts, it also absorbs and dissipates some of the engine heat produced by internal combustion. If the engine oil level should fall too low, an abnormally high engine oil temperature indication may result.

On the ground or in the air, excessively high engine temperatures can cause excessive oil consumption, loss of power, and possible permanent internal engine damage.

If the engine oil temperature and cylinder head temperature gauges have exceeded their normal operating range, or if the pilot suspects that the engine (with a fixed-pitch propeller) is detonating during climb-out, the pilot may have been operating with either too much power and the mixture set too lean, using fuel of too low a grade, or operating the engine with an insufficient amount of oil in it. Reducing the rate of climb and increasing airspeed, enriching the fuel mixture, or retarding the throttle will aid in cooling an engine that is overheating.

The most important rule to remember in the event of a power failure after becoming airborne is to maintain safe airspeed.

AIR, RTC

**3221.** Excessively high engine temperatures will

A—cause damage to heat-conducting hoses and warping of the cylinder cooling fins.
B—cause loss of power, excessive oil consumption, and possible permanent internal engine damage.
C—not appreciably affect an aircraft engine.

*Operating an engine at a higher temperature than it was designed for will cause loss of power, excessive oil consumption, and detonation. It will also lead to serious permanent injury to the engine including scoring of cylinder walls, damage to pistons and rings, and burning and warping of valves. (H307) — AC 61-23C, Chapter 2*

Answer (A) is incorrect because internal engine damage is more likely to result before external damage occurs. Answer (C) is incorrect because excessively high engine temperatures seriously affect an aircraft engine.

AIR, RTC

**3222.** If the engine oil temperature and cylinder head temperature gauges have exceeded their normal operating range, the pilot may have been operating with

A—the mixture set too rich.
B—higher-than-normal oil pressure.
C—too much power and with the mixture set too lean.

*Excessively high engine temperatures can result from insufficient cooling caused by too lean a mixture, too low a grade of fuel, low oil, or insufficient airflow over the engine. (H307) — AC 61-23C, Chapter 2*

Answer (A) is incorrect because a richer fuel mixture will normally cool an engine. Answer (B) is incorrect because high oil pressure does not cause high engine temperatures.

AIR

**3239.** If a pilot suspects that the engine (with a fixed-pitch propeller) is detonating during climb-out after takeoff, the initial corrective action to take would be to

A—lean the mixture.
B—lower the nose slightly to increase airspeed.
C—apply carburetor heat.

*To prevent detonation, the pilot should use the correct grade of fuel, maintain a sufficiently rich mixture, open the throttle smoothly, and keep the temperature of the engine within recommended operating limits. Some aircraft have an automatically enriched mixture for enhanced cooling in takeoff and climb-out at full throttle. Lowering the nose will allow the aircraft to gain airspeed, which eventually lowers the engine temperature. (H307) — AC 61-23C, Chapter 2*

Answer (A) is incorrect because leaning the mixture increases engine temperatures; detonation results from excessively high engine temperatures. Answer (C) is incorrect because although a richer fuel mixture results from applying carburetor heat, the heat may offset the cooling effect of the mixture change. The most efficient initial action would be to increase airspeed.

**Answers**

3221 [B]      3222 [C]      3239 [B]

**AIR, RTC**
**3241.** Which would most likely cause the cylinder head temperature and engine oil temperature gauges to exceed their normal operating ranges?

A— Using fuel that has a lower-than-specified fuel rating.
B— Using fuel that has a higher-than-specified fuel rating.
C— Operating with higher-than-normal oil pressure.

*Excessively high engine temperatures result from insufficient cooling caused by too lean a mixture, too low a grade of fuel, low oil, or insufficient airflow over the engine. (H307) — AC 61-23C, Chapter 2*

Answer (B) is incorrect because higher octane fuel will burn at lower temperatures, keeping the engine cooler. Answer (C) is incorrect because high oil pressure does not cause high engine temperatures.

**AIR, RTC**
**3244.** For internal cooling, reciprocating aircraft engines are especially dependent on

A— a properly functioning thermostat.
B— air flowing over the exhaust manifold.
C— the circulation of lubricating oil.

*Oil, used primarily to lubricate the moving parts of the engine, also cools the internal parts of the engine as it circulates. (H307) — AC 61-23C, Chapter 2*

Answer (A) is incorrect because most air-cooled aircraft engines do not have thermostats. Answer (B) is incorrect because, although air-cooling is important, internal cooling is more reliant on oil circulation. Air cools the cylinders, not the exhaust manifold.

**AIR, RTC**
**3245.** An abnormally high engine oil temperature indication may be caused by

A— the oil level being too low.
B— operating with a too high viscosity oil.
C— operating with an excessively rich mixture.

*Oil, used primarily to lubricate the moving parts of the engine, also helps reduce engine temperature by removing some of the heat from the cylinders. Therefore, if the oil level is too low, the transfer of heat to less oil would cause the oil temperature to rise. (H307) — AC 61-23C, Chapter 2*

Answer (B) is incorrect because the higher the viscosity, the better the lubricating and cooling capability of the oil. Answer (C) is incorrect because a rich fuel/air mixture usually decreases engine temperature.

**AIR, RTC**
**3651.** What action can a pilot take to aid in cooling an engine that is overheating during a climb?

A— Reduce rate of climb and increase airspeed.
B— Reduce climb speed and increase RPM.
C— Increase climb speed and increase RPM.

*To avoid excessive cylinder head temperatures, a pilot can open the cowl flaps, increase airspeed, enrich the mixture, or reduce power. Any of these procedures will aid in reducing the engine temperature. Establishing a shallower climb (increasing airspeed) increases the airflow through the cooling system, reducing high engine temperatures. (H307) — AC 61-23C, Chapter 2*

Answer (B) is incorrect because reducing airspeed hinders cooling, and increasing RPM will further increase engine temperature. Answer (C) is incorrect because increasing RPM will increase engine temperature.

**AIR, RTC**
**3652.** What is one procedure to aid in cooling an engine that is overheating?

A— Enrich the fuel mixture.
B— Increase the RPM.
C— Reduce the airspeed.

*To avoid excessive cylinder head temperatures, a pilot can open the cowl flaps, increase airspeed, enrich the mixture, or reduce power. Any of these procedures will aid in reducing the engine temperature. (H307) — AC 61-23C, Chapter 2*

Answer (B) is incorrect because increasing the RPM increases the engine's internal heat. Answer (C) is incorrect because reducing the airspeed decreases the airflow needed for cooling, thus increasing the engine's temperature.

**AIR, RTC**
**3711.** The most important rule to remember in the event of a power failure after becoming airborne is to

A— immediately establish the proper gliding attitude and airspeed.
B— quickly check the fuel supply for possible fuel exhaustion.
C— determine the wind direction to plan for the forced landing.

*Maintaining the proper glide speed (safe airspeed) is the most important rule to remember in the event of a power failure. (H582) — FAA-H-8083-3, Chapter 12*

Answers (B) and (C) are incorrect because these steps should be taken only after establishing the proper glide speed.

**Answers**

3241 [A]    3244 [C]    3245 [A]    3651 [A]    3652 [A]    3711 [A]

# Propellers

A propeller provides thrust to propel the airplane through the air. Some aircraft are equipped with a **constant-speed propeller**. This type of propeller allows the pilot to select the most efficient propeller blade angle for each phase of flight. In these aircraft, the throttle controls the power output as registered on the manifold pressure gauge, and the propeller control regulates the engine RPM.

A pilot should avoid a high manifold pressure setting with low RPM on engines equipped with a constant-speed propeller. To avoid high manifold pressure combined with low RPM, reduce the manifold pressure before reducing RPM when decreasing power settings (or increase the RPM before increasing the manifold pressure when increasing power settings).

AIR
**3653.** How is engine operation controlled on an engine equipped with a constant-speed propeller?

A—The throttle controls power output as registered on the manifold pressure gauge and the propeller control regulates engine RPM.
B—The throttle controls power output as registered on the manifold pressure gauge and the propeller control regulates a constant blade angle.
C—The throttle controls engine RPM as registered on the tachometer and the mixture control regulates the power output.

*On aircraft equipped with a constant-speed propeller, the throttle controls the engine power output which is registered on the manifold pressure gauge. The propeller control changes the pitch angle of the propeller and governs the RPM which is indicated on the tachometer. (H308) — AC 61-23C, Chapter 2*

*Answer (B) is incorrect because the propeller control does not maintain a constant pitch, it changes pitch in order to hold a constant RPM. Answer (C) is incorrect because the throttle does not directly control RPM, and mixture control does not regulate power.*

AIR
**3654.** What is an advantage of a constant-speed propeller?

A—Permits the pilot to select and maintain a desired cruising speed.
B—Permits the pilot to select the blade angle for the most efficient performance.
C—Provides a smoother operation with stable RPM and eliminates vibrations.

*A constant-speed propeller permits the pilot to select the blade angle that will result in the most efficient performance for a particular flight condition. A low blade angle allows higher RPM and horsepower, desirable for take-offs. An intermediate position can be used for subsequent climb. After airspeed is attained during cruising flight, the propeller blade may be changed to a higher angle for lower RPM, reduced engine noise, generally lower vibration, and greater fuel efficiency. (H308) — AC 61-23C, Chapter 2*

*Answer (A) is incorrect because a constant-speed propeller is not used to maintain airspeed, but rather constant engine RPM. Answer (C) is incorrect because a constant-speed propeller may not be smoother or operate with less vibration than a fixed-pitch propeller.*

AIR
**3655.** A precaution for the operation of an engine equipped with a constant-speed propeller is to

A—avoid high RPM settings with high manifold pressure.
B—avoid high manifold pressure settings with low RPM.
C—always use a rich mixture with high RPM settings.

*On aircraft equipped with a constant-speed propeller, the throttle controls the engine power output which is registered on the manifold pressure gauge. The propeller control changes the pitch angle of the propeller and governs the RPM which is indicated on the tachometer. On most airplanes, for any given RPM, there is a manifold pressure that should not be exceeded. If an excessive amount of manifold pressure is carried for a given RPM, the maximum allowable pressure within the engine cylinders could be exceeded, thus putting undue strain on them. (H308) — AC 61-23C, Chapter 2*

*Answer (A) is incorrect because high manifold pressure is allowable with high RPM settings, within specification limits. Answer (C) is incorrect because the mixture should be leaned for best performance.*

**Answers**

3653 [A]        3654 [B]        3655 [B]

# Torque

An airplane of standard configuration has an insistent tendency to turn to the left. This tendency is called torque, and is a combination of four forces: namely, reactive force, spiraling slipstream, gyroscopic precession, and P-factor.

**Reactive force** is based on Newton's Law of action and reaction. A propeller rotating in a clockwise direction (as seen from the rear) produces a force which tends to roll the airplane in a counterclockwise direction. *See* Figure 2-2.

The **spiraling slipstream** is the reaction of the air to a rotating propeller. (The propeller forces the air to spiral in a clockwise direction around the fuselage.) This spiraling slipstream strikes the vertical stabilizer on the left side. This pushes the tail of the airplane to the right and the nose of the airplane to the left. *See* Figure 2-3.

**Gyroscopic precession** is the result of a deflective force applied to a rotating body (such as a propeller). The resultant action occurs 90° later in the direction of rotation. *See* Figure 2-4.

Asymmetric propeller loading, called **P-factor**, is caused by the downward moving blade on the right side of the propeller having a higher angle of attack, a greater action and reaction, and therefore a higher thrust than the upward moving opposite blade. This results in a tendency for the airplane to yaw to the left around the vertical axis. Additional left-turning tendency from torque will be greatest when the airplane is operating at low airspeed with a high power setting.

**Figure 2-2.** Reactive force

**Figure 2-3.** Spiraling slipstream

**Figure 2-4.** Gyroscopic precession

AIR

**3207.** In what flight condition is torque effect the greatest in a single-engine airplane?

A—Low airspeed, high power, high angle of attack.
B—Low airspeed, low power, low angle of attack.
C—High airspeed, high power, high angle of attack.

*The effect of torque increases in direct proportion to the engine power, airspeed, and airplane attitude. If the power setting is high, the airspeed slow, and the angle of attack high, the effect of torque is greater. (H300) — AC 61-23C, Chapter 1*

*Answer (B) is incorrect because the least amount of torque effect is produced under these conditions. Answer (C) is incorrect because torque effect is negligible at higher airspeeds due to increased stability generated by more airflow moving over all airfoils.*

AIR

**3208.** The left turning tendency of an airplane caused by P-factor is the result of the

A—clockwise rotation of the engine and the propeller turning the airplane counter-clockwise.
B—propeller blade descending on the right, producing more thrust than the ascending blade on the left.
C—gyroscopic forces applied to the rotating propeller blades acting 90° in advance of the point the force was applied.

*The downward-moving blade on the right side of the propeller has a higher angle of attack and greater action and reaction than the upward moving blade on the left. This results in a tendency for the airplane to yaw around the vertical axis to the left. (H301) — AC 61-23C, Chapter 1*

*Answer (A) is incorrect because it describes the characteristics involved with torque effect. Answer (C) is incorrect because it describes gyroscopic precession.*

AIR

**3209.** When does P-factor cause the airplane to yaw to the left?

A—When at low angles of attack.
B—When at high angles of attack.
C—When at high airspeeds.

*The effects of P-factor, or asymmetric propeller loading, usually occur when the airplane is flown at high angles of attack and at high power settings. (H301) — AC 61-23C, Chapter 1*

*Answer (A) is incorrect because the thrust differential between ascending and descending propeller blades at low angles of attack is slight. Answer (C) is incorrect because at higher airspeeds, an aircraft's angle of attack decreases in straight-and-level flight; therefore propeller-blade differential thrust becomes negligible.*

**Answers**

3207 [A]     3208 [B]     3209 [B]

# Preflight Inspection Procedures

A thorough **preflight inspection** should be performed on an aircraft to help ensure that the aircraft is prepared for safe flight and should be a thorough and systematic means by which the pilot determines the airplane is ready for safe flight. Prior to every flight, a pilot should at least perform a walk-around inspection of the aircraft.

After an aircraft has been stored for an extended period of time, a special check should be made during preflight for damage or obstructions caused by animals, birds, or insects.

The use of a written checklist for preflight inspection and starting the engine is recommended to ensure that all necessary items are checked in a logical sequence.

Although 14 CFR Part 91 places primary responsibility on the owner or operator for maintaining an aircraft in an airworthy condition, the pilot-in-command is responsible for determining whether that aircraft is in condition for safe flight.

ALL
**3658.** During the preflight inspection who is responsible for determining the aircraft is safe for flight?

A—The pilot in command.
B—The owner or operator.
C—The certificated mechanic who performed the annual inspection.

*The pilot-in-command of an aircraft is responsible for determining whether that aircraft is in condition for safe flight. (H311) — 14 CFR §91.7*

ALL
**3659.** How should an aircraft preflight inspection be accomplished for the first flight of the day?

A—Quick walk around with a check of gas and oil.
B—Thorough and systematic means recommended by the manufacturer.
C—Any sequence as determined by the pilot-in-command.

*The preflight inspection should be a thorough and systematic means by which the pilot determines that the airplane is ready for safe flight. Most Aircraft Flight Manuals or Pilot's Operating Handbooks contain a section devoted to a systematic method of performing a preflight inspection that should be used by the pilot for guidance. (H311) — AC 61-23C, Chapter 2*

ALL
**3660.** Who is primarily responsible for maintaining an aircraft in airworthy condition?

A—Pilot-in-command.
B—Owner or operator.
C—Mechanic.

*14 CFR Part 91 places primary responsibility on the owner or operator for maintaining an aircraft in an airworthy condition. (H311) — AC 61-23C, Chapter 2*

**Answers**

3658 [A]    3659 [B]    3660 [B]

# Helicopter Systems

RTC
**3318.** (Refer to Figure 10.) During flight, if cyclic control pressure is applied which results in a maximum increase in pitch angle of the rotor blade at position A, the rotor disc will tilt

A—forward.
B—aft.
C—left.

*Gyroscopic precession is the resultant action of a spinning object when a force is applied to the object. The action occurs approximately 90° later in the direction of rotation. Thus, if the maximum increase in angle of attack occurs at point A, maximum deflection takes place 90° later. This is maximum upward deflection at the rear, and the tip-path plane tips forward. (H703) — FAA-H-8083-21, Chapter 3*

RTC
**3319.** The lift differential that exists between the advancing main rotor blade and the retreating main rotor blade is known as

A—transverse flow effect.
B—dissymmetry of lift.
C—hunting tendency.

*The difference in lift that exists between the advancing blade half of the disc and retreating blade half, created by horizontal flight or by wind during hovering flight, is called dissymmetry of lift. (H703) — FAA-H-8083-21, Chapter 3*

RTC
**3320.** During forward cruising flight at constant airspeed and altitude, the individual rotor blades, when compared to each other, are operating

A—with increased lift on the retreating blade.
B—with a decreasing angle of attack on the advancing blade.
C—at unequal airspeed, unequal angles of attack, and equal lift moment.

*As the helicopter moves into forward flight, the relative wind moving over each rotor blade becomes a combination of the rotational speed of the rotor and the forward movement of the helicopter. Increased lift on the advancing blade will cause the blade to flap, decreasing the angle of attack. Decreased lift on the retreating blade will cause the blade to flap down, increasing the angle of attack. The combination of decreased angle of attack on the advancing blade and increased angle of attack on the retreating blade through blade flapping action tends to equalize lift over the two halves of the rotor disc. (H703) — FAA-H-8083-21, Chapter 3*

RTC
**3321.** The upward bending of the rotor blades resulting from the combined forces of lift and centrifugal force is known as

A—coning.
B—blade slapping.
C—inertia.

*As a vertical takeoff is made, two major forces are acting at the same time—centrifugal force acting outward, perpendicular to the rotor mast, and lift, acting upward and parallel to the mast. The result of these two forces is that the blades assume a conical path instead of remaining in the plane perpendicular to the mast. (H703) — FAA-H-8083-21, Chapter 3*

RTC
**3322.** When a blade flaps up, the CG moves closer to its axis of rotation giving that blade a tendency to

A—decelerate.
B—accelerate.
C—stabilize its rotational velocity.

*When a rotor blade flaps up, the center of mass of that blade moves closer to the axis of rotation and blade acceleration takes place. (H703) — FAA-H-8083-21, Chapter 3*

RTC
**3323.** During a hover, a helicopter tends to drift to the right. To compensate for this, some helicopters have the

A—tail rotor tilted to the left.
B—tail rotor tilted to the right.
C—rotor mast rigged to the left side.

*To counteract drift, the rotor mast in some helicopters is rigged slightly to the left side so that the tip-path plane has a built-in tilt to the left, thus producing a small sideward thrust. (H703) — FAA-H-8083-21, Chapter 3*

**Answers**

| 3318 [A] | 3319 [B] | 3320 [C] | 3321 [A] | 3322 [B] | 3323 [C] |
| --- | --- | --- | --- | --- | --- |

RTC

**3325.** Translational lift is the result of

A—decreased rotor efficiency.
B—airspeed.
C—both airspeed and groundspeed.

*Translational lift is that additional lift obtained when entering horizontal flight due to the increased efficiency of the rotor system. Translational lift depends upon airspeed rather than ground speed. (H703) — FAA-H-8083-21, Chapter 3*

RTC

**3326.** The primary purpose of the tail rotor system is to

A—assist in making a coordinated turn.
B—maintain heading during forward flight.
C—counteract the torque effect of the main rotor.

*The force that compensates for torque and keeps the fuselage from turning in the direction opposite to the main rotor is produced by means of an auxiliary rotor located on the end of the tail boom. (H705) — FAA-H-8083-21, Chapter 4*

RTC

**3327.** If RPM is low and manifold pressure is high, what initial corrective action should be taken?

A—Increase the throttle.
B—Lower the collective pitch.
C—Raise the collective pitch.

*Lowering the collective pitch will reduce the manifold pressure, decrease drag on the rotor, and therefore increase the RPM. (H705) — FAA-H-8083-21, Chapter 4*

RTC

**3328.** The purpose of the lead-lag (drag) hinge in a three-bladed, fully articulated helicopter rotor system is to compensate for

A—Coriolis effect.
B—coning.
C—geometric unbalance.

*In a fully-articulated rotor system, each rotor blade is attached to the hub by a vertical hinge called a drag or lag hinge that permits each blade, independently of the others, to move back and forth in the plane of the rotor disc. This movement is called dragging, lead-lag, or hunting. The purpose of the drag hinge and dampers is to absorb the acceleration and deceleration of the rotor blades caused by Coriolis effect. (H703) — FAA-H-8083-21, Chapter 3*

RTC

**3329.** High airspeeds, particularly in turbulent air, should be avoided primarily because of the possibility of

A—an abrupt pitchup.
B—retreating blade stall.
C—a low-frequency vibration developing.

*A tendency for the retreating blade to stall in forward flight is a major factor in limiting a helicopter's forward airspeed. When operating at high airspeeds, stalls are more liable to occur under conditions of high gross weight, low RPM, high density altitude, steep or abrupt turns, and/or turbulent flight. (H748) — FAA-H-8083-21, Chapter 11*

RTC

**3330.** The maximum forward speed of a helicopter is limited by

A—retreating blade stall.
B—the rotor RPM red line.
C—solidity ratio.

*A tendency for the retreating blade to stall in forward flight is a major factor in limiting a helicopter's forward airspeed. When operating at high airspeeds, stalls are more liable to occur under conditions of high gross weight, low RPM, high density altitude, steep or abrupt turns, and/or turbulent flight. (H748) — FAA-H-8083-21, Chapter 11*

RTC

**3331.** When operating at high forward airspeeds, retreating blade stalls are more likely to occur under which condition?

A—Low gross weight and low density altitude.
B—High RPM and low density altitude.
C—Steep turns in turbulent air.

*A tendency for the retreating blade to stall in forward flight is a major factor in limiting a helicopter's forward airspeed. When operating at high airspeeds, stalls are more liable to occur under conditions of high gross weight, low RPM, high density altitude, steep or abrupt turns, and/or turbulent flight. (H748) — FAA-H-8083-21, Chapter 11*

**Answers**

| 3325 [B] | 3326 [C] | 3327 [B] | 3328 [A] | 3329 [B] | 3330 [A] |
| 3331 [C] | | | | | |

RTC
**3332.** Ground resonance is most likely to develop when

A—on the ground and harmonic vibrations develop between the main and tail rotors.
B—a series of shocks causes the rotor system to become unbalanced.
C—there is a combination of a decrease in the angle of attack on the advancing blade and an increase in the angle of attack on the retreating blade.

*When one landing gear of the helicopter strikes the surface first, a shock is transmitted through the fuselage to the rotor. This shock may cause the blades straddling the contact point to be forced closer together. When one of the other landing gears strikes, the unbalance could be aggravated. This sets up a resonance of the fuselage. (H749) — FAA-H-8083-21, Chapter 11*

RTC
**3333.** While in level cruising flight in a helicopter, a pilot experiences low-frequency vibrations (100 to 400 cycles per minute). These vibrations are normally associated with the

A—engine.
B—cooling fan.
C—main rotor.

*Low-frequency vibrations are always associated with the main rotor. (H745) — FAA-H-8083-21, Chapter 11*

RTC
**3334.** Select the helicopter component that, if defective, would cause medium-frequency vibrations.

A—Tail rotor.
B—Main rotor.
C—Engine.

*Medium-frequency vibrations are a result of trouble with the tail rotor in most helicopters. (H745) — FAA-H-8083-21, Chapter 11*

RTC
**3335.** The principal reason the shaded area of a Height vs. Velocity Chart should be avoided is

A—turbulence near the surface can dephase the blade dampers.
B—rotor RPM may decay before ground contact is made if an engine failure should occur.
C—insufficient airspeed would be available to ensure a safe landing in case of an engine failure.

*The chart can be used to determine those altitude-airspeed combinations from which it would be impossible to successfully complete an autorotative landing. The altitude-airspeed combinations that should be avoided are represented by the shaded areas of the chart. (H747) — FAA-H-8083-21, Chapter 11*

RTC
**3336.** During surface taxiing, the collective pitch is used to control

A—drift during a crosswind.
B—rate of speed.
C—ground track.

*Collective pitch is used to control rate of speed during taxi. The higher the collective pitch, the faster will be the taxi speed. (H727) — FAA-H-8083-21, Chapter 9*

RTC
**3337.** During surface taxiing, the cyclic pitch stick is used to control

A—forward movement.
B—heading.
C—ground track.

*Cyclic pitch is used to control ground track during surface taxi. (H727) — FAA-H-8083-21, Chapter 9*

RTC
**3338.** If the pilot experiences ground resonance during rotor spin-up, what action should the pilot take?

A—Taxi to a smooth area.
B—Close the throttle and slowly raise the spin-up lever.
C—Make a normal takeoff immediately.

*Corrective action for ground resonance could be an immediate takeoff if RPM is in proper range, or an immediate closing of the throttle and placing the blades in low pitch if RPM is low. "During rotor spin-up" implies low RPM. (H767) — FAA-H-8083-21, Chapter 21*

**Answers**

| 3332 [B] | 3333 [C] | 3334 [A] | 3335 [C] | 3336 [B] | 3337 [C] |
| 3338 [B] | | | | | |

RTC
**3339.** What precaution should be taken while taxiing a gyroplane?

A—The cyclic stick should be held in the neutral position at all times.
B—Avoid abrupt control movements when blades are turning.
C—The cyclic stick should be held slightly aft of neutral at all times.

*Avoid abrupt control motions while taxiing. (H766) — FAA-H-8083-21, Chapter 20*

RTC
**3733.** With calm wind conditions, which flight operation would require the most power?

A—A right-hovering turn.
B—A left-hovering turn.
C—Hovering out of ground effect.

*During a hovering turn to the left, the RPM will decrease if throttle is not added. In a hovering turn to the right, RPM will increase if throttle is not reduced slightly. (This is due to the amount of engine power that is being absorbed by the tail rotor, which is dependent upon the pitch angle at which the tail rotor blades are operating.) (H720) — FAA-H-8083-21, Chapter 8*

RTC
**3734.** If the pilot were to make a near-vertical power approach into a confined area with the airspeed near zero, what hazardous condition may develop?

A—Ground resonance when ground contact is made.
B—A settling-with-power condition.
C—Blade stall vibration could develop.

*The following combination of conditions are likely to cause settling with power:*

*1. A vertical, or nearly vertical, descent of at least 300 feet per minute. Actual critical rate depends on the gross weight, RPM, density altitude, and other pertinent factors.*

*2. The rotor system must be using some of the available engine power (from 20 to 100 percent).*

*3. The horizontal velocity must be no greater than approximately 10 miles per hour.*

*(H745) — FAA-H-8083-21, Chapter 11*

RTC
**3736-1.** (Refer to Figure 47.) Which airspeed/altitude combination should be avoided during helicopter operations?

A—30 MPH/200 feet AGL.
B—50 MPH/300 feet AGL.
C—60 MPH/20 feet AGL.

*Use the following steps:*

*1. Note the shaded "avoid operation" areas of FAA Figure 47.*

*2. Locate each of the three height-above-terrain and airspeed points on the diagram.*

*3. The 60 MPH/20 feet AGL point is located within the low-altitude high airspeed area.*

*(H747) — FAA-H-8083-21, Chapter 11*

RTC
**3736-2.** (Refer to Figure 47.) Which airspeed/altitude combination should be avoided during helicopter operations?

A—20 MPH/200 feet AGL.
B—40 MPH/75 feet AGL.
C—35 MPH/175 feet AGL.

*Use the following steps:*

*1. Note the shaded "avoid operation" areas of FAA Figure 47.*

*2. Locate each of the three height-above-terrain and airspeed points on the diagram.*

*3. The 20 MPH/200 feet AGL point is located within the low-altitude high airspeed area.*

*(H747) — FAA-H-8083-21, Chapter 11*

**Answers**

3339 [B]    3733 [B]    3734 [B]    3736-1 [C]    3736-2 [A]

RTC
**3737.** (Refer to Figure 47.) Which airspeed/altitude combination should be avoided during helicopter operations?

A—20 MPH/200 feet AGL.
B—35 MPH/175 feet AGL.
C—40 MPH/75 feet AGL.

*Use the following steps:*

*1. Note the shaded "avoid operation" areas of FAA Figure 47.*

*2. Locate each of the three height-above-terrain and airspeed points on the diagram.*

*3. The 20 MPH/200 feet AGL point is located within the high-altitude low airspeed area.*

*(H78) — FAA-H-8083-21*

RTC
**3738.** If anti-torque failure occurred during the landing touchdown, what could be done to help straighten out a left yaw prior to touchdown?

A—A flare to zero airspeed and a vertical descent to touchdown should be made.
B—Apply available throttle to help swing the nose to the right just prior to touchdown.
C—A normal running landing should be made.

*If sufficient forward speed is maintained, the fuselage remains fairly well streamlined. However, if descent is attempted at slow speeds, a continuous turning movement to the left can be expected. (Know the manufacturer's recommendations in case of tail rotor failure for each particular helicopter you fly. This information will generally be found under Emergency Procedures in the helicopter flight manual.) Directional control should be maintained primarily with cyclic control and, secondarily, by gently applying throttle momentarily, with needles joined, to swing the nose to the right. (H78) — FAA-H-8083-21*

RTC
**3739.** Which flight technique is recommended for use during hot weather?

A—Use minimum allowable RPM and maximum allowable manifold pressure during all phases of flight.
B—During hovering flight, maintain minimum engine RPM during left pedal turns, and maximum engine RPM during right pedal turns.
C—During takeoff, accelerate slowly into forward flight.

*The following techniques should be used in hot weather:*

*1. Make full use of wind and translational lift.*

*2. Hover as low as possible and no longer than necessary.*

*3. Maintain maximum allowable engine RPM.*

*4. Accelerate very slowly into forward flight.*

*5. Employ running takeoffs and landings when necessary.*

*6. Use caution in maximum performance takeoffs and steep approaches.*

*7. Avoid high rates of descent in all approaches.*

*(H738) — FAA-H-8083-21, Chapter 10*

RTC
**3740.** Under what condition should a helicopter pilot consider using a running takeoff?

A—When gross weight or density altitude prevents a sustained hover at normal hovering altitude.
B—When a normal climb speed is assured between 10 and 20 feet.
C—When the additional airspeed can be quickly converted to altitude.

*A running takeoff is used when conditions of load and/or density altitude prevent a sustained hover at normal hovering altitude. It is often referred to as a high-altitude takeoff. With insufficient power to hover at least momentarily or at a very low altitude, a running takeoff is not advisable. No takeoff should be attempted if the helicopter cannot be lifted off the surface momentarily at full power. (H738) — FAA-H-8083-21, Chapter 10*

RTC
**3741.** What action should the pilot take if engine failure occurs at altitude?

A—Open the throttle as the collective pitch is raised.
B—Reduce cyclic back stick pressure during turns.
C—Lower the collective pitch control, as necessary, to maintain rotor RPM.

*By immediately lowering collective pitch (which must be done in case of engine failure), lift and drag will be reduced and the helicopter will begin an immediate descent, thus producing an upward flow of air through the rotor system. The impact of this upward flow of air provides sufficient thrust to maintain rotor RPM throughout the descent. (H746) — FAA-H-8083-21, Chapter 11*

**Answers**

| 3737 | [A] | 3738 | [B] | 3739 | [C] | 3740 | [A] | 3741 | [C] |

RTC
**3742.** Which is a precaution to be observed during an autorotative descent?

A—Normally, the airspeed is controlled with the collective pitch.
B—Normally, only the cyclic control is used to make turns.
C—Do not allow the rate of descent to get too low at zero airspeed.

*When making turns during an autorotative descent, generally use cyclic control only. Use of antitorque pedals to assist or speed the turn causes loss of airspeed and downward pitching of the nose. This is especially true when the left pedal is used. When the autorotation is initiated, sufficient right pedal pressure should be used to maintain straight flight and prevent yawing to the left. This pressure should not be changed to assist the turn. (H746) — FAA-H-8083-21, Chapter 11*

RTC
**3743.** The proper action to initiate a quick stop is to apply

A—forward cyclic and lower the collective pitch.
B—aft cyclic and raise the collective pitch.
C—aft cyclic and lower the collective pitch.

*A quick stop is initiated by applying aft cyclic to reduce forward speed. Simultaneously, the collective pitch should be lowered as necessary, to counteract any climbing tendency. The timing must be exact. If too little down collective is applied for the amount of aft cyclic applied, a climb will result. If too much down collective is applied for the amount of aft cyclic applied, a descent will result. A rapid application of aft cyclic requires an equally rapid application of down collective. As collective pitch is lowered, the right pedal should be increased to maintain heading, and throttle should be adjusted to maintain RPM. (H739) — FAA-H-8083-21, Chapter 10*

RTC
**3744.** What is the procedure for a slope landing?

A—When the downslope skid is on the ground, hold the collective pitch at the same position.
B—Minimum RPM shall be held until the full weight of the helicopter is on the skid.
C—When parallel to the slope, slowly lower the upslope skid to the ground prior to lowering the downslope skid.

*A downward pressure on the collective pitch will start the helicopter descending. As the upslope skid touches the ground, apply cyclic stick in the direction of the slope. This will hold the skid against the slope while the downslope skid is continuing to be let down with the collective pitch. (H742) — FAA-H-8083-21, Chapter 10*

RTC
**3745.** Takeoff from a slope is normally accomplished by

A—moving the cyclic in a direction away from the slope.
B—bringing the helicopter to a level attitude before completely leaving the ground.
C—moving the cyclic stick to a full up position as the helicopter nears a level attitude.

*Recommended slope takeoff technique is to:*

1. *Adjust throttle to obtain takeoff RPM and move the cyclic stick in the direction of the slope so that the rotor rotation is parallel to the true horizontal rather than the slope.*

2. *Apply up-collective pitch. As the helicopter becomes light on the skids, apply the pedal as needed to maintain heading.*

3. *As the downslope skid is rising and the helicopter approaches a level attitude, move the cyclic stick back to the neutral position, keeping the rotor disc parallel to the true horizon. Continue to apply up-collective pitch and take the helicopter straight up to a hover before moving away from the slope. In moving away from the slope, the tail should not be turned upslope because of the danger of the tail rotor striking the surface.*

*(H742) — FAA-H-8083-21, Chapter 10*

RTC
**3746.** Which action would be appropriate for confined area operations?

A—Takeoffs and landings must be made into the wind.
B—Plan the flightpath over areas suitable for a forced landing.
C—A very steep angle of descent should be used to land on the selected spot.

*In any type of confined area operation, plan a flight path over areas suitable for forced landings if possible. (H743) — FAA-H-8083-21, Chapter 10*

**Answers**

| 3742 [B] | 3743 [C] | 3744 [C] | 3745 [B] | 3746 [B] |
|---|---|---|---|---|

RTC

**3747.** If possible, when departing a confined area, what type of takeoff is preferred?

A—A normal takeoff from a hover.
B—A vertical takeoff.
C—A normal takeoff from the surface.

*If possible, a normal takeoff from a hover should be made when departing a confined area. (H743) — FAA-H-8083-21, Chapter 10*

RTC

**3748.** Which is a correct general rule for pinnacle and ridgeline operations?

A—Gaining altitude on takeoff is more important than gaining airspeed.
B—The approach path to a ridgeline is usually perpendicular to the ridge.
C—A climb to a pinnacle or ridgeline should be performed on the upwind side.

*If necessary to climb to a pinnacle or ridgeline, the climb should be performed on the upwind side, when practicable, to take advantage of any updrafts. (H744) — FAA-H-8083-21, Chapter 10*

RTC

**3749.** Before beginning a confined area or pinnacle landing, the pilot should first

A—execute a high reconnaissance.
B—execute a low reconnaissance.
C—fly around the area to discover areas of turbulence.

*The purpose of the high reconnaissance is to determine the suitability of an area for landing. In a high reconnaissance, the following items should be accomplished:*

1. *Determine wind direction and speed.*

2. *Select the most suitable flight paths into and out of the area, with particular consideration being given to forced landing areas.*

3. *Plan the approach and select a point for touchdown.*

4. *Locate and determine the size of barriers, if any.*

*The approach path should be generally into the wind. The purpose of the low reconnaissance is to verify what was seen in the high reconnaissance.*

*(H743) — FAA-H-8083-21, Chapter 10*

# Glider Operations

GLI

**3174.** The minimum allowable strength of a towline used for an aerotow of a glider having a certificated gross weight of 700 pounds is

A—560 pounds.
B—700 pounds.
C—1,000 pounds.

*No person may operate a civil aircraft towing a glider unless the towline used has a breaking strength not less than 80% of the maximum certificated operating weight of the glider, and not greater than twice this operating weight unless safety links are used.*

$$\begin{array}{r} 700 \text{ lbs} \\ \underline{\times\ 0.80} \\ 560 \text{ lbs} \end{array}$$

*(B12) — 14 CFR §91.309(a)(3)*

GLI

**3175.** The minimum allowable strength of a towline used for an aerotow of a glider having a certificated gross weight of 1,040 pounds is

A—502 pounds.
B—832 pounds.
C—1,040 pounds.

*No person may operate a civil aircraft towing a glider unless the towline used has a breaking strength not less than 80% of the maximum certificated operating weight of the glider, and not greater than twice this operating weight unless safety links are used.*

$$\begin{array}{r} 1,040 \text{ lbs} \\ \underline{\times\ 0.80} \\ 832 \text{ lbs} \end{array}$$

*(B12) — 14 CFR §91.309(a)(3)*

**Answers**

| 3747 [A] | 3748 [C] | 3749 [A] | 3174 [A] | 3175 [B] |
|---|---|---|---|---|

**GLI**
**3177.** When using a towline having a breaking strength more than twice the maximum certificated operating weight of the glider, an approved safety link must be installed at what point(s)?

A—Only the point where the towline is attached to the glider.
B—The point where the towline is attached to the glider and the point of attachment of the towline to the towplane.
C—Only the point where the towline is attached to the towplane.

*The towline may have a breaking strength of more than twice the maximum certificated operating weight of the glider if a safety link is installed at the point of attachment of the towline to the glider, and a safety link is installed at the point of attachment of the towline to the towing aircraft. (B12) — 14 CFR §91.309(a)(3)*

**GLI**
**3176.** For the aerotow of a glider that weighs 700 pounds, which towrope tensile strength would require the use of safety links at each end of the rope?

A—850 pounds.
B—1,040 pounds.
C—1,450 pounds.

*No person may operate a civil aircraft towing a glider unless the towline used has a breaking strength not less than 80% of the maximum certificated operating weight of the glider, and not greater than twice this operating weight unless safety links are used.*

$$\begin{array}{r} 700 \ lbs \\ \underline{\times 2} \\ 1,400 \ lbs \end{array}$$

*(B12) — 14 CFR §91.309(a)(3)*

**GLI**
**3340.** What force provides the forward motion necessary to move a glider through the air?

A—Lift.
B—Centripetal force.
C—Gravity.

*The pull of gravity provides the forward motion necessary to move the wings through the air. (N20) — Soaring Flight Manual, Chapter 1*

**GLI**
**3341.** To obtain maximum distance over the ground, the airspeed to use is the

A—minimum control speed.
B—best lift/drag speed.
C—minimum sink speed.

*If the maximum distance over the ground is desired, the airspeed for best L/D should be used. (N21) — Soaring Flight Manual, Chapter 2*

**GLI**
**3342.** What effect would gusts and turbulence have on the load factor of a glider with changes in airspeed?

A—Load factor decreases as airspeed increases.
B—Load factor increases as airspeed increases.
C—Load factor increases as airspeed decreases.

*Both positive and negative gust load factors increase with increasing airspeed. (N21) — Soaring Flight Manual, Chapter 2*

**GLI**
**3343.** (Refer to Figure 11.) Which yaw string and inclinometer illustrations indicate a slipping right turn?

A—3 and 6.
B—2 and 6.
C—2 and 4.

*In the case of a slipping right turn, the yaw string moves outside left and the ball moves inside, or right, as illustrated by 2 and 6 of FAA Figure 11. (N22) — Soaring Flight Manual, Chapter 3*

**GLI**
**3344.** (Refer to Figure 11.) Which of the illustrations depicts the excessive use of right rudder during the entry of a right turn?

A—2 only.
B—2 and 4.
C—3 and 4.

*In the case of a skidding right turn, the yaw string moves inside right and the ball moves outside, or left, as illustrated by 3 and 4 of FAA Figure 11. (N22) — Soaring Flight Manual, Chapter 3*

**Answers**
3177 [B]    3176 [C]    3340 [C]    3341 [B]    3342 [B]    3343 [B]
3344 [C]

GLI
**3345.** A sailplane has a best glide ratio of 23:1. How many feet will the glider lose in 8 nautical miles?

A—1,840 feet.
B—2,100 feet.
C—2,750 feet.

*L/D is lift divided by drag. This significant ratio is numerically the same as glide ratio, the ratio of forward to downward motion. Hence, 23 to 1 glide ratio would indicate:*

1. $\dfrac{23}{1} = \dfrac{6{,}000 \ (feet/NM - forward)}{X \ (feet/NM - downward)}$

2. $\dfrac{23}{1} \times X = 6{,}000$

3. *X = 261 feet downward for each 6,000 feet (1 NM) forward.*

4. *The total sink is 8 NM x 261 feet/NM or about 2,100 feet in 8 NM in calm air.*

*(N27) — Soaring Flight Manual, Chapter 9*

GLI
**3346.** A sailplane has a best glide ratio of 30:1. How many nautical miles will the glider travel while losing 2,000 feet?

A—10 nautical miles.
B—15 nautical miles.
C—21 nautical miles.

*L/D is lift divided by drag. This significant ratio is numerically the same as glide ratio, the ratio of forward to downward motion. Hence, 30 to 1 glide ratio would indicate:*

1. $\dfrac{30}{1} = \dfrac{X \ (feet/NM - forward)}{2{,}000 \ (feet/NM - downward)}$

2. $\dfrac{30}{1} \times 2{,}000 = X$

3. *X = 60,000 feet (10 NM) forward for each 2,000 feet downward.*

*(N27) — Soaring Flight Manual, Chapter 9*

GLI
**3347.** A sailplane has lost 2,000 feet in 9 nautical miles. The best glide ratio for this sailplane is approximately

A—24:1.
B—27:1.
C—30:1.

*L/D is lift divided by drag. This significant ratio is numerically the same as glide ratio, the ratio of forward to downward motion. Assuming that 1 NM is approximately 6,000 feet, the glide ratio and L/D may be expressed as:*

$$\dfrac{9 \times 6{,}000 \ feet \ forward}{2{,}000 \ feet \ downward} = \dfrac{54{,}000}{2{,}000} = \dfrac{54}{2} = \dfrac{27}{1} \ or \ 27{:}1$$

*(N27) — Soaring Flight Manual, Chapter 9*

GLI
**3348.** How many feet will a sailplane sink in 15 nautical miles if its lift/drag ratio is 22:1?

A—2,700 feet.
B—3,600 feet.
C—4,100 feet.

*L/D is lift divided by drag. This significant ratio is numerically the same as glide ratio, the ratio of forward to downward motion. Hence, 22 to 1 glide ratio would indicate:*

1. $\dfrac{22}{1} = \dfrac{6{,}000 \ (feet/NM - forward)}{X \ (feet/NM - downward)}$

2. $\dfrac{22}{1} \times X = 6{,}000$

3. *X = 273 feet downward for each 6,000 feet (1 NM) forward.*

4. *The total sink is 15 NM x 273 feet/NM, or about 4,095 feet in 15 NM in calm air.*

*(N27) — Soaring Flight Manual, Chapter 9*

---

**Answers**

3345  [B]          3346  [A]          3347  [B]          3348  [C]

GLI
**3349.** How many feet will a glider sink in 10 nautical miles if its lift/drag ratio is 23:1?

A—2,400 feet.
B—2,600 feet.
C—4,300 feet.

*L/D is lift divided by drag. This significant ratio is numerically the same as glide ratio, the ratio of forward to downward motion. Hence, 23 to 1 glide ratio would indicate:*

1. $\dfrac{23}{1} = \dfrac{6{,}000 \ (feet/NM - forward)}{X \ (feet/NM - downward)}$

2. $\dfrac{23}{1} \times X = 6{,}000$

3. *X = 261 feet downward for each 6,000 feet (1 NM) forward.*

4. *The total sink is 10 NM x 261 feet/NM, or about 2,610 feet in 10 NM in calm air.*

*(N27) — Soaring Flight Manual, Chapter 9*

GLI
**3750.** What minimum upward current must a glider encounter to maintain altitude?

A—At least 2 feet per second.
B—The same as the glider's sink rate.
C—The same as the adjacent down currents.

*Zero sink occurs when upward currents are just strong enough to hold altitude. For a sink rate of about 2 feet per second, there must be an upward air current of at least 2 feet per second. (I35) — AC 00-6A, Chapter 16*

GLI
**3751.** On which side of a rocky knoll, that is surrounded by vegetation, should a pilot find the best thermals?

A—On the side facing the Sun.
B—On the downwind side.
C—Exactly over the center.

*If a rocky knoll protrudes above a grassy plane, the most likely area for thermals to occur is over the eastern slope in the forenoon and over the western slope in the afternoon. (I35) — AC 00-6A, Chapter 16*

GLI
**3752.** What is one recommended method for locating thermals?

A—Fly an ever increasing circular path.
B—Maintain a straight track downwind.
C—Look for converging streamers of dust or smoke.

*Look for converging streamers of dust and smoke. (I35) — AC 00-6A, Chapter 16*

GLI
**3753.** What is a recommended procedure for entering a dust devil for soaring?

A—Enter above 500 feet and circle the edge in the same direction as the rotation.
B—Enter below 500 feet and circle the edge opposite the direction of rotation.
C—Enter at or above 500 feet and circle the edge opposite the direction of rotation.

*At around 500 feet, the pilot makes a circle on the outside of the dust devil against the direction of rotation. (I35) — AC 00-6A, Chapter 16*

GLI
**3754.** What is an important precaution when soaring in a dust devil?

A—Avoid the eye of the vortex.
B—Avoid the clear area at the outside edge of the dust.
C—Maintain the same direction as the rotation of the vortex.

*The rarefied air in the eye provides very little lift, and the wall of the hollow core is very turbulent. (I35) — AC 00-6A, Chapter 16*

GLI
**3755.** What is the best visual indication of a thermal?

A—Fragmented cumulus clouds with concave bases.
B—Smooth cumulus clouds with concave bases.
C—Scattered to broken sky with cumulus clouds.

*Look for a cumulus with a concave base, and with a firm, sharp, unfragmented outline. (I35) — AC 00-6A, Chapter 16*

GLI
**3756.** How can a pilot locate bubble thermals?

A—Look for wet areas where recent showers have occurred.
B—Look for birds that are soaring in areas of intermittent heating.
C—Fly the area just above the boundary of a temperature inversion.

*Birds may be soaring in a "bubble" thermal that has been pinched off and forced upward through intermittent shading. (I35) — AC 00-6A, Chapter 16*

GLI
**3757.** Where may the most favorable type thermals for cross-country soaring be found?

A—Just ahead of a warm front.
B—Along thermal streets.
C—Under mountain waves.

*Thermal streeting is a real boon to speed and distance. (I35) — AC 00-6A, Chapter 16*

GLI
**3758.** Where and under what condition can enough lift be found for soaring when the weather is generally stable?

A—On the upwind side of hills or ridges with moderate winds present.
B—In mountain waves that form on the upwind side of the mountains.
C—Over isolated peaks when strong winds are present.

*Stability affects the continuity and extent of lift over hills or ridges, allowing relatively streamlined upslope flow. An upslope wind of 15 knots creates lift of about 6 feet per second. (I35) — AC 00-6A, Chapter 16*

GLI
**3857.** Which is an advantage of using a CG hook for a winch tow rather than the nose hook?

A—A greater percent of the line length can be used to reach altitude.
B—Maximum release altitude is limited.
C—It is the safest method of launching.

*A distinct advantage of a CG hook is that the sailplane can gain a greater altitude with a given line length. (N31) — Soaring Flight Manual, Chapter 13*

GLI
**3858.** To stop pitch oscillation (porpoising) during a winch launch, the pilot should

A—release back pressure and then pull back against the cycle of pitching oscillation to get in phase with the undulations.
B—signal the ground crew to increase the speed of the tow.
C—relax the back pressure on the control stick and shallow the angle of climb.

*"Porpoising" is caused by the horizontal stabilizer oscillating in and out of a stalled condition during a winch tow. The cure is to relax back pressure on the stick and shallow the climb angle. (N31) — Soaring Flight Manual, Chapter 13*

GLI
**3859.** A pilot plans to fly solo in the front seat of a two-place glider which displays the following placards on the instrument panel:

MINIMUM PILOT WEIGHT: 135 LB
MAXIMUM PILOT WEIGHT: 220 LB

NOTE: Seat ballast should be used as necessary.

The recommended towing speed for all tows is 55 – 65 knots. What action should be taken if the pilot's weight is 115 pounds?

A—Add 20 pounds of seat ballast to the rear seat.
B—Add 55 pounds of seat ballast to obtain the average pilot weight of 170 pounds.
C—Add 20 pounds of seat ballast.

*Two criteria must be satisfied in the loading of a glider:*

*1. The total weight must be within limits, and*

*2. Within those limits, placement of the weight with respect to the aerodynamic center of the wing must satisfy total moment conditions (Weight x Arm = Moment).*

*To satisfy the conditions specified in the question, first calculate the weight required:*

$$135 – 115 = 20 \text{ lbs}$$

*In order for that weight to provide the same moment as the "pilot weight" it replaces, it will also need to be at the same (that is, the forward) seat location. (N21) — Soaring Flight Manual, Chapter 2*

**Answers**

3756　[B]　　　3757　[B]　　　3758　[A]　　　3857　[A]　　　3858　[C]　　　3859　[C]

GLI
**3860.** A pilot plans to fly solo in the front seat of a two-place glider which displays the following placards on the instrument panel:

MINIMUM PILOT WEIGHT: 135 LB
MAXIMUM PILOT WEIGHT: 220 LB

NOTE: Seat ballast should be used as necessary.

The recommended towing speed for all tows is 55 – 65 knots. What action should be taken if the pilot's weight is 125 pounds?

A—Add 10 pounds of seat ballast to the rear seat.
B—Add 10 pounds of seat ballast.
C—Add 45 pounds of seat ballast to obtain the average pilot weight of 170 pounds.

*Two criteria must be satisfied in the loading of a glider:*

*1. The total weight must be within limits, and*

*2. Within those limits, placement of the weight with respect to the aerodynamic center of the wing must satisfy total moment conditions (Weight x Arm = Moment).*

*To satisfy the conditions specified in the question, first calculate the weight required:*

*135 – 125 = 10 lbs*

*In order for that weight to provide the same moment as the "pilot weight" it replaces, it will also need to be at the same (that is, the forward) seat location. (N21) — Soaring Flight Manual, Chapter 2*

GLI
**3869.** (Refer to Figure 56.) Illustration 2 means

A—release towline.
B—ready to tow.
C—hold position.

*During all glider operations there should be a wing runner, if possible. Lowering the wing and raising the hands is the signal to hold position. (N30) — Soaring Flight Manual, Chapter 12*

GLI
**3870.** (Refer to Figure 56.) Illustration 3 means

A—stop operations.
B—release towline.
C—take up slack.

*The wing runner moving his/her hand across the throat is the signal to release the towline. (N30) — Soaring Flight Manual, Chapter 12*

GLI
**3871.** (Refer to Figure 56.) Which illustration is a signal to stop operation?

A—2.
B—3.
C—7.

*Wing runners should use a paddle, flag or some signaling device that is easily visible to the tow pilot. Moving the signaling device and free hand back and forth over the head is the signal to stop operation. (N30) — Soaring Flight Manual, Chapter 12*

GLI
**3872.** (Refer to Figure 56.) Which illustration is a signal from the sailplane for the towplane to turn right?

A—5.
B—6.
C—11.

*To signal the towplane to turn, move the glider to the side opposite the direction of turn and gently pull the towplane's tail out. (N30) — Soaring Flight Manual, Chapter 12*

GLI
**3873.** (Refer to Figure 56.) Which illustration is a signal that the glider is unable to release?

A—8.
B—10.
C—11.

*If the glider cannot release, he/she should move to the left and rock the wings. (N30) — Soaring Flight Manual, Chapter 12*

GLI
**3874.** (Refer to Figure 56.) Which illustration is a signal to the towplane to reduce airspeed?

A—7.
B—10.
C—12.

*To signal the towplane or ground launch crew to reduce airspeed or ground launch speed, fishtail the glider. (N30) — Soaring Flight Manual, Chapter 12*

**Answers**

| | | | | |
|---|---|---|---|---|
| 3860 [B] | 3869 [C] | 3870 [B] | 3871 [C] | 3872 [A] | 3873 [B] |
| 3874 [C] | | | | |

GLI
**3875.** (Refer to Figure 56.) Which illustration means the towplane cannot release?

A—6.
B—8.
C—9.

*After the glider has signaled that he/she cannot release, the towplane will attempt to release the glider. If the towplane cannot release, he/she should fishtail the towplane. A landing on tow will then be necessary. (N30) — Soaring Flight Manual, Chapter 12*

GLI
**3876.** What corrective action should the sailplane pilot take during takeoff if the towplane is still on the ground and the sailplane is airborne and drifting to the left?

A—Crab into the wind by holding upwind (right) rudder pressure.
B—Crab into the wind so as to maintain a position directly behind the towplane.
C—Establish a right wing low drift correction to remain in the flightpath of the towplane.

*Crab into the wind to maintain a position directly behind the towplane. (N30) — Soaring Flight Manual, Chapter 12*

GLI
**3877.** An indication that the glider has begun a turn too soon on aerotow is that the

A—glider's nose is pulled to the outside of the turn.
B—towplane's nose is pulled to the outside of the turn.
C—towplane will pitch up.

*When a turn is begun too soon, the towplane's nose is pulled to the outside of the turn. (N30) — Soaring Flight Manual, Chapter 12*

GLI
**3878.** The sailplane has become airborne and the towplane loses power before leaving the ground. The sailplane should release immediately,

A—and maneuver to the right of the towplane.
B—extend the spoilers, and land straight ahead.
C—and maneuver to the left of the towplane.

*The glider should maneuver to the right of the towplane. The towplane should move over to the left. If there is a narrow runway, a full spoiler landing should be made as soon as possible. (N30) — Soaring Flight Manual, Chapter 12*

GLI
**3879.** What should a glider pilot do if a towline breaks below 200 feet AGL?

A—Turn into the wind, then back to the runway for a downwind landing.
B—Turn away from the wind, then back to the runway for a downwind landing.
C—Land straight ahead or make slight turns to reach a suitable landing area.

*At low altitude, the only alternative to landing straight ahead may be slight turns in order to reach a suitable landing area. (N30) — Soaring Flight Manual, Chapter 12*

GLI
**3880.** A pilot unintentionally enters a steep diving spiral to the left. What is the proper way to recover from this attitude without overstressing the glider?

A—Apply up-elevator pressure to raise the nose.
B—Apply more up-elevator pressure and then use right aileron pressure to control the overbanking tendency.
C—Relax the back pressure and shallow the bank; then apply up-elevator pressure until the nose has been raised to the desired position.

*The correct recovery from a spiral dive is to relax back pressure on the stick and at the same time reduce the bank angle with coordinated aileron and rudder. When the bank is less than 45°, the stick may be moved back while continuing to decrease bank. (N32) — Soaring Flight Manual, Chapter 14*

**Answers**

3875 [C]    3876 [B]    3877 [B]    3878 [A]    3879 [C]    3880 [C]

GLI

**3881.** What corrective action should be taken if, while thermalling at minimum sink speed in turbulent air, the left wing drops while turning to the left?

A—Apply more opposite (right) aileron pressure than opposite (right) rudder pressure to counteract the overbanking tendency.

B—Apply opposite (right) rudder pressure to slow the rate of turn.

C—Lower the nose before applying opposite (right) aileron pressure.

*If a wing begins to drop during a turn, it is an indication of a stall. The nose of the sailplane should be lowered before applying coordinated opposite aileron and rudder to break the stall. (N32) — Soaring Flight Manual, Chapter 14*

GLI

**3882.** A sailplane pilot can differentiate between a spin and a spiral dive because in a spiral dive,

A—the speed remains constant.

B—the G loads increase.

C—there is a small loss of altitude in each rotation.

*A spiral dive, as contrasted to a spin, can be recognized by rapidly increasing speed and G loading. (N32) — Soaring Flight Manual, Chapter 14*

GLI

**3883.** How are forward slips normally performed?

A—With the direction of the slip away from any crosswind that exists.

B—With dive brakes or spoilers fully open.

C—With rudder and aileron deflection on the same side.

*When using the forward slip to increase an angle of descent without acceleration, the dive brakes or spoilers are normally fully open. (N32) — Soaring Flight Manual, Chapter 14*

GLI

**3884.** What would be a proper action or procedure to use if the pilot is getting too low on a cross-country flight in a sailplane?

A—Continue on course until descending to 1,000 feet above the ground and then plan the landing approach.

B—Fly directly into the wind and make a straight-in approach at the end of the glide.

C—Have a suitable landing area selected upon reaching 2,000 feet AGL, and a specific field chosen upon reaching 1,500 feet AGL.

*It is always necessary to have a suitable landing site in mind. As altitude decreases, the plans have to get more specific. The area should be narrowed down at 2,000 feet and a specific field should be selected by 1,500 feet. (N34) — Soaring Flight Manual, Chapter 16*

**Answers**

| 3881 | [C] | 3882 | [B] | 3883 | [B] | 3884 | [C] |

# Lighter-Than-Air Operations

LTA
**3351.** The part of a balloon that bears the entire load is the

A—envelope material.
B—envelope seams.
C—load tapes (or cords).

*The load tape supports the weight of the balloon and minimizes the strain on the envelope fabric. (O155) — Balloon Digest*

LTA
**3352.** In hot air balloons, propane is preferred to butane or other hydrocarbons because it

A—is less volatile.
B—is slower to vaporize.
C—has a lower boiling point.

*Propane is preferred over butane and other hydrocarbons in balloon design because propane has a lower boiling point (-44°F). (O170) — Balloon Digest*

LTA
**3353.** The initial temperature at which propane boils is

A—+32°F.
B—-44°F.
C—-60°F.

*Propane is preferred over butane and other hydrocarbons in balloon design because propane has a lower boiling point (-44°F). (O170) — Balloon Digest*

LTA
**3354.** On cold days, it may be necessary to preheat the propane tanks because

A—the temperature of the liquid propane controls the burner pressure during combustion.
B—there may be ice in the lines to the burner.
C—the propane needs to be thawed from a solid to a liquid state.

*On very cold days, it may be necessary to preheat the propane tanks since the temperature of the liquid propane controls the burner pressure during combustion. (O170) — Balloon Digest*

LTA
**3355.** When ample liquid propane is available, propane will vaporize sufficiently to provide proper operation between the temperatures of

A—+30 to +90°F.
B—-44 to +25°F.
C—-51 to +20°F.

*When ample liquid propane is available, propane will vaporize sufficiently to provide proper operation between 30°F and 90°F. (O220) — Balloon Ground School*

LTA
**3356.** If ample propane is available, within which temperature range will propane vaporize sufficiently to provide enough pressure for burner operation during flight?

A—0 to 30°F.
B—10 to 30°F.
C—30 to 90°F.

*When ample liquid propane is available, propane will vaporize sufficiently to provide proper operation between 30°F and 90°F. (O220) — Balloon Ground School*

LTA
**3357.** The valve located on the top of the propane tank which opens automatically when the pressure in the tank exceeds maximum allowable pressure is the

A—pressure release valve.
B—metering valve.
C—blast valve.

*The pressure release valve is located on top of the fuel tank and opens automatically when the pressure in the tank exceeds the maximum allowable pressure. (O220) — Balloon Ground School*

---

**Answers**

| | | | | | |
|---|---|---|---|---|---|
| 3351  [C] | 3352  [C] | 3353  [B] | 3354  [A] | 3355  [A] | 3356  [C] |
| 3357  [A] | | | | | |

**LTA**
**3358.** The valve located on each tank that indicates when the tank is filled to 80 percent capacity is the

A—main tank valve.
B—vapor-bleed valve.
C—pilot valve.

*A vapor-bleed valve, or "spit tube," is located on each tank and indicates when the tank is filled to 80% of capacity. (O220) — Balloon Ground School*

**LTA**
**3359.** The lifting forces which act on a hot air balloon are primarily the result of the interior air temperature being

A—greater than ambient temperature.
B—less than ambient temperature.
C—equal to ambient temperature.

*A hot air balloon derives lift from the fact that air inside the envelope is warmer and therefore, "lighter" than the air around the balloon. (O220) — Balloon Ground School*

**LTA**
**3360.** Burner efficiency of a hot air balloon decreases approximately what percent for each 1,000 feet above MSL?

A—4 percent.
B—8 percent.
C—15 percent.

*Burner efficiency of a hot air balloon system decreases at approximately 4% per 1,000 feet above MSL. (O220) — Balloon Ground School*

**LTA**
**3361.** While in flight, ice begins forming on the outside of the fuel tank in use. This would most likely be caused by

A—water in the fuel.
B—a leak in the fuel line.
C—vaporized fuel instead of liquid fuel being drawn from the tank into the main burner.

*If large quantities of vapor are withdrawn rapidly from a propane cylinder, the cooling effect of the vaporization in the tank cools the propane and lowers the vapor pressure and the rate of vaporization. (O220) — Balloon Ground School*

**LTA**
**3362.** For what reason is methanol added to the propane fuel of hot air balloons?

A—To check for fuel leaks.
B—As a fire retardant.
C—As an anti-icing additive.

*Since propane holds little water in solution, there is a tendency for free water to collect in the bottom of the tanks where it may reach the dip tube, be piped into the burner system, and freeze up the regulators. If water contamination is suspected, methyl alcohol (methanol) should be added to the system. (O220) — Balloon Ground School*

**LTA**
**3363.** On a balloon equipped with a blast valve, the blast valve is used for

A—climbs and descents only.
B—altitude control.
C—emergencies only.

*The blast valve is located on the burner and controls ascent or descent by use of short bursts of power. When reaching the desired altitude, the pilot should reduce the frequency of blasts. As the envelope cools, the desired altitude can be maintained by using short blasts of heat evenly spaced. (O220) — Balloon Ground School*

**LTA**
**3364.** The term "weigh-off" means to determine the

A—static equilibrium of the balloon as loaded for flight.
B—amount of gas required for an ascent to a preselected altitude.
C—standard weight and balance of the balloon.

*A weigh-off is used to determine the static equilibrium of the balloon. (O30) — Powerline Excerpts*

**Answers**
3358 [B]        3359 [A]        3360 [A]        3361 [C]        3362 [C]        3363 [B]
3364 [A]

LTA
**3365.** What causes false lift which sometimes occurs during launch procedures?

A—Closing the maneuvering vent too rapidly.
B—Excessive temperature within the envelope.
C—Venturi effect of the wind on the envelope.

*False lift is caused by the venturi effect produced by the wind blowing across an inflated but stationary envelope. This is "dynamic lift" created by relative air movement. If the balloon is released, the relative wind decreases as the balloon accelerates to the speed of the wind and false lift decreases. (O30) — Powerline Excerpts*

LTA
**3366.** What is the relationship of false lift with the wind?

A—False lift increases as the wind accelerates the balloon.
B—False lift does not exist if the surface winds are calm.
C—False lift decreases as the wind accelerates the balloon.

*False lift is caused by the venturi effect produced by the wind blowing across an inflated but stationary envelope. This is "dynamic lift" created by relative air movement. If the balloon is released, the relative wind decreases as the balloon accelerates to the speed of the wind and false lift decreases. (O30) — Powerline Excerpts*

LTA
**3367.** What would cause a gas balloon to start a descent if a cold air mass is encountered and the envelope becomes cooled?

A—A density differential.
B—A barometric pressure differential.
C—The contraction of the gas.

*As the gas is cooled, it contracts and becomes more dense and so displaces less air. (O150) — Balloon Digest*

LTA
**3368.** Under which condition will an airship float in the air?

A—When buoyant force equals horizontal equilibrium existing between propeller thrust and airship drag.
B—When buoyant force is less than the difference between airship weight and the weight of the air volume being displaced.
C—When buoyant force equals the difference between airship weight and the weight of the air volume being displaced.

*A lighter-than-air craft is in equilibrium when buoyancy equals weight. The buoyant force is equal to the weight of the air volume displaced. (P01) — Goodyear Airship Operations Manual*

LTA
**3369.** During flight in an airship, when is vertical equilibrium established?

A—When buoyancy is greater than airship weight.
B—When buoyancy equals airship weight.
C—When buoyancy is less than airship weight.

*A lighter-than-air craft is in equilibrium when buoyancy equals weight. The buoyant force is equal to the weight of the air volume displaced. (P01) — Goodyear Airship Operations Manual*

LTA
**3370.** An airship descending through a steep temperature inversion will

A—show no change in superheat as altitude is lost.
B—show a decrease in superheat as altitude is lost.
C—become progressively lighter, thus becoming increasingly more difficult to drive down.

*As the airship descends into the colder temperature of the inversion, the weight of the displaced air volume is increasing, thereby increasing buoyancy. (P01) — Goodyear Airship Operations Manual*

**Answers**

| | | | | | |
|---|---|---|---|---|---|
| 3365 [C] | 3366 [C] | 3367 [C] | 3368 [C] | 3369 [B] | 3370 [C] |

LTA
**3371.** What is airship superheat?

A—A condition of excessive exterior temperature of the envelope.
B—The temperature of the lifting gas exceeding the red line.
C—The difference between outside air temperature and the temperature inside the envelope.

*Superheat is the difference between outside air temperature and the temperature in the airship envelope. (P01) — Goodyear Airship Operations Manual*

LTA
**3372.** In relation to the operation of an airship, what is the definition of aerostatics?

A—The gravitational factors involving equilibrium of a body freely suspended in the atmosphere.
B—The science of the dynamics involved in the expansion and contraction of hydrogen gas.
C—The expansion and contraction of the lifting gas helium.

*Aerostatics are the gravitational factors involving equilibrium of a body freely suspended in the atmosphere. (P04) — Goodyear Airship Operations Manual*

LTA
**3373.** Below pressure height, each 5°F of positive superheat amounts to approximately

A—1 percent of gross lift.
B—2 percent of net lift.
C—2 percent of total lift.

*Each 5°F amounts to about 1% of gross lift. (P04) — Goodyear Airship Operations Manual*

LTA
**3374.** When the airship is at pressure height and superheat increases, constant pressure must be maintained by valving

A—gas from the envelope.
B—air from the envelope.
C—gas from the ballonets.

*Expansion of the gas will cause the ballonets to completely deflate at pressure height. Gas must be valved from the envelope to maintain constant pressure. (P04) — Goodyear Airship Operations Manual*

LTA
**3375.** How does the pilot know when pressure height has been reached?

A—Liquid in the gas manometer will rise and the liquid in the air manometer will fall below normal levels.
B—Liquid in the gas and air manometers will fall below the normal level.
C—Liquid in the gas manometer will fall and the liquid in the air manometer will rise above normal levels.

*When pressure height has been reached, the liquid in the gas manometer will rise and the liquid in the air manometer will fall below normal levels. (P04) — Goodyear Airship Operations Manual*

LTA
**3376.** The pressure height of an airship is the altitude at which

A—the airship would be unable to gain more altitude.
B—gas pressure would reach 3 inches of water.
C—the ballonet(s) would be empty.

*Expansion of the gas will cause the ballonets to completely deflate at pressure height. Thus, no further increase in displaced air volume is possible. (P04) — Goodyear Airship Operations Manual*

LTA
**3377.** The maximum altitude that a rigid airship can reach (under a given atmospheric condition) and then return safely to the surface is determined by

A—the disposable load.
B—ballonet capacity.
C—pressure altitude.

*Expansion of the gas will cause the ballonets to completely deflate at pressure height. Thus, no further increase in displaced air volume is possible. (P04) — Goodyear Airship Operations Manual*

LTA
**3378.** An unbalanced condition of an airship in flight must be overcome by

A—valving air from the ballonets.
B—valving gas from the envelope.
C—a negative or a positive dynamic force.

*Dynamic force, created by movement through the air, must be used to overcome any out-of-equilibrium condition. (P04) — Goodyear Airship Operations Manual*

**Answers**
3371 [C]     3372 [A]     3373 [A]     3374 [A]     3375 [A]     3376 [C]
3377 [C]     3378 [C]

**LTA**
**3379.** Air damper valves should normally be kept closed during climbs because any air forced into the system would

A—increase the amount of gas that must be exhausted to prevent the airship from ascending at an excessively high rate.
B—increase the amount of air to be exhausted, resulting in a lower rate of ascent.
C—decrease the purity of the gas within the envelope.

*Any air entering the ballonets through the damper valves will have to be exhausted overboard as the gas expands. This slows the rate of ascent. (P11) — Goodyear Airship Operations Manual*

**LTA**
**3380.** To check the gas pressures (pressure height) of an airship during a climb, the air damper valves should be

A—opened forward and closed aft.
B—opened aft and closed forward.
C—closed.

*If damper valves are open, ram air pressure will keep the ballonets inflated longer than they should be inflated. (P11) — Goodyear Airship Operations Manual*

**LTA**
**3396.** What condition does a rising barometer indicate for balloon operations?

A—Decreasing clouds and wind.
B—Chances of thunderstorms.
C—Approaching frontal activity.

*Within a high-pressure system, flying conditions are generally more favorable than in low-pressure areas because there are normally fewer clouds, better visibility, calm or light winds, and less turbulence. (I23) — AC 00-6A, Chapter 4*

**LTA**
**3885.** Why should propane tanks not be refueled in a closed trailer or truck?

A—Propane vapor is one and one-half times heavier than air and will linger in the floor of the truck or trailer.
B—The propane vapor is odorless and the refuelers may be overcome by the fumes.
C—Propane is very cold and could cause damage to the truck or trailer.

*Since propane vapor is 1-1/2 times heavier than air, it can linger on the floor. (O220) — Balloon Ground School*

**LTA**
**3886.** Why should special precautions be taken when filling the propane bottles?

A—Propane is transferred from the storage tanks to the propane bottles under high pressure.
B—During transfer, propane reaches a high temperature and can cause severe burns.
C—Propane is super-cold and may cause severe freeze burns.

*Precautions, such as wearing gloves, should be taken when filling the propane bottles because propane is super-cold and may cause severe freeze burns. (O220) — Balloon Ground School*

**LTA**
**3895.** All fuel tanks should be fired during preflight to determine

A—the burner pressure and condition of the valves.
B—that the pilot light functions properly on each tank.
C—if there are any leaks in the tank.

*Burner output is dependent on fuel pressure. Proper valve operation is critical to safety and control. (O220) — Balloon Ground School*

**LTA**
**3896.** What is a recommended ascent upon initial launch?

A—Maximum ascent to altitude to avoid low-level thermals.
B—Shallow ascent to avoid flashbacks of flames as the envelope is cooled.
C—A moderate-rate ascent to determine wind directions at different levels.

*A moderate-rate ascent is recommended initially to accurately determine the wind direction at various altitudes. (O220) — Balloon Ground School*

**Answers**

| 3379 | [B] | 3380 | [C] | 3396 | [A] | 3885 | [A] | 3886 | [C] | 3895 | [A] |
| 3896 | [C] | | | | | | | | | | |

LTA
**3897.** What is a potential hazard when climbing at maximum rate?

A—The envelope may collapse.
B—Deflation ports may be forced open.
C—The rapid flow of air may extinguish the burner and pilot light.

*The positive pressure on the top of the envelope could force the deflation ports open. (O220) — Balloon Ground School*

LTA
**3898.** How should a roundout from a moderate-rate ascent to level flight be made?

A—Reduce the amount of heat gradually as the balloon is approaching altitude.
B—Cool the envelope by venting and add heat just before arriving at altitude.
C—Vent at altitude and add heat upon settling back down to altitude.

*The most efficient roundout is to reduce the frequency of blasts so that the envelope cools to a level flight temperature just as the balloon reaches the desired altitude. (O220) — Balloon Ground School*

LTA
**3899.** What is one procedure for relighting the burner while in flight?

A—Open the regulator or blast valve full open and light the pilot light.
B—Close the tank valves, vent the fuel lines, reopen the tank valves, and light the pilot light.
C—Open another tank valve, open the regulator or blast valve, and light the main jets with reduced flow.

*The pilot should open another tank valve, open the regular, or blast valve and light off the main jet with reduced flow. (O220) — Balloon Ground School*

LTA
**3900.** The windspeed is such that it is necessary to deflate the envelope as rapidly as possible during a landing. When should the deflation port (rip panel) be opened?

A—The instant the gondola contacts the surface.
B—As the balloon skips off the surface the first time and the last of the ballast has been discharged.
C—Just prior to ground contact.

*In a high-wind landing, the envelope should be ripped just prior to ground contact. (O220) — Balloon Ground School*

LTA
**3901.** When landing a free balloon, what should the occupants do to minimize landing shock?

A—Be seated on the floor of the basket.
B—Stand with knees slightly bent, in the center of the gondola, facing the direction of movement.
C—Stand back-to-back and hold onto the load ring.

*By facing forward with knees bent, the body is balanced and the legs act as springs, absorbing the landing shock. (O265) — How to Fly a Balloon*

LTA
**3902.** Prior to a high-wind landing, the pilot in command should brief the passengers to prepare for the landing by

A—kneeling on the floor and facing aft.
B—crouching on the floor and jumping out of the basket upon contact with the ground.
C—crouching while hanging on in two places, and remaining in the basket until advised otherwise.

*By facing forward with knees bent, the body is balanced and the legs act as springs absorbing the landing shock. It is important that everyone remain in the basket until the envelope cannot lift the balloon back into the air. (O220) — Balloon Ground School*

**Answers**
3897 [B]      3898 [A]      3899 [C]      3900 [C]      3901 [B]      3902 [C]

**LTA**

**3903.** Which precaution should be exercised if confronted with the necessity of having to land a balloon when the air is turbulent?

A—Land in any available lake close to the upwind shore.
B—Land in the center of the largest available field.
C—Land in the trees to absorb shock forces, thus cushioning the landing.

*At one time or another a balloonist will be faced with the necessity of having to land in turbulent air. When this happens, the landing should be attempted in the middle of the largest field available. (O220) — Balloon Ground School*

**LTA**

**3904.** What action is most appropriate when an envelope over-temperature condition occurs?

A—Throw all unnecessary equipment overboard.
B—Descend; hover in ground effect until the envelope cools.
C—Land as soon as practical.

*An envelope over-temperature can seriously degrade the strength of the envelope, so land as soon as is practical. (O220) — Balloon Ground School*

**LTA**

**3905.** In addition to the required documents, what carry-on equipment should be accounted for during preflight?

A—Flotation gear.
B—Emergency locator transmitter.
C—Two means of burner ignition.

*As a precaution against flameout, an ignitor must be carried to relight the burner. A second ignitor is necessary in case the first malfunctions or is lost overboard. (O10) — Flight Instructor Manual*

**LTA**

**3906.** How should a balloon fuel system be checked for leaks prior to flight?

A—Listen and smell.
B—Check all connections with a lighted match.
C—Cover all connections and tubing with soapy water.

*Propane is under pressure and has an artificial odor. If a leak exists, the fuel will "hiss" out and can be smelled. (O220) — Balloon Ground School*

**LTA**

**3907.** In a balloon, best fuel economy in level flight can be accomplished by

A—riding the haze line in a temperature inversion.
B—short blasts of heat at high frequency.
C—long blasts of heat at low frequency.

*The desired envelope temperature for level flight is best maintained by short blasts at high frequency. (O220) — Balloon Ground School*

**LTA**

**3908.** The minimum size a launch site should be is at least

A—twice the height of the balloon.
B—100 feet for every 1 knot of wind.
C—500 feet on the downwind side.

*A free balloon will move about 100 feet per minute for every knot of wind. A pilot should allow 100 feet of travel for each knot of wind speed. (O30) — Powerline Excerpts*

**LTA**

**3909.** What is a hazard of rapid descents?

A—Wind shear can cavitate one side of the envelope, forcing air out of the mouth.
B—The pilot light cannot remain lit with the turbulent air over the basket.
C—Aerodynamic forces may collapse the envelope.

*Turbulent airflow may extinguish the pilot light. (O30) — Powerline Excerpts*

**LTA**

**3910.** It may be possible to make changes in the direction of flight in a hot air balloon by

A—flying a constant atmospheric pressure gradient.
B—operating at different flight altitudes.
C—operating above the friction level, if there is no gradient wind.

*A free balloon has no propulsion and so must take advantage of differing wind directions at various altitudes. (O263) — How to Fly a Balloon*

**Answers**

| | | | | | |
|---|---|---|---|---|---|
| 3903 [B] | 3904 [C] | 3905 [C] | 3906 [A] | 3907 [B] | 3908 [B] |
| 3909 [B] | 3910 [B] | | | | |

LTA
**3911.** What action should be taken if a balloon encounters unforecast weather and shifts direction abruptly while in the vicinity of a thunderstorm?

A—Land immediately.
B—Descend to and maintain the lowest altitude possible.
C—Ascend to an altitude which will ensure adequate obstacle clearance in all directions.

*Weather conditions during flight may take a sudden and unpredictable change. When this occurs and if powerful wind gusts, thermals, wind shears, or precipitation and lightning, are encountered, the appropriate action is to land as soon as possible. (P03) — Goodyear Operations Manual*

LTA
**3912.** To land an airship that is 250 pounds heavy when the wind is calm, the best landing can usually be made if the airship is

A—in trim.
B—nose heavy approximately 20°
C—tail heavy approximately 20°.

*A heavy airship should be trimmed tail heavy to provide dynamic lift during approach. (P11) — Goodyear Operations Manual*

LTA
**3913.** Which takeoff procedure is considered to be most hazardous for an airship?

A—Maintaining only 50 percent of the maximum permissible positive angle of inclination.
B—Failing to apply full engine power properly on all takeoffs, regardless of wind.
C—Maintaining a negative angle of inclination during takeoff after elevator response is adequate for controllability.

*It is necessary to apply full power at the correct moment in an "upship" maneuver. (P11) — Goodyear Operations Manual*

LTA
**3914.** Which action is necessary in order to perform a normal descent in an airship?

A—Valve gas.
B—Valve air.
C—Take air into the aft ballonets.

*An airship is normally flown heavy, so a power reduction would cause a descent. Air should be taken into the forward ballonets. (P11) — Goodyear Operations Manual*

LTA
**3915.** If an airship should experience failure of both engines during flight and neither engine can be restarted, what initial immediate action must the pilot take?

A—The airship must be driven down to a landing before control and envelope shape are lost.
B—The emergency auxiliary power unit must be started for electrical power to the airscoop blowers so that ballonet inflation can be maintained.
C—Immediate preparations to operate the airship as a free balloon are necessary.

*An airship without power must be operated as a free balloon. (P11) — Goodyear Operations Manual*

**Answers**

3911  [A]      3912  [C]      3913  [B]      3914  [A]      3915  [C]

# Chapter 3
# Flight Instruments

# Pitot-Static Instruments

The pressure altimeter, vertical-speed indicator, and airspeed indicator operate in response to pressures through the **pitot-static system**. *See* Figure 3-1.

**Static** (atmospheric) **pressure** is taken from the static vents and is provided to all three instruments. Clogging of the static vents or line will cause all three instruments to become inoperative or to display erroneous readings.

**Impact** (ram) **pressure** is taken from the pitot tube and furnished to the airspeed indicator only. Clogging of the pitot opening will not affect operation of the altimeter or vertical speed indicator.

**Figure 3-1.** Pitot-static system

---

AIR, GLI, RTC

**3247.** If the pitot tube and outside static vents become clogged, which instruments would be affected?

A—The altimeter, airspeed indicator, and turn-and-slip indicator.
B—The altimeter, airspeed indicator, and vertical speed indicator.
C—The altimeter, attitude indicator, and turn-and-slip indicator.

*Airspeed, altimeter and vertical speed all receive static input and would indicate inaccurately if the static sources became plugged. (H312) — AC 61-23C, Chapter 3*

Answers (A) and (C) are incorrect because the turn-and-slip indicator and attitude indicator are gyroscopic instruments, and are not part of the pitot-static system.

ALL

**3248.** Which instrument will become inoperative if the pitot tube becomes clogged?

A—Altimeter.
B—Vertical speed.
C—Airspeed.

*The pitot tube provides input for the airspeed indicator only. (H312) — AC 61-23C, Chapter 3*

Answers (A) and (B) are incorrect because the altimeter and vertical speed indicator operate off the static system and are not affected by a clogged pitot tube.

---

**Answers**

3247    [B]          3248    [C]

ALL
**3249.** Which instrument(s) will become inoperative if the static vents become clogged?

A—Airspeed only.
B—Altimeter only.
C—Airspeed, altimeter, and vertical speed.

*Airspeed, altimeter and vertical speed all receive static input and would indicate inaccurately if the static sources became plugged. (H312) — AC 61-23C, Chapter 3*

AIR, GLI, RTC
**3262.** The pitot system provides impact pressure for which instrument?

A—Altimeter.
B—Vertical-speed indicator.
C—Airspeed indicator.

*The pitot tube provides input for the airspeed indicator only. (H312) — AC 61-23C, Chapter 3*

Answers (A) and (B) are incorrect because the altimeter and vertical speed indicator operate off the static system.

# Airspeeds and the Airspeed Indicator

A pilot must be familiar with the following airspeed terms and abbreviations:

**Indicated Airspeed (IAS)**—the uncorrected reading obtained from the airspeed indicator.

**Calibrated Airspeed (CAS)**—indicated airspeed corrected for installation and instrument error.

**True Airspeed (TAS)**—calibrated airspeed corrected for temperature and pressure variations.

A number of airspeed limitations, abbreviated as "V" speeds, are indicated by color-coded marking on the airspeed indicator (*See* Figure 3-2 on the next page):

$V_{SO}$—stall speed or minimum steady flight speed in the landing configuration (the lower limit of the white arc).

$V_{FE}$—maximum flap extended speed (the upper limit of the white arc). The entire white arc defines the flap operating range.

$V_{S1}$—the stall speed or minimum steady flight speed in a specified configuration (the lower limit of the green arc). The entire green arc defines the normal operating range.

$V_{NO}$—the maximum structural cruising speed (the upper limit of the green arc and lower limit of the yellow arc). The yellow arc defines the caution range, which should be avoided unless in smooth air.

$V_{NE}$—never exceed speed (the upper limit of the yellow arc) marked in red.

There are other important airspeed limitations that are not color-coded on the airspeed indicator:

$V_{LE}$—the maximum landing gear extended speed.

$V_A$—the design maneuvering speed. If rough air or severe turbulence is encountered, airspeed should be reduced to maneuvering speed or less to minimize stress on the airplane structure.

$V_Y$—the best rate-of-climb speed (the airspeed that will result in the most altitude in a given period of time).

$V_X$—the best angle-of-climb speed (the airspeed that will result in the most altitude in a given distance).

**Answers**

3249   [C]          3262   [C]

**Figure 3-2.** Airspeed indicator

ALL
**3006.** Which V-speed represents maneuvering speed?

A—$V_A$.
B—$V_{LO}$.
C—$V_{NE}$.

*$V_A$ is design maneuvering speed. (A02) — 14 CFR §1.2*

Answer (B) is incorrect because this is the maximum landing gear operating speed. Answer (C) is incorrect because this is the never exceed speed.

AIR, GLI
**3007.** Which V-speed represents maximum flap extended speed?

A—$V_{FE}$.
B—$V_{LOF}$.
C—$V_{FC}$.

*$V_{FE}$ is the highest calibrated airspeed permissible with the wing flaps in a prescribed extended position. (A02) — 14 CFR §1.2*

Answer (B) is incorrect because this is the liftoff speed. Answer (C) is incorrect because this is the maximum speed for stability characteristics.

AIR, GLI
**3008.** Which V-speed represents maximum landing gear extended speed?

A—$V_{LE}$.
B—$V_{LO}$.
C—$V_{FE}$.

*$V_{LE}$ is the maximum calibrated airspeed at which the airplane can be safely flown with the landing gear extended. (A02) — 14 CFR §1.2*

Answer (B) is incorrect because $V_{LO}$ is maximum landing gear operating speed. Answer (C) is incorrect because $V_{FE}$ is maximum flap extended speed.

AIR, GLI
**3009.** $V_{NO}$ is defined as the

A—normal operating range.
B—never-exceed speed.
C—maximum structural cruising speed.

*$V_{NO}$ is the maximum calibrated airspeed for normal operation, or the maximum structural cruising speed. (A02) — 14 CFR §1.2*

Answer (A) is incorrect because this is not designated a V-speed; but rather it is the green arc on the airspeed indicator. Answer (B) is incorrect because this is $V_{NE}$.

AIR, GLI
**3010.** $V_{SO}$ is defined as the

A—stalling speed or minimum steady flight speed in the landing configuration.
B—stalling speed or minimum steady flight speed in a specified configuration.
C—stalling speed or minimum takeoff safety speed.

*$V_{SO}$ is the calibrated power-off stalling speed or the minimum steady-flight speed at which the aircraft is controllable in the landing configuration. (A02) — 14 CFR §1.2*

Answer (B) is incorrect because this is $V_{S1}$. Answer (C) is incorrect because $V_S$ is stalling speed, and $V_2$ is the minimum takeoff safety speed.

**Answers**

3006  [A]          3007  [A]          3008  [A]          3009  [C]          3010  [A]

AIR

**3011.** Which would provide the greatest gain in altitude in the shortest distance during climb after takeoff?

A—$V_Y$.

B—$V_A$.

C—$V_X$.

$V_X$ (best angle) is the calibrated airspeed at which the aircraft will attain the highest altitude in a given horizontal distance. (A02) — 14 CFR §1.2

Answer (A) is incorrect because $V_Y$ is best rate of climb. Answer (B) is incorrect because $V_A$ is design maneuvering speed.

AIR

**3012-1.** After takeoff, which airspeed would the pilot use to gain the most altitude in a given period of time?

A—$V_Y$.

B—$V_X$.

C—$V_A$.

$V_Y$ (best rate) is the calibrated airspeed at which the airplane will obtain the maximum increase in altitude per unit of time (feet per minute) after takeoff. (A02) — 14 CFR §1.2

Answer (B) is incorrect because $V_X$ is the best angle of climb. Answer (C) is incorrect because $V_A$ is the design maneuvering speed.

ALL

**3264.** What does the red line on an airspeed indicator represent?

A—Maneuvering speed.

B—Turbulent or rough-air speed.

C—Never-exceed speed.

The upper end of the arc is marked by a red radial line which is the never-exceed speed ($V_{NE}$). (H312) — AC 61-23C, Chapter 3

Answers (A) and (B) are incorrect because the maneuvering speed and turbulent or rough-air speed is not indicated on the airspeed indicator.

AIR

**3265.** (Refer to Figure 4.) What is the full flap operating range for the airplane?

A—60 to 100 MPH.

B—60 to 208 MPH.

C—65 to 165 MPH.

The flap operating range is marked by the white arc. The low end is $V_{SO}$ (stall speed in a landing configuration), and the high end is $V_{FE}$ (maximum flap extended speed). (H312) — AC 61-23C, Chapter 3

Answer (B) is incorrect because 60 to 208 MPH is the entire operating range of this airplane, from the stall speed to the never-exceed speed. Answer (C) is incorrect because 65 to 165 MPH is the normal operating range for this airplane (green arc).

AIR, GLI

**3266.** (Refer to Figure 4.) What is the caution range of the airplane?

A—0 to 60 MPH.

B—100 to 165 MPH.

C—165 to 208 MPH.

The caution range (yellow arc) includes speeds which should only be flown in smooth air, and is 165 to 208 MPH for this airplane. (H312) — AC 61-23C, Chapter 3

Answer (A) is incorrect because 0 to 60 MPH is less than stall speed. Answer (B) is incorrect because 100 to 165 MPH is the normal operating airspeed range from maximum flap extension speed to maximum structural cruising speed, the upper limit of the green arc and lower limit of the yellow arc.

AIR

**3267.** (Refer to Figure 4.) The maximum speed at which the airplane can be operated in smooth air is

A—100 MPH.

B—165 MPH.

C—208 MPH.

The caution range (yellow arc) includes speeds which should only be flown in smooth air; the maximum speed in the caution range is 208 MPH for this airplane. (H312) — AC 61-23C, Chapter 3

Answer (A) is incorrect because 100 MPH is the upper limit of the white arc, which is the maximum flaps-extended speed. Answer (B) is incorrect because 165 MPH is the upper limit of the green arc, which is the maximum structural cruising speed.

**Answers**

| | | | | | |
|---|---|---|---|---|---|
| 3011 [C] | 3012-1 [A] | 3264 [C] | 3265 [A] | 3266 [C] | 3267 [C] |

**ALL**
**3268.** (Refer to Figure 4.) Which color identifies the never-exceed speed?

A—Lower limit of the yellow arc.
B—Upper limit of the white arc.
C—The red radial line.

*The upper end of the arc is marked by a red radial line which is the never-exceed speed ($V_{NE}$). (H312) — AC 61-23C, Chapter 3*

Answer (A) is incorrect because the lower limit of the yellow arc is the beginning of the caution range. Answer (B) is incorrect because the upper limit of the white arc is the maximum speed at which flaps may be extended.

**ALL**
**3269.** (Refer to Figure 4.) Which color identifies the power-off stalling speed in a specified configuration?

A—Upper limit of the green arc.
B—Upper limit of the white arc.
C—Lower limit of the green arc.

*The green arc is the normal operating range. The lower end of the arc ($V_{S1}$) is the stalling speed in a specified configuration. (H312) — AC 61-23C, Chapter 3*

Answer (A) is incorrect because the upper limit of the green arc indicates the maximum structural cruising speed. Answer (B) is incorrect because the upper limit of the white arc is the maximum flaps-extended speed.

**AIR**
**3270.** (Refer to Figure 4.) What is the maximum flaps-extended speed?

A—65 MPH.
B—100 MPH.
C—165 MPH.

*The flap operating range is marked by the white arc. The high end is $V_{FE}$ (maximum flap extended speed), which is 100 MPH for this airplane. (H312) — AC 61-23C, Chapter 3*

Answer (A) is incorrect because 65 MPH is the lower limit of the green arc, which is the power-off stall speed, $V_{S1}$. Answer (C) is incorrect because 165 MPH is the upper limit of the green arc, which is $V_{NO}$.

**AIR**
**3271.** (Refer to Figure 4.) Which color identifies the normal flap operating range?

A—The lower limit of the white arc to the upper limit of the green arc.
B—The green arc.
C—The white arc.

*The flap operating range is marked by the white arc. The low end is $V_{SO}$ (stall speed in a landing configuration), and the high end is $V_{FE}$ (maximum flap extended speed). (H312) — AC 61-23C, Chapter 3*

Answer (A) is incorrect because the upper limit of the green arc is well above the white arc and represents $V_{NO}$. Answer (B) is incorrect because the green arc indicates the normal operating range.

**AIR**
**3272.** (Refer to Figure 4.) Which color identifies the power-off stalling speed with wing flaps and landing gear in the landing configuration?

A—Upper limit of the green arc.
B—Upper limit of the white arc.
C—Lower limit of the white arc.

*The flap operating range is marked by the white arc. The low end is $V_{SO}$ (stall speed in a landing configuration). (H312) — AC 61-23C, Chapter 3*

Answer (A) is incorrect because the upper limit of the green arc is $V_{NO}$. Answer (B) is incorrect because the upper limit of the white arc is $V_{FE}$.

**AIR**
**3273.** (Refer to Figure 4.) What is the maximum structural cruising speed?

A—100 MPH.
B—165 MPH.
C—208 MPH.

*The green arc is the normal operating range. The upper end of the arc ($V_{NO}$) is defined as the "maximum structural cruising speed." (H312) — AC 61-23C, Chapter 3*

Answer (A) is incorrect because 100 MPH is the upper limit of the white arc, which is the maximum flaps extended speed. Answer (C) is incorrect because 208 MPH is the never-exceed speed.

**AIR**
**3274.** What is an important airspeed limitation that is not color coded on airspeed indicators?

A—Never-exceed speed.
B—Maximum structural cruising speed.
C—Maneuvering speed.

*Maneuvering speed ($V_A$) is not displayed on the airspeed indicator. (H312) — AC 61-23C, Chapter 3*

Answer (A) is incorrect because the never-exceed speed is indicated by a red line on the airspeed indicator. Answer (B) is incorrect because the maximum structural cruising speed can be found on the airspeed indicator by the upper limit of the green arc.

**Answers**

| 3268 | [C] | 3269 | [C] | 3270 | [B] | 3271 | [C] | 3272 | [C] | 3273 | [B] |
| 3274 | [C] | | | | | | | | | | |

# The Altimeter and Altitudes

An **altimeter** is an instrument used to measure height (altitude) by responding to atmospheric pressure changes. *See* Figure 3-3 on the next page.

Altitude is indicated by three hands on the face of the altimeter. The shortest hand indicates altitude in tens of thousands of feet; the intermediate hand, in thousands of feet; and the longest hand in hundreds of feet. The altimeter is subdivided into 20-foot increments.

"Altitude" means elevation with respect to any assumed reference level, and different terms identify the reference level used. *See* Figure 3-4 on the next page.

**Indicated altitude**—the altitude read on the altimeter after it is set to the current local altimeter setting.

**Absolute altitude**—the height above the surface.

**True altitude**—the true height above Mean Sea Level (MSL) normally measured in feet.

**Pressure altitude**—the altitude that is indicated whenever the altimeter setting dial (Kohlsman window) is adjusted to 29.92. This is the Standard Datum Plane; a theoretical level where air pressure is equal to 29.92 inches of mercury (in. Hg). The Standard Datum Plane may be above, at, or below sea level.

**Density altitude**—the pressure altitude corrected for non-standard temperature and/or pressure. Rotating the setting knob on the altimeter simultaneously rotates the setting dial and the altimeter hands at a rate of one inch per 1,000 feet of altitude. Thus, increasing the setting dial from 29.15 to 29.85 would cause the hands of the altimeter to show an increase of 700 feet.

Prior to takeoff, the altimeter should be set to the current local altimeter setting. This is the value to which the scale of the altimeter is set so that the altimeter indicates true altitude at field elevation. If the altimeter setting is not available, the altimeter should be set to the elevation of the departure airport.

After takeoff, the altimeter should remain set to the current local altimeter setting until climbing through 18,000 feet MSL. At that time, the altimeter should be set to 29.92.

On a standard day (29.92" Hg and +15°C) at sea level, pressure altitude, true altitude, indicated altitude, and density altitude are all equal. Any variation from standard temperature or pressure will have an effect on the altimeter.

To compensate for the effect of nonstandard conditions, the altimeter must be set to the altimeter setting of a station within 100 NM of the aircraft (unless it is above 18,000 feet MSL).

If a flight is made from an area of low pressure/low temperature to an area of high pressure/high temperature without adjusting the altimeter setting, the altimeter will indicate *lower* than the actual altitude above ground level. If a flight is made from an area of high pressure/high temperature to an area of low pressure/low temperature without adjusting the altimeter setting, the altimeter will indicate *higher* than the actual altitude above mean sea level.

**Figure 3-3.** Altimeter components

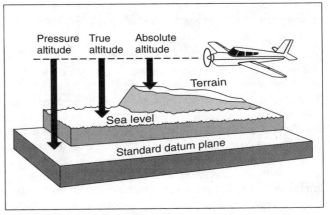

**Figure 3-4.** Types of altitude

ALL
**3105.** If an altimeter setting is not available before flight, to which altitude should the pilot adjust the altimeter?

A—The elevation of the nearest airport corrected to mean sea level.
B—The elevation of the departure area.
C—Pressure altitude corrected for nonstandard temperature.

*The altimeter should be set to the elevation of the departure airport for airplanes, and the departure area for other aircraft. (B08) — 14 CFR §91.121(a)(1)(iii)*

Answer (A) is incorrect because airport elevation is always expressed in feet above MSL. Answer (C) is incorrect because pressure altitude adjusted for nonstandard temperature is not true altitude, but density altitude.

ALL
**3106.** Prior to takeoff, the altimeter should be set to which altitude or altimeter setting?

A—The current local altimeter setting, if available, or the departure airport elevation.
B—The corrected density altitude of the departure airport.
C—The corrected pressure altitude for the departure airport.

*The altimeter should be set to the elevation of the departure airport for airplanes, and the departure area for other aircraft. (B08) — 14 CFR §91.121(a)(1)*

Answer (B) is incorrect because density altitude is pressure altitude corrected for nonstandard temperature variations and only concerns the performance of the aircraft. Answer (C) is incorrect because pressure altitude is the altitude indicated on the altimeter when the altimeter is set to 29.92.

ALL
**3107.** At what altitude shall the altimeter be set to 29.92, when climbing to cruising flight level?

A—14,500 feet MSL.
B—18,000 feet MSL.
C—24,000 feet MSL.

*The altimeter should be set to 29.92" Hg at 18,000 feet MSL and above. (B08) — 14 CFR §91.121(a)(2)*

Answer (A) is incorrect because 14,500 feet is the base of Class E airspace, when not designated lower. Answer (C) is incorrect because 24,000 feet MSL is the altitude at which DME is required.

ALL
**3254.** Altimeter setting is the value to which the barometric pressure scale of the altimeter is set so the altimeter indicates

A—calibrated altitude at field elevation.
B—absolute altitude at field elevation.
C—true altitude at field elevation.

*The local altimeter setting corrects for the difference between existing pressure and standard atmospheric pressure. Whether local pressure is higher or lower than standard, it will indicate true altitude (MSL) at ground level, when the aircraft altimeter is set to the local altimeter setting (assuming no setting scale error). (H312) — AC 61-23C, Chapter 3*

Answer (A) is incorrect because "calibrated" does not apply to altitudes; it only applies to airspeeds. Answer (B) is incorrect because absolute altitude is the height above the ground.

**Answers**

| 3105 | [B] | 3106 | [A] | 3107 | [B] | 3254 | [C] |

ALL

**3255.** How do variations in temperature affect the altimeter?

A—Pressure levels are raised on warm days and the indicated altitude is lower than true altitude.
B—Higher temperatures expand the pressure levels and the indicated altitude is higher than true altitude.
C—Lower temperatures lower the pressure levels and the indicated altitude is lower than true altitude.

*On a warm day, the expanded air is lighter than on a cold day, and consequently the pressure levels are raised. For example, the pressure level where the altimeter indicates 10,000 feet will be higher on a warm day than under standard conditions. On a cold day the reverse is true. (H312) — AC 61-23C, Chapter 3*

Answer (B) is incorrect because raising the pressure levels would not cause the indicated altitude to be higher than the true altitude. Answer (C) is incorrect because lowering the pressure levels would not cause the indicated altitude to be lower than the true altitude.

ALL

**3256.** What is true altitude?

A—The vertical distance of the aircraft above sea level.
B—The vertical distance of the aircraft above the surface.
C—The height above the standard datum plane.

*True altitude is height above sea level. Airport terrain and obstacle elevations found on aeronautical charts are true altitudes. (H312) — AC 61-23C, Chapter 3*

Answer (B) is incorrect because the vertical distance above the surface is absolute altitude. Answer (C) is incorrect because the height above the standard datum plane is pressure altitude.

ALL

**3392.** Under what condition will true altitude be lower than indicated altitude?

A—In colder than standard air temperature.
B—In warmer than standard air temperature.
C—When density altitude is higher than indicated altitude.

*True altitude will be lower than indicated altitude in colder than standard air temperature, even with an accurate altimeter set to 29.92. (I22) — AC 00-6A, Chapter 3*

ALL

**3257.** What is absolute altitude?

A—The altitude read directly from the altimeter.
B—The vertical distance of the aircraft above the surface.
C—The height above the standard datum plane.

*Absolute altitude is height above the surface. This height may be indicated directly on a radar altimeter. Absolute altitude may be approximately computed from indicated altitude and chart elevation data. (H312) — AC 61-23C, Chapter 3*

Answer (A) is incorrect because the altitude read from the altimeter is indicated altitude. Answer (C) is incorrect because the height above the standard datum plane is pressure altitude.

ALL

**3258.** What is density altitude?

A—The height above the standard datum plane.
B—The pressure altitude corrected for nonstandard temperature.
C—The altitude read directly from the altimeter.

*Under standard atmospheric conditions, each level of air in the atmosphere has a specific density, and under standard conditions, pressure altitude and density altitude identify the same level. At temperatures higher or lower than standard, density altitude cannot be determined directly from the altimeter. (H312) — AC 61-23C, Chapter 3*

Answer (A) is incorrect because the height above the standard datum plane is pressure altitude. Answer (C) is incorrect because the altitude read from the altimeter is indicated altitude.

ALL

**3259.** What is pressure altitude?

A—The indicated altitude corrected for position and installation error.
B—The altitude indicated when the barometric pressure scale is set to 29.92.
C—The indicated altitude corrected for nonstandard temperature and pressure.

**Answers**

3255 [A]      3256 [A]      3392 [A]      3257 [B]      3258 [B]      3259 [B]

The pressure altitude can be determined by either of two methods:

1. Setting the barometric scale of the altimeter to 29.92 and reading the indicated altitude, or

2. Applying a correction factor to the elevation (true altitude) according to the reported "altimeter setting."

*(H312) — AC 61-23C, Chapter 3*

*Answer (A) is incorrect because the altimeter is not corrected for position and installation error. Answer (C) is incorrect because indicated altitude corrected for nonstandard temperature and pressure defines density altitude.*

ALL
**3260.** Under what condition is indicated altitude the same as true altitude?

A— If the altimeter has no mechanical error.
B— When at sea level under standard conditions.
C— When at 18,000 feet MSL with the altimeter set at 29.92.

*On a standard day (29.92" Hg and +15°C) at sea level, pressure altitude, indicated altitude, and density altitude are all equal. Any variation from standard temperature or pressure will have an effect on the altimeter. (H312) — AC 61-23C, Chapter 3*

*Answer (A) is incorrect because mechanical error does not apply to true altitude. Answer (C) is incorrect because when the altimeter is set to 29.92, it indicates pressure altitude.*

ALL
**3261.** If it is necessary to set the altimeter from 29.15 to 29.85, what change occurs?

A— 70-foot increase in indicated altitude.
B— 70-foot increase in density altitude.
C— 700-foot increase in indicated altitude.

*When the knob on the altimeter is rotated, the pressure scale moves simultaneously with the altimeter pointers. The numerical values of pressure indicated in the window increase while the altimeter indicates an increase in altitude; or decrease while the altimeter indicates a decrease in altitude. This is contrary to the reaction on the pointers when air pressure changes, and is based solely on the mechanical makeup of the altimeter. The difference between the two settings is equal to 0.70" Hg (29.85 – 29.15). At the standard pressure lapse rate of 1" Hg = 1,000 feet in altitude, the amount of change equals 700 feet. (H312) — AC 61-23C, Chapter 3*

AIR, GLI, RTC
**3387.** If a pilot changes the altimeter setting from 30.11 to 29.96, what is the approximate change in indication?

A— Altimeter will indicate .15" Hg higher.
B— Altimeter will indicate 150 feet higher.
C— Altimeter will indicate 150 feet lower.

*When the knob on the altimeter is rotated, the altimeter setting pressure scale moves simultaneously with the altimeter pointers. The numerical values of pressure indicated in the window increase while the altimeter indicates an increase in altitude, or decrease while the altimeter indicates a decrease in altitude. This is contrary to the reaction on the pointers when air pressure changes and is based solely on the mechanical makeup of the altimeter. The difference between the two settings is equal to 0.15" Hg (30.11 – 29.96 = 0.15). At the standard pressure lapse rate of 1" Hg = 1,000 feet in altitude, the amount of change equals 150 feet. (I22) — AC 00-6A, Chapter 3*

ALL
**3388.** Under which condition will pressure altitude be equal to true altitude?

A— When the atmospheric pressure is 29.92" Hg.
B— When standard atmospheric conditions exist.
C— When indicated altitude is equal to the pressure altitude.

*Pressure altitude is equal to true altitude under standard atmospheric conditions. (I22) — AC 00-6A, Chapter 3*

ALL
**3389.** Under what condition is pressure altitude and density altitude the same value?

A— At sea level, when the temperature is 0°F.
B— When the altimeter has no installation error.
C— At standard temperature.

*When conditions are standard, pressure altitude and density altitude are the same. (I22) — AC 00-6A, Chapter 3*

*Answer (A) is incorrect because standard temperature at sea level is 59°F. Answer (B) is incorrect because installation errors apply to airspeed indicators, not altimeters.*

**Answers**
3260　[B]　　3261　[C]　　3387　[C]　　3388　[B]　　3389　[C]

ALL
**3390.** If a flight is made from an area of low pressure into an area of high pressure without the altimeter setting being adjusted, the altimeter will indicate

A—the actual altitude above sea level.
B—higher than the actual altitude above sea level.
C—lower than the actual altitude above sea level.

*If a flight is made from a high-pressure area to a low-pressure area without adjusting the altimeter, the actual altitude of the airplane will be lower than the indicated altitude, and when flying from a low-pressure area to high-pressure area, the actual altitude of the airplane will be higher than the indicated altitude. (I22) — AC 00-6A, Chapter 3*

*Answer (A) is incorrect because a correct altimeter setting must be used and/or standard atmospheric conditions must exist. Answer (B) is incorrect because the altimeter will indicate a lower altitude than actual.*

ALL
**3391.** If a flight is made from an area of high pressure into an area of lower pressure without the altimeter setting being adjusted, the altimeter will indicate

A—lower than the actual altitude above sea level.
B—higher than the actual altitude above sea level.
C—the actual altitude above sea level.

*If a flight is made from a high-pressure area to a low-pressure area without adjusting the altimeter, the actual altitude of the airplane will be lower than the indicated altitude, and when flying from a low-pressure area to high-pressure area, the actual altitude of the airplane will be higher than the indicated altitude. (I22) — AC 00-6A, Chapter 3*

*Answer (A) is incorrect because this change would indicate a flight into a high-pressure area from a low-pressure area. Answer (C) is incorrect because the lack of change would indicate constant pressure, thus actual altitude.*

ALL
**3393.** Which condition would cause the altimeter to indicate a lower altitude than true altitude?

A—Air temperature lower than standard.
B—Atmospheric pressure lower than standard.
C—Air temperature warmer than standard.

*The altimeter will indicate a lower altitude than actually flown, in air temperature warmer than standard. (I22) — AC 00-6A, Chapter 3*

*Answer (A) is incorrect because if the air temperature was lower, this would indicate a higher indicated altitude and a lower true altitude. Answer (B) is incorrect because when atmospheric pressure is lower than standard, the same conditions exist as described in Answer (A).*

ALL
**3250.** (Refer to Figure 3.) Altimeter 1 indicates

A—500 feet.
B—1,500 feet.
C—10,500 feet.

*On altimeter #1 the 10,000-foot pointer (shortest hand) is just above 10,000 feet, the 1,000-foot pointer (fat hand) is between 0 and 1,000 feet, and the 100-foot pointer is on 500 feet. (H312) — AC 61-23C, Chapter 3*

ALL
**3251.** (Refer to Figure 3.) Altimeter 2 indicates

A—1,500 feet.
B—4,500 feet.
C—14,500 feet.

*On altimeter #2 the 10,000-foot pointer is between 10,000 feet and 20,000 feet. The 1,000-foot pointer is between 4,000 feet and 5,000 feet, and the 100-foot pointer is on 500 feet. (H312) — AC 61-23C, Chapter 3*

ALL
**3252.** (Refer to Figure 3.) Altimeter 3 indicates

A—9,500 feet.
B—10,950 feet.
C—15,940 feet.

*On altimeter #3 the 10,000-foot pointer is not quite to 10,000 feet. The 1,000-foot pointer is halfway between 9,000 and 10,000 feet, and the 100-foot pointer is on 500 feet. (H312) — AC 61-23C, Chapter 3*

ALL
**3253.** (Refer to Figure 3.) Which altimeter(s) indicate(s) more than 10,000 feet?

A—1, 2, and 3.
B—1 and 2 only.
C—1 only.

*The shortest hand (10,000 foot) in #1 is between 1 and 2, indicating 10,000 feet plus. The shortest hand in #2 also indicates 10,000 feet plus. The shortest hand in #3 indicates less than 10,000 feet. (H312) — AC 61-23C, Chapter 3*

**Answers**

| | | | | | |
|---|---|---|---|---|---|
| 3390 [C] | 3391 [B] | 3393 [C] | 3250 [C] | 3251 [C] | 3252 [A] |
| 3253 [B] | | | | | |

# Gyroscopic Instruments

Some aircraft instruments use gyroscopes. Simply stated, gyroscopes are rapidly spinning wheels or disks which resist any attempt to move them from their plane of rotation. This is called "rigidity in space." Three aircraft instruments which use gyroscopes are the **attitude indicator**, the **turn coordinator**, and the **heading indicator.**

## Attitude Indicator

The rigidity in space principle makes the gyroscope an excellent "artificial horizon" around which the attitude indicator (and the airplane) pivot.

When viewing the attitude indicator, the direction of bank is determined by the relationship of the miniature airplane to the horizon bar. The miniature airplane may be moved up or down from the horizon with an adjustment knob. Normally, the miniature airplane will be adjusted so that the wings overlap the horizon bar whenever the airplane is in straight-and-level flight.

## Turn Coordinator

The turn coordinator (also using the principle of the gyroscope) uses a miniature airplane to provide information concerning rate of roll and rate of turn. As the airplane enters a turn, movement of the miniature aircraft indicates rate of roll. When the bank is held constant, rate of turn is indicated. Simultaneously, the quality of turn, or movement about the yaw axis, is indicated by the ball of the inclinometer.

## Heading Indicator

The heading indicator is a gyroscopic instrument designed to avoid many of the errors inherent in a magnetic compass. However, the heading indicator does suffer from precession, caused mainly by bearing friction. Because of this precessional error, the heading indicator must periodically be realigned with the magnetic compass during straight-and-level, unaccelerated flight.

AIR, RTC
**3277.** (Refer to Figure 7.) The proper adjustment to make on the attitude indicator during level flight is to align the

A—horizon bar to the level-flight indication.
B—horizon bar to the miniature airplane.
C—miniature airplane to the horizon bar.

*The miniature airplane "C" is adjusted so that the wings overlap the horizon bar "B" when the airplane is in straight-and-level cruising flight. (H313) — AC 61-23C, Chapter 3*

Answers (A) and (B) are incorrect because adjustment is only made to the miniature airplane.

ALL
**3278.** (Refer to Figure 7.) How should a pilot determine the direction of bank from an attitude indicator such as the one illustrated?

A— By the direction of deflection of the banking scale (A).
B— By the direction of deflection of the horizon bar (B).
C— By the relationship of the miniature airplane (C) to the deflected horizon bar (B).

*The relationship of the miniature aircraft C to the horizon bar B is the same as the relationship of the real aircraft to the actual horizon. (H313) — AC 61-23C, Chapter 3*

Answer (A) is incorrect because the bank scale shows degrees, and not direction of bank. Answer (B) is incorrect because the horizon line deflects opposite the direction of turn, in order to correct horizon representation.

**Answers**

3277    [C]                3278    [C]

AIR

**3275.** (Refer to Figure 5.) A turn coordinator provides an indication of the

A—movement of the aircraft about the yaw and roll axes.

B—angle of bank up to but not exceeding 30°.

C—attitude of the aircraft with reference to the longitudinal axis.

*The movement of the miniature airplane on the instrument is proportional to the roll rate of the airplane. When the roll rate is reduced to zero, i.e., the bank is held constant, the instrument provides an indication of the rate of turn. This design features a realignment of the gyro in such a manner that it senses airplane movement about the yaw and roll axis. (H313) — AC 61-23C, Chapter 3*

*Answers (B) and (C) are incorrect because the miniature aircraft indicates rate of turn, not angle of bank or attitude.*

AIR, RTC

**3276.** (Refer to Figure 6.) To receive accurate indications during flight from a heading indicator, the instrument must be

A—set prior to flight on a known heading.

B—calibrated on a compass rose at regular intervals.

C—periodically realigned with the magnetic compass as the gyro precesses.

*Because the heading indicator is run by a gyroscope instead of a magnetic source, precession will cause creep or drift from a heading to which it is set. It is important to check the indications frequently and reset the heading indicator to align it with the magnetic compass when required. (H313) — AC 61-23C, Chapter 3*

*Answers (A) and (B) are incorrect because they don't do anything to correct for precession in flight.*

# Magnetic Compass (Northern Hemisphere)

The magnetic compass, attracted to a magnetic field in the earth, points down as well as north. This downward pointing tendency, called "**magnetic dip**," causes errors in compass indications.

When turning toward north from an easterly or westerly heading, the compass lags behind the actual aircraft heading. When a turn is initiated while on a northerly heading, the compass first indicates a turn in the opposite direction. The compass lags whenever turns are made to or from north.

When turning toward south from an easterly or westerly heading, the compass leads the actual aircraft heading. When a turn is initiated while on a southerly heading, the compass shows an immediate lead in the same direction as the turn. The compass leads whenever turns are made to or from south.

Accelerating or decelerating while heading either east or west will also cause compass errors. If acceleration occurs on a heading of east or west, the compass will indicate a turn to the north, while deceleration will cause an indication of a turn to the south. Therefore, it becomes apparent that the indications of a magnetic compass are accurate only during straight-and-level, unaccelerated flight.

The magnetic compass is also influenced by lines of force from magnetic fields within the aircraft. These errors are called deviations.

ALL

**3279.** Deviation in a magnetic compass is caused by the

A—presence of flaws in the permanent magnets of the compass.

B—difference in the location between true north and magnetic north.

C—magnetic fields within the aircraft distorting the lines of magnetic force.

*Magnetic disturbances from magnetic fields produced by metals and electrical accessories in an aircraft disturb the compass card and produce an additional error which is referred to as deviation. (H314) — AC 61-23C, Chapter 3*

*Answer (A) is incorrect because deviation is not caused by magnet flaws. Answer (B) is incorrect because the difference between magnetic north and true north is called variation.*

**Answers**

3275 [A]          3276 [C]          3279 [C]

AIR, GLI, RTC

**3280.** In the Northern Hemisphere, a magnetic compass will normally indicate initially a turn toward the west if

A—a left turn is entered from a north heading.
B—a right turn is entered from a north heading.
C—an aircraft is accelerated while on a north heading.

*If on a northerly heading and a turn is made toward east or west, the initial indication of the compass lags, or indicates a turn in the opposite direction. (H314) — AC 61-23C, Chapter 3*

Answer (A) is incorrect because a left turn would indicate a turn toward the east, while turning west. Answer (C) is incorrect because acceleration error does not occur on a north or south heading.

AIR, GLI, RTC

**3281.** In the Northern Hemisphere, a magnetic compass will normally indicate initially a turn toward the east if

A—an aircraft is decelerated while on a south heading.
B—an aircraft is accelerated while on a north heading.
C—a left turn is entered from a north heading.

*If on a northerly heading and a turn is made toward east or west, the initial indication of the compass lags, or indicates a turn in the opposite direction. (H314) — AC 61-23C, Chapter 3*

Answers (A) and (B) are incorrect because acceleration error does not occur on north or south headings.

ALL

**3282.** In the Northern Hemisphere, a magnetic compass will normally indicate a turn toward the north if

A—a right turn is entered from an east heading.
B—a left turn is entered from a west heading.
C—an aircraft is accelerated while on an east or west heading.

*While on an east or west heading, an increase in airspeed or acceleration will cause the compass to indicate a turn toward the north and a deceleration will cause the compass to indicate a turn to the south. If on a north or south heading, no error will be apparent because of acceleration or deceleration. (Remember **ANDS** = Accelerate North Decelerate South). (H314) — AC 61-23C, Chapter 3*

Answers (A) and (B) are incorrect because on east and west headings, turning error is negligible.

ALL

**3283.** In the Northern Hemisphere, the magnetic compass will normally indicate a turn toward the south when

A—a left turn is entered from an east heading.
B—a right turn is entered from a west heading.
C—the aircraft is decelerated while on a west heading.

*While on an east or west heading, an increase in airspeed or acceleration will cause the compass to indicate a turn toward the north and a deceleration will cause the compass to indicate a turn to the south. If on a north or south heading, no error will be apparent because of acceleration or deceleration. (Remember **ANDS** = Accelerate North Decelerate South). (H314) — AC 61-23C, Chapter 3*

Answers (A) and (B) are incorrect because on east and west heading, turning error is negligible.

ALL

**3284.** In the Northern Hemisphere, if an aircraft is accelerated or decelerated, the magnetic compass will normally indicate

A—a turn momentarily.
B—correctly when on a north or south heading.
C—a turn toward the south.

*While on an east or west heading, an increase in airspeed or acceleration will cause the compass to indicate a turn toward the north and a deceleration will cause the compass to indicate a turn to the south. If on a north or south heading, no error will be apparent because of acceleration or deceleration. (Remember **ANDS** = Accelerate North Decelerate South). (H314) — AC 61-23C, Chapter 3*

Answers (A) and (C) are incorrect because these conditions only occur on a north or south heading.

AIR, GLI, RTC

**3286.** During flight, when are the indications of a magnetic compass accurate?

A—Only in straight-and-level unaccelerated flight.
B—As long as the airspeed is constant.
C—During turns if the bank does not exceed 18°.

*The magnetic compass should be read only when the aircraft is flying straight-and-level at a constant speed. This will help reduce errors to the minimum. (H314) — AC 61-23C, Chapter 3*

Answer (B) is incorrect because airspeed can remain constant in a turn, and the compass is subject to turning errors. Answer (C) is incorrect because no matter how steep the turn, the compass is still susceptible to turning errors.

**Answers**

| 3280 | [B] | 3281 | [C] | 3282 | [C] | 3283 | [C] | 3284 | [B] | 3286 | [A] |

GLI

**3285.** In the Northern Hemisphere, if a glider is accelerated or decelerated, the magnetic compass will normally indicate

A—a turn toward north while decelerating on an east heading.

B—correctly only when on a north or south heading.

C—a turn toward south while accelerating on a west heading.

While on an east or west heading, an increase in airspeed or acceleration will cause the compass to indicate a turn toward the north and a deceleration will cause the compass to indicate a turn to the south. If on a north or south heading, no error will be apparent because of acceleration or deceleration. (Remember **ANDS** = Accelerate North Decelerate South). (H314) — AC 61-23C, Chapter 3

**Answers**

3285    [B]

# Chapter 4
# Regulations

# Introduction

Although "FAR" is used as the acronym for "Federal Aviation Regulations," and found throughout the regulations themselves and hundreds of other publications, the FAA is now actively discouraging its use. "FAR" also means "Federal Acquisition Regulations." To eliminate any possible confusion, the FAA cites the federal aviation regulations with reference to Title 14 of the Code of Federal Regulations. For example, "FAR Part 91.3" is referenced as "14 CFR Part 91 Section 3."

While **Federal Aviation Regulations** are many and varied, some are of particular interest to all pilots.

**14 CFR Part 1** contains definitions and abbreviations of many terms commonly used in aviation. For example, the term "night" means "the time between the end of evening civil twilight and the beginning of morning civil twilight, as published in the American Air Almanac, converted to local time" and is used for logging night time.

**14 CFR Part 61**, entitled "Certification: Pilots, Flight Instructors and Ground Instructors," prescribes the requirements for issuing pilot and flight instructor certificates and ratings, the conditions of issue, and the privileges and limitations of those certificates and ratings.

**14 CFR Part 91,** entitled "General Operating and Flight Rules," describes rules governing the operation of aircraft (with certain exceptions) within the United States.

The **National Transportation Safety Board (NTSB)** has established rules and requirements for notification and reporting of aircraft accidents and incidents. These are contained in **NTSB Part 830.**

ALL
**3005.** The definition of nighttime is

A—sunset to sunrise.
B—1 hour after sunset to 1 hour before sunrise.
C—the time between the end of evening civil twilight and the beginning of morning civil twilight.

*Night is the time between the end of evening civil twilight and the beginning of morning civil twilight converted to local time, as published in the American Air Almanac. (A01) — 14 CFR §1.1*

Answer (A) is incorrect because it refers to the time when lighted position lights are required. Answer (B) is incorrect because it refers to the currency requirement to carry passengers.

# Pilot Certificate Privileges and Limitations

The types of pilot certificates and the attendant privileges are contained in 14 CFR Part 61 and are briefly stated as follows:

• The holder of a student pilot certificate is limited to solo flights or flights with an instructor.

• Recreational pilots may not carry more than one passenger, pay less than the pro rata share of the operating expenses of a flight with a passenger (provided the expenses involve only fuel, oil, airport expenses, or aircraft rental fees), fly an aircraft with more than 4 seats or high-performance characteristics, demonstrate an aircraft to a prospective buyer, fly between sunset and sunrise, or fly in airspace in which communication with air traffic control is required. Recreational pilots may fly beyond 50 NM from the departure airport with additional training and endorsements from an authorized instructor.

• A private pilot has unlimited solo privileges, and may carry passengers or cargo as long as the flying is for the pilots' pleasure or personal business and is not done for hire. A private pilot may fly in conjunction with his/her job as long as that flying is incidental to his/her employment.

*Continued*

**Answers**
3005   [C]

- A private pilot may not pay less than the pro rata share of the operating expenses of a flight with passengers, provided the expenses involve only fuel, oil, airport expenditures, or rental fees. The only time passengers may pay for the entire flight is if a donation is made by the passengers to the charitable organization which is sponsoring the flight.

- Commercial pilots may fly for compensation or hire.

- An Airline Transport Pilot may act as pilot-in-command (PIC) of airline and scheduled commuter operations.

- All pilot certificates (except student pilot) are valid indefinitely unless surrendered, superseded or revoked.

ALL
**3064.** In regard to privileges and limitations, a private pilot may

A—not pay less than the pro rata share of the operating expenses of a flight with passengers provided the expenses involve only fuel, oil, airport expenditures, or rental fees.

B—act as pilot in command of an aircraft carrying a passenger for compensation if the flight is in connection with a business or employment.

C—not be paid in any manner for the operating expenses of a flight.

*A private pilot may not pay less than the pro rata share of the operating expenses of a flight with passengers, provided the expenses involve only fuel, oil, airport expenditures, or rental fees. (A23) — 14 CFR §61.113*

ALL
**3065.** According to regulations pertaining to privileges and limitations, a private pilot may

A—be paid for the operating expenses of a flight if at least three takeoffs and three landings were made by the pilot within the preceding 90 days.

B—not be paid in any manner for the operating expenses of a flight.

C—not pay less than the pro rata share of the operating expenses of a flight with passengers provided the expenses involve only fuel, oil, airport expenditures, or rental fees.

*A private pilot may not pay less than the pro rata share of the operating expenses of a flight with passengers, provided the expenses involve only fuel, oil, airport expenditures, or rental fees. (A23) — 14 CFR §61.113*

AIR, RTC
**3066.** What exception, if any, permits a private pilot to act as pilot in command of an aircraft carrying passengers who pay for the flight?

A—If the passengers pay all the operating expenses.

B—If a donation is made to a charitable organization for the flight.

C—There is no exception.

*A private pilot may act as pilot-in-command of an aircraft used in a passenger-carrying airlift sponsored by a charitable organization, and for which the passengers make a donation to the organization. This can be done if the sponsor of the airlift notifies the FAA General Aviation District Office having jurisdiction over the area concerned, at least 7 days before the flight, and furnishes any essential information that the office requests. (A23) — 14 CFR §61.113*

REC
**3044.** According to regulations pertaining to privileges and limitations, a recreational pilot may

A—be paid for the operating expenses of a flight.

B—not pay less than the pro rata share of the operating expenses of a flight with a passenger.

C—not be paid in any manner for the operating expenses of a flight.

*A recreational pilot may not pay less than the pro rata share of the operating expenses of a flight with a passenger, provided the expenses involve only fuel, oil, airport expenditures, or rental fees. (A29) — 14 CFR §61.101*

**Answers**

| | | | |
|---|---|---|---|
| 3064 [A] | 3065 [C] | 3066 [B] | 3044 [B] |

REC

**3045.** In regard to privileges and limitations, a recreational pilot may

A—fly for compensation or hire within 50 nautical miles from the departure airport with a logbook endorsement.

B—not be paid in any manner for the operating expenses of a flight from a passenger.

C—not pay less than the pro rata share of the operating expenses of a flight with a passenger.

*A recreational pilot may not pay less than the pro rata share of the operating expenses of a flight with a passenger, provided the expenses involve only fuel, oil, airport expenditures, or rental fees. (A29) — 14 CFR §61.101*

REC

**3046.** When may a recreational pilot act as pilot in command on a cross-country flight that exceeds 50 nautical miles from the departure airport?

A—After receiving ground and flight instructions on cross-country training and a logbook endorsement.

B—12 calendar months after receiving his or her recreational pilot certificate and a logbook endorsement.

C—After attaining 100 hours of pilot-in-command time and a logbook endorsement.

*A person who holds a recreational pilot certificate may act as pilot-in-command of an aircraft on a flight that exceeds 50 nautical miles from the departure airport, provided that person has received ground and flight training from an authorized instructor, been found proficient in cross-country flying, and received an endorsement, which is carried in the person's possession in the aircraft. (A29) — 14 CFR §61.101*

REC

**3047.** A recreational pilot may act as pilot in command of an aircraft that is certificated for a maximum of how many occupants?

A—Two.

B—Three.

C—Four.

*A recreational pilot may not act as pilot-in-command of an aircraft that is certificated for more than four occupants. (A29) — 14 CFR §61.101*

REC

**3048.** A recreational pilot may act as pilot in command of an aircraft with a maximum engine horsepower of

A—160.

B—180.

C—200.

*A recreational pilot may not act as pilot-in-command of an aircraft that is certificated with a powerplant of more than 180 horsepower. (A29) — 14 CFR §61.101*

REC

**3049.** What exception, if any, permits a recreational pilot to act as pilot in command of an aircraft carrying a passenger for hire?

A—If the passenger pays no more than the operating expenses.

B—If a donation is made to a charitable organization for the flight.

C—There is no exception.

*A recreational pilot may not act as pilot-in-command of an aircraft that is carrying a passenger or property for compensation or hire, in furtherance of a business, or for a charitable organization. (A29) — 14 CFR §61.101*

Answer (A) is incorrect because the passenger may only pay an equal share of the operating expenses. Answer (B) is incorrect because a recreational pilot may not carry passengers for hire, even if the flight is a donation to a charitable organization.

REC

**3050.** May a recreational pilot act as pilot in command of an aircraft in furtherance of a business?

A—Yes, if the flight is only incidental to that business.

B—Yes, providing the aircraft does not carry a person or property for compensation or hire.

C—No, it is not allowed.

*A recreational pilot may not act as pilot-in-command of an aircraft in furtherance of a business. (A29) — 14 CFR §61.101*

REC

**3051.** With respect to daylight hours, what is the earliest time a recreational pilot may take off?

A—One hour before sunrise.

B—At sunrise.

C—At the beginning of morning civil twilight.

*Continued*

**Answers**

| 3045 | [C] | | 3046 | [A] | | 3047 | [C] | | 3048 | [B] | | 3049 | [C] | | 3050 | [C] |
| 3051 | [B] | | | | | | | | | | | | | | | | |

**2004 Private Pilot Test Prep** ASA **4–5**

*A recreational pilot may not act as pilot-in-command of an aircraft between sunset and sunrise. The earliest a recreational pilot may takeoff is at sunrise. (A29) — 14 CFR §61.101*

REC
**3052.** If sunset is 2021 and the end of evening civil twilight is 2043, when must a recreational pilot terminate the flight?

A—2021.
B—2043.
C—2121.

*A recreational pilot may not act as pilot-in-command of an aircraft between sunset and sunrise. A recreational pilot must land by sunset. (A29) — 14 CFR §61.101*

REC
**3053.** When may a recreational pilot operate to or from an airport that lies within Class C airspace?

A—Anytime the control tower is in operation.
B—When the ceiling is at least 1,000 feet and the surface visibility is at least 3 miles.
C—For the purpose of obtaining an additional certificate or rating while under the supervision of an authorized flight instructor.

*A recreational pilot may not operate in airspace where air traffic control is required, unless under the supervision of an authorized instructor in airspace with air traffic control for the purpose of obtaining an additional certificate or rating. (A29) — 14 CFR §61.101*

REC
**3054.** Under what conditions may a recreational pilot operate at an airport that lies within Class D airspace and that has a part-time control tower in operation?

A—Between sunrise and sunset when the tower is in operation, the ceiling is at least 2,500 feet, and the visibility is at least 3 miles.
B—Any time when the tower is in operation, the ceiling is at least 3,000 feet, and the visibility is more than 1 mile.
C—Between sunrise and sunset when the tower is closed, the ceiling is at least 1,000 feet, and the visibility is at least 3 miles.

*A recreational pilot may not act as pilot-in-command of an aircraft in airspace in which communication with ATC is required. If the tower is closed, no communication is required and it reverts to Class E airspace. The visibility and cloud clearances for Class E airspace require a ceiling at least 1,000 feet and the visibility at least 3 miles. (A29) — 14 CFR §61.101*

*Answers (A) and (B) are incorrect because a recreational pilot may not operate in airspace that requires communication with ATC.*

REC
**3055.** When may a recreational pilot fly above 10,000 feet MSL?

A—When 2,000 feet AGL or below.
B—When 2,500 feet AGL or below.
C—When outside of controlled airspace.

*A recreational pilot may not act as pilot-in-command of an aircraft at an altitude of more than 10,000 feet MSL or 2,000 feet AGL, whichever is higher. (A29) — 14 CFR §61.101*

REC
**3056.** During daytime, what is the minimum flight or surface visibility required for recreational pilots in Class G airspace below 10,000 feet MSL?

A—1 mile.
B—3 miles.
C—5 miles.

*A recreational pilot may not act as pilot-in-command of an aircraft when the flight or surface visibility is less than 3 statute miles. (A29) — 14 CFR §61.101*

REC
**3057.** During daytime, what is the minimum flight visibility required for recreational pilots in controlled airspace below 10,000 feet MSL?

A—1 mile.
B—3 miles.
C—5 miles.

*A recreational pilot may not act as pilot-in-command of an aircraft when the flight or surface visibility is less than 3 statute miles. (A29) — 14 CFR §61.101*

**Answers**

| | | | | | |
|---|---|---|---|---|---|
| 3052 [A] | 3053 [C] | 3054 [C] | 3055 [A] | 3056 [B] | 3057 [B] |

**REC**
**3058.** Under what conditions, if any, may a recreational pilot demonstrate an aircraft in flight to a prospective buyer?

A—The buyer pays all the operating expenses.
B—The flight is not outside the United States.
C—None.

*A recreational pilot may not act as pilot-in-command of an aircraft to demonstrate that aircraft in flight to a prospective buyer. (A29) — 14 CFR §61.101*

**REC**
**3059.** When, if ever, may a recreational pilot act as pilot in command in an aircraft towing a banner?

A—If the pilot has logged 100 hours of flight time in powered aircraft.
B—If the pilot has an endorsement in his/her pilot logbook from an authorized flight instructor.
C—It is not allowed.

*A recreational pilot may not act as pilot-in-command of an aircraft that is towing any object. (A29) — 14 CFR §61.101*

**REC**
**3043.** How many passengers is a recreational pilot allowed to carry on board?

A—One.
B—Two.
C—Three.

*A recreational pilot may not carry more than one passenger. (A29) — 14 CFR §61.101*

**REC**
**3060.** When must a recreational pilot have a pilot-in-command flight check?

A—Every 400 hours.
B—Every 180 days.
C—If the pilot has less than 400 total flight hours and has not flown as pilot in command in an aircraft within the preceding 180 days.

*A recreational pilot who has logged fewer than 400 flight hours and who has not logged pilot-in-command time in an aircraft within the preceding 180 days may not act as pilot-in-command of an aircraft until flight instruction is received from an authorized flight instructor who certifies in the pilot's logbook that the pilot is competent to*

*act as pilot-in-command of the aircraft. This requirement can be met in combination with the requirements of flight reviews, at the discretion of the instructor. (A29) — 14 CFR §61.101*

**REC**
**3061.** A recreational pilot may fly as sole occupant of an aircraft at night while under the supervision of a flight instructor provided the flight or surface visibility is at least

A—3 miles.
B—4 miles.
C—5 miles.

*For the purpose of obtaining additional certificates or ratings, while under the supervision of an authorized flight instructor, a recreational pilot may fly as sole occupant of an aircraft between sunset and sunrise, provided the flight or surface visibility is at least 5 statute miles. (A29) — 14 CFR §61.101*

**REC**
**3134.** What minimum visibility and clearance from clouds are required for a recreational pilot in Class G airspace at 1,200 feet AGL or below during daylight hours?

A—1 mile visibility and clear of clouds.
B—3 miles visibility and clear of clouds.
C—3 miles visibility, 500 feet below the clouds.

*Minimum flight or surface visibility for recreational pilots is 3 miles and minimum cloud clearance for all pilots in Class G airspace, below 1,200 AGL, is clear of clouds. (B09) — 14 CFR §61.101*

*Answer (A) is incorrect because this would be for private pilots. Answer (C) is incorrect because this is for controlled airspace.*

**REC**
**3135.** Outside controlled airspace, the minimum flight visibility requirement for a recreational pilot flying VFR above 1,200 feet AGL and below 10,000 feet MSL during daylight hours is

A—1 mile.
B—3 miles.
C—5 miles.

*Minimum flight or surface visibility for recreational pilots is 3 miles. (B09) — 14 CFR §61.101*

**Answers**
3058 [C]   3059 [C]   3043 [A]   3060 [C]   3061 [C]   3134 [B]
3135 [B]

# Pilot Ratings

When a pilot certificate is issued, it lists the category, class, and type (if appropriate) of aircraft in which the certificate holder is qualified. *See* Figure 4-1.

The term "**category**" means a broad classification of aircraft, such as airplane, rotorcraft, glider, and lighter-than-air. The term "**class**" means a classification within a category having similar operating characteristics, such as single-engine, multi-engine, land, water, helicopter, and balloon. The term "**type**" means a specific make and basic model of aircraft, such as F-27, or DC-7.

A type rating must be held by the pilot-in-command of a large aircraft. "Large aircraft" means aircraft of more than 12,500 pounds maximum certificated takeoff weight.

All turbojet-powered airplanes, regardless of weight, require the PIC to have a type rating.

In addition to the category, class, and type ratings, if a pilot wishes to fly IFR, an instrument rating is required.

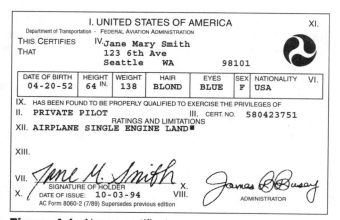

**Figure 4-1.** Airman certificate

ALL

**3001.** With respect to the certification of airmen, which is a category of aircraft?

A—Gyroplane, helicopter, airship, free balloon.
B—Airplane, rotorcraft, glider, lighter-than-air.
C—Single-engine land and sea, multiengine land and sea.

*With respect to the certification of airmen, "category" means a broad classification of aircraft such as airplane, rotorcraft, glider, and lighter-than-air. (A01) — 14 CFR §1.1*

Answer (A) is incorrect because it refers to classes of rotorcraft and lighter-than-air craft. Answer (C) is incorrect because it refers to classes of airplanes.

ALL

**3002.** With respect to the certification of airmen, which is a class of aircraft?

A—Airplane, rotorcraft, glider, lighter-than-air.
B—Single-engine land and sea, multiengine land and sea.
C—Lighter-than-air, airship, hot air balloon, gas balloon.

*With respect to the certification of airmen, a "class" refers to aircraft with similar operating characteristics such as single-engine land/sea and multi-engine land/sea, gyroplane, helicopter, airship, and free balloon. (A01) — 14 CFR §1.1*

Answer (A) is incorrect because it refers to categories of aircraft. Answer (C) is incorrect because it refers to lighter-than-air category. Airship and free balloon are lighter-than-air class ratings, but hot air balloon and gas balloon are not.

AIR, RTC

**3024.** The pilot in command is required to hold a type rating in which aircraft?

A—Aircraft operated under an authorization issued by the Administrator.
B—Aircraft having a gross weight of more than 12,500 pounds.
C—Aircraft involved in ferry flights, training flights, or test flights.

*A type rating is required in order for a pilot to act as pilot-in-command of a large aircraft (except lighter-than-air) which is further defined as more than 12,500 pounds maximum certificated takeoff weight or a turbojet-powered aircraft. (A20) — 14 CFR §61.31(a)(1)*

Answers (A) and (C) are incorrect because they don't address the weight or type of propulsion.

---

**Answers**

3001    [B]        3002    [B]        3024    [B]

# Medical Certificates

Student pilot, recreational pilot, and private pilot operations, other than glider and balloon pilots, require a Third-Class Medical Certificate. A Third-Class Medical Certificate issued before September 16, 1996, expires at the end of the 24th month after the month of the date of examination shown on the certificate. Certificates issued on or after September 16, 1996, expire at the end of:

1. The 36th month after the month of the date of the examination shown on the certificate if the person has not reached his or her 40th birthday on or before the date of examination; or

2. The 24th month after the month of the date of examination shown on the certificate if the person has reached his or her 40th birthday on or before the date of the examination.

The holder of a Second-Class Medical Certificate may exercise commercial privileges during the first 12 calendar months, but the certificate is valid only for private pilot privileges during the following (12 or 24) calendar months, depending on the applicant's age.

The holder of a First-Class Medical Certificate may exercise Airline Transport Pilot privileges during the first 6 calendar months, commercial privileges during the following 6 calendar months, and private pilot privileges during the following (12 or 24) calendar months, depending on the applicant's age.

AIR, RTC, REC, LTA
**3020.** A Third-Class Medical Certificate is issued to a 36-year-old pilot on August 10, this year. To exercise the privileges of a Private Pilot Certificate, the medical certificate will be valid until midnight on

A—August 10, 2 years later.
B—August 31, 3 years later.
C—August 31, 2 years later.

*A Third-Class Medical Certificate expires at the end of the last day of the 36th month after the month of the date of the examination shown on the certificate if the person has not reached his or her 40th birthday on or before the date of examination, for operations requiring a Private Pilot Certificate. (A20) — 14 CFR §61.23*

AIR, RTC, REC, LTA
**3021.** A Third-Class Medical Certificate is issued to a 51-year-old pilot on May 3, this year. To exercise the privileges of a Private Pilot Certificate, the medical certificate will be valid until midnight on

A—May 3, 1 year later.
B—May 31, 1 year later.
C—May 31, 2 years later.

*A Third-Class Medical Certificate expires at the end of the last day of the 24th month after the month of the date of the examination shown on the certificate if the person has reached his or her 40th birthday on or before the date of examination, for operations requiring a Private Pilot Certificate. (A20) — 14 CFR §61.23*

AIR, RTC, REC, LTA
**3022.** For private pilot operations, a Second-Class Medical Certificate issued to a 42-year-old pilot on July 15, this year, will expire at midnight on

A—July 15, 2 years later.
B—July 31, 1 year later.
C—July 31, 2 years later.

*A Second-Class Medical Certificate expires at the end of the last day of the 24th month after the month of the date of the examination shown on the certificate if the person has reached his or her 40th birthday on or before the date of examination, for operations requiring a Private Pilot Certificate. (A20) — 14 CFR §61.23*

AIR, RTC, REC, LTA
**3023.** For private pilot operations, a First-Class Medical Certificate issued to a 23-year-old pilot on October 21, this year, will expire at midnight on

A—October 21, 2 years later.
B—October 31, next year.
C—October 31, 3 years later.

*A First-Class Medical Certificate expires at the end of the last day of the 36th month after the month of the date of the examination shown on the certificate if the person has not reached his or her 40th birthday on or before the date of examination, for operations requiring a Private Pilot Certificate. (A20) — 14 CFR §61.23*

**Answers**
3020 [B]     3021 [C]     3022 [C]     3023 [C]

**ALL**
**3039.** A Third-Class Medical Certificate was issued to a 19-year-old pilot on August 10, this year. To exercise the privileges of a Recreational or Private Pilot Certificate, the medical certificate will expire at midnight on

A—August 10, 2 years later.
B—August 31, 3 years later.
C—August 31, 2 years later.

*A Third-Class Medical Certificate expires at the end of the last day of the 36th month after the month of the date of the examination shown on the certificate if the person has not reached his or her 40th birthday on or before the date of examination, for operations requiring a Recreational or Private Pilot Certificate. (A20) — 14 CFR §61.23*

**GLI**
**3062.** Prior to becoming certified as a private pilot with a glider rating, the pilot must have in his or her possession what type of medical?

A—A statement from a designated medical examiner.
B—A third-class medical certificate.
C—A medical certificate is not required.

*A person is not required to hold a medical certificate when exercising the privileges of a pilot certificate with a glider category rating. (A20) — 14 CFR §61.23*

**LTA**
**3063.** Prior to becoming certified as a private pilot with a balloon rating, the pilot must have in his or her possession what class of medical?

A—A third-class medical certificate.
B—A medical certificate is not required.
C—A statement from a designated medical examiner.

*A person is not required to hold a medical certificate when exercising the privileges of a pilot certificate with a balloon class rating. (A20) — 14 CFR §61.23*

# Required Certificates

When acting as pilot-in-command, a pilot must have a current pilot license and a current medical certificate in his/her physical possession or readily accessible in the aircraft. Glider and balloon pilots do not need a medical certificate. A recreational pilot acting as PIC must have a current logbook endorsement in his/her personal possession within flights 50 NM from the departure airport.

A pilot must present his/her pilot license and medical certificate for inspection upon request of any FAA, NTSB or federal, state, or local law enforcement officer.

**ALL**
**3016.** What document(s) must be in your personal possession or readily accessible in the aircraft while operating as pilot in command of an aircraft?

A—Certificates showing accomplishment of a checkout in the aircraft and a current biennial flight review.
B—A pilot certificate with an endorsement showing accomplishment of an annual flight review and a pilot logbook showing recency of experience.
C—An appropriate pilot certificate and an appropriate current medical certificate if required.

*No person may act as pilot-in-command (PIC), or in any other capacity as a required pilot flight crewmember, of a civil aircraft of United States registry unless he/she has in possession or readily accessible in the aircraft a current pilot certificate. Except for free balloon pilots piloting balloons and glider pilots piloting gliders, no person may act as pilot-in-command or in any other capacity as a required pilot flight crewmember of an aircraft unless he/she has in possession or readily accessible in the aircraft an appropriate current medical certificate. (A20) — 14 CFR §61.3(a), (c)*

*Answers (A) and (B) are incorrect because aircraft checkouts don't need to be recorded, and a BFR record and currency proof don't need to be in your possession.*

**Answers**

| 3039 | [B] | 3062 | [C] | 3063 | [B] | 3016 | [C] |

ALL

**3017.** When must a current pilot certificate be in the pilot's personal possession or readily accessible in the aircraft?

A—When acting as a crew chief during launch and recovery.
B—Only when passengers are carried.
C—Anytime when acting as pilot in command or as a required crewmember.

*No person may act as pilot-in-command (PIC), or in any other capacity as a required pilot flight crewmember, of a civil aircraft of United States registry unless he/she has in possession or readily accessible in the aircraft a current pilot certificate. (A20) — 14 CFR §61.3(a)*

*Answers (A) and (B) are incorrect because a crew chief does not require a pilot certificate, and pilots must have certificates, regardless of whether carrying passengers or not.*

ALL

**3018.** A recreational or private pilot acting as pilot in command, or in any other capacity as a required pilot flight crewmember, must have in their personal possession or readily accessible in the aircraft a current

A—logbook endorsement to show that a flight review has been satisfactorily accomplished.
B—medical certificate if required and an appropriate pilot certificate.
C—endorsement on the pilot certificate to show that a flight review has been satisfactorily accomplished.

*No person may act as pilot-in-command (PIC), or in any other capacity as a required pilot flight crewmember, of a civil aircraft of United States registry unless he/she has in possession or readily accessible in the aircraft a current pilot certificate. Except for free balloon pilots piloting balloons and glider pilots piloting gliders, no person may act as pilot-in-command or in any other capacity as a required pilot flight crewmember of an aircraft unless he/she has in possession or readily accessible in the aircraft an appropriate current medical certificate. (A20) — 14 CFR §61.3(a), (c)*

*Answers (A) and (C) are incorrect because proof of a flight review does not need to be in your possession while acting as pilot-in-command.*

ALL

**3019.** Each person who holds a pilot certificate or a medical certificate shall present it for inspection upon the request of the Administrator, the National Transportation Safety Board, or any

A—authorized representative of the Department of Transportation.
B—person in a position of authority.
C—federal, state, or local law enforcement officer.

*Each person who holds a pilot or medical certificate shall present it for inspection upon the request of the FAA Administrator, an NTSB representative, or any Federal, State, or local law enforcement officer. (A20) — 14 CFR §61.3*

REC

**3038.** A recreational pilot acting as pilot in command must have in his/her personal possession while aboard the aircraft

A—a current logbook endorsement to show that a flight review has been satisfactorily accomplished.
B—a current logbook endorsement that permits flights within 50 NM from the departure airport.
C—the pilot logbook to show recent experience requirements to serve as pilot in command have been met.

*A recreational pilot may act as PIC on a flight within 50 NM from the departure airport, provided they receive from an authorized instructor a logbook endorsement, which is carried in the person's possession in the aircraft. (A29) — 14 CFR §61.101*

# Recent Flight Experience

No person may act as pilot-in-command of an aircraft unless within the preceding 24 calendar months he/she has accomplished a **flight review**. This review is given in an aircraft for which the pilot is rated by an appropriately-rated instructor or other person designated by the FAA. A logbook entry will document satisfactory accomplishment of this requirement. If the pilot takes a proficiency check (as for a certificate or a new rating), it counts for the flight review.

No person may act as PIC of an aircraft carrying passengers unless, within the preceding 90 days, he/she has made three takeoffs and three landings as the sole manipulator of the controls in an aircraft of the same category, class, and if a type rating is required, in the same type. Touch and go landings are acceptable unless the passengers are to be carried in a tailwheel airplane, in which case the landing must be to a full stop, and they must be in a tailwheel airplane.

If passengers are to be carried during the period from 1 hour after sunset to 1 hour before sunrise, the PIC must have made, within the preceding 90 days, at least three takeoffs and three landings during that period. The landings must have been to a full stop and in the same category and class of aircraft to be used.

ALL
**3028.** To act as pilot in command of an aircraft carrying passengers, a pilot must show by logbook endorsement the satisfactory completion of a flight review or completion of a pilot proficiency check within the preceding

A—6 calendar months.
B—12 calendar months.
C—24 calendar months.

*Each pilot must complete a flight review every 24 calendar months. (A20) — 14 CFR §61.56(c)(1)*

ALL
**3029.** If recency of experience requirements for night flight are not met and official sunset is 1830, the latest time passengers may be carried is

A—1829.
B—1859.
C—1929.

*No person may act as pilot-in-command of an aircraft carrying passengers during the period beginning one hour after sunset and ending one hour before sunrise (as published in the American Air Almanac) unless, within the preceding 90 days, he/she has made at least three takeoffs and three landings to a full stop during that period in the category and class of aircraft to be used.*

*1830 + 59 minutes = 1929*

*(A20) — 14 CFR §61.57*

ALL
**3030.** To act as pilot in command of an aircraft carrying passengers, the pilot must have made at least three takeoffs and three landings in an aircraft of the same category, class, and if a type rating is required, of the same type, within the preceding

A—90 days.
B—12 calendar months.
C—24 calendar months.

*No person may act as pilot-in-command of an aircraft carrying passengers, unless, within the preceding 90 days, he/she has made three takeoffs and three landings as the sole manipulator of the flight controls in an aircraft of the same category and class and, if a type rating is required, of the same type. If the aircraft is a tailwheel airplane, the landings must have been made to a full stop. (A20) — 14 CFR §61.57*

ALL
**3031.** To act as pilot in command of an aircraft carrying passengers, the pilot must have made three takeoffs and three landings within the preceding 90 days in an aircraft of the same

A—make and model.
B—category and class, but not type.
C—category, class, and type, if a type rating is required.

*No person may act as pilot-in-command of an aircraft carrying passengers, unless, within the preceding 90 days, he/she has made three takeoffs and three landings as the sole manipulator of the flight controls in an aircraft of the same category and class and, if a type*

**Answers**

3028  [C]          3029  [C]          3030  [A]          3031  [C] rating is required, of the same type. If the aircraft is a tailwheel airplane, the landings must have been made to a full stop. (A20) — 14 CFR §61.57

**AIR**

**3032.** The takeoffs and landings required to meet the recency of experience requirements for carrying passengers in a tailwheel airplane

A—may be touch and go or full stop.
B—must be touch and go.
C—must be to a full stop.

No person may act as pilot-in-command of an aircraft carrying passengers, unless, within the preceding 90 days, he/she has made three takeoffs and three landings as the sole manipulator of the flight controls in an aircraft of the same category and class and, if a type rating is required, of the same type. If the aircraft is a tailwheel airplane, the landings must have been made to a full stop. (A20) — 14 CFR §61.57

**AIR, RTC**

**3033.** The three takeoffs and landings that are required to act as pilot in command at night must be done during the time period from

A—sunset to sunrise.
B—1 hour after sunset to 1 hour before sunrise.
C—the end of evening civil twilight to the beginning of morning civil twilight.

No person may act as pilot-in-command of an aircraft carrying passengers during the period beginning one hour after sunset and ending one hour before sunrise (as published in the American Air Almanac) unless, within the preceding 90 days, he/she has made at least three takeoffs and three landings to a full stop during that period in the category and class of aircraft to be used. (A20) — 14 CFR §61.57

Answer (A) is incorrect because this is the requirement for position lights. Answer (C) is incorrect because it refers to the time which may be logged as night flight.

**ALL**

**3034.** To meet the recency of experience requirements to act as pilot in command carrying passengers at night, a pilot must have made at least three takeoffs and three landings to a full stop within the preceding 90 days in

A—the same category and class of aircraft to be used.
B—the same type of aircraft to be used.
C—any aircraft.

No person may act as pilot-in-command of an aircraft carrying passengers during the period beginning one hour after sunset and ending one hour before sunrise (as published in the American Air Almanac) unless, within the preceding 90 days, he/she has made at least three takeoffs and three landings to a full stop during that period in the category and class of aircraft to be used. (A20) — 14 CFR §61.57

**ALL**

**3040.** If a recreational or private pilot had a flight review on August 8, this year, when is the next flight review required?

A—August 8, 2 years later.
B—August 31, next year.
C—August 31, 2 years later.

Each pilot must have completed a biennial flight review since the beginning of the 24th calendar month before the month in which that pilot acts as pilot-in-command. A calendar month always ends at midnight of the last day of the month. If a pilot had a flight review on August 8, the next flight review would be due on August 31, two years later. (A20) — 14 CFR §61.56

**ALL**

**3041.** Each recreational or private pilot is required to have

A—a biennial flight review.
B—an annual flight review.
C—a semiannual flight review.

Each pilot must have completed a biennial flight review since the beginning of the 24th calendar month before the month in which that pilot acts as pilot-in-command. (A20) — 14 CFR §61.56

**ALL**

**3042.** If a recreational or private pilot had a flight review on August 8, this year, when is the next flight review required?

A—August 8, next year.
B—August 31, 1 year later.
C—August 31, 2 years later.

Each pilot must have completed a biennial flight review since the beginning of the 24th calendar month before the month in which that pilot acts as pilot-in-command. A calendar month always ends at midnight of the last day of the month. If a pilot had a flight review on August 8, the next flight review would be due on August 31, two years later. (A20) — 14 CFR §61.56

**Answers**

| 3032 [C] | 3033 [B] | 3034 [A] | 3040 [C] | 3041 [A] | 3042 [C] |

# High-Performance Airplanes

No person holding a Private or Commercial Pilot Certificate may act as pilot-in-command of an airplane that has more than 200 horsepower, unless he/she has received instruction from an authorized flight instructor who has certified in his/her logbook that he/she is competent to pilot a high-performance airplane.

AIR
**3025.** What is the definition of a high-performance airplane?

A—An airplane with an engine of more than 200 horsepower.
B—An airplane with 180 horsepower, or retractable landing gear, flaps, and a fixed-pitch propeller.
C—An airplane with a normal cruise speed in excess of 200 knots.

*A high-performance airplane is one with an engine of more than 200 horsepower. (A20) — 14 CFR §61.31*

AIR
**3026.** Before a person holding a Private Pilot Certificate may act as pilot in command of a high-performance airplane, that person must have

A—passed a flight test in that airplane from an FAA inspector.
B—an endorsement in that person's logbook that he or she is competent to act as pilot in command.
C—received ground and flight instruction from an authorized flight instructor who then endorses that person's logbook.

*No person holding a Private or Commercial pilot certificate may pilot a high-performance aircraft unless he or she has received instruction and has been certified competent in his/her logbook. (A20) — 14 CFR §61.31*

Answer (A) is incorrect because a flight test is not required. Answer (B) is incorrect because instruction is required.

AIR
**3027.** In order to act as pilot in command of a high-performance airplane, a pilot must have

A—made and logged three solo takeoffs and landings in a high-performance airplane.
B—passed a flight test in a high-performance airplane.
C—received and logged ground and flight instruction in an airplane that has more than 200 horsepower.

*A high-performance airplane is one with more than 200 horsepower. No person holding a Private or Commercial pilot certificate may pilot a high-performance aircraft unless he or she has received ground and flight instruction and has been certified proficient in his/her logbook. (A20) — 14 CFR §61.31*

Answer (A) is incorrect because landings are only required in order to carry passengers, and they don't need to be solo. Answer (B) is incorrect because a flight test is not required.

**Answers**
3025　[A]　　3026　[C]　　3027　[C]

# Glider Towing

A private pilot may not act as pilot-in-command of an aircraft towing a glider unless at least 100 hours of pilot flight time is logged in the aircraft category, class, and type (if required), or 200 hours total pilot time. Also, within the preceding 12 months he/she has made at least three actual/simulated glider tows while accompanied by a qualified pilot or has made three flights as PIC of a towed glider.

AIR, GLI

**3036.** A certificated private pilot may not act as pilot in command of an aircraft towing a glider unless there is entered in the pilot's logbook a minimum of

A— 100 hours of pilot flight time in any aircraft, that the pilot is using to tow a glider.
B— 100 hours of pilot-in-command time in the aircraft category, class, and type, if required, that the pilot is using to tow a glider.
C— 200 hours of pilot-in-command time in the aircraft category, class, and type, if required, that the pilot is using to tow a glider.

*With a Private pilot certificate, no person may act as PIC of an aircraft towing a glider unless he/she has had, and entered in his/her logbook, at least:*

1. *100 hours of pilot flight time in the aircraft category, class, and type (if required), or*
2. *200 hours of pilot flight time in powered or other aircraft.*

*(A21) — 14 CFR §61.69(d)*

AIR, GLI

**3037.** To act as pilot in command of an aircraft towing a glider, a person is required to have made within the preceding 12 months.

A— at least three flights as observer in a glider being towed by an aircraft.
B— at least three flights in a powered glider.
C— at least three actual or simulated glider tows while accompanied by a qualified pilot.

*No person may act as a pilot-in-command of an aircraft towing a glider unless within the preceding 12 months he/she has—*

1. *Made at least three actual or simulated glider tows while accompanied by a qualified pilot who meets the requirements of this 14 CFR §61.69, or*
2. *Made at least three flights as pilot-in-command of a glider towed by an aircraft.*

*(A21) — 14 CFR §61.69(d)*

# Change of Address

If a pilot changes his/her permanent mailing address without notifying the FAA Airmen's Certification Branch, in writing, within 30 days, then he/she may not exercise the privileges of his/her certificate.

ALL

**3035.** If a certificated pilot changes permanent mailing address and fails to notify the FAA Airmen Certification Branch of the new address, the pilot is entitled to exercise the privileges of the pilot certificate for a period of only

A— 30 days after the date of the move.
B— 60 days after the date of the move.
C— 90 days after the date of the move.

*The holder of a Pilot or Flight Instructor Certificate who has made a change in his/her permanent mailing address may not, after 30 days from the date moved, exercise the privileges of his/her certificate unless he/she has notified in writing the Department of Transportation, Federal Aviation Administration, Airmen Certification Branch, Box 25082, Oklahoma City, OK 73125, of the new address. (A20) — 14 CFR §61.60*

**Answers**

3036 [B]    3037 [C]    3035 [A]

# Responsibility and Authority of the Pilot-in-Command

The pilot-in-command (PIC) of an aircraft is directly responsible, and is the final authority, for the safety and operation of that aircraft. Should an emergency require immediate action, the PIC may deviate from 14 CFR Part 91 to the extent necessary in the interest of safety. Upon request, a written report of any deviation from the rules must be sent to the Administrator.

If a pilot receives a clearance that would cause a deviation from a rule, he/she should query the controller and request that the clearance be amended.

ALL
**3070.** The final authority as to the operation of an aircraft is the

A—Federal Aviation Administration.
B—pilot in command.
C—aircraft manufacturer.

*The pilot-in-command of an aircraft is directly responsible for, and is the final authority as to the operation of that aircraft. (B07) — 14 CFR §91.3(a)*

ALL
**3072.** If an in-flight emergency requires immediate action, the pilot in command may

A—deviate from the FAR's to the extent required to meet the emergency, but must submit a written report to the Administrator within 24 hours.
B—deviate from the FAR's to the extent required to meet that emergency.
C—not deviate from the FAR's unless prior to the deviation approval is granted by the Administrator.

*If an emergency requires immediate action, the pilot-in-command may deviate from the operating rules of Part 91 to the extent necessary to meet that emergency. No report of such deviation is required unless the FAA requests one. (B07) — 14 CFR §91.3(b)*

ALL
**3073.** When must a pilot who deviates from a regulation during an emergency send a written report of that deviation to the Administrator?

A—Within 7 days.
B—Within 10 days.
C—Upon request.

*Each pilot-in-command who deviates from a rule in an emergency shall, **upon request**, send a written report of that deviation to the Administrator. (B07) — 14 CFR §91.3(c)*

ALL
**3074.** Who is responsible for determining if an aircraft is in condition for safe flight?

A—A certificated aircraft mechanic.
B—The pilot in command.
C—The owner or operator.

*The pilot-in-command of an aircraft is responsible for determining whether that aircraft is in condition for safe flight. The pilot shall discontinue the flight when unairworthy mechanical, electrical or structural conditions occur. (B07) — 14 CFR §91.7(b)*

LTA
**3071.** The person directly responsible for the pre-launch briefing of passengers for a flight is the

A—safety officer.
B—pilot in command.
C—ground crewmember.

*The pilot-in-command is responsible for briefing crewmembers and occupants in all areas of the flight, including inflation, tether, in-flight, landing, emergency, and recovery procedures. (B07) — 14 CFR §91.3(a)*

**Answers**

| | | | | |
|---|---|---|---|---|
| 3070 [B] | 3072 [B] | 3073 [C] | 3074 [B] | 3071 [B] |

# Preflight Action

Before beginning a flight, the pilot-in-command is required to become familiar with all available information concerning that flight. This information must include the following:

1. Runway lengths, and
2. Takeoff and landing information for airports of intended use, including aircraft performance data.

If the flight will not be in the vicinity of an airport, the pilot must also consider the following:

1. Weather reports and forecasts,
2. Fuel requirements (enough fuel to fly to the first point of intended landing, and at normal cruising speed, to fly after that for at least 30 minutes if during the day, or for at least 45 minutes at night), and
3. Alternatives available if the flight cannot be completed as planned.

ALL
**3080.** Which preflight action is specifically required of the pilot prior to each flight?

A—Check the aircraft logbooks for appropriate entries.
B—Become familiar with all available information concerning the flight.
C—Review wake turbulence avoidance procedures.

*Each pilot-in-command shall, before each flight, become familiar with all available information concerning that flight. This information must include:*

*(a) For a flight under IFR or a flight not in the vicinity of an airport, weather reports and forecasts, fuel requirements, alternatives available if the planned flight cannot be completed, and any known traffic delays of which the pilot has been advised by ATC;*

*(b) For any flight, runway lengths of airports of intended use, and the following takeoff and landing distance information:*

*1. For civil aircraft for which an approved airplane or rotorcraft flight manual containing takeoff and landing distance data is required, the takeoff and landing distance data contained therein; and*

*2. For civil aircraft other than those specified in paragraph (b)(1) of this section, other reliable information appropriate to the aircraft, relating to aircraft performance under expected values of airport elevation and runway slope, aircraft gross weight, and wind and temperature.*

*(B07) — 14 CFR §91.103*

ALL
**3081.** Preflight action, as required for all flights away from the vicinity of an airport, shall include

A—the designation of an alternate airport.
B—a study of arrival procedures at airports/ heliports of intended use.
C—an alternate course of action if the flight cannot be completed as planned.

*Each pilot-in-command shall, before each flight, become familiar with all available information concerning that flight. This information must include:*

*(a) For a flight under IFR or a flight not in the vicinity of an airport, weather reports and forecasts, fuel requirements, alternatives available if the planned flight cannot be completed, and any known traffic delays of which the pilot has been advised by ATC;*

*(b) For any flight, runway lengths of airports of intended use, and the following takeoff and landing distance information:*

*1. For civil aircraft for which an approved airplane or rotorcraft flight manual containing takeoff and landing distance data is required, the takeoff and landing distance data contained therein; and*

*2. For civil aircraft other than those specified in paragraph (b)(1) of this section, other reliable information appropriate to the aircraft, relating to aircraft performance under expected values of airport elevation and runway slope, aircraft gross weight, and wind and temperature.*

*(B07) — 14 CFR §91.103*

**Answers**
3080 [B]      3081 [C]

ALL
**3082.** In addition to other preflight actions for a VFR flight away from the vicinity of the departure airport, regulations specifically require the pilot in command to

A—review traffic control light signal procedures.
B—check the accuracy of the navigation equipment and the emergency locator transmitter (ELT).
C—determine runway lengths at airports of intended use and the aircraft's takeoff and landing distance data.

*Each pilot-in-command shall, before each flight, become familiar with all available information concerning that flight. This information must include:*

*(a) For a flight under IFR or a flight not in the vicinity of an airport, weather reports and forecasts, fuel requirements, alternatives available if the planned flight cannot be completed, and any known traffic delays of which the pilot has been advised by ATC;*

*(b) For any flight, runway lengths of airports of intended use, and the following takeoff and landing distance information:*

*1. For civil aircraft for which an approved airplane or rotorcraft flight manual containing takeoff and landing distance data is required, the takeoff and landing distance data contained therein; and*

*2. For civil aircraft other than those specified in paragraph (b)(1) of this section, other reliable information appropriate to the aircraft, relating to aircraft performance under expected values of airport elevation and runway slope, aircraft gross weight, and wind and temperature.*

*(B07) — 14 CFR §91.103(b)*

AIR, REC
**3131.** What is the specific fuel requirement for flight under VFR during daylight hours in an airplane?

A—Enough to complete the flight at normal cruising speed with adverse wind conditions.
B—Enough to fly to the first point of intended landing and to fly after that for 30 minutes at normal cruising speed.
C—Enough to fly to the first point of intended landing and to fly after that for 45 minutes at normal cruising speed.

*No person may begin a flight in an airplane under VFR unless (considering wind and forecast weather conditions) there is enough fuel to fly to the first point of intended landing and, assuming normal cruising speed, and day operations, to fly after that for at least 30 minutes. (B09) — 14 CFR §91.151(a)(1)*

AIR
**3132.** What is the specific fuel requirement for flight under VFR at night in an airplane?

A—Enough to complete the flight at normal cruising speed with adverse wind conditions.
B—Enough to fly to the first point of intended landing and to fly after that for 30 minutes at normal cruising speed.
C—Enough to fly to the first point of intended landing and to fly after that for 45 minutes at normal cruising speed.

*No person may begin a flight in an airplane under VFR unless (considering wind and forecast weather conditions) there is enough fuel to fly to the first point of intended landing and, assuming normal cruising speed, and night operations, to fly after that for at least 45 minutes. (B09) — 14 CFR §91.151(a)(2)*

RTC
**3133.** No person may begin a flight in a rotorcraft under VFR unless there is enough fuel to fly to the first point of intended landing and, assuming normal cruising speed, to fly thereafter for at least

A—20 minutes.
B—30 minutes.
C—1 hour.

*No person may begin a flight in a rotorcraft under VFR unless (considering wind and forecast weather conditions) there is enough fuel to fly to the first point of intended landing and, assuming normal cruising speed, to fly after that for at least 20 minutes. (B09) — 14 CFR §91.151(b)*

---

**Answers**

| | | | |
|---|---|---|---|
| 3082 [C] | 3131 [B] | 3132 [C] | 3133 [A] |

# Seatbelts

All required flight crewmembers must remain in their seats with seatbelts secured during the entire flight unless absent in connection with duties or physiological needs. When shoulder harnesses are installed they must be used during takeoffs and landings.

Prior to takeoff, the pilot-in-command must ensure that each person on board has been briefed on the use of seatbelts. In addition, he/she must ensure that the passengers are notified to fasten their seatbelts during taxi, takeoffs, and landings. A child who has not reached his/her second birthday may be held by an adult who is occupying a seat or berth.

ALL
**3083.** Flight crewmembers are required to keep their safety belts and shoulder harnesses fastened during

A—takeoffs and landings.
B—all flight conditions.
C—flight in turbulent air.

*During takeoff and landing, and while en route, each required flight crewmember shall keep his/her seatbelt fastened while at the station. During takeoff and landing this includes shoulder harness (if installed) unless it interferes with required duties. (B07) — 14 CFR §91.105*

ALL
**3084.** Which best describes the flight conditions under which flight crewmembers are specifically required to keep their safety belts and shoulder harnesses fastened?

A—Safety belts during takeoff and landing; shoulder harnesses during takeoff and landing.
B—Safety belts during takeoff and landing; shoulder harnesses during takeoff and landing and while en route.
C—Safety belts during takeoff and landing and while en route; shoulder harnesses during takeoff and landing.

*During takeoff and landing, and while en route, each required flight crewmember shall keep his/her seatbelt fastened while at his/her station. During takeoff and landing this includes shoulder harness (if installed) unless it interferes with required duties. (B07) — 14 CFR §91.105*

AIR, GLI, RTC, REC
**3085.** With respect to passengers, what obligation, if any, does a pilot in command have concerning the use of safety belts?

A—The pilot in command must instruct the passengers to keep their safety belts fastened for the entire flight.
B—The pilot in command must brief the passengers on the use of safety belts and notify them to fasten their safety belts during taxi, takeoff, and landing.
C—The pilot in command has no obligation in regard to passengers' use of safety belts.

*Unless otherwise authorized by the Administrator, no pilot may takeoff in a civil aircraft unless the pilot-in-command of that aircraft ensures that each person on board is briefed on how to fasten and unfasten that person's seatbelt, and that each person has been notified to fasten the seatbelt during taxi, takeoff and landing. (B07) — 14 CFR §91.107(a)*

AIR, GLI, RTC, REC
**3086.** With certain exceptions, safety belts are required to be secured about passengers during

A—taxi, takeoffs, and landings.
B—all flight conditions.
C—flight in turbulent air.

*During taxi, takeoff and landing, each person on board the aircraft must occupy a seat or berth with a seatbelt and shoulder harness, properly secured if installed. (B07) — 14 CFR §91.107(b)*

**Answers**
3083 [A]    3084 [C]    3085 [B]    3086 [A]

**AIR, GLI, RTC, REC**
**3087.** Safety belts are required to be properly secured about which persons in an aircraft and when?

A—Pilots only, during takeoffs and landings.
B—Passengers, during taxi, takeoffs, and landings only.
C—Each person on board the aircraft during the entire flight.

*During taxi, takeoff and landing, each person on board the aircraft must occupy a seat or berth with a safety belt and shoulder harness, properly secured if installed. However, a person who has not reached his/her second birthday may be held by an adult who is occupying a seat or a berth, and a person on board for the purpose of engaging in sport parachuting may use the floor of the aircraft as a seat. (B07) — 14 CFR §91.107(b)*

# Alcohol and Drugs

No person may act as a crewmember on an aircraft under the following conditions:

1. Within 8 hours after the consumption of any alcoholic beverage;
2. While under the influence of alcohol (.04 percent by weight or more alcohol in the blood);
3. While using any drug that affects his/her faculties in any way contrary to safety.

Except in an emergency, no pilot of an aircraft may allow a person who appears to be intoxicated or under the influence of drugs (except a medical patient under proper care) to be carried in that aircraft.

**ALL**
**3077.** A person may not act as a crewmember of a civil aircraft if alcoholic beverages have been consumed by that person within the preceding

A—8 hours.
B—12 hours.
C—24 hours.

*No person may act or attempt to act as a crewmember of a civil aircraft within 8 hours after the consumption of any alcoholic beverage. Remember "8 hours bottle to throttle." (B07) — 14 CFR §91.17(a)(1)*

**ALL**
**3079.** No person may attempt to act as a crewmember of a civil aircraft with

A—.008 percent by weight or more alcohol in the blood.
B—.004 percent by weight or more alcohol in the blood.
C—.04 percent by weight or more alcohol in the blood.

*No person may act, or attempt to act, as a crewmember of a civil aircraft while having .04 percent or more, by weight, alcohol in the blood. (B07) — 14 CFR §91.17(a)(4)*

**ALL**
**3078.** Under what condition, if any, may a pilot allow a person who is obviously under the influence of drugs to be carried aboard an aircraft?

A—In an emergency or if the person is a medical patient under proper care.
B—Only if the person does not have access to the cockpit or pilot's compartment.
C—Under no condition.

*Except in an emergency, or a medical patient under proper care, no pilot of a civil aircraft may allow a person who appears to be intoxicated, or who demonstrates by manner or physical indications that the individual is under the influence of drugs, to be carried in that aircraft. (B07) — 14 CFR §91.17(b)*

**Answers**

| | | | |
|---|---|---|---|
| 3087 [B] | 3077 [A] | 3078 [A] | 3079 [C] |

# Right-of-Way Rules

When weather conditions permit, vigilance must be maintained so as to see and avoid other aircraft.

An aircraft in distress has the right-of-way over all other air traffic. When aircraft of the same category are converging at approximately the same altitude (except head-on, or nearly so), the aircraft on the other's right has the right-of-way. *See* Figure 4-2.

If the aircraft are of different categories, the following applies:

1. A balloon has the right-of-way over any other category of aircraft;
2. A glider has the right-of-way over an airship, airplane, or rotorcraft; and
3. An airship has the right-of-way over an airplane or rotorcraft.

An aircraft towing or refueling other aircraft has the right-of-way over all other engine driven aircraft.

When aircraft are approaching each other head-on, or nearly so, each pilot of each aircraft (regardless of category), shall alter course to the right. *See* Figure 4-3.

An aircraft being overtaken has the right-of-way. The overtaking aircraft shall alter course to the right to pass well clear. *See* Figure 4-4.

When two or more aircraft are approaching an airport for landing, the aircraft at the lower altitude has the right-of-way, but it shall not take advantage of this rule to cut in front of, or overtake another aircraft.

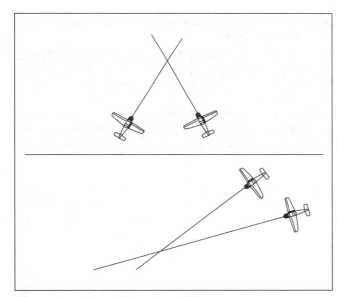

**Figure 4-2.** Aircraft on converging courses

**Figure 4-3.** Aircraft approaching head-on

**Figure 4-4.** One aircraft overtaking another

ALL
**3089.** Which aircraft has the right-of-way over all other air traffic?

A—A balloon.
B—An aircraft in distress.
C—An aircraft on final approach to land.

*An aircraft in distress has the right-of-way over all other air traffic. (B08) — 14 CFR §91.113(c)*

ALL
**3090.** What action is required when two aircraft of the same category converge, but not head-on?

A—The faster aircraft shall give way.
B—The aircraft on the left shall give way.
C—Each aircraft shall give way to the right.

*When two aircraft of the same "right-of-way" category converge at approximately the same altitude, the aircraft to the other's right has the right-of-way. (B08) — 14 CFR §91.113(d)*

Answer (A) is incorrect because speed has nothing to do with right-of-way. Answer (C) is incorrect because "each aircraft giving way to the right" is the rule when approaching head-on.

ALL
**3093.** Which aircraft has the right-of-way over the other aircraft listed?

A—Airship.
B—Aircraft towing other aircraft.
C—Gyroplane.

*An aircraft towing or refueling other aircraft has the right-of-way over all other engine driven aircraft. (B08) — 14 CFR §91.113(d)(3)*

ALL
**3092.** An airplane and an airship are converging. If the airship is left of the airplane's position, which aircraft has the right-of-way?

A—The airship.
B—The airplane.
C—Each pilot should alter course to the right.

*An airship has the right-of-way over an airplane or rotorcraft. (B08) — 14 CFR §91.113(d)(3)*

ALL
**3091.** Which aircraft has the right-of-way over the other aircraft listed?

A—Gyroplane.
B—Airship.
C—Aircraft towing other aircraft.

*An aircraft towing or refueling other aircraft has the right-of-way over all other engine-driven aircraft. (B08) — 14 CFR §91.113(d)(2)*

AIR, GLI, REC
**3094.** What action should the pilots of a glider and an airplane take if on a head-on collision course?

A—The airplane pilot should give way to the left.
B—The glider pilot should give way to the right.
C—Both pilots should give way to the right.

*When two aircraft are approaching each other from head-on, or nearly so, each pilot must alter course to the right. This rule does not give right-of-way by categories. (B08) — 14 CFR §91.113(e)*

ALL
**3095.** When two or more aircraft are approaching an airport for the purpose of landing, the right-of-way belongs to the aircraft

A—that has the other to its right.
B—that is the least maneuverable.
C—at the lower altitude, but it shall not take advantage of this rule to cut in front of or to overtake another.

*When two aircraft are approaching an airport for landing, the lower aircraft has the right-of-way. A pilot shall not take advantage of that rule to overtake or cut in front of another aircraft. (B08) — 14 CFR §91.113(f)*

AIR
**3096.** A seaplane and a motorboat are on crossing courses. If the motorboat is to the left of the seaplane, which has the right-of-way?

A—The motorboat.
B—The seaplane.
C—Both should alter course to the right.

*For water operation, when aircraft, or an aircraft and a vessel, are on crossing courses, the aircraft or vessel to the other's right has the right-of-way. (B08) — 14 CFR §91.115(b)*

**Answers**

| | | | | | | | |
|---|---|---|---|---|---|---|---|
| 3089 | [B] | 3090 | [B] | 3093 | [B] | 3092 | [A] |
| 3095 | [C] | 3096 | [B] | | | | |

3091 [C]  3094 [C]

# Acrobatic Flight

Acrobatic flight means an intentional maneuver involving an abrupt change in an aircraft's altitude, an abnormal attitude, or abnormal acceleration, not necessary for normal flight. Acrobatic flight is prohibited:

1. Over any congested area of a city, town, or settlement;
2. Over an open-air assembly of people;
3. Within the lateral boundaries of Class B, C, D or E airspace designated for an airport;
4. Within 4 nautical miles of the centerline of a federal airway;
5. Below an altitude of 1,500 feet above the surface, or;
6. When flight visibility is less than 3 statute miles.

AIR, GLI, REC
**3167.** No person may operate an aircraft in acrobatic flight when

A—flight visibility is less than 5 miles.
B—over any congested area of a city, town, or settlement.
C—less than 2,500 feet AGL.

*No person may operate an aircraft in acrobatic flight—*

*1. Over any congested area of a city, town, or settlement;*
*2. Over an open-air assembly of persons;*
*3. Within the lateral boundaries of Class B, C, D or E airspace designated for an airport;*
*4. Within 4 nautical miles of the centerline of a federal airway;*
*5. Below an altitude of 1,500 feet above the surface; or*
*6. When flight visibility is less than 3 statute miles.*
*(B12) — 14 CFR §91.303*

AIR, GLI, REC
**3168.** In which class of airspace is acrobatic flight prohibited?

A—Class G airspace above 1,500 feet AGL.
B—Class E airspace below 1,500 feet AGL.
C—Class E airspace not designated for Federal Airways above 1,500 feet AGL.

*No person may operate an aircraft in acrobatic flight in any class of airspace below an altitude of 1,500 feet above the surface. (B12) — 14 CFR §91.303*

Answers (A) and (C) are incorrect because acrobatic flight is permitted in both these locations.

AIR, GLI, REC
**3169.** What is the lowest altitude permitted for acrobatic flight?

A—1,000 feet AGL.
B—1,500 feet AGL.
C—2,000 feet AGL.

*No person may operate an aircraft in acrobatic flight—*

*1. Over any congested area of a city, town, or settlement;*
*2. Over an open-air assembly of persons;*
*3. Within the lateral boundaries of Class B, C, D or E airspace designated for an airport;*
*4. Within 4 nautical miles of the centerline of a federal airway;*
*5. Below an altitude of 1,500 feet above the surface; or*
*6. When flight visibility is less than 3 statute miles.*
*(B12) — 14 CFR §91.303*

**Answers**
3167 [B]     3168 [B]     3169 [B]

AIR, GLI, REC
**3170.** No person may operate an aircraft in acrobatic flight when the flight visibility is less than

A—3 miles.
B—5 miles.
C—7 miles.

*No person may operate an aircraft in acrobatic flight—*

1. *Over any congested area of a city, town, or settlement;*

2. *Over an open-air assembly of persons;*

3. *Within the lateral boundaries of Class B, C, D or E airspace designated for an airport;*

4. *Within 4 nautical miles of the centerline of a Federal airway;*

5. *Below an altitude of 1,500 feet above the surface; or*

6. *When flight visibility is less than 3 statute miles.*

*(B12) — 14 CFR §91.303*

# Parachutes

If any passengers are carried, the pilot of an aircraft may not intentionally exceed 60° of bank or 30° of pitch unless each occupant is wearing an approved parachute. However, this requirement does not apply when a Certified Flight Instructor is giving instruction in spins or any other flight maneuver required by regulations for a rating.

If the parachute is of the chair type, it must have been packed by a certificated and appropriately-rated parachute rigger within the preceding 120 days.

AIR, GLI, REC, RTC
**3171.** A chair-type parachute must have been packed by a certificated and appropriately rated parachute rigger within the preceding

A—60 days.
B—90 days.
C—120 days.

*No pilot of a civil aircraft may allow a parachute that is available for emergency use to be carried in that aircraft unless, if a chair type, it has been packed by a certificated and appropriately-rated parachute rigger within the preceding 120 days. (B12) — 14 CFR §91.307(a)(1)*

AIR, GLI, REC, RTC
**3172.** An approved chair-type parachute may be carried in an aircraft for emergency use if it has been packed by an appropriately rated parachute rigger within the preceding

A—120 days.
B—180 days.
C—365 days.

*No pilot of a civil aircraft may allow a parachute that is available for emergency use to be carried in that aircraft unless, if a chair type, it has been packed by a certificated and appropriately-rated parachute rigger within the preceding 120 days. (B12) — 14 CFR §91.307(a)(1)*

AIR, GLI, REC, RTC
**3173.** With certain exceptions, when must each occupant of an aircraft wear an approved parachute?

A—When a door is removed from the aircraft to facilitate parachute jumpers.
B—When intentionally pitching the nose of the aircraft up or down 30° or more.
C—When intentionally banking in excess of 30°.

*Unless each occupant of the aircraft is wearing an approved parachute, no pilot of a civil aircraft, carrying any person (other than a crewmember) may execute an intentional maneuver that exceeds 60° bank or 30° nose up or down, relative to the horizon. (B12) — 14 CFR §91.307(c)(2)*

**Answers**

3170 [A]     3171 [C]     3172 [A]     3173 [B]

# Deviation from Air Traffic Control Instructions

An ATC clearance is authorization for an aircraft to proceed under specified traffic conditions within controlled airspace. When an ATC clearance has been obtained, no pilot-in-command may deviate from that clearance, except in an emergency, unless he/she obtains an amended clearance. If a pilot does deviate from a clearance or ATC instruction during an emergency, he/she must notify ATC of the deviation as soon as possible. If, in an emergency, a pilot is given priority over other aircraft by ATC, he/she may be requested to submit a detailed report even though no deviation from a rule occurred. The requested report shall be submitted within 48 hours to the chief of the ATC facility which granted the priority.

ALL

**3108.** When an ATC clearance has been obtained, no pilot in command may deviate from that clearance, unless that pilot obtains an amended clearance. The one exception to this regulation is

A—when the clearance states "at pilot's discretion."
B—an emergency.
C—if the clearance contains a restriction.

*Except in an emergency, no person may operate an aircraft contrary to an ATC clearance or instruction. (B08) — 14 CFR §91.123*

ALL

**3109.** When would a pilot be required to submit a detailed report of an emergency which caused the pilot to deviate from an ATC clearance?

A—When requested by ATC.
B—Immediately.
C—Within 7 days.

*Each pilot-in-command who deviated from an ATC clearance during an emergency must submit a detailed report when requested by ATC. (B08) — 14 CFR §91.123(d)*

ALL

**3110.** What action, if any, is appropriate if the pilot deviates from an ATC instruction during an emergency and is given priority?

A—Take no special action since you are pilot in command.
B—File a detailed report within 48 hours to the chief of the appropriate ATC facility, if requested.
C—File a report to the FAA Administrator, as soon as possible.

*Each pilot-in-command who (though not deviating from a rule of 14 CFR Part 91) is given priority by ATC in an emergency shall, if requested by ATC, submit a detailed report of that emergency within 48 hours to the chief of that ATC facility. (B08) — 14 CFR §91.123*

ALL

**3837.** An ATC clearance provides

A—priority over all other traffic.
B—adequate separation from all traffic.
C—authorization to proceed under specified traffic conditions in controlled airspace.

*An ATC Clearance is an authorization by air traffic control, for the purpose of preventing collisions between known aircraft, for an aircraft to proceed under specified traffic conditions within controlled airspace. (J33) — Pilot/Controller Glossary*

Answer (A) is incorrect because a clearance does not provide priority. Answer (B) is incorrect because a clearance does not relieve the pilot of the responsibility for collision avoidance with aircraft not in instrument meteorological conditions (IMC).

**Answers**

| | | | |
|---|---|---|---|
| 3108 [B] | 3109 [A] | 3110 [B] | 3837 [C] |

# Minimum Safe Altitudes

No minimum altitude applies during takeoff or landing. During other phases of flight, however, the following minimum altitudes apply:

**Anywhere**—The pilot must maintain an altitude which, in the event of engine failure, will allow an emergency landing without undue hazard to persons or property on the surface.

**Over congested areas**—An altitude of at least 1,000 feet above the highest obstacle within a horizontal radius of 2,000 feet of the aircraft must be maintained over any congested area of a city, town, or settlement or over any open-air assembly of people.

**Over other than congested areas**—An altitude of 500 feet above the surface must be maintained except over open water or sparsely populated areas. In that case, the aircraft may not be operated closer than 500 feet to any person, vessel, vehicle or structure.

ALL
**3101.** Except when necessary for takeoff or landing, what is the minimum safe altitude for a pilot to operate an aircraft anywhere?

A—An altitude allowing, if a power unit fails, an emergency landing without undue hazard to persons or property on the surface.
B—An altitude of 500 feet above the surface and no closer than 500 feet to any person, vessel, vehicle, or structure.
C—An altitude of 500 feet above the highest obstacle within a horizontal radius of 1,000 feet.

*Except when necessary for takeoff or landing, no person may operate an aircraft anywhere below an altitude allowing, if a power unit fails, an emergency landing without undue hazard to persons or property on the surface. (B08) — 14 CFR §91.119(a),(b),(c)*

AIR, GLI, LTA, REC
**3102.** Except when necessary for takeoff or landing, what is the minimum safe altitude required for a pilot to operate an aircraft over congested areas?

A—An altitude of 1,000 feet above any person, vessel, vehicle, or structure.
B—An altitude of 500 feet above the highest obstacle within a horizontal radius of 1,000 feet of the aircraft.
C—An altitude of 1,000 feet above the highest obstacle within a horizontal radius of 2,000 feet of the aircraft.

*Except when necessary for takeoff or landing, no person may operate an aircraft over any congested area of a city, town, or settlement, or over any open air assembly of persons, below an altitude of 1,000 feet above the highest obstacle within a horizontal radius of 2,000 feet of the aircraft. (B08) — 14 CFR §91.119(a),(b),(c)*

AIR, GLI, LTA, REC
**3103.** Except when necessary for takeoff or landing, what is the minimum safe altitude required for a pilot to operate an aircraft over other than a congested area?

A—An altitude allowing, if a power unit fails, an emergency landing without undue hazard to persons or property on the surface.
B—An altitude of 500 feet AGL, except over open water or a sparsely populated area, which requires 500 feet from any person, vessel, vehicle, or structure.
C—An altitude of 500 feet above the highest obstacle within a horizontal radius of 1,000 feet.

*Except when necessary for takeoff or landing, no person may operate an aircraft over other than congested areas below an altitude of 500 feet above the surface except over open water or sparsely populated areas. In that case, the aircraft may not be operated closer than 500 feet to any person, vessel, vehicle, or structure. (B08) — 14 CFR §91.119(a),(b),(c)*

AIR, GLI, LTA, REC
**3104.** Except when necessary for takeoff or landing, an aircraft may not be operated closer than what distance from any person, vessel, vehicle, or structure?

A—500 feet.
B—700 feet.
C—1,000 feet.

*Except when necessary for takeoff or landing, no person may operate an aircraft closer than 500 feet to any person, vessel, vehicle, or structure. (B08) — 14 CFR §91.119(a),(b),(c)*

**Answers**
3101 [A]    3102 [C]    3103 [B]    3104 [A]

# Basic VFR Weather Minimums

Rules governing flight under **Visual Flight Rules (VFR)** have been adopted to assist the pilot in meeting his/her responsibility to see and avoid other aircraft. *See* the figure for Questions 3136 through 3147.

In addition, when operating within the lateral boundaries of the surface area of Class B, C, D or E airspace designated for an airport, the ceiling must not be less than 1,000 feet. If the pilot intends to land, take off, or enter a traffic pattern within such airspace, the ground visibility must be at least 3 miles at that airport. If ground visibility is not reported, 3 miles flight visibility is required in the pattern.

| Airspace | Flight Visibility | Distance from Clouds |
|---|---|---|
| **Class A** | Not Applicable | Not Applicable |
| **Class B** | 3 statute miles | Clear of clouds |
| **Class C** | 3 statute miles | 500 feet below<br>1,000 feet above<br>2,000 feet horizontal |
| **Class D** | 3 statute miles | 500 feet below<br>1,000 feet above<br>2,000 feet horizontal |
| **Class E**<br>Less than<br>10,000 feet MSL | 3 statute miles | 500 feet below<br>1,000 feet above<br>2,000 feet horizontal |
| At or above<br>10,000 feet MSL | 5 statute miles | 1,000 feet below<br>1,000 feet above<br>1 statute mile horizontal |
| **Class G**<br>1,200 feet or less<br>above the surface<br>(regardless of<br>MSL altitude)<br>Day, except as provided<br>in § 91.155(b) | 1 statute mile | Clear of clouds |
| Night, except as pro-<br>vided in § 91.155(b) | 3 statute miles | 500 feet below<br>1,000 feet above<br>2,000 feet horizontal |
| More than 1,200 feet<br>above the surface<br>but less than<br>10,000 feet MSL<br>Day | 1 statute mile | 500 feet below<br>1,000 feet above<br>2,000 feet horizontal |
| Night | 3 statute miles | 500 feet below<br>1,000 feet above<br>2,000 feet horizontal |
| More than 1,200 feet<br>above the surface<br>and at or above<br>10,000 feet MSL | 5 statute miles | 1,000 feet below<br>1,000 feet above<br>1 statute mile horizontal |

**Questions 3136 through 3147**

ALL
**3136.** During operations within controlled airspace at altitudes of less than 1,200 feet AGL, the minimum horizontal distance from clouds requirement for VFR flight is

A—1,000 feet.
B—1,500 feet.
C—2,000 feet.

*Minimum horizontal distance from clouds within Class C, D, or E airspace below 10,000 feet is 2,000 feet. See the figure to the left. (B09) — 14 CFR §91.155*

AIR, GLI, LTA
**3137.** What minimum visibility and clearance from clouds are required for VFR operations in Class G airspace at 700 feet AGL or below during daylight hours?

A—1 mile visibility and clear of clouds.
B—1 mile visibility, 500 feet below, 1,000 feet above, and 2,000 feet horizontal clearance from clouds.
C—3 miles visibility and clear of clouds.

*Minimum visibility and cloud clearance for Class G airspace at 700 feet AGL or below during daylight hours is 1 mile visibility and clear of clouds. See the figure to the left. (B09) — 14 CFR §91.155*

*Answer (B) is incorrect because this is for Class C, D, or E airspace. Answer (C) is incorrect because this is for Class B airspace.*

ALL
**3138.** What minimum flight visibility is required for VFR flight operations on an airway below 10,000 feet MSL?

A—1 mile.
B—3 miles.
C—4 miles.

*An airway below 10,000 feet MSL is in either Class B, C, or D, or E airspace, and requires 3 miles flight visibility. See the figure to the left. (B09) — 14 CFR §91.155*

**Answers**

3136   [C]        3137   [A]        3138   [B]

ALL
**3139.** The minimum distance from clouds required for VFR operations on an airway below 10,000 feet MSL is

A—remain clear of clouds.
B—500 feet below, 1,000 feet above, and 2,000 feet horizontally.
C—500 feet above, 1,000 feet below, and 2,000 feet horizontally.

*An airway below 10,000 feet MSL is in either Class B, C, or D, or E airspace, and requires a cloud clearance of 500 feet below, 1,000 feet above, and 2,000 feet horizontally. See the previous figure. (B09) — 14 CFR §91.155*

ALL
**3140.** During operations within controlled airspace at altitudes of more than 1,200 feet AGL, but less than 10,000 feet MSL, the minimum distance above clouds requirement for VFR flight is

A—500 feet.
B—1,000 feet.
C—1,500 feet.

*Class B, C, D, and E airspace are all controlled airspace in which VFR flight is allowed, and requires a cloud clearance of 1,000 feet above at altitudes of more than 1,200 feet AGL, but less than 10,000 feet MSL. See the previous figure. (B09) — 14 CFR §91.155*

ALL
**3141.** VFR flight in controlled airspace above 1,200 feet AGL and below 10,000 feet MSL requires a minimum visibility and vertical cloud clearance of

A—3 miles, and 500 feet below or 1,000 feet above the clouds in controlled airspace.
B—5 miles, and 1,000 feet below or 1,000 feet above the clouds at all altitudes.
C—5 miles, and 1,000 feet below or 1,000 feet above the clouds only in Class A airspace.

*Class B, C, D, and E airspace are all controlled airspace in which VFR flight is allowed, and requires 3 miles visibility and cloud clearance of 500 feet below or 1,000 feet above when operating above 1,200 feet AGL and below 10,000 feet MSL. See the previous figure. (B09) — 14 CFR §91.155*

AIR, GLI, RTC, LTA
**3142.** During operations outside controlled airspace at altitudes of more than 1,200 feet AGL, but less than 10,000 feet MSL, the minimum flight visibility for VFR flight at night is

A—1 mile.
B—3 miles.
C—5 miles.

*At altitudes of more than 1,200 feet AGL but less than 10,000 feet MSL, Class G airspace requires 3 miles visibility at night. See the previous figure. (B09) — 14 CFR §91.155*

AIR, GLI, LTA, REC
**3143.** Outside controlled airspace, the minimum flight visibility requirement for VFR flight above 1,200 feet AGL and below 10,000 feet MSL during daylight hours is

A—1 mile.
B—3 miles.
C—5 miles.

*At altitudes of more than 1,200 feet AGL but less than 10,000 feet MSL, Class G airspace requires 1 mile visibility during the day. See the previous figure. (B09) — 14 CFR §91.155*

AIR, GLI, LTA
**3144.** During operations outside controlled airspace at altitudes of more than 1,200 feet AGL, but less than 10,000 feet MSL, the minimum distance below clouds requirement for VFR flight at night is

A—500 feet.
B—1,000 feet.
C—1,500 feet.

*At altitudes of more than 1,200 feet AGL but less than 10,000 feet MSL, Class G airspace requires a cloud clearance of 500 feet below, 1,000 feet above, and 2,000 feet horizontal, during the day. See the previous figure. (B09) — 14 CFR §91.155*

ALL
**3145.** The minimum flight visibility required for VFR flights above 10,000 feet MSL and more than 1,200 feet AGL in controlled airspace is

A—1 mile.
B—3 miles.
C—5 miles.

**Answers**

| | | | | | |
|---|---|---|---|---|---|
| 3139 [B] | 3140 [B] | 3141 [A] | 3142 [B] | 3143 [A] | 3144 [A] |
| 3145 [C] | | | | | |

*Controlled airspace above 10,000 feet which allows VFR is Class E airspace, and requires 5 miles visibility above 10,000 feet MSL and more than 1,200 feet AGL. See the previous figure. (B09) — 14 CFR §91.155*

ALL
**3146.** For VFR flight operations above 10,000 feet MSL and more than 1,200 feet AGL, the minimum horizontal distance from clouds required is

A—1,000 feet.
B—2,000 feet.
C—1 mile.

*Controlled airspace above 10,000 feet which allows VFR is Class E airspace, and requires cloud clearance of 1,000 feet below, 1,000 feet above, and 1 SM horizontal during operations above 10,000 feet MSL and more than 1,200 feet AGL. See the previous figure. (B09) — 14 CFR §91.155*

ALL
**3147.** During operations at altitudes of more than 1,200 feet AGL and at or above 10,000 feet MSL, the minimum distance above clouds requirement for VFR flight is

A—500 feet.
B—1,000 feet.
C—1,500 feet.

*Controlled airspace above 10,000 feet which allows VFR is Class E airspace, and requires cloud clearance of 1,000 feet below, 1,000 feet above, and 1 SM horizontal during operations above 10,000 feet MSL and more than 1,200 feet AGL. See the previous figure. (B09) — 14 CFR §91.155*

AIR, GLI, RTC, LTA
**3148.** No person may take off or land an aircraft under basic VFR at an airport that lies within Class D airspace unless the

A—flight visibility at that airport is at least 1 mile.
B—ground visibility at that airport is at least 1 mile.
C—ground visibility at that airport is at least 3 miles.

*Except for Special VFR procedures, no person may operate an aircraft under VFR within Class D airspace, beneath the ceiling when the ceiling is less than 1,000 feet. No person may takeoff or land an aircraft, or enter the traffic pattern of an airport under VFR, within Class D airspace unless ground visibility at that airport is at least 3 statute miles. (B09) — 14 CFR §91.155(d)(1)*

AIR, GLI, RTC, LTA
**3149.** The basic VFR weather minimums for operating an aircraft within Class D airspace are

A—500-foot ceiling and 1 mile visibility.
B—1,000-foot ceiling and 3 miles visibility.
C—clear of clouds and 2 miles visibility.

*Except for Special VFR procedures, no person may operate an aircraft under VFR within Class D airspace, beneath the ceiling when the ceiling is less than 1,000 feet. No person may takeoff or land an aircraft, or enter the traffic pattern of an airport under VFR, within Class D airspace unless ground visibility at that airport is at least 3 statute miles. (B09) — 14 CFR §91.155(c), (d)(1)*

ALL
**3620-1.** (Refer to Figure 23, area 1.) The visibility and cloud clearance requirements to operate VFR during daylight hours over Sandpoint Airport at 1,200 feet AGL are

A—1 mile and 1,000 feet above, 500 feet below, and 2,000 feet horizontally from each cloud.
B—1 mile and clear of clouds.
C—3 miles and 1,000 feet above, 500 feet below, and 2,000 feet horizontally from each cloud.

*The Sandpoint Airport Class E airspace starts at 700 feet AGL. The visibility and cloud clearance requirements to operate VFR during daylight hours over Sandpoint Airport at 1,200 feet AGL are 3 SM, 500 feet below, 1,000 feet above, and 2,000 feet horizontal. (J37) — AIM 3-1-3*

ALL
**3620-2.** (Refer to Figure 23, area 1.) The visibility and cloud clearance requirements to operate over Sandpoint Airport at less than 700 feet AGL are

A—3 miles and 1,000 feet above, 500 feet below, and 2,000 feet horizontally from each cloud.
B—3 miles and clear of clouds.
C—1 mile and 1,000 feet above, 500 feet below, and 2,000 feet horizontally from each cloud.

*The Sandpoint Airport Class E airspace starts at 700 feet AGL. Below 700 feet AGL, the visibility and cloud clearance requirements to operate VFR during daylight hours is 1 mile visibility and clear of clouds. At night, the requirements are 3 SM, 500 feet below, 1,000 feet above, and 2,000 feet horizontal. (J37) — AIM 3-1-3*

**Answers**

| 3146 | [C] | 3147 | [B] | 3148 | [C] | 3149 | [B] | 3620-1 | [C] | 3620-2 | [A] |

ALL

**3621-1.** (Refer to Figure 27, area 2.) The visibility and cloud clearance requirements to operate VFR during daylight hours over the town of Cooperstown between 1,200 feet AGL and 10,000 feet MSL are

A— 1 mile and clear of clouds.
B— 1 mile and 1,000 feet above, 500 feet below, and 2,000 feet horizontally from clouds.
C— 3 miles and 1,000 feet above, 500 feet below, and 2,000 feet horizontally from clouds.

*For VFR flight during daylight hours, between 1,200 feet AGL and 10,000 feet MSL, in Class E airspace, visibility and cloud clearances require 3 miles and 1,000 feet above, 500 feet below, and 2,000 feet horizontally. (J37) — AIM 3-2-1*

ALL

**3621-2.** (Refer to Figure 27, area 2.) The visibility and cloud clearance requirements to operate over the town of Cooperstown below 700 feet AGL are

A— 3 miles and clear of clouds.
B— 1 mile and 1,000 feet above, 500 feet below, and 2,000 feet horizontally from clouds.
C— 1 mile and clear of clouds.

*Cooperstown is in Class G airspace from the surface to 700 feet AGL. Therefore, the visibility and cloud clearance requirements are 1 mile and clear of clouds. (J37) — AIM 3-2-1*

# Special VFR Weather Minimums

If an appropriate ATC clearance (**Special VFR**) has been received, an aircraft may be operated within the lateral boundaries of the surface area of Class B, C, D, or E airspace designated for an airport when the ceiling is less than 1,000 feet and/or the visibility is less than 3 miles.

Special VFR requires the aircraft to be operated clear of clouds with flight visibility of at least 1 statute mile.

For Special VFR operation between sunset and sunrise, the pilot must hold an instrument rating and the airplane must be equipped for instrument flight.

Requests for Special VFR arrival or departure clearance should be directed to the airport traffic control tower if one is in operation.

AIR

**3150.** A special VFR clearance authorizes the pilot of an aircraft to operate VFR while within Class D airspace when the visibility is

A— less than 1 mile and the ceiling is less than 1,000 feet.
B— at least 1 mile and the aircraft can remain clear of clouds.
C— at least 3 miles and the aircraft can remain clear of clouds.

*No person may operate an aircraft (other than a helicopter) in a Class D airspace under Special VFR unless clear of clouds and flight visibility is at least 1 statute mile. (B09) — 14 CFR §91.157(b),(c)*

AIR

**3151.** What is the minimum weather condition required for airplanes operating under special VFR in Class D airspace?

A— 1 mile flight visibility.
B— 1 mile flight visibility and 1,000-foot ceiling.
C— 3 miles flight visibility and 1,000-foot ceiling.

*No person may operate an aircraft (other than a helicopter) in a Class D airspace under special VFR unless clear of clouds and flight visibility is at least 1 statute mile. (B09) — 14 CFR §91.157(b),(c)*

**Answers**

3621-1   [C]          3621-2   [C]          3150   [B]          3151   [A]

AIR

**3153.** What are the minimum requirements for airplane operations under special VFR in Class D airspace at night?

A—The airplane must be under radar surveillance at all times while in Class D airspace.
B—The airplane must be equipped for IFR with an altitude reporting transponder.
C—The pilot must be instrument rated, and the airplane must be IFR equipped.

*No person may operate an aircraft (other than a helicopter) in a Class D airspace under special weather minimums between sunset and sunrise unless the pilot and airplane are certified for instrument flight. (B09) — 14 CFR §91.157, §91.205*

Answers (A) and (B) are incorrect because radar and transponder are not required in Class D airspace.

AIR

**3154.** No person may operate an airplane within Class D airspace at night under special VFR unless the

A—flight can be conducted 500 feet below the clouds.
B—airplane is equipped for instrument flight.
C—flight visibility is at least 3 miles.

*No person may operate an aircraft (other than a helicopter) in a Class D airspace under special weather minimums between sunset and sunrise unless the airplane and pilot are certified for instrument flight. (B09) — 14 CFR §91.155(d)(1),(2)*

AIR, RTC

**3813.** What ATC facility should the pilot contact to receive a special VFR departure clearance in Class D airspace?

A—Automated Flight Service Station.
B—Air Traffic Control Tower.
C—Air Route Traffic Control Center.

*When a control tower is in operation, requests for special VFR clearances should be to the tower. (J14) — AIM ¶4-4-5*

RTC

**3152.** Under what conditions, if any, may a private pilot operate a helicopter under special VFR at night within Class D airspace?

A—The helicopter must be fully instrument equipped and the pilot must be instrument rated.
B—The flight visibility must be at least 1 mile.
C—There are no conditions; regulations permit this.

*There are no restrictions on helicopters for Special VFR operations within Class D airspace. (B09) — 14 CFR §91.157(e)*

**Answers**

3153 [C]          3154 [B]          3813 [B]          3152 [C]

# VFR Cruising Altitudes

When operating an aircraft under VFR in level cruising flight more than 3,000 feet above the surface and below 18,000 feet MSL, a pilot is required to maintain an appropriate altitude in accordance with certain rules. This requirement is sometimes called the "Hemispherical Cruising Rule," and is based on magnetic course, not magnetic heading. *See* Figure 4-5.

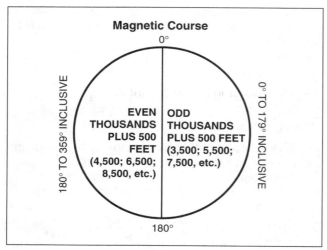

**Magnetic Course**

**Figure 4-5.** VFR cruising altitudes

AIR, RTC
**3155.** Which cruising altitude is appropriate for a VFR flight on a magnetic course of 135°?

A—Even thousandths.
B—Even thousandths plus 500 feet.
C—Odd thousandths plus 500 feet.

*When operating below 18,000 feet MSL in VFR cruising flight more than 3,000 feet above the surface and on a magnetic course of 0° through 179°, any odd thousand-foot MSL altitude plus 500 feet (i.e., 3,500, 5,500, etc.) is appropriate. On a course of 180° through 359°, even thousands plus 500 feet (4,500, 6,500, etc.) is appropriate. (B09) — 14 CFR §91.159(a)*

AIR, RTC
**3156.** Which VFR cruising altitude is acceptable for a flight on a Victor Airway with a magnetic course of 175°? The terrain is less than 1,000 feet.

A—4,500 feet.
B—5,000 feet.
C—5,500 feet.

*When operating below 18,000 feet MSL in VFR cruising flight more than 3,000 feet above the surface and on a magnetic course of 0° through 179°, any odd thousand-foot MSL altitude plus 500 feet (i.e., 3,500, 5,500, etc.) is appropriate. On a course of 180° through 359°, even thousands plus 500 feet (4,500, 6,500, etc.) is appropriate. (B09) — 14 CFR §91.159*

AIR, RTC
**3157.** Which VFR cruising altitude is appropriate when flying above 3,000 feet AGL on a magnetic course of 185°?

A—4,000 feet.
B—4,500 feet.
C—5,000 feet.

*When operating below 18,000 feet MSL in VFR cruising flight more than 3,000 feet above the surface and on a magnetic course of 0° through 179°, any odd thousand-foot MSL altitude plus 500 feet (i.e., 3,500, 5,500, etc.) is appropriate. On a course of 180° through 359°, even thousands plus 500 feet (4,500, 6,500, etc.) is appropriate. (B09) — 14 CFR §91.159*

AIR, RTC
**3158.** Each person operating an aircraft at a VFR cruising altitude shall maintain an odd-thousand plus 500-foot altitude while on a

A—magnetic heading of 0° through 179°.
B—magnetic course of 0° through 179°.
C—true course of 0° through 179°.

*When operating below 18,000 feet MSL in VFR cruising flight more than 3,000 feet above the surface and on a magnetic course of 0° through 179°, any odd thousand-foot MSL altitude plus 500 feet (i.e., 3,500, 5,500, etc.) is appropriate. On a course of 180° through 359°, even thousands plus 500 feet (4,500, 6,500, etc.) is appropriate. (B09) — 14 CFR §91.159*

*Answers (A) and (C) are incorrect because VFR altitudes are based on a magnetic course.*

**Answers**

3155   [C]        3156   [C]        3157   [B]        3158   [B]

# Categories of Aircraft

The term "**category**," when used with respect to the certification of aircraft, means a grouping of aircraft based upon intended use or operating limitations. Examples include normal, utility, acrobatic, restricted, experimental, transport, limited and provisional categories.

Both restricted and experimental category aircraft are prohibited from carrying persons or property for compensation or hire. In addition, both categories are normally prohibited from flying over densely populated areas or in congested airways.

ALL
**3003.** With respect to the certification of aircraft, which is a category of aircraft?

A—Normal, utility, acrobatic.
B—Airplane, rotorcraft, glider.
C—Landplane, seaplane.

*With respect to the certification of aircraft, "a category of aircraft" means a grouping of aircraft based upon intended use or operating limitations. Examples include normal, utility, acrobatic, transport, limited, restricted, and provisional. (A01) — 14 CFR §1.1*

Answer (B) is incorrect because it refers to the certification of airmen, not aircraft. Answer (C) is incorrect because it is not any kind of category.

ALL
**3004.** With respect to the certification of aircraft, which is a class of aircraft?

A—Airplane, rotorcraft, glider, balloon.
B—Normal, utility, acrobatic, limited.
C—Transport, restricted, provisional.

*With respect to the certification of aircraft, "class" is a broad grouping of aircraft having similar means of propulsion, flight, or landing. Examples include airplane, rotorcraft, glider, balloon, landplane, and seaplane. (A01) — 14 CFR §1.1*

Answers (B) and (C) are incorrect because they refer to category of aircraft rather than class.

AIR, GLI, RTC
**3178.** Which is normally prohibited when operating a restricted category civil aircraft?

A—Flight under instrument flight rules.
B—Flight over a densely populated area.
C—Flight within Class D airspace.

*No person may operate a restricted category civil aircraft within the United States:*

1. *Over a densely populated area.*

2. *In a congested airway.*

3. *Near a busy airport where passenger transport operations are conducted.*

*(B12) — 14 CFR §91.313(e)*

ALL
**3179.** Unless otherwise specifically authorized, no person may operate an aircraft that has an experimental certificate

A—beneath the floor of Class B airspace.
B—over a densely populated area or in a congested airway.
C—from the primary airport within Class D airspace.

*Unless otherwise authorized by the Administrator in special operating limitations, no person may operate an aircraft that has an experimental certificate over a densely populated area or in a congested airway. (B12) — 14 CFR §91.319(c)*

**Answers**

3003  [A]        3004  [A]        3178  [B]        3179  [B]

# Formation Flight and Dropping Objects

Flying so close to another aircraft as to create a collision hazard is prohibited. If the intent is to fly formation, prior arrangement with the pilot-in-command of each aircraft is required. In any case, no person may operate an aircraft carrying passengers for hire in formation flight.

The PIC of an aircraft may not allow any object to be dropped while in flight unless reasonable precautions are taken to avoid injury or damage to persons or property on the surface.

ALL
**3088.** No person may operate an aircraft in formation flight

A—over a densely populated area.
B—in Class D airspace under special VFR.
C—except by prior arrangement with the pilot in command of each aircraft.

*No person may operate an aircraft in formation flight except by arrangement with the pilot-in-command of each aircraft in the formation. The only restriction to formation flight is when carrying passengers for hire. (B08) — 14 CFR §91.111*

ALL
**3076.** Under what conditions may objects be dropped from an aircraft?

A—Only in an emergency.
B—If precautions are taken to avoid injury or damage to persons or property on the surface.
C—If prior permission is received from the Federal Aviation Administration.

*No pilot-in-command of a civil aircraft may allow any object to be dropped from an aircraft in flight that creates a hazard to persons or property. However, this does not prohibit the dropping of any object if reasonable precautions are taken to avoid injury or damage to persons or property. (B07) — 14 CFR §91.15*

# VFR Flight Plans

Although filing a VFR flight plan is not mandatory (except under certain circumstances), it is considered good operating practice.

When a VFR flight plan is filed, the information provided should include the following:

- In Block 7 enter the initial cruising altitude (even if more than one cruising altitude is intended).
- In Block 9, for maximum protection, file only to the point of first intended landing, and re-file for each leg to final destination. Enter the name or coded identifier of the destination airport. When a "stopover" flight is anticipated, it is recommended that a separate flight plan be filed for each "leg" when the stop is expected to be more than 1 hour duration.
- In Block 12, enter the total amount of usable fuel on board, expressed in hours.

The pilot must close a VFR flight plan at the completion of a flight. This can be done by contacting the nearest flight service station (FSS) or other FAA facility upon landing.

**Answers**
3088 [C]     3076 [B]

AIR, RTC
**3815.** (Refer to Figure 52.) If more than one cruising altitude is intended, which should be entered in block 7 of the flight plan?

A—Initial cruising altitude.
B—Highest cruising altitude.
C—Lowest cruising altitude.

*Block 7 of the flight plan is the place to enter the "initial cruising altitude." (J15) — AIM ¶5-1-4*

AIR, RTC
**3816.** (Refer to Figure 52.) What information should be entered in block 9 for a VFR day flight?

A—The name of the airport of first intended landing.
B—The name of destination airport if no stopover for more than 1 hour is anticipated.
C—The name of the airport where the aircraft is based.

*Enter the destination airport identifier code or name, or separate flight plans for each leg if a stopover will be more than one hour. (J15) — AIM ¶5-1-4*

AIR, RTC
**3817.** (Refer to Figure 52.) What information should be entered in block 12 for a VFR day flight?

A—The estimated time en route plus 30 minutes.
B—The estimated time en route plus 45 minutes.
C—The amount of usable fuel on board expressed in time.

*Specify the fuel on board in hours and minutes. (J15) — AIM ¶5-1-4*

ALL
**3818.** How should a VFR flight plan be closed at the completion of the flight at a controlled airport?

A—The tower will automatically close the flight plan when the aircraft turns off the runway.
B—The pilot must close the flight plan with the nearest FSS or other FAA facility upon landing.
C—The tower will relay the instructions to the nearest FSS when the aircraft contacts the tower for landing.

*The pilot-in-command, upon canceling or completing the flight under the flight plan, shall notify an FAA Flight Service Station or ATC facility. (J15) — AIM ¶5-1-12*

## Speed Limits

The following maximum speed limits for aircraft have been established in the interest of safety:

1. Below 10,000 feet MSL, the speed limit is 250 knots indicated air speed (KIAS). *See* Figure 4-6a.
2. The speed limit within Class B airspace (Figure 4-6b) is also 250 KIAS.
3. The maximum speed authorized in a VFR corridor through Class B airspace (Figure 4-6c) or in airspace underlying Class B airspace (Figure 4-6d) is 200 KIAS.
4. In Class D airspace, aircraft are restricted to a maximum of 200 KIAS (Figure 4-6e).

AIR, RTC
**3097.** Unless otherwise authorized, what is the maximum indicated airspeed at which a person may operate an aircraft below 10,000 feet MSL?

A—200 knots.
B—250 knots.
C—288 knots.

*Maximum speed below 10,000 feet MSL is 250 knots. (B08) — 14 CFR §91.117(a)*

AIR, RTC
**3098.** Unless otherwise authorized, the maximum indicated airspeed at which aircraft may be flown when at or below 2,500 feet AGL and within 4 nautical miles of the primary airport of Class C airspace is

A—200 knots.
B—230 knots.
C—250 knots.

*Unless otherwise authorized or required by ATC, no person may operate an aircraft at or below 2,500 feet AGL within 4 NM of the primary airport of a Class C or Class D airspace area at an indicated airspeed of more than 200 knots. (B08) — 14 CFR §91.117(b)*

**Answers**

| | | | | | |
|---|---|---|---|---|---|
| 3815 [A] | 3816 [B] | 3817 [C] | 3818 [B] | 3097 [B] | 3098 [A] |

AIR, RTC

**3099.** When flying in the airspace underlying Class B airspace, the maximum speed authorized is

A—200 knots.
B—230 knots.
C—250 knots.

*No person may operate an aircraft in the airspace underlying Class B airspace at a speed of more than 200 knots. (B08) — 14 CFR §91.117(b)*

AIR, RTC

**3100.** When flying in a VFR corridor designated through Class B airspace, the maximum speed authorized is

A—180 knots.
B—200 knots.
C—250 knots.

*Maximum speed in a VFR corridor through Class B airspace is 200 KIAS. (B08) — 14 CFR §91.117(b)*

**Figure 4-6.** Maximum speed limits

# Airworthiness

Each aircraft is issued an Airworthiness Certificate, which remains valid as long as the aircraft is maintained and operated as required by regulations. This Airworthiness Certificate, along with the Aircraft Registration Certificate and the operating limitations, must be aboard the aircraft during flight.

The aircraft's operating limitations may be found in the airplane flight manual, approved manual material, markings, and placards, or any combination thereof.

ALL
**3075.** Where may an aircraft's operating limitations be found?

A—On the Airworthiness Certificate.
B—In the current, FAA-approved flight manual, approved manual material, markings, and placards, or any combination thereof.
C—In the aircraft airframe and engine logbooks.

*No person may operate a civil aircraft without complying with the limitations found in the approved flight manual, markings, and placards. (B07) — 14 CFR §91.9(a)*

ALL
**3159.** In addition to a valid Airworthiness Certificate, what documents or records must be aboard an aircraft during flight?

A—Aircraft engine and airframe logbooks, and owner's manual.
B—Radio operator's permit, and repair and alteration forms.
C—Operating limitations and Registration Certificate.

*No person may operate an aircraft unless it has within it:*

1. *An appropriate and current Airworthiness Certificate, displayed at the cabin or cockpit entrance so that it is legible to passengers or crew.*
2. *A Registration Certificate issued to its owner.*
3. *An approved flight manual, manual material, markings and placards or any combination thereof, which show the operating limitations of the aircraft.*

*(B11) — 14 CFR §91.203*

ALL
**3187.** How long does the Airworthiness Certificate of an aircraft remain valid?

A—As long as the aircraft has a current Registration Certificate.
B—Indefinitely, unless the aircraft suffers major damage.
C—As long as the aircraft is maintained and operated as required by Federal Aviation Regulations.

*Unless sooner surrendered, suspended, revoked, or a termination date is otherwise established by the Administrator, Standard Airworthiness Certificates and Airworthiness Certificates issued for restricted or limited category aircraft are effective as long as the maintenance, preventive maintenance, and alterations are performed in accordance with Parts 43 and 91 and the aircraft are registered in the United States. (B13) — 14 CFR §21.181*

**Answers**

3075 [B]     3159 [C]     3187 [C]

# Maintenance and Inspections

The owner or operator of an aircraft is primarily responsible for maintaining that aircraft in an airworthy condition, including compliance with airworthiness directives. He/she is also responsible for all records of maintenance, repairs, and alterations. (The pilot-in-command is responsible for determining that the aircraft is in an airworthy condition prior to flight.) The airworthiness of an aircraft can be determined by a preflight inspection and a review of the maintenance records.

The holder of a pilot certificate is allowed (within certain limits) to perform preventive maintenance on any aircraft owned and operated by that pilot. Preventive maintenance is limited to tasks such as replacing defective safety wire, servicing landing gear wheel bearings, replacing safety belts, and other tasks listed in 14 CFR Part 43, Appendix A. After preventive maintenance has been performed on an aircraft, the signature, certificate type and certificate number of the person approving the aircraft for return to service, and a description of the work, must be entered in the aircraft maintenance records.

An aircraft may not be operated unless, within the preceding 12 calendar months, it has had an annual inspection and has been approved for return to service. This will be indicated by the appropriate notation in the aircraft maintenance records. To determine the expiration date of the last annual inspection, refer to the aircraft maintenance records. For example, if the aircraft's last annual inspection was performed on July 12, 1993, the next annual inspection will be due no later than midnight, July 31, 1994.

If an aircraft is used to carry passengers for hire or used for flight instruction for hire, it must have, in addition to the annual inspection, an inspection each 100 hours of flight time. (An annual inspection may be substituted for the 100-hour inspection, but a 100-hour inspection may not be substituted for an annual inspection.) The 100-hour limitation may be exceeded by not more than 10 hours if necessary to reach a place at which the inspection can be done. The excess time, however, is included in computing the next 100 hours of time in service. For example: a 100-hour inspection was due at 3,302.5 hours on the tachometer. The 100-hour inspection was actually done at 3,309.5 hours. The next 100-hour inspection is due at 3,402.5 hours, (100 hours after the previous inspection was due, not after the time the inspection was actually completed).

The transponder cannot be operated unless within the preceding 24 calendar months, it has been inspected and found satisfactory.

If an aircraft has been maintained, rebuilt, or altered in any manner that may have appreciably changed its flight characteristics or operation in flight, no passengers may be carried until it has been flight tested by an appropriately-rated pilot (with at least a Private Pilot Certificate) and approved for return to service.

ALL
**3180-1.** The responsibility for ensuring that an aircraft is maintained in an airworthy condition is primarily that of the

A—pilot in command.
B—owner or operator.
C—mechanic who performs the work.

*The owner or operator of an aircraft is primarily responsible for maintaining the aircraft in an airworthy condition. The pilot-in-command of a civil aircraft is responsible for determining whether that aircraft is in condition for safe flight. (B13) — 14 CFR §91.403(a)*

ALL
**3180-2.** The airworthiness of an aircraft can be determined by a preflight inspection and a

A—statement from the owner or operator that the aircraft is airworthy.
B—log book endorsement from a flight instructor.
C—review of the maintenance records.

*The airworthiness of an aircraft can be determined by a preflight inspection and a review of the maintenance records. Each owner or operator shall ensure that maintenance personnel make appropriate entries in the aircraft maintenance records indicating maintenance done and the aircraft has been approved for return to service. (B13) — 14 CFR §91.405*

**Answers**

3180-1   [B]       3180-2   [C]

**ALL**
**3181-1.** The responsibility for ensuring that maintenance personnel make the appropriate entries in the aircraft maintenance records indicating the aircraft has been approved for return to service lies with the

A—owner or operator.
B—pilot in command.
C—mechanic who performed the work.

*The registered owner or operator shall ensure that the aircraft maintenance records include the signature and the certificate number of the person approving the aircraft for return to service. (B13) — 14 CFR §91.417(a)(1)(i-iii)*

**ALL**
**3181-2.** Who is responsible for ensuring appropriate entries are made in maintenance records indicating the aircraft has been approved for return to service?

A—Owner or operator.
B—Certified mechanic.
C—Repair station.

*Each owner or operator shall ensure that maintenance personnel make appropriate entries in the aircraft maintenance records indicating maintenance done and the aircraft has been approved for return to service. (B13) — 14 CFR §91.405*

**ALL**
**3182.** Completion of an annual inspection and the return of the aircraft to service should always be indicated by

A—the relicensing date on the Registration Certificate.
B—an appropriate notation in the aircraft maintenance records.
C—an inspection sticker placed on the instrument panel that lists the annual inspection completion date.

*Each registered owner or operator shall keep records of the maintenance and alteration, and records of the 100-hour, annual, progressive, and other required or approved inspections, as appropriate, for each aircraft (including the airframe) and each engine, propeller, rotor, and appliance of an aircraft. The records must include:*

1. *A description (or reference to data acceptable to the Administrator) of the work performed;*

2. *The date of completion of the work performed; and*

3. *The signature and certificate number of the person approving the aircraft for return to service.*

*(B13) — 14 CFR §91.417(a)*

**ALL**
**3185.** An aircraft's annual inspection was performed on July 12, this year. The next annual inspection will be due no later than

A—July 1, next year.
B—July 13, next year.
C—July 31, next year.

*No person may operate an aircraft unless, within the preceding 12 calendar months, it has had an annual inspection in accordance with Part 43 and has been approved for return to service by an authorized person. (B13) — 14 CFR §91.409*

**ALL**
**3186.** To determine the expiration date of the last annual aircraft inspection, a person should refer to the

A—Airworthiness Certificate.
B—Registration Certificate.
C—aircraft maintenance records.

*Each registered owner or operator shall keep records of the maintenance and alteration, and records of the 100-hour, annual, progressive, and other required or approved inspections, as appropriate, for each aircraft (including the airframe) and each engine, propeller, rotor, and appliance of an aircraft. (B13) — 14 CFR §91.417(a)*

**ALL**
**3188.** What aircraft inspections are required for rental aircraft that are also used for flight instruction?

A—Annual and 100-hour inspections.
B—Biannual and 100-hour inspections.
C—Annual and 50-hour inspections.

*No person may operate an aircraft carrying any person for hire, and no person may give flight instruction for hire in an aircraft which that person provides, unless within the preceding 100 hours of time in service it has received an annual or 100-hour inspection and been approved for return to service. (B13) — 14 CFR §91.409(b)*

**Answers**

| 3181-1 [A] | 3181-2 [A] | 3182 [B] | 3185 [C] | 3186 [C] | 3188 [A] |
|---|---|---|---|---|---|

AIR, RTC

**3189.** An aircraft had a 100-hour inspection when the tachometer read 1259.6. When is the next 100-hour inspection due?

A—1349.6 hours.
B—1359.6 hours.
C—1369.6 hours.

*The 100-hour limitation may be exceeded by not more than 10 hours if necessary to reach a place at which the inspection can be done. The excess time, however, is included in computing the next 100 hours in service.*

> 1259.6 *time at 100-hour inspection*
> + 100.0 *time in service*
> 1359.6 *time next inspection due*

*(B13) — 14 CFR §91.409(b)*

AIR, RTC

**3190.** A 100-hour inspection was due at 3302.5 hours. The 100-hour inspection was actually done at 3309.5 hours. When is the next 100-hour inspection due?

A—3312.5 hours.
B—3402.5 hours.
C—3409.5 hours.

*The 100-hour limitation may be exceeded by not more than 10 hours if necessary to reach a place at which the inspection can be done. The excess time, however, is included in computing the next 100 hours in service.*

> 3302.5 *time inspection was due*
> + 100.0 *time in service*
> 3402.5 *time next inspection due*

*(B13) — 14 CFR §91.409(b)*

ALL

**3191.** No person may use an ATC transponder unless it has been tested and inspected within at least the preceding

A—6 calendar months.
B—12 calendar months.
C—24 calendar months.

*No person may use an ATC transponder unless within the preceding 24 calendar months, the ATC transponder has been tested and inspected and found to comply with Appendix F of Part 43. (B13) — 14 CFR §91.413(a)*

ALL

**3192.** Maintenance records show the last transponder inspection was performed on September 1, 1993. The next inspection will be due no later than

A—September 30, 1994.
B—September 1, 1995.
C—September 30, 1995.

*No person may use an ATC transponder unless within the preceding 24 calendar months, the ATC transponder has been tested and inspected and found to comply with Appendix F of Part 43. (B13) — 14 CFR §91.413(a)*

ALL

**3013-1.** Preventive maintenance has been performed on an aircraft. What paperwork is required?

A—A full, detailed description of the work done must be entered in the airframe logbook.
B—The date the work was completed, and the name of the person who did the work must be entered in the airframe and engine logbook.
C—The signature, certificate number, and kind of certificate held by the person approving the work and a description of the work must be entered in the aircraft maintenance records.

*Each registered owner or operator shall keep records of preventative maintenance. The records must include:*

1. *A description of the work performed;*

2. *The date of completion of the work performed; and*

3. *The signature and certificate number of the person approving the aircraft for return to service (could be pilot certificate number for Part 43 when you are doing your own preventative maintenance).*

*(A15) — 14 CFR §91.417(a)*

*Answer (A) is incorrect because it is incomplete. Answer (B) is incorrect because it refers to who performed the work rather than who approved it.*

ALL
**3013-2.** What regulation allows a private pilot to perform preventive maintenance?

A—14 CFR Part 91.403.
B—14 CFR Part 43.7.
C—14 CFR Part 61.113.

*14 CFR §43.7 Persons authorized to approve aircraft, airframes, aircraft engines, propellers, appliances, or component parts for return to service after maintenance, preventive maintenance, rebuilding, or alteration says a person holding at least a private pilot certificate may approve an aircraft for return to service after performing preventive maintenance under the provisions of §43.3(g). (A15) — 14 CFR §43.7*

*Answer (A) is incorrect because 14 CFR §91.403 explains that the owner or operator must maintain the aircraft in airworthy condition. Answer (C) is incorrect because 14 CFR §61.113 details the private pilot privileges and limitations while operating as pilot-in-command.*

ALL
**3013-3.** Who may perform preventive maintenance on an aircraft and approve it for return to service?

A—None of these.
B—Private or Commercial pilot.
C—Student or Recreational pilot.

*A person holding at least a private pilot certificate may approve an aircraft for return to service after performing preventive maintenance. (A15) — 14 CFR §43.7*

ALL
**3014.** Which operation would be described as preventive maintenance?

A—Replenishing hydraulic fluid.
B—Repair of portions of skin sheets by making additional seams.
C—Repair of landing gear brace struts.

*Preventative maintenance items which can be performed by the pilot are listed in Part 43 and include such basic items as oil changes, wheel bearing lubrication, and hydraulic fluid (brakes, landing gear system) refills. (A16) — 14 CFR Part 43*

*Answers (B) and (C) are incorrect because they both list major maintenance.*

ALL
**3015.** Which operation would be described as preventive maintenance?

A—Repair of landing gear brace struts.
B—Replenishing hydraulic fluid.
C—Repair of portions of skin sheets by making additional seams.

*Preventative maintenance items which can be performed by the pilot are listed in Part 43 and include such basic items as oil changes, wheel bearing lubrication, and hydraulic fluid (brakes, landing gear system) refills. (A16) — 14 CFR Part 43*

*Answers (A) and (C) are incorrect because they both list major maintenance.*

ALL
**3183.** If an alteration or repair substantially affects an aircraft's operation in flight, that aircraft must be test flown by an appropriately-rated pilot and approved for return to service prior to being operated

A—by any private pilot.
B—with passengers aboard.
C—for compensation or hire.

*No person may carry any person (other than crewmembers) in an aircraft that has been maintained, rebuilt, or altered in a manner that may have appreciably changed its flight characteristics or substantially affected its operation in flight until an appropriately-rated pilot with at least a Private Pilot Certificate flies the aircraft, makes an operational check of the maintenance performed or alteration made, and logs the flight in the aircraft records. (B13) — 14 CFR §91.407(b)*

**Answers**
3013-2 [B]   3013-3 [B]   3014 [A]   3015 [B]   3183 [B]

ALL

**3184.** Before passengers can be carried in an aircraft that has been altered in a manner that may have appreciably changed its flight characteristics, it must be flight tested by an appropriately-rated pilot who holds at least a

A—Commercial Pilot Certificate with an instrument rating.
B—Private Pilot Certificate.
C—Commercial Pilot Certificate and a mechanic's certificate.

*No person may carry any person (other than crewmembers) in an aircraft that has been maintained, rebuilt, or altered in a manner that may have appreciably changed its flight characteristics or substantially affected its operation in flight until an appropriately-rated pilot with at least a Private Pilot Certificate flies the aircraft, makes an operational check of the maintenance performed or alteration made, and logs the flight in the aircraft records. (B13) — 14 CFR §91.407*

# Airworthiness Directives (ADs) and Advisory Circulars (ACs)

Airworthiness Directives (ADs) identify unsafe aircraft conditions and prescribe regulatory actions (such as inspections or modifications) or limitations under which the affected aircraft may continue to be operated and are mandatory. Compliance with an applicable Airworthiness Directive must be entered in the appropriate aircraft maintenance records. The owner or operator is responsible for ensuring ADs are complied with. Pilots may operate an aircraft not in compliance with an AD, if the AD allows for this.

Advisory Circulars are issued by the FAA to inform the aviation community in a systematic way of non-regulatory material of interest. In many cases, they are the result of a need to fully explain a particular subject (wake turbulence, for example). They are issued in a numbered-subject system corresponding to the subject areas of the Federal Aviation Regulations. Advisory Circulars (some free, others at cost) may be obtained by ordering from the Government Printing Office (GPO).

ALL

**3193.** Which records or documents shall the owner or operator of an aircraft keep to show compliance with an applicable Airworthiness Directive?

A—Aircraft maintenance records.
B—Airworthiness Certificate and Pilot's Operating Handbook.
C—Airworthiness and Registration Certificates.

*Each registered owner or operator shall keep records of the maintenance and alteration, and records of the 100-hour, annual, progressive, and other required or approved inspections, as appropriate, for each aircraft (including the airframe) and each engine, propeller, rotor, and appliance of an aircraft. (B13) — 14 CFR §91.417*

ALL

**3012-2.** What should an owner or operator know about Airworthiness Directives (AD's)?

A—For Informational purposes only.
B—They are mandatory.
C—They are voluntary.

*Airworthiness Directives (ADs) are mandatory. No person may operate a product to which an airworthiness directive applies except in accordance with the requirements of that airworthiness directive. (A13) — 14 CFR §39.3*

ALL

**3012-3.** May a pilot operate an aircraft that is not in compliance with an Airworthiness Directive (AD)?

A—Yes, under VFR conditions only.
B—Yes, AD's are only voluntary.
C—Yes, if allowed by the AD.

*No person may operate a product to which an airworthiness directive applies except in accordance with the requirements of that airworthiness directive. (A13) — 14 CFR §39.3*

**Answers**

3184    [B]          3193    [A]          3012-2    [B]          3012-3    [C]

ALL
**3181-3.** Who is responsible for ensuring Airworthiness Directives (AD's) are compiled with?

A—Owner or operator.
B—Repair station.
C—Mechanic with inspection authorization (IA).

*The owner or operator of an aircraft is primarily responsible for maintaining that aircraft in an airworthy condition, including compliance with the Airworthiness Directives (ADs) found in 14 CFR Part 39. (B13) — 14 CFR §91.403*

ALL
**3709.** FAA advisory circulars (some free, others at cost) are available to all pilots and are obtained by

A—distribution from the nearest FAA district office.
B—ordering those desired from the Government Printing Office.
C—subscribing to the Federal Register.

*Advisory circulars which are offered for sale or free may be ordered from the Superintendent of Documents, U.S. Government Printing Office. (M52) — AC 00-2*

ALL
**3854.** FAA advisory circulars containing subject matter specifically related to Airmen are issued under which subject number?

A—60.
B—70.
C—90.

*Appendix II of the Advisory Circular Checklist contains the Circular Numbering System wherein advisory circular numbers relate to Federal Aviation Regulations subchapter titles and correspond to the Parts and/or sections of the regulations. The four to remember are:*

*20 — Aircraft;*
*60 — Airmen;*
*70 — Airspace; and*
*90 — Air Traffic and General Operating Rules*

*(M52) — AC 00-2*

ALL
**3855.** FAA advisory circulars containing subject matter specifically related to Airspace are issued under which subject number?

A—60.
B—70.
C—90.

*Appendix II of the Advisory Circular Checklist contains the Circular Numbering System wherein advisory circular numbers relate to Federal Aviation Regulations subchapter titles and correspond to the Parts and/or sections of the regulations. The four to remember are:*

*20 — Aircraft;*
*60 — Airmen;*
*70 — Airspace; and*
*90 — Air Traffic and General Operating Rules*

*(M52) — AC 00-2*

ALL
**3856.** FAA advisory circulars containing subject matter specifically related to Air Traffic Control and General Operations are issued under which subject number?

A—60.
B—70.
C—90.

*Appendix II of the Advisory Circular Checklist contains the Circular Numbering System wherein advisory circular numbers relate to Federal Aviation Regulations subchapter titles and correspond to the Parts and/or sections of the regulations. The four to remember are:*

*20 — Aircraft;*
*60 — Airmen;*
*70 — Airspace; and*
*90 — Air Traffic and General Operating Rules*

*(M52) — AC 00-2*

**Answers**

3181-3 [A]     3709 [B]     3854 [A]     3855 [B]     3856 [C]

# National Transportation Safety Board (NTSB) Part 830

NTSB Part 830 contains rules pertaining to notification and reporting of aircraft accidents and incidents. It also addresses preservation of aircraft wreckage, mail, cargo, and records.

The term "accident" means "an occurrence in which any person suffers death or serious injury, or in which the aircraft receives substantial damage."

The term "incident" means "an occurrence other than an accident, which affects or could affect the safety of operations."

Immediate notification of the NTSB is required when an aircraft accident occurs, and any of a specified list of incidents, which include:

1. Inability of a flight crewmember to perform his/her duties due to illness or injury;
2. In-flight fire;
3. An aircraft is overdue and believed to have been involved in an accident; or
4. Flight control system malfunction or failure.

The operator of an aircraft involved in an accident or incident which requires notification of the NTSB is responsible for preserving the wreckage, mail, or cargo until the NTSB takes custody. These items may be moved to protect the wreckage from further damage.

The operator of an aircraft involved in an accident is required to file an accident report within 10 days. A report of an incident must be reported only upon request.

ALL
**3194.** If an aircraft is involved in an accident which results in substantial damage to the aircraft, the nearest NTSB field office should be notified

A—immediately.
B—within 48 hours.
C—within 7 days.

*The operator of an aircraft shall immediately, and by the most expeditious means available, notify the nearest NTSB field office when an aircraft accident occurs. (G11) — NTSB §830.5*

ALL
**3195.** Which incident requires an immediate notification to the nearest NTSB field office?

A—A forced landing due to engine failure.
B—Landing gear damage, due to a hard landing.
C—Flight control system malfunction or failure.

*A flight control system malfunction or failure requires immediate NTSB notification. (G11) — NTSB §830.5*

ALL
**3196.** Which incident would necessitate an immediate notification to the nearest NTSB field office?

A—An in-flight generator/alternator failure.
B—An in-flight fire.
C—An in-flight loss of VOR receiver capability.

*Immediate notification of the NTSB is necessary if an in-flight fire occurs. (G11) — NTSB §830.5*

ALL
**3197.** Which incident requires an immediate notification be made to the nearest NTSB field office?

A—An overdue aircraft that is believed to be involved in an accident.
B—An in-flight radio communications failure.
C—An in-flight generator or alternator failure.

*When an aircraft is overdue and believed to have been involved in an accident, the NTSB must be notified immediately. (G11) — NTSB §830.5*

**Answers**

3194 [A]         3195 [C]         3196 [B]         3197 [A]

ALL
**3198.** May aircraft wreckage be moved prior to the time the NTSB takes custody?

A—Yes, but only if moved by a federal, state, or local law enforcement officer.
B—Yes, but only to protect the wreckage from further damage.
C—No, it may not be moved under any circumstances.

*Prior to the time the Board and its authorized representative takes custody of aircraft wreckage, it may not be disturbed or moved except to remove persons injured or trapped, to protect the wreckage from further damage, or to protect the public from injury. (G12) — NTSB §830.10*

ALL
**3199.** The operator of an aircraft that has been involved in an accident is required to file an accident report within how many days?

A—5.
B—7.
C—10.

*The operator of an aircraft shall file a report on Board Form 6120.1 or 6120.2 within 10 days of an accident. (G13) — NTSB §830.15*

ALL
**3200.** The operator of an aircraft that has been involved in an incident is required to submit a report to the nearest field office of the NTSB

A—within 7 days.
B—within 10 days.
C—when requested.

*A report on an incident for which notification is required shall be filed only as requested by an authorized representative of the Board. (G13) — NTSB §830.15*

# Chapter 5
# Procedures and Airport Operations

# Uncontrolled and Tower-Controlled Airports

Airport Traffic Control Towers (ATCT) are established to promote the safe, orderly, and expeditious flow of air traffic. The tower controller will issue instructions for aircraft to follow the desired flight path while in the airport traffic area whenever necessary by using terminology as shown in Figure 5-1.

The ATCT will also direct aircraft taxiing on the surface movement area of the airport. In all instances, an appropriate clearance must be received from the tower before taking off or landing.

At airports without an operating control tower, pilots of fixed-wing aircraft must circle the airport to the left ("left traffic") unless visual indicators indicate right traffic.

A common visual indicator is the segmented circle system, which consists of the following components (*See* Figure 5-2):

**Figure 5-1**

- The **segmented circle** is located in a position readily visible to pilots in the air and on the ground.
- A **tetrahedron** may be used to indicate the direction of landings and takeoffs. The small end of the tetrahedron points in the direction of landing. Pilots are cautioned against using the tetrahedron to determine wind direction, because it may not indicate the correct direction in light winds.
- A **wind cone**, **wind sock**, or **wind tee** may be installed near the operational runway to indicate wind direction. The large end of the wind cone or sock points into the wind as does the cross bar of the wind tee. *See* Figure 5-3.

**Figure 5-2.** Segmented circle and landing direction indicator

**Figure 5-3.** Wind/landing direction indicators

The tetrahedron, wind cone, wind sock, or wind tee may be located in the center of the segmented circle and may be lit for night operations.

Landing runway (landing strip) indicators are installed in pairs and used to show alignment of runways. *See* Figure 5-4(a). Traffic pattern indicators are installed in pairs in conjunction with landing strip indicators, and are used to indicate the direction of turns. *See* Figure 5-4(b).

Approaching to land at an airport without a control tower, or when the control tower is not in operation, the pilot should observe the indicator for the approach end of the runway to be used. VFR landings at night should be made the same as during daytime.

Aircraft departing an uncontrolled airport must comply with any FAA traffic pattern established for that airport.

**Figure 5-4.** Landing runway and traffic pattern indicators

ALL
**3123.** Which is the correct traffic pattern departure procedure to use at a noncontrolled airport?

A— Depart in any direction consistent with safety, after crossing the airport boundary.
B— Make all turns to the left.
C— Comply with any FAA traffic pattern established for the airport.

*In the case of an aircraft departing an airport without an operating control tower, comply with any FAA traffic pattern for that airport. (B08) — 14 CFR §91.127*

AIR, RTC
**3719.** VFR approaches to land at night should be accomplished

A— at a higher airspeed.
B— with a steeper descent.
C— the same as during daytime.

*Inexperienced pilots often have a tendency to make approaches and landings at night with excessive airspeed. Every effort should be made to execute the approach and landing in the same manner as during the day. (H573) — FAA-H-8083-3, Chapter 10*

ALL
**3807.** (Refer to Figure 51.) The segmented circle indicates that the airport traffic is

A— left-hand for Runway 36 and right-hand for Runway 18.
B— left-hand for Runway 18 and right-hand for Runway 36.
C— right-hand for Runway 9 and left-hand for Runway 27.

*The traffic pattern indicators on a segmented circle are used to indicate the direction of turns. The traffic pattern indicators, shown as extensions from the segmented circle, represent the base and final approach legs. (J13) — AIM ¶4-3-3*

ALL
**3808.** (Refer to Figure 51.) The traffic patterns indicated in the segmented circle have been arranged to avoid flights over an area to the

A— south of the airport.
B— north of the airport.
C— southeast of the airport.

*No flights cross the southeast area of the airport. (J13) — AIM ¶4-3-3*

ALL
**3809.** (Refer to Figure 51.) The segmented circle indicates that a landing on Runway 26 will be with a

A— right-quartering headwind.
B— left-quartering headwind.
C— right-quartering tailwind.

*The large end of the wind cone (wind sock) points into the wind. The wind cone in FAA Figure 51 indicates a wind from the northwest. When landing on RWY 26, this would be a right quartering headwind. (J13) — AIM ¶4-3-3*

**Answers**
3123 [C]      3719 [C]      3807 [A]      3808 [C]      3809 [A]

ALL
**3810.** (Refer to Figure 51.) Which runway and traffic pattern should be used as indicated by the wind cone in the segmented circle?

A—Right-hand traffic on Runway 9.
B—Right-hand traffic on Runway 18.
C—Left-hand traffic on Runway 36.

*The large end of the wind cone (wind sock) points into the wind. The wind cone in FAA Figure 51 indicates a wind from the northwest. Landing into the wind can be accomplished on either Runway 27 or Runway 36. The traffic pattern indicators require right traffic to Runway 27 and left traffic to Runway 36. (J13) — AIM ¶4-3-3*

RTC
**3122.** Which is appropriate for a helicopter approaching an airport for landing?

A—Remain below the airplane traffic pattern altitude.
B—Avoid the flow of fixed-wing traffic.
C—Fly right-hand traffic.

*Helicopters must avoid the flow of fixed-wing aircraft. (B08) — 14 CFR §91.127(b), §91.129(f)(2)*

# Airport Markings

Runway numbers and letters are determined from the approach direction. The number is the magnetic heading of the runway rounded to the nearest 10°. For example, an azimuth of 183° would result in a runway number of 18; a magnetic azimuth of 076° would result in a runway numbered 8. Runway letters differentiate between left (L), right (R), or center (C). *See* Figure 5-5.

The designated beginning of the runway that is available and suitable for the landing of aircraft is called the **threshold** (Figure 5-6a). A threshold that is not at the beginning of the full-strength runway pavement is a **displaced threshold**. The paved area behind the displaced threshold is marked by arrows (Figure 5-6b) and is available for taxiing, takeoff, and landing rollout, but is not to be used for landing, usually because of an obstruction in the approach path. *See* Figure 5-6.

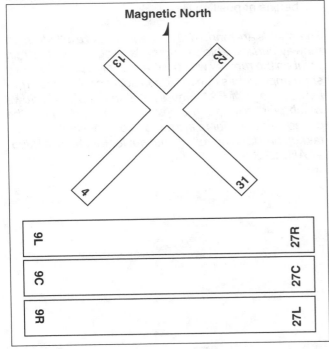

**Figure 5-5.** Runway numbers and letters

**Figure 5-6.** Threshold marking

**Answers**
3810    [C]                3122    [B]

Stopways are found extending beyond some usable runways. These areas are marked by chevrons, and while they appear usable, they are suitable only as overrun areas. *See* Figure 5-7.

A closed runway which is unusable and may be hazardous, even though it may appear usable, will be marked by an "X."

LAHSO is an acronym for "Land And Hold Short Operations." These operations include landing and holding short of an intersecting runway, an intersecting taxiway, or some other designated point on a runway other than an intersecting runway or taxiway. LAHSO is an air traffic control procedure that requires pilot participation to balance the needs for increased airport capacity and system efficiency, consistent with safety. Student pilots or pilots not familiar with LAHSO should not participate in the program. The pilot-in-command has the final authority to accept or decline any land and hold short clearance. The safety and operation of the aircraft remain the responsibility of the pilot. Pilots are expected to decline a LAHSO clearance if they determine it will compromise safety. Available Landing Distance (ALD) data are published in the special notices section of the Airport/Facility Directory (A/FD) and in the U.S. Terminal Procedures Publications. Pilots should only receive a LAHSO clearance when there is a minimum ceiling of 1,000 feet and 3 statute miles visibility. The intent of having "basic" VFR weather conditions is to allow pilots to maintain visual contact with other aircraft and ground vehicle operations.

**Figure 5-7.** Stopway marking

AIR, RTC, LTA
**3773.** (Refer to Figure 49.) That portion of the runway identified by the letter A may be used for

A—landing.
B—taxiing and takeoff.
C—taxiing and landing.

*Thresholds are marked at the beginning of a full-strength runway surface able to endure landing impacts or at a point on the runway which will encourage pilots to avoid short approaches due to hidden noise or obstacle problems. Area A of FAA Figure 49 is marked with arrows which point towards a displaced threshold. Thus, the paved surface prior to the threshold is available for taxi, takeoff and landing rollout, but not for touchdown. (J05) — AIM ¶2-3-3*

AIR, GLI, RTC, REC
**3774.** (Refer to Figure 49.) According to the airport diagram, which statement is true?

A—Runway 30 is equipped at position E with emergency arresting gear to provide a means of stopping military aircraft.
B—Takeoffs may be started at position A on Runway 12, and the landing portion of this runway begins at position B.
C—The takeoff and landing portion of Runway 12 begins at position B.

*Thresholds are marked at the beginning of a full-strength runway surface able to endure landing impacts or at a point on the runway which will encourage pilots to avoid short approaches due to hidden noise or obstacle problems. Area A of FAA Figure 49 is marked with arrows which point towards a displaced threshold. Thus, the paved surface prior to the threshold is available for taxi, takeoff and landing rollout, but not for touchdown. (J05) — AIM ¶2-3-3*

**Answers**

3773  [B]                    3774  [B]

AIR, GLI, RTC, REC
**3775.** (Refer to Figure 49.) What is the difference between area A and area E on the airport depicted?

A—"A" may be used for taxi and takeoff; "E" may be used only as an overrun.
B—"A" may be used for all operations except heavy aircraft landings; "E" may be used only as an overrun.
C—"A" may be used only for taxiing; "E" may be used for all operations except landings.

*The paved area behind the displaced threshold is available for taxiing, landing rollout, and takeoff. The stopway, extending beyond the usable runway, is unusable due to the nature of its construction. Area E of FAA Figure 49, marked with chevrons, is used for overrun only. (J05) — AIM ¶2-3-3*

AIR, GLI, RTC, REC
**3776.** (Refer to Figure 49.) Area C on the airport depicted is classified as a

A—stabilized area.
B—multiple heliport.
C—closed runway.

*An "X" painted on the end of runway means it is closed. (J05) — AIM ¶2-3-3*

AIR, GLI, RTC, REC
**3777.** (Refer to Figure 50.) The arrows that appear on the end of the north/south runway indicate that the area

A—may be used only for taxiing.
B—is usable for taxiing, takeoff, and landing.
C—cannot be used for landing, but may be used for taxiing and takeoff.

*The paved area behind the displaced runway threshold is available for taxiing, landing rollout, and the takeoff of aircraft. (J05) — AIM ¶2-3-3*

ALL
**3778.** The numbers 9 and 27 on a runway indicate that the runway is oriented approximately

A—009° and 027° true.
B—090° and 270° true.
C—090° and 270° magnetic.

*The runway number is the whole number nearest one-tenth the **magnetic** azimuth of the centerline of the runway, measured clockwise from magnetic north. For example: 272° = RWY 27; 087° = RWY 9. (J05) — AIM ¶2-3-3*

AIR, GLI, RTC, REC
**3805.** (Refer to Figure 50.) Select the proper traffic pattern and runway for landing.

A—Left-hand traffic and Runway 18.
B—Right-hand traffic and Runway 18.
C—Left-hand traffic and Runway 22.

*The small end of the tetrahedron points into the wind, indicating the direction of landing. The wind is coming from the southwest. However, the runway most nearly aligned into the wind is closed (X), leaving RWY 18 as the most suitable runway. The traffic pattern indicators on a segmented circle are used to indicate the direction of turns. The traffic pattern indicators, shown as extensions from the segmented circle, represent the base and final approach legs. The traffic pattern indicator shows right traffic for RWY 18. (J13) — AIM ¶4-3-4*

AIR, GLI, RTC, REC
**3806.** (Refer to Figure 50.) If the wind is as shown by the landing direction indicator, the pilot should land on

A—Runway 18 and expect a crosswind from the right.
B—Runway 22 directly into the wind.
C—Runway 36 and expect a crosswind from the right.

*The small end of the tetrahedron points into the wind indicating the direction of landing. Landing to the south on RWY 18, the pilot could expect a right crosswind. (J13) — AIM ¶4-3-3*

**Answers**

| 3775 [A] | 3776 [C] | 3777 [C] | 3778 [C] | 3805 [B] | 3806 [A] |

ALL
**3951.** Who should not participate in the Land and Hold Short Operations (LAHSO) program?

A—Recreational pilots only.
B—Military pilots.
C—Student pilots.

*Student pilots or pilots not familiar with LAHSO should not participate in the program. (J13) — AIM ¶4-3-11*

ALL
**3952.** Who has final authority to accept or decline any land and hold short (LAHSO) clearance?

A—Pilot-in-command.
B—Owner/operator.
C—Second-in-command.

*The pilot-in-command has the final authority to accept or decline any land and hold short clearance. The safety and operation of the aircraft remain the responsibility of the pilot. (J13) — AIM ¶4-3-11*

ALL
**3953.** When should pilots decline a land and hold short (LAHSO) clearance?

A—When it will compromise safety.
B—Only when the tower operator concurs.
C—Pilots can not decline clearance.

*Pilots are expected to decline a LAHSO clearance if they determine it will compromise safety. (J13) — AIM ¶4-3-11*

ALL
**3954.** Where is the "Available Landing Distance" (ALD) data published for an airport that utilizes Land and Hold Short Operations (LAHSO) published?

A—Airport/Facility Directory (A/FD).
B—14 CFR Part 91, General Operating and Flight Rules.
C—Aeronautical Information Manual (AIM).

*ALD data are published in the special notices section of the Airport/Facility Directory (A/FD) and in the U.S. Terminal Procedures Publications. (J13) — AIM ¶4-3-11*

ALL
**3955.** What is the minimum visibility for a pilot to receive a land and hold short (LAHSO) clearance?

A—3 nautical miles.
B—3 statute miles.
C—1 statute mile.

*Pilots should only receive a LAHSO clearance when there is a minimum ceiling of 1,000 feet and 3 statute miles visibility. The intent of having "basic" VFR weather conditions is to allow pilots to maintain visual contact with other aircraft and ground vehicle operations. (J13) — AIM ¶4-3-11*

**Answers**

| | | | | |
|---|---|---|---|---|
| 3951 [C] | 3952 [A] | 3953 [A] | 3954 [A] | 3955 [B] |

# Airport Lighting

At night, the location of an airport can be determined by the presence of an airport **rotating beacon** light. The colors and color combinations that denote the type of airports are:

White and green .................. Lighted land airport

*Green alone ....................... Lighted land airport

White and yellow ................ Lighted water airport

*Yellow alone ...................... Lighted water airport

Green, yellow, white ........... Lighted heliport

*Note:* Green alone or amber alone is used only in connection with a white-and-green or white-and-amber beacon display, respectively.

A civil-lighted land airport beacon will show alternating white and green flashes. A military airfield will be identified by dual-peaked (two quick) white flashes between green flashes.

In Class B, C, D, or E airspace, operation of the airport beacon during the hours of daylight often indicates the ceiling is less than 1,000 feet and/or the visibility is less than 3 miles. However, pilots should not rely solely on the operation of the airport beacon to indicate if weather conditions are IFR or VFR.

**Runway edge lights** are used to outline the runway at night or during periods of low visibility. For the most part, runway edge lights are white, and may be high-, medium-, or low-intensity, while taxiways are outlined by blue omnidirectional lights.

Radio control of lighting is available at some airports, providing airborne control of lights by keying the aircraft's microphone. The control system is responsive to 7, 5, or 3 microphone clicks. Keying the microphone 7 times within 5 seconds will turn the lighting to its highest intensity; 5 times in 5 seconds will set the lights to medium intensity; low intensity is set by keying 3 times in 5 seconds.

AIR, RTC

**3718.** Airport taxiway edge lights are identified at night by

A—white directional lights.
B—blue omnidirectional lights.
C—alternate red and green lights.

*A taxiway-edge lighting system consists of omnidirectional blue lights which outline the usable limits of taxi paths. (H568) — FAA-H-8083-3, Chapter 10*

AIR, RTC

**3768.** To set the high intensity runway lights on medium intensity, the pilot should click the microphone seven times, then click it

A—one time.
B—three times.
C—five times.

*To save money at low-usage airports, pilot-controlled lighting is installed. Key the mike seven times to set the highest level, then adjust to medium with five clicks. (J03) — AIM ¶2-1-7*

ALL

**3769.** An airport's rotating beacon operated during daylight hours indicates

A—there are obstructions on the airport.
B—that weather at the airport located in Class D airspace is below basic VFR weather minimums.
C—the Air Traffic Control tower is not in operation.

*In Class B, C, D or E airspace, operation of the airport beacon during the hours of daylight often indicates that the weather in the airspace is below basic VFR weather minimums (ground visibility is less than 3 miles and/or the ceiling is less than 1,000 feet). (J03) — AIM ¶2-1-8*

**Answers**

3718 **[B]**        3768 **[C]**        3769 **[B]**

AIR, RTC, LTA

**3770.** A lighted heliport may be identified by a

A—green, yellow, and white rotating beacon.
B—flashing yellow light.
C—blue lighted square landing area.

*A lighted heliport has a green, yellow and white beacon flashing 30 to 60 times per minute. A flashing yellow light identifies a lighted water port. (J03) — AIM ¶2-1-8*

AIR, RTC, LTA

**3771.** A military air station can be identified by a rotating beacon that emits

A—white and green alternating flashes.
B—two quick, white flashes between green flashes.
C—green, yellow, and white flashes.

*Military airport beacons flash alternately white and green, but are differentiated from civil beacons by dual-peaked (two quick) white flashes between the green flashes. (J03) — AIM ¶2-1-8*

AIR, RTC, LTA

**3772.** How can a military airport be identified at night?

A—Alternate white and green light flashes.
B—Dual peaked (two quick) white flashes between green flashes.
C—White flashing lights with steady green at the same location.

*Military airport beacons flash alternately white and green, but are differentiated from civil beacons by dual-peaked (two quick) white flashes between the green flashes. (J03) — AIM ¶2-1-8*

**Answers**

3770 [A]     3771 [B]     3772 [B]

# Visual Approach Slope Indicator (VASI)

The **Visual Approach Slope Indicator (VASI)** is a lighting system arranged so as to provide visual-descent guidance information during approach to a runway. The lights are visible for up to 5 miles during the day. The VASI glide path provides obstruction clearance, while lateral guidance is provided by the runway or runway lights. When operating to an airport with an operating control tower, the pilot of an airplane approaching to land on a runway served by a VASI is required to maintain an altitude at or above the glide slope until a lower altitude is necessary for landing.

Most VASI installations consist of two bars, near and far, which provide one visual glide path. On final approach flying toward the runway of intended landing, if the pilot sees both bars as red, the aircraft is below the glide path (Figure 5-8A). Maintaining altitude, the pilot will see the near bar turn pink and then white, while the far bar remains red, indicating the glide path is being intercepted (Figure 5-8B). If the aircraft is above the glide path, the pilot will see both near and far bars as white (Figure 5-8C).

Tri-color visual approach slope indicators normally consist of a single light unit projecting a three-color visual approach path. The below-glide path indication is red, the above-glide path indication is amber, and the on-glide path indication is green. See Figure 5-9.

Pulsating VASIs normally consist of a single light unit projecting a two-color visual approach path. The below-glide path indication is normally red or pulsating red, and the above-glide path indication is normally pulsating white. The on-glide path indication is usually steady white. See Figure 5-10.

*Continued*

**Figure 5-8.** A 2-bar VASI

**Figure 5-9.** Tri-color VASI

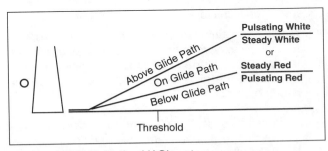

**Figure 5-10.** Pulsating VASI system

The **Precision Approach Path Indicator (PAPI)** uses a single row of lights. Four white lights means "too high." One red light and three white lights means "slightly high," etc. *See* Figure 5-11.

**Figure 5-11.** Precision approach path indicator (PAPI)

AIR, RTC

**3120.** Each pilot of an aircraft approaching to land on a runway served by a visual approach slope indicator (VASI) shall

A—maintain a 3° glide to the runway.

B—maintain an altitude at or above the glide slope.

C—stay high until the runway can be reached in a power-off landing.

*An airplane approaching to land on a runway served by a visual approach indicator, shall maintain an altitude at or above the glide slope until a lower altitude is necessary for a safe landing. (B08) — 14 CFR §91.129(e)(3)*

AIR, RTC

**3121.** When approaching to land on a runway served by a visual approach slope indicator (VASI), the pilot shall

A—maintain an altitude that captures the glide slope at least 2 miles downwind from the runway threshold.

B—maintain an altitude at or above the glide slope.

C—remain on the glide slope and land between the two-light bar.

*An airplane approaching to land on a runway served by a visual approach indicator, shall maintain an altitude at or above the glide slope until a lower altitude is necessary for a safe landing. (B08) — 14 CFR §91.129(e)(3)*

AIR, RTC

**3760.** A slightly high glide slope indication from a precision approach path indicator is

A—four white lights.

B—three white lights and one red light.

C—two white lights and two red lights.

*The precision approach path indicator (PAPI) uses light units similar to the VASI but are installed in a single row of either two or four light units. Four white lights means you are above the glide slope, three white lights and one red light means you are slightly high, two red and two white lights means you are on the glide slope, three reds and one white light means you are slightly low and four red lights means you are below the glide slope. (J03) — AIM ¶2-1-2(b)*

AIR, RTC

**3761.** A below glide slope indication from a tri-color VASI is a

A—red light signal.

B—pink light signal.

C—green light signal.

*A tri-color VASI normally is a single light unit projecting a three-color visual approach path. Below the glide path is red, on the glide path is green, and above the glide path is amber. (J03) — AIM ¶2-1-2(c)*

**Answers**

3120    [B]             3121    [B]             3760    [B]             3761    [A]

AIR
**3762.** An above glide slope indication from a tri-color VASI is

A—a white light signal.
B—a green light signal.
C—an amber light signal.

*A tri-color VASI normally is a single light unit projecting a three-color visual approach path. Below the glide path is red, on the glide path is green, and above the glide path is amber. (J03) — AIM ¶2-1-2(c)*

AIR
**3763.** An on glide slope indication from a tri-color VASI is

A—a white light signal.
B—a green light signal.
C—an amber light signal.

*A tri-color VASI normally is a single light unit projecting a three-color visual approach path. Below the glide path is red, on the glide path is green, and above the glide path is amber. (J03) — AIM ¶2-1-2(c)*

AIR
**3764.** A below glide slope indication from a pulsating approach slope indicator is a

A—pulsating white light.
B—steady white light.
C—pulsating red light.

*Pulsating visual approach slope indicators normally consist of a single light unit projecting a two-color visual approach path. The below-glide path indication is red or pulsating red. The on-glide path indication is a steady white light for one type of system, while for another system it is an alternating red and white light. (J03) — AIM ¶2-1-2(d)*

AIR, RTC
**3765.** (Refer to Figure 48.) Illustration A indicates that the aircraft is

A—below the glide slope.
B—on the glide slope.
C—above the glide slope.

*The two-bar VASI on-glide slope indication is red over white lights. (J03) — AIM ¶2-1-2*

AIR, RTC
**3766.** (Refer to Figure 48.) VASI lights as shown by illustration C indicate that the airplane is

A—off course to the left.
B—above the glide slope.
C—below the glide slope.

*The two-bar VASI above-glide slope indication is white over white lights. VASI lights do not give horizontal direction. (J03) — AIM ¶2-1-2(a)*

AIR, RTC
**3767.** (Refer to Figure 48.) While on final approach to a runway equipped with a standard 2-bar VASI, the lights appear as shown by illustration D. This means that the aircraft is

A—above the glide slope.
B—below the glide slope.
C—on the glide slope.

*The below-glide slope indication from a two-bar VASI is red over red lights. (J03) — AIM ¶2-1-2*

**Answers**
3762 [C]    3763 [B]    3764 [C]    3765 [B]    3766 [B]    3767 [B]

# Surface Operations

Taxiing to or from the runway generally presents no problems during calm or light wind conditions. However, when taxiing in moderate to strong wind conditions, the airplane's control surfaces must be used to counteract the effects of wind. In airplanes equipped with a nose wheel (tricycle-gear), use the following taxi procedures:

1. The elevator should be in the neutral position when taxiing into a head wind.

2. The upwind aileron should be held in the up position when taxiing in a crosswind, (or the upwind wing will tend to be lifted).

3. The elevator should be held in the down position and the upwind aileron down when taxiing with a quartering tailwind (the most critical condition for a nosewheel-type airplane). *See* Figure 5-12.

When an airplane equipped with a tailwheel is taxied into a headwind, the elevator should be held in the up position to hold the tail down. In a quartering tailwind, both the upwind aileron and the elevator should be in the down position.

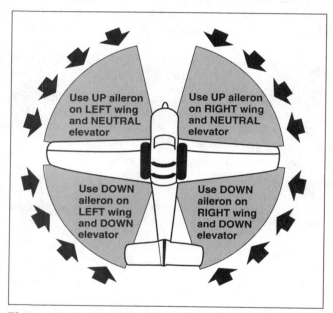

**Figure 5-12.** Control position while taxiing

AIR
**3302.** When taxiing with strong quartering tailwinds, which aileron positions should be used?

A—Aileron down on the downwind side.
B—Ailerons neutral.
C—Aileron down on the side from which the wind is blowing.

*Taxiing with a quartering tailwind provides the most hazardous conditions. In this case, the elevator should be in the down position and the aileron on the upwind side should also be in the down position to keep the wing from lifting. (H516) — FAA-H-8083-3, Chapter 2*

AIR
**3303.** Which aileron positions should a pilot generally use when taxiing in strong quartering headwinds?

A—Aileron up on the side from which the wind is blowing.
B—Aileron down on the side from which the wind is blowing.
C—Ailerons neutral.

*When taxiing a nosewheel aircraft in the presence of moderate to strong winds, extra caution should be taken. For a quartering headwind, the elevator should be held in the neutral position, and the aileron on the upwind side should be in the up position. (H516) — FAA-H-8083-3, Chapter 2*

**Answers**
3302  [C]                3303  [A]

AIR
**3304.** Which wind condition would be most critical when taxiing a nosewheel equipped high-wing airplane?

A—Quartering tailwind.
B—Direct crosswind.
C—Quartering headwind.

*When taxiing a nosewheel aircraft in the presence of moderate to strong winds, extra caution should be taken. Taxiing with a quartering tailwind produces the most hazardous conditions. (H516) — FAA-H-8083-3, Chapter 2*

AIR
**3305.** (Refer to Figure 9, area A.) How should the flight controls be held while taxiing a tricycle-gear equipped airplane into a left quartering headwind?

A—Left aileron up, elevator neutral.
B—Left aileron down, elevator neutral.
C—Left aileron up, elevator down.

*When taxiing a nosewheel aircraft in the presence of moderate to strong winds, extra caution should be taken. For a quartering headwind, the elevator should be held in the neutral position, and the aileron on the upwind side should be in the up position. (H516) — FAA-H-8083-3, Chapter 2*

AIR
**3306.** (Refer to Figure 9, area B.) How should the flight controls be held while taxiing a tailwheel airplane into a right quartering headwind?

A—Right aileron up, elevator up.
B—Right aileron down, elevator neutral.
C—Right aileron up, elevator down.

*When taxiing a tailwheel airplane with a quartering headwind, the aileron on the upwind side should be up, and the elevator held in the up position to hold the tail down. (H516) — FAA-H-8083-3, Chapter 2*

AIR
**3307.** (Refer to Figure 9, area C.) How should the flight controls be held while taxiing a tailwheel airplane with a left quartering tailwind?

A—Left aileron up, elevator neutral.
B—Left aileron down, elevator neutral.
C—Left aileron down, elevator down.

*When taxiing a tailwheel aircraft with a quartering tailwind, the upwind aileron should be down to keep that wing from lifting, and the elevator should also be down. (H516) — FAA-H-8083-3, Chapter 2*

AIR
**3308.** (Refer to Figure 9, area C.) How should the flight controls be held while taxiing a tricycle-gear equipped airplane with a left quartering tailwind?

A—Left aileron up, elevator neutral.
B—Left aileron down, elevator down.
C—Left aileron up, elevator down.

*Taxiing with a quartering tailwind produces the most hazardous conditions. In this case, the elevator should be in the down position, and the aileron on the upwind side should also be in the down position to keep the wing from lifting. (H516) — FAA-H-8083-3, Chapter 2*

**Answers**
3304  [A]          3305  [A]          3306  [A]          3307  [C]          3308  [B]

# Airport/Facility Directory

The Airport/Facility Directory (A/FD) is a publication designed primarily as a pilot's operational manual containing all airports, seaplane bases, and heliports open to the public including communications data, navigational facilities, and certain special notices and procedures. Directories are reissued in their entirety each 56 days.

Because of the wealth of information provided, an extensive legend is required for the Airport/Facility section. *See* FAA Legends 2 through 9.

**ALL**
**3619.** (Refer to Figure 23, area 2 and Legend 1.) For information about the parachute jumping and glider operations at Silverwood Airport, refer to

A—notes on the border of the chart.
B—the Airport/Facility Directory.
C—the Notices to Airmen (NOTAM) publication.

*Tabulations of parachute jump areas in the U.S. are contained in the Airport/Facility Directory. (J34) — AIM ¶3-5-5*

**AIR, RTC**
**3838.** (Refer to Figure 53.) When approaching Lincoln Municipal from the west at noon for the purpose of landing, initial communications should be with

A—Lincoln Approach Control on 124.0 MHz.
B—Minneapolis Center on 128.75 MHz.
C—Lincoln Tower on 118.5 MHz.

*Arriving aircraft landing at airports within Class C airspace should contact Approach Control from outside the Class C airspace on the specified frequency.*

1. *Determine which of the two Approach Controls should be contacted based on the time of day. Convert noon local time by adding the appropriate UTC conversion.*

    *1200 local*
    *+ 0600 UTC conversion*
    _____
    *1800 Z*

    *Lincoln Muni approach should be contacted since its hours of operation are 1130 – 0630Z.*

2. *Identify the appropriate frequency for the aircraft's arrival from the west, 270°. Two frequencies are available. Aircraft approaching from any direction between 170° and 349° should make contact on 124.0 MHz.*

*(J34) — AIM ¶4-1-8*

**AIR, RTC**
**3839.** (Refer to Figure 53.) Which type radar service is provided to VFR aircraft at Lincoln Municipal?

A—Sequencing to the primary Class C airport and standard separation.
B—Sequencing to the primary Class C airport and conflict resolution so that radar targets do not touch, or 1,000 feet vertical separation.
C—Sequencing to the primary Class C airport, traffic advisories, conflict resolution, and safety alerts.

*Radar service in Class C airspace consists of sequencing to the primary airport, standard IFR/IFR separation, IFR/VFR separation (so that targets do not touch or have less than 500-foot separation), and providing traffic advisories and safety alerts. (J34) — AIM ¶3-2-4*

**AIR, RTC, REC**
**3840.** (Refer to Figure 53.) What is the recommended communications procedure for landing at Lincoln Municipal during the hours when the tower is not in operation?

A—Monitor airport traffic and announce your position and intentions on 118.5 MHz.
B—Contact UNICOM on 122.95 MHz for traffic advisories.
C—Monitor ATIS for airport conditions, then announce your position on 122.95 MHz.

*At an airport where the tower is operated on a part-time basis, a pilot should self-announce on the CTAF. (J34) — AIM ¶4-1-8*

**Answers**

3619  [B]          3838  [A]          3839  [C]          3840  [A]

ALL
**3841.** (Refer to Figure 53.) Where is Loup City Municipal located with relation to the city?

A—Northeast approximately 3 miles.
B—Northwest approximately 1 mile.
C—East approximately 10 miles.

*Airport location is expressed as distance and direction from the center of the associated city in NM and cardinal points. The first item in parentheses is the airport identifier and the second item is the relation from the city. In this case, "1 NW." (J34) — A/FD Legend*

ALL
**3842.** (Refer to Figure 53.) Traffic patterns in effect at Lincoln Municipal are

A—to the right on Runway 17L and Runway 35L; to the left on Runway 17R and Runway 35R.
B—to the left on Runway 17L and Runway 35L; to the right on Runway 17R and Runway 35R.
C—to the right on Runways 14 – 32.

*Traffic is to the left unless otherwise stated in the Airport/Facility Directory as "Rgt tfc." (J34) — A/FD Legend*

# Fitness for Flight

Pilot performance can be seriously degraded by a number of physiological factors. While some of the factors may be beyond the control of the pilot, awareness of cause and effect can help minimize any adverse effects.

**Hypoxia**, a state of oxygen deficiency, impairs functions of the brain and other organs. Headache, drowsiness, dizziness, and euphoria are all symptoms of hypoxia.

For optimum protection, pilots should avoid flying above 10,000 feet MSL for prolonged periods without using supplemental oxygen. Federal Aviation Regulations require that when operating an aircraft at cabin pressure altitudes above 12,500 feet MSL up to and including 14,000 feet MSL, **supplemental oxygen** shall be used by the minimum flight crew during that time in excess of 30 minutes at those altitudes. Every occupant of the aircraft must be provided with supplemental oxygen above 15,000 feet.

Aviation-breathing oxygen should be used to replenish an aircraft oxygen system for high-altitude flight. Oxygen used for medical purposes or welding normally should not be used because it may contain too much water. The excess water could condense and freeze in oxygen lines when flying at high altitudes. This could block oxygen flow. Also, constant use of oxygen containing too much water may cause corrosion in the system. Specifications for "aviators' breathing oxygen" are 99.5% pure oxygen and not more than .005 mg. of water per liter of oxygen.

**Hyperventilation**, a deficiency of carbon dioxide within the body, can be the result of rapid or extra deep breathing due to emotional tension, anxiety, or fear. Symptoms will subside after the rate and depth of breathing are brought under control. A pilot should be able to overcome the symptoms or avoid future occurrences of hyperventilation by talking aloud, breathing into a bag, or slowing the breathing rate.

**Carbon monoxide** is a colorless, odorless, and tasteless gas contained in exhaust fumes. Symptoms of carbon monoxide poisoning include headache, drowsiness, or dizziness. Large accumulations of carbon monoxide in the human body result in a loss of muscular power. Susceptibility increases as altitude increases.

A pilot who detects symptoms of carbon monoxide poisoning should immediately shut off the heater and open air vents.

Various complex motions, forces, and visual scenes encountered in flight may result in misleading information being sent to the brain by various sensory organs. Spatial disorientation may result if these body signals are used to interpret flight attitude. The best way to overcome **spatial disorientation** is by relying on the flight instruments rather than taking a chance on the sensory organs.

**Answers**

3841　[B]　　　　3842　[B]

ALL

**3163.** When operating an aircraft at cabin pressure altitudes above 12,500 feet MSL up to and including 14,000 feet MSL, supplemental oxygen shall be used during

A—the entire flight time at those altitudes.
B—that flight time in excess of 10 minutes at those altitudes.
C—that flight time in excess of 30 minutes at those altitudes.

*No person may operate civil aircraft at cabin pressure altitudes above 12,500 feet MSL up to and including 14,000 feet MSL, unless the required minimum flight crew uses supplemental oxygen for that part of the flight at those altitudes that is more than 30 minutes duration. (B11) — 14 CFR §91.211(a)(1)*

ALL

**3164.** Unless each occupant is provided with supplemental oxygen, no person may operate a civil aircraft of U.S. registry above a maximum cabin pressure altitude of

A—12,500 feet MSL.
B—14,000 feet MSL.
C—15,000 feet MSL.

*No person may operate a civil aircraft at cabin pressure altitudes above 15,000 feet MSL unless each occupant is provided with supplemental oxygen. (B11) — 14 CFR §91.211(a)(3)*

ALL

**3832.** Large accumulations of carbon monoxide in the human body result in

A—tightness across the forehead.
B—loss of muscular power.
C—an increased sense of well-being.

*A large accumulation of carbon monoxide in the body results in loss of muscular power, vomiting, convulsions, and coma. (J31) — AIM ¶8-1-4*

*Answers (A) and (C) are incorrect because hypoxia gives you an increased sense of well-being; stress could result in tightness across the forehead.*

ALL

**3844.** Which statement best defines hypoxia?

A—A state of oxygen deficiency in the body.
B—An abnormal increase in the volume of air breathed.
C—A condition of gas bubble formation around the joints or muscles.

*Hypoxia is an oxygen deficiency in the body usually caused by flight at higher altitudes. For optimum protection from hypoxia, pilots are encouraged to use supplemental oxygen above 10,000 feet during the day, and above 5,000 feet at night. (J31) — AIM ¶8-1-2*

*Answer (B) is incorrect because it describes hyperventilation. Answer (C) is incorrect because it describes the bends.*

ALL

**3845.** Rapid or extra deep breathing while using oxygen can cause a condition known as

A—hyperventilation.
B—aerosinusitis.
C—aerotitis.

*An abnormal increase in the volume of air breathed in and out of the lungs flushes an excessive amount of carbon dioxide from the lungs and blood, causing hyperventilation. (J31) — AIM ¶8-1-3*

ALL

**3846.** Which would most likely result in hyperventilation?

A—Emotional tension, anxiety, or fear.
B—The excessive consumption of alcohol.
C—An extremely slow rate of breathing and insufficient oxygen.

*Hyperventilation is most likely to occur during periods of stress or anxiety. (J31) — AIM ¶8-1-3*

**Answers**

| | | | | | |
|---|---|---|---|---|---|
| 3163 [C] | 3164 [C] | 3832 [B] | 3844 [A] | 3845 [A] | 3846 [A] |

ALL
**3847.** A pilot should be able to overcome the symptoms or avoid future occurrences of hyperventilation by

A—closely monitoring the flight instruments to control the airplane.
B—slowing the breathing rate, breathing into a bag, or talking aloud.
C—increasing the breathing rate in order to increase lung ventilation.

*The symptoms of hyperventilation subside within a few minutes after the rate and depth of breathing are consciously brought back under control. The buildup of carbon dioxide in the body can be hastened by controlled breathing in and out of a paper bag held over the nose and mouth. Talking aloud often helps, while normally-paced breathing at all times prevents hyperventilation. (J31) — AIM ¶8-1-3*

ALL
**3848.** Susceptibility to carbon monoxide poisoning increases as

A—altitude increases.
B—altitude decreases.
C—air pressure increases.

*Susceptibility to carbon monoxide poisoning increases with altitude. As altitude increases, air pressure decreases and the body has difficulty getting oxygen. Add carbon monoxide, which further deprives the body of oxygen, and the situation can become critical. (J31) — AIM ¶8-1-4*

ALL
**3850.** The danger of spatial disorientation during flight in poor visual conditions may be reduced by

A—shifting the eyes quickly between the exterior visual field and the instrument panel.
B—having faith in the instruments rather than taking a chance on the sensory organs.
C—leaning the body in the opposite direction of the motion of the aircraft.

*Even if the natural horizon or surface reference is clearly visible, rely on instrument indications to overcome the effects of spatial disorientation. Shifting the eyes quickly from outside to inside, and leaning, will only compound the problem. (J31) — AIM ¶8-1-5*

ALL
**3851.** A state of temporary confusion resulting from misleading information being sent to the brain by various sensory organs is defined as

A—spatial disorientation.
B—hyperventilation.
C—hypoxia.

*Disorientation, or vertigo, is actually a state of temporary spatial confusion resulting from misleading information sent to the brain by various sensory organs. (J31) — AIM ¶8-1-5*

ALL
**3852.** Pilots are more subject to spatial disorientation if

A—they ignore the sensations of muscles and inner ear.
B—body signals are used to interpret flight attitude.
C—eyes are moved often in the process of cross-checking the flight instruments.

*Sight, supported by other senses, allows the pilot to maintain orientation. However, during periods of low visibility, the supporting senses sometimes conflict with what is seen. When this happens, a pilot is particularly vulnerable to disorientation and must rely more on flight instruments. (J31) — AIM ¶8-1-6*

ALL
**3853.** If a pilot experiences spatial disorientation during flight in a restricted visibility condition, the best way to overcome the effect is to

A—rely upon the aircraft instrument indications.
B—concentrate on yaw, pitch, and roll sensations.
C—consciously slow the breathing rate until symptoms clear and then resume normal breathing rate.

*Even if the natural horizon or surface reference is clearly visible, rely on instrument indications to overcome the effects of spatial disorientation. Shifting the eyes quickly from outside to inside, and leaning, will only compound the problem. (J31) — AIM ¶8-1-6*

**Answers**

| 3847 [B] | 3848 [A] | 3850 [B] | 3851 [A] | 3852 [B] | 3853 [A] |

# Aeronautical Decision Making

The pilot is responsible for determining whether he/she is fit to fly for a particular flight. Mot preventable accidents have one common factor: human error, rather than a mechanical malfunction. Good aeronautical decision making (ADM) is necessary to prevent human error. ADM is a systematic approach to the mental process used by aircraft pilots to consistently determine the best course of action in response to a given set of circumstances.

The ADM process addresses all aspects of decision making in the cockpit and identifies the steps involved in good decision making. Steps for good decision making are:

1. Identifying personal attitudes hazardous to safe flight.
2. Learning behavior modification techniques.
3. Learning how to recognize and cope with stress.
4. Developing risk assessment skills.
5. Using all resources in a multicrew situation.
6. Evaluating the effectiveness of one's ADM skills.

There are a number of classic behavioral traps into which pilots have been known to fall. Pilots, particularly those with considerable experience, as a rule always try to complete a flight as planned, please passengers, meet schedules, and generally demonstrate that they have the "right stuff." These tendencies ultimately may lead to practices that are dangerous and often illegal, and may lead to a mishap. All experienced pilots have fallen prey to, or have been tempted by, one or more of these tendencies in their flying careers. These dangerous tendencies or behavior patterns, which must be identified and eliminated, include:

**Peer Pressure.** Poor decision making based upon emotional response to peers rather than evaluating a situation objectively.

**Mind Set.** The inability to recognize and cope with changes in the situation different from those anticipated or planned.

**Get-There-Itis.** This tendency, common among pilots, clouds the vision and impairs judgment by causing a fixation on the original goal or destination combined with a total disregard for any alternative course of action.

**Duck-Under Syndrome.** The tendency to sneak a peek by descending below minimums during an approach. Based on a belief that there is always a built-in "fudge" factor that can be used or on an unwillingness to admit defeat and shoot a missed approach.

**Scud Running.** Pushing the capabilities of the pilot and the aircraft to the limits by trying to maintain visual contact with the terrain while trying to avoid physical contact with it. This attitude is characterized by the old pilot's joke: "If it's too bad to go IFR, we'll go VFR."

**Continuing Visual Flight Rules (VFR)** into instrument conditions often leads to spatial disorientation or collision with ground/obstacles. It is even more dangerous if the pilot is not instrument qualified or current.

**Getting Behind the Aircraft.** Allowing events or the situation to control your actions rather than the other way around. Characterized by a constant state of surprise at what happens next.

**Loss of Positional or Situation Awareness.** Another case of getting behind the aircraft which results in not knowing where you are, an inability to recognize deteriorating circumstances, and/or the misjudgment of the rate of deterioration.

**Operating Without Adequate Fuel Reserves.** Ignoring minimum fuel reserve requirements, either VFR or Instrument Flight Rules (IFR), is generally the result of overconfidence, lack of flight planning, or ignoring the regulations.

**Descent Below the Minimum Enroute Altitude.** The duck-under syndrome (mentioned above) manifesting itself during the enroute portion of an IFR flight.

**Flying Outside the Envelope.** Unjustified reliance on the (usually mistaken) belief that the aircraft's high performance capability meets the demands imposed by the pilot's (usually overestimated) flying skills.

**Neglect of Flight Planning, Preflight Inspections, Checklists, Etc.** Unjustified reliance on the pilot's short and long term memory, regular flying skills, repetitive and familiar routes, etc.

Each ADM student should take the Self-Assessment Hazardous Attitude Inventory Test in order to gain a realistic perspective on his/her attitudes toward flying. The inventory test requires the pilot to provide a response which most accurately reflects the reasoning behind his/her decision. The pilot must choose one of the five given reasons for making that decision, even though the pilot may not consider any of the five choices acceptable. The inventory test presents extreme cases of incorrect pilot decision making in an effort to introduce the five types of hazardous attitudes.

ADM addresses the following five hazardous attitudes:

1. **Antiauthority (don't tell me!).** This attitude is found in people who do not like anyone telling them what to do. In a sense they are saying "no one can tell me what to do." They may be resentful of having someone tell them what to do or may regard rules, regulations, and procedures as silly or unnecessary. However, it is always your prerogative to question authority if you feel it is in error. The antidote for this attitude is: Follow the rules. They are usually right.

2. **Impulsivity (do something quickly!)** is the attitude of people who frequently feel the need to do something—*anything*—immediately. They do not stop to think about what they are about to do, they do not select the best alternative, and they do the first thing that comes to mind. The antidote for this attitude is: Not so fast. Think first.

3. **Invulnerability (it won't happen to me).** Many people feel that accidents happen to others, but never to them. They know accidents can happen, and they know that anyone can be affected. They never really feel or believe that they will be personally involved. Pilots who think this way are more likely to take chances and increase risk. The antidote for this attitude is: It could happen to me.

4. **Macho (I can do it).** Pilots who are always trying to prove that they are better than anyone else are thinking "I can do it—I'll show them." Pilots with this type of attitude will try to prove themselves by taking risks in order to impress others. While this pattern is thought to be a male characteristic, women are equally susceptible. The antidote for this attitude is: taking chances is foolish.

5. **Resignation (what's the use?).** Pilots who think "what's the use?" do not see themselves as being able to make a great deal of difference in what happens to them. When things go well, the pilot is apt to think that's good luck. When things go badly, the pilot may feel that "someone is out to get me," or attribute it to bad luck. The pilot will leave the action to others, for better or worse. Sometimes, such pilots will even go along with unreasonable requests just to be a "nice guy." The antidote for this attitude is: I'm not helpless. I can make a difference.

*Continued*

Hazardous attitudes which contribute to poor pilot judgment can be effectively counteracted by redirecting that hazardous attitude so that appropriate action can be taken. Recognition of hazardous thoughts is the first step in neutralizing them in the ADM process. Pilots should become familiar with a means of counteracting hazardous attitudes with an appropriate antidote thought. When a pilot recognizes a thought as hazardous, the pilot should label that thought as hazardous, then correct that thought by stating the corresponding antidote.

If you hope to succeed at reducing stress associated with crisis management in the air or with your job, it is essential to begin by making a personal assessment of stress in all areas of your life. Good **cockpit stress management** begins with good life stress management. Many of the stress coping techniques practiced for life stress management are not usually practical in flight. Rather, you must condition yourself to relax and think rationally when stress appears. The following checklist outlines some thoughts on cockpit stress management.

1. Avoid situations that distract you from flying the aircraft.

2. Reduce your workload to reduce stress levels. This will create a proper environment in which to make good decisions.

3. If an emergency does occur, be calm. Think for a moment, weigh the alternatives, then act.

4. Maintain proficiency in your aircraft; proficiency builds confidence. Familiarize yourself thoroughly with your aircraft, its systems, and emergency procedures.

5. Know and respect your own personal limits.

6. Do not let little mistakes bother you until they build into a big thing. Wait until after you land, then "debrief" and analyze past actions.

7. If flying is adding to your stress, either stop flying or seek professional help to manage your stress within acceptable limits.

**The DECIDE Model**, comprised of a six-step process, is intended to provide the pilot with a logical way of approaching decision making. The six elements of the DECIDE Model represent a continuous loop decision process which can be used to assist a pilot in the decision making process when he/she is faced with a change in a situation that requires a judgment. This DECIDE Model is primarily focused on the intellectual component, but can have an impact on the motivational component of judgment as well. If a pilot practices the DECIDE Model in all decision making, its use can become very natural and could result in better decisions being made under all types of situations.

1. **D**etect. The decisionmaker detects the fact that change has occurred.

2. **E**stimate. The decisionmaker estimates the need to counter or react to the change.

3. **C**hoose. The decisionmaker chooses a desirable outcome (in terms of success) for the flight.

4. **I**dentify. The decisionmaker identifies actions which could successfully control the change.

5. **D**o. The decisionmaker takes the necessary action.

6. **E**valuate. The decisionmaker evaluates the effect(s) of his/her action countering the change.

ALL
**3931.** What is it often called when a pilot pushes his or her capabilities and the aircraft's limits by trying to maintain visual contact with the terrain in low visibility and ceiling?

A—Scud running.
B—Mind set.
C—Peer pressure.

*Scud running is pushing the capabilities of the pilot and the aircraft to the limits by trying to maintain visual contact with the terrain while trying to avoid physical contact with it. (L05) — AC 60-22*

ALL
**3932.** What is the antidote when a pilot has a hazardous attitude, such as "Antiauthority"?

A—Rules do not apply in this situation.
B—I know what I am doing.
C—Follow the rules.

*The antiauthority (don't tell me!) attitude is found in people who do not like anyone telling them what to do. The antidote for this attitude is: follow the rules, they are usually right. (L05) — AC 60-22*

ALL
**3933.** What is the antidote when a pilot has a hazardous attitude, such as "Impulsivity"?

A—It could happen to me.
B—Do it quickly to get it over with.
C—Not so fast, think first.

*Impulsivity (do something quickly!) is the attitude of people who frequently feel the need to do something, anything, immediately. They do not stop to think about what they are about to do, they do not select the best alternative, and they do the first thing that comes to mind. The antidote for this attitude is: Not so fast. Think first. (L05) — AC 60-22*

ALL
**3934.** What is the antidote when a pilot has a hazardous attitude, such as "Invulnerability"?

A—It will not happen to me.
B—It can not be that bad.
C—It could happen to me.

*Invulnerability (it won't happen to me) is found in people who think accidents happen to others, but never to them. Pilots who think this way are more likely to take chances and increase risk. The antidote for this attitude is: It could happen to me. (L05) — AC 60-22*

ALL
**3935.** What is the antidote when a pilot has a hazardous attitude, such as "Macho"?

A—I can do it.
B—Taking chances is foolish.
C—Nothing will happen.

*Macho (I can do it) is the attitude found in pilots who are always trying to prove they are better than anyone else. Pilots with this type of attitude will try to prove themselves by taking risks in order to impress others. The antidote for this attitude is: taking chances is foolish. (L05) — AC 60-22*

ALL
**3936.** What is the antidote when a pilot has a hazardous attitude, such as "Resignation"?

A—What is the use.
B—Someone else is responsible.
C—I am not helpless.

*Resignation (what's the use) is the attitude in pilots who do not see themselves as being able to make a great deal of difference in what happens to them. When things go well, the pilot is apt to think it's due to good luck. When things go badly, the pilot may feel that "someone is out to get me," or attribute it to bad luck. The antidote for this attitude is: I'm not helpless. I can make a difference. (L05) — AC 60-22*

ALL

**3937.** Who is responsible for determining whether a pilot is fit to fly for a particular flight, even though he or she holds a current medical certificate?

A—The FAA.
B—The medical examiner.
C—The pilot.

*The pilot is responsible for determining whether he/she is fit to fly for a particular flight. (L05) — AC 60-22*

ALL

**3938.** What is the one common factor which affects most preventable accidents?

A—Structural failure.
B—Mechanical malfunction.
C—Human error.

*Most preventable accidents have one common factor: human error, rather than a mechanical malfunction. (L05) — AC 60-22*

ALL

**3939.** What often leads to spatial disorientation or collision with ground/obstacles when flying under Visual Flight Rules (VFR)?

A—Continual flight into instrument conditions.
B—Getting behind the aircraft.
C—Duck-under syndrome.

*Continuing visual flight rules (VFR) into instrument conditions often leads to spatial disorientation or collision with ground/obstacles. It is even more dangerous if the pilot is not instrument qualified or current. (L05) — AC 60-22*

ALL

**3940.** What is one of the neglected items when a pilot relies on short and long term memory for repetitive tasks?

A—Checklists.
B—Situation awareness.
C—Flying outside the envelope.

*Unjustified reliance on the pilot's short and long term memory, regular flying skills, repetitive and familiar routes usually results in neglect of flight planning, pre-flight inspections, and checklists. (L05) — AC 60-22*

**Answers**

3937 [C]　　　　3938 [C]　　　　3939 [A]　　　　3940 [A]

# Collision Avoidance

Vision is the most important body sense for safe flight. Major factors that determine how effectively vision can be used are the level of illumination and the technique of scanning the sky for other aircraft.

**Atmospheric haze** reduces the ability to see traffic or terrain during flight, making all features appear to be farther away than they actually are.

In preparation for a night flight, the pilot should avoid bright white lights for at least 30 minutes before the flight.

**Scanning** the sky for other aircraft is a key factor in collision avoidance. Pilots must develop an effective scanning technique which maximizes visual capabilities. Because the eyes focus only on a narrow viewing area, effective scanning is accomplished with a series of short, regularly spaced eye movements. Each movement should not exceed 10°, and each area should be observed for at least one second. At night, scan slowly to permit the use of off-center vision.

Prior to starting any maneuver, a pilot should visually scan the entire area for collision avoidance. Any aircraft that appears to have no relative motion and stays in one scan quadrant is likely to be on a collision course. If a target shows neither lateral nor vertical motion, but increases in size, take evasive action.

When climbing or descending VFR on an airway, execute gentle banks, right and left, to provide for visual scanning of the airspace.

ALL
**3710.** Prior to starting each maneuver, pilots should

A—check altitude, airspeed, and heading indications.
B—visually scan the entire area for collision avoidance.
C—announce their intentions on the nearest CTAF.

*Scanning the sky for other aircraft is a key factor in collision avoidance. (H507) — AC 61-23C, Chapter 2*

Answer (A) is incorrect because checking your instruments is important but secondary to collision avoidance. Answer (C) is incorrect because announcing your intentions on the nearest CTAF does not guarantee that anyone is listening.

AIR, RTC, LTA
**3712.** What is the most effective way to use the eyes during night flight?

A—Look only at far away, dim lights.
B—Scan slowly to permit offcenter viewing.
C—Concentrate directly on each object for a few seconds.

*During daylight, an object can be seen best by looking directly at it, but at night, a scanning procedure to permit "off-center" viewing of the object is more effective. In addition, the pilot should consciously practice moving the eyes more slowly than in daylight to optimize night vision. Off-center viewing must be utilized during night flying because of the distribution of rods and cones in the eye. (H564) — FAA-H-8083-3, Chapter 10*

AIR, RTC, LTA
**3713.** The best method to use when looking for other traffic at night is to

A—look to the side of the object and scan slowly.
B—scan the visual field very rapidly.
C—look to the side of the object and scan rapidly.

*During daylight, an object can be seen best by looking directly at it, but at night, a scanning procedure to permit "off-center" viewing of the object is more effective. In addition, the pilot should consciously practice moving the eyes more slowly than in daylight to optimize night vision. Off-center viewing must be utilized during night flying because of the distribution of rods and cones in the eye. (H564) — FAA-H-8083-3, Chapter 10*

**Answers**

| | | |
|---|---|---|
| 3710 [B] | 3712 [B] | 3713 [A] |

AIR, RTC, LTA
**3714.** The most effective method of scanning for other aircraft for collision avoidance during nighttime hours is to use

A—regularly spaced concentration on the 3-, 9-, and 12-o'clock positions.
B—a series of short, regularly spaced eye movements to search each 30-degree sector.
C—peripheral vision by scanning small sectors and utilizing offcenter viewing.

*During daylight, an object can be seen best by looking directly at it, but at night, a scanning procedure to permit "off-center" viewing of the object is more effective. In addition, the pilot should consciously practice moving the eyes more slowly than in daylight to optimize night vision. Off-center viewing must be utilized during night flying because of the distribution of rods and cones in the eye. (H564) — FAA-H-8083-3, Chapter 10*

ALL
**3833.** What effect does haze have on the ability to see traffic or terrain features during flight?

A—Haze causes the eyes to focus at infinity.
B—The eyes tend to overwork in haze and do not detect relative movement easily.
C—All traffic or terrain features appear to be farther away than their actual distance.

*Atmospheric haze can create the illusion of being at a greater distance from objects on the ground and in the air. (J31) — AIM ¶8-1-5*

ALL
**3834.** The most effective method of scanning for other aircraft for collision avoidance during daylight hours is to use

A—regularly spaced concentration on the 3-, 9-, and 12-o'clock positions.
B—a series of short, regularly spaced eye movements to search each 10-degree sector.
C—peripheral vision by scanning small sectors and utilizing offcenter viewing.

*Effective scanning is accomplished with a series of short, regularly spaced eye movements that bring successive areas of the sky into the central visual field. Each movement should not exceed 10°, and each area should be observed for at least one second to enable detection. (J31) — AIM ¶8-1-6*

ALL
**3835.** Which technique should a pilot use to scan for traffic to the right and left during straight-and-level flight?

A—Systematically focus on different segments of the sky for short intervals.
B—Concentrate on relative movement detected in the peripheral vision area.
C—Continuous sweeping of the windshield from right to left.

*Effective scanning is accomplished with a series of short, regularly spaced eye movements that bring successive areas of the sky into the central visual field. Each movement should not exceed 10°, and each area should be observed for at least one second to enable detection. (J31) — AIM ¶8-1-6*

ALL
**3836.** How can you determine if another aircraft is on a collision course with your aircraft?

A—The other aircraft will always appear to get larger and closer at a rapid rate.
B—The nose of each aircraft is pointed at the same point in space.
C—There will be no apparent relative motion between your aircraft and the other aircraft.

*Any aircraft that appears to have no relative motion and stays in one scan quadrant is likely to be on a collision course. (J31) — AIM ¶8-1-8*

ALL
**3849.** What preparation should a pilot make to adapt the eyes for night flying?

A—Wear sunglasses after sunset until ready for flight.
B—Avoid red lights at least 30 minutes before the flight.
C—Avoid bright white lights at least 30 minutes before the flight.

*Exposure to total darkness for at least 30 minutes is required for complete dark adaptation. Any degree of dark adaptation is lost within a few seconds of viewing a bright light. Red lights do not affect night vision. (J31) — AIM ¶8-1-6*

**Answers**

3714 [C]      3833 [C]      3834 [B]      3835 [A]      3836 [C]      3849 [C]

# Aircraft Lighting

When an aircraft is being operated during the period from sunset to sunrise (except in Alaska), it must display lighted position lights and an anticollision light. The anticollision light may be either aviation red or aviation white. *See* Figure 5-13.

For collision avoidance, a pilot must know where each colored light is located on an aircraft. For example, if a pilot observes a steady red light and a flashing red light ahead and at the same altitude, the other aircraft is crossing to the left; a steady white and a flashing red light indicates that the other aircraft is headed away from the observer; and steady red and green lights at the same altitude as the observer indicates that the other aircraft is approaching head-on.

**Left Wing —** Red Light

**Right Wing —** Green Light

**Tail —** White Light

**Figure 5-13.** Aircraft lighting

ALL
**3162.** Except in Alaska, during what time period should lighted position lights be displayed on an aircraft?

A—End of evening civil twilight to the beginning of morning civil twilight.
B—1 hour after sunset to 1 hour before sunrise.
C—Sunset to sunrise.

*An aircraft must display lighted position lights from sunset to sunrise. (B11) — 14 CFR §91.209(a)*

Answer (A) is incorrect because it applies to logging of night time. Answer (B) is incorrect because it applies to the night landing requirement.

AIR, RTC, LTA
**3715.** During a night flight, you observe a steady red light and a flashing red light ahead and at the same altitude. What is the general direction of movement of the other aircraft?

A—The other aircraft is crossing to the left.
B—The other aircraft is crossing to the right.
C—The other aircraft is approaching head-on.

*Airplanes have a red light on the left wing tip, a green light on the right wing tip and a white light on the tail. The flashing red light is the rotating beacon which can be seen from all directions around the aircraft. If the only steady light seen is red, then the airplane is crossing from right to left in relation to the observing pilot. (H567) — FAA-H-8083-3, Chapter 10*

AIR, RTC, LTA
**3716.** During a night flight, you observe a steady white light and a flashing red light ahead and at the same altitude. What is the general direction of movement of the other aircraft?

A—The other aircraft is flying away from you.
B—The other aircraft is crossing to the left.
C—The other aircraft is crossing to the right.

*Airplanes have a red light on the left wing tip, a green light on the right wing tip and a white light on the tail. The flashing red light is the rotating beacon which can be seen from all directions around the aircraft. When the only steady light seen is white, then the airplane is headed away from the observing pilot. (H567) — FAA-H-8083-3, Chapter 10*

AIR, RTC, LTA
**3717.** During a night flight, you observe steady red and green lights ahead and at the same altitude. What is the general direction of movement of the other aircraft?

A—The other aircraft is crossing to the left.
B—The other aircraft is flying away from you.
C—The other aircraft is approaching head-on.

*When both a red and green light of another airplane are observed, the airplane would be flying in a general direction toward you. Airplanes have a red light on the left wing tip, a green light on the right wing tip and a white light on the tail. (H567) — FAA-H-8083-3, Chapter 10*

**Answers**

3162 [C]    3715 [A]    3716 [A]    3717 [C]

# Chapter 6
# **Weather**

# The Heating of the Earth

The major source of all weather is the sun. Changes or variations of weather patterns are caused by the unequal heating of the Earth's surface.

Every physical process of weather is accompanied by or is a result of unequal heating of the Earth's surface. The heating of the Earth (and therefore the heating of the air surrounding the Earth) is unequal around the entire planet. Both north or south of the equator, one square foot of sunrays is not concentrated over one square foot of the surface, but over a larger area. This lower concentration of sunrays produces less radiation of heat over a given surface area; therefore, less atmospheric heating takes place in that area.

The unequal heating of the Earth's atmosphere creates a large air-cell circulation pattern (wind) because the warmer air has a tendency to rise (low pressure) and the colder air has a tendency to settle or descend (high pressure) and replace the rising warmer air. This unequal heating, which causes pressure variations, will also cause variations in altimeter settings between weather reporting points.

Because the Earth rotates, this large, simple air-cell circulation pattern is greatly distorted by a phenomenon known as the **Coriolis force**. When the wind (which is created by high pressure trying to flow into low pressure) first begins to move at higher altitudes, the Coriolis force deflects it to the right (in the Northern Hemisphere) causing it to flow parallel to the isobars (lines of equal pressure). These deflections of the large-cell circulation pattern create general wind patterns as depicted in Figure 6-1.

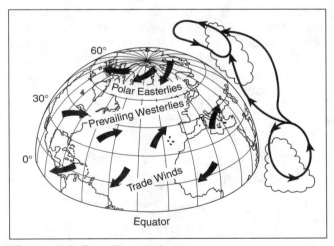

**Figure 6-1.** Prevailing wind systems

ALL
**3381.** Every physical process of weather is accompanied by, or is the result of, a

A—movement of air.
B—pressure differential.
C—heat exchange.

*Every physical process of weather is accompanied by, or is a result of, unequal heating of the Earth's surface. (I21) — AC 00-6A, Chapter 2*

ALL
**3382.** What causes variations in altimeter settings between weather reporting points?

A—Unequal heating of the Earth's surface.
B—Variation of terrain elevation.
C—Coriolis force.

*All altimeter settings are corrected to sea level. Unequal heating of the Earth's surface causes pressure differences. (I21) — AC 00-6A, Chapter 2*

GLI
**3448.** The development of thermals depends upon

A—a counterclockwise circulation of air.
B—temperature inversions.
C—solar heating.

*Thermals are updrafts in convective currents dependent on solar heating. A temperature inversion would result in stable air with very little, if any, convective activity. (I35) — AC 00-6A, Chapter 16*

**Answers**
3381  [C]          3382  [A]          3448  [C]

GLI
**3647.** (Refer to Figure 21.) Over which area should a glider pilot expect to find the best lift under normal conditions?

A—6.
B—7.
C—5.

*One fundamental point is that dry areas get hotter than moist areas. Dry fields or dry ground of any nature are better thermal sources than moist areas. This applies to woods or forests, which are poor sources of thermals because of the large amount of moisture given off by foliage. (N23) — American Soaring Handbook, page 5-10*

# Circulation and Wind

The general circulation and wind rules in the Northern Hemisphere are as follows:

1.  Air circulates in a clockwise direction around a high;

2.  Air circulates in a counterclockwise direction around a low;

3.  The closer the isobars are together, the stronger the wind speed; and

4.  Due to surface friction (up to about 2,000 feet AGL), surface winds do not exactly parallel the isobars, but move outward from the center of the high toward lower pressure. *See* Figure 6-2.

Knowing that air flows out of the high in a clockwise direction and into the low in a counterclockwise direction is useful in preflight planning. Assume a flight from point A to point B as shown in Figure 6-3. Going direct would involve fighting the wind flowing around the low. However, by traveling south of the low-pressure area, the circulation pattern could help instead of hinder. Generally speaking, in the Northern Hemisphere, when traveling west to east, the most favorable winds can be found by flying north of high-pressure areas and south of low-pressure areas. Conversely, when flying east to west, the most favorable winds can be found south of high-pressure areas and north of low-pressure areas.

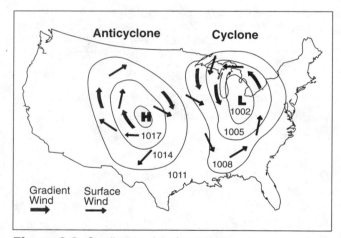

**Figure 6-2.** Gradient and surface wind

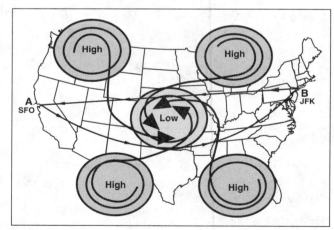

**Figure 6-3.** Circulation and wind

**Answers**

3647 [A]

**ALL**
**3395.** The wind at 5,000 feet AGL is southwesterly while the surface wind is southerly. This difference in direction is primarily due to

A—stronger pressure gradient at higher altitudes.
B—friction between the wind and the surface.
C—stronger Coriolis force at the surface.

*Friction between the wind and the surface slows the wind. The Coriolis force has less affect on slower winds, therefore there will be less deflection with surface winds than with winds at 5,000 feet AGL. (I23) — AC 00-6A, Chapter 4*

Answer (A) is incorrect because pressure gradient is not the reason for wind direction differences; it is the force which causes wind. Answer (C) is incorrect because slower wind speed results in weaker Coriolis force at the surface.

**ALL**
**3450.** Convective circulation patterns associated with sea breezes are caused by

A—warm, dense air moving inland from over the water.
B—water absorbing and radiating heat faster than the land.
C—cool, dense air moving inland from over the water.

*Caused by the heating of land on warm, sunny days, the sea breeze usually begins during early forenoon, reaches a maximum during the afternoon, and subsides around dusk after the land has cooled. The leading edge of the cool sea breeze forces warmer air inland to rise. Rising air from over land returns seaward at higher altitude to complete the convective cell. (I35) — AC 00-6A, Chapter 16*

Answer (A) is incorrect because there will be cooler air over the water. Answer (B) is incorrect because land absorbs and radiates heat faster.

**GLI**
**3350.** What is the proper airspeed to use when flying between thermals on a cross-country flight against a headwind?

A—The best lift/drag speed increased by one-half the estimated wind velocity.
B—The minimum sink speed increased by one-half the estimated wind velocity.
C—The best lift/drag speed decreased by one-half the estimated wind velocity.

*When gliding into a headwind, maximum distance will be achieved by adding approximately one-half the estimated headwind velocity to the best L/D speed. (N34) — Soaring Flight Manual, Chapter 2*

# Temperature

In aviation, temperature is measured in degrees Celsius (°C). The standard temperature at sea level is 59°F (15°C). The average decrease in temperature with altitude (standard lapse rate) is 2°C (3.5°F) per 1,000 feet. Since this is an average, the exact value seldom exists; in fact, temperature sometimes increases with altitude (an inversion). The most frequent type of ground- or surface-based **temperature inversion** is one that is produced by terrestrial radiation on a clear, relatively still night.

**ALL**
**3383.** A temperature inversion would most likely result in which weather condition?

A—Clouds with extensive vertical development above an inversion aloft.
B—Good visibility in the lower levels of the atmosphere and poor visibility above an inversion aloft.
C—An increase in temperature as altitude is increased.

*An increase in temperature with altitude is defined as an inversion. An inversion often develops near the ground on clear, cool nights when wind is light. The ground radiates heat and cools much faster than the overlying air. Air in contact with the ground becomes cold while the temperature a few hundred feet above changes very little. Thus, the temperature increases with height. A ground-based inversion usually means poor visibility. (I21) — AC 00-6A, Chapter 2*

Answer (A) is incorrect because a temperature inversion will not result in vertical development, since warm air will not rise if the air above is warmer. Answer (B) is incorrect because a temperature inversion will trap dust, smoke, and other particles, thus causing reduced visibilities.

**Answers**

| | | | |
|---|---|---|---|
| 3395 [B] | 3450 [C] | 3350 [A] | 3383 [C] |

ALL
**3384.** The most frequent type of ground or surface-based temperature inversion is that which is produced by

A—terrestrial radiation on a clear, relatively still night.
B—warm air being lifted rapidly aloft in the vicinity of mountainous terrain.
C—the movement of colder air under warm air, or the movement of warm air over cold air.

*An inversion often develops near the ground on clear, cool nights when wind is light. The ground radiates heat and cools much faster than the overlying air. Air in contact with the ground becomes cold while the temperature a few hundred feet above changes very little. Thus, the temperature increases with height. (I21) — AC 00-6A, Chapter 2*

*Answer (B) is incorrect because this is an example of convective activity. Answer (C) is incorrect because this describes a cold front and a warm front.*

# Moisture

Air has moisture (water vapor) in it. The water vapor content of air can be expressed in two different ways. The two commonly used terms are **relative humidity** and **dew point**.

Relative humidity relates the actual water vapor present in the air to that which could be present in the air. Temperature largely determines the maximum amount of water vapor air can hold. Warm air can hold more water vapor than can cold air. *See* Figure 6-4.

Air with 100% relative humidity is said to be saturated, and less than 100% is unsaturated.

Dew point is the temperature to which air must be cooled to become saturated by the water already present in the air. *See* Figure 6-5.

**Moisture** can be added to the air by either evaporation or sublimation. Moisture is removed from the air by either condensation or sublimation.

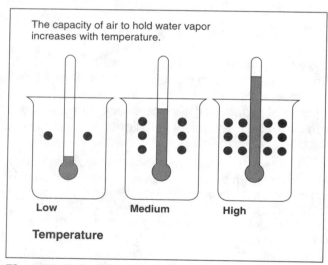

**Figure 6-4.** Capacity of air to hold water

**Figure 6-5.** Relative humidity and dew point

When water vapor condenses on large objects such as leaves, windshields, or airplanes, it will form **dew**; and when it condenses on microscopic particles such as salt, dust, or combustion by-products (condensation nuclei), it will form clouds or fog.

To summarize, relative humidity can be increased either by lowering the air temperature or by increasing the amount of moisture in the air. If the temperature and dew point spread is small and decreasing, condensation is about to occur. If the temperature is above freezing, the weather most likely to develop will be fog or low clouds.

ALL
**3397.** What is meant by the term "dewpoint"?

A—The temperature at which condensation and evaporation are equal.
B—The temperature at which dew will always form.
C—The temperature to which air must be cooled to become saturated.

*Dew point is the temperature to which air must be cooled to become saturated by the water vapor already present in the air. (I24) — AC 00-6A, Chapter 5*

Answer (A) is incorrect because evaporation is not directly related to the dew point. Answer (B) is incorrect because dew will form only when an object cools below the dew point of the surrounding air.

ALL
**3398.** The amount of water vapor which air can hold depends on the

A—dewpoint.
B—air temperature.
C—stability of the air.

*Temperature largely determines the maximum amount of water vapor air can hold. (I24) — AC 00-6A, Chapter 5*

ALL
**3399.** Clouds, fog, or dew will always form when

A—water vapor condenses.
B—water vapor is present.
C—relative humidity reaches 100 percent.

*As water vapor condenses or sublimates on condensation nuclei, liquid or ice particles begin to grow. Some condensation nuclei have an affinity for water and can induce condensation or sublimation even when air is almost, but not completely, saturated. (I24) — AC 00-6A, Chapter 5*

Answer (B) is incorrect because the presence of water vapor does not result in clouds, fog, or dew unless condensation occurs. Answer (C) is incorrect because it is possible to have 100% humidity without the occurrence of condensation, which is necessary for clouds, fog, or dew to form.

ALL
**3400.** What are the processes by which moisture is added to unsaturated air?

A—Evaporation and sublimation.
B—Heating and condensation.
C—Supersaturation and evaporation.

*Evaporation is the changing of liquid water to invisible water vapor. Sublimation is the changing of solid water directly to the vapor phase or water vapor to ice, by passing the liquid state in each process. (I24) — AC 00-6A, Chapter 5*

Answer (B) is incorrect because heating and condensation alone do not add moisture to unsaturated air. Answer (C) is incorrect because "supersaturation" does not fit the context of the question.

ALL
**3444.** If the temperature/dewpoint spread is small and decreasing, and the temperature is 62°F, what type weather is most likely to develop?

A—Freezing precipitation.
B—Thunderstorms.
C—Fog or low clouds.

*With a small temperature/dew point spread, the air is close to saturation. This will usually result in fog or low clouds. Anticipate fog when the temperature/dew point spread is 5°F or less and decreasing. (I31) — AC 00-6A, Chapter 12*

Answer (A) is incorrect because precipitation will not freeze at a temperature of 62°F. Answer (B) is incorrect because temperature/dew point spread does not relate to the development of thunderstorms.

**Answers**

| | | | | |
|---|---|---|---|---|
| 3397 [C] | 3398 [B] | 3399 [A] | 3400 [A] | 3444 [C] |

# Air Masses and Fronts

When a body of air comes to rest on, or moves slowly over, an extensive area having fairly uniform properties of temperature and moisture, the air takes on these properties. The area over which the air mass acquires its identifying distribution of temperature and moisture is its "source region." As this air mass moves from its source region, it tends to take on the properties of the new underlying surface. The trend toward change is called air mass modification.

A **ridge** is an elongated area of high pressure. A **trough** is an elongated area of low pressure. All fronts lie in troughs. A **cold front** is the leading edge of an advancing cold air mass. A **warm front** is the leading edge of an advancing warm air mass. Warm fronts move about half as fast as cold fronts. **Frontal waves** and **cyclones** (areas of low pressure) usually form on slow-moving cold fronts or stationary fronts. Figure 6-6 shows the symbols that would appear on a weather map.

The physical manifestations of a warm or cold front can be different with each front. They vary with the speed of the air mass on the move and the degree of stability of the air mass being overtaken. A stable air mass forced aloft will continue to exhibit stable characteristics, while an unstable air mass forced to ascend will continue to be characterized by cumulus clouds, turbulence, showery precipitation, and good visibility.

Frontal passage will be indicated by the following discontinuities:

1. A temperature change (the most easily recognizable discontinuity);

2. A continuous decrease in pressure followed by an increase as the front passes; and

3. A shift in the wind direction, speed, or both.

**Symbols on Surface Analysis (Surface Weather Maps)**

| Color | Symbol | Description |
|---|---|---|
| Blue | | Cold front |
| Blue | | Cold front aloft |
| Red | | Warm front |
| Red/Blue | | Stationary front |
| Purple | | Occluded front |
| Purple | | Squall line |
| Brown | | Trough |
| Yellow | | Ridge |

**Figure 6-6.** Weather map symbols

ALL
**3421.** The boundary between two different air masses is referred to as a

A—frontolysis.
B—frontogenesis.
C—front.

*A front is the boundary between two different air masses. (I27) — AC 00-6A, Chapter 8*

ALL
**3422.** One of the most easily recognized discontinuities across a front is

A—a change in temperature.
B—an increase in cloud coverage.
C—an increase in relative humidity.

*Temperature is one of the most easily recognized discontinuities across a front. (I27) — AC 00-6A, Chapter 8*

Answer (B) is incorrect because cloud coverage is not always present across a front. Answer (C) is incorrect because relative humidity is not an easily recognized discontinuity across a front.

ALL
**3423.** One weather phenomenon which will always occur when flying across a front is a change in the

A—wind direction.
B—type of precipitation.
C—stability of the air mass.

*Wind direction always changes across a front. (I27) — AC 00-6A, Chapter 8*

Answer (B) is incorrect because precipitation does not always exist with a front. Answer (C) is incorrect because the stability on both sides of the front may be the same.

**Answers**

3421　[C]　　　　3422　[A]　　　　3423　[A]

GLI
**3451.** During which period is a sea breeze front most suitable for soaring flight?

A—Shortly after sunrise.
B—During the early forenoon.
C—During the afternoon.

*A sea breeze begins during early afternoon and reaches a maximum in the afternoon, subsiding around dusk. (I35) — AC 00-6A, Chapter 16*

# Stability of the Atmosphere

Atmospheric stability is defined as the resistance of the atmosphere to vertical motion. A stable atmosphere resists any upward or downward movement. An unstable atmosphere allows an upward or downward disturbance to grow into a vertical (convective) current.

Determining the stability of the atmosphere requires measuring the difference between the actual existing (ambient) temperature lapse rate of a given parcel of air and the dry adiabatic (3°C per 1,000 feet) lapse rate.

A stable layer of air would be associated with a temperature inversion. Warming from below, on the other hand, would decrease the stability of an air mass.

The conditions shown in Figure 6-7 can be characteristic of stable or unstable air masses.

| Unstable Air | Stable Air |
|---|---|
| Cumuliform clouds | Stratiform clouds and fog |
| Showery precipitation | Continuous precipitation |
| Rough air (turbulence) | Smooth air |
| Good visibility except in blowing obstructions | Fair to poor visibility in haze and smoke |

**Figure 6-7**

ALL
**3385.** Which weather conditions should be expected beneath a low-level temperature inversion layer when the relative humidity is high?

A—Smooth air, poor visibility, fog, haze, or low clouds.
B—Light wind shear, poor visibility, haze, and light rain.
C—Turbulent air, poor visibility, fog, low stratus type clouds, and showery precipitation.

*A ground-based inversion leads to poor visibility by trapping fog, smoke, and other restrictions into low levels of the atmosphere. The layer is stable and convection is suppressed. (I21) — AC 00-6A, Chapter 2*

Answer (B) is incorrect because wind shears would occur above the inversion. Answer (C) is incorrect because showery precipitation and turbulent air are not associated with the presence of a low-level temperature inversion.

ALL
**3403.** What measurement can be used to determine the stability of the atmosphere?

A—Atmospheric pressure.
B—Actual lapse rate.
C—Surface temperature.

*The difference between the existing lapse rate of a given mass of air and the adiabatic rates of cooling in upward moving air determines if the air is stable or unstable. (I25) — AC 00-6A, Chapter 6*

ALL
**3404.** What would decrease the stability of an air mass?

A—Warming from below.
B—Cooling from below.
C—Decrease in water vapor.

*When air near the surface is warm and moist, suspect instability. Surface heating, cooling aloft, converging or upslope winds, or an invading mass of colder air may lead to instability and cumuliform clouds. (I25) — AC 00-6A, Chapter 6*

Answer (B) is incorrect because cooling from the air below would increase the stability of the air. Answer (C) is incorrect because an increase in water vapor will result in a decrease in stability.

**Answers**

| | | | |
|---|---|---|---|
| 3451 [C] | 3385 [A] | 3403 [B] | 3404 [A] |

ALL
**3405.** What is a characteristic of stable air?

A—Stratiform clouds.
B—Unlimited visibility.
C—Cumulus clouds.

*Since stable air resists convection, clouds in stable air form in horizontal, sheet-like layers or "strata." (I25) — AC 00-6A, Chapter 6*

Answers (B) and (C) are incorrect because unlimited visibility and cumulus clouds are characteristics of unstable air.

ALL
**3408.** What feature is associated with a temperature inversion?

A—A stable layer of air.
B—An unstable layer of air.
C—Chinook winds on mountain slopes.

*If the temperature increases with altitude through a layer (an inversion), the layer is stable and convection is suppressed. (I25) — AC 00-6A, Chapter 6*

ALL
**3412.** What are characteristics of a moist, unstable air mass?

A—Cumuliform clouds and showery precipitation.
B—Poor visibility and smooth air.
C—Stratiform clouds and showery precipitation.

*Characteristics of a moist, unstable air mass include cumuliform clouds, showery precipitation, rough air (turbulence), and good visibility (except in blowing obstructions). (I25) — AC 00-6A, Chapter 6*

ALL
**3413.** What are characteristics of unstable air?

A—Turbulence and good surface visibility.
B—Turbulence and poor surface visibility.
C—Nimbostratus clouds and good surface visibility.

*Characteristics of an unstable air mass include cumuliform clouds, showery precipitation, rough air (turbulence), and good visibility (except in blowing obstructions). (I25) — AC 00-6A, Chapter 6*

ALL
**3414.** A stable air mass is most likely to have which characteristic?

A—Showery precipitation.
B—Turbulent air.
C—Smooth air.

*Characteristics of a stable air mass include stratiform clouds and fog, continuous precipitation, smooth air, and fair to poor visibility in haze and smoke. (I25) — AC-00-6A, Chapter 6*

# Clouds

Stability determines which of two types of clouds will be formed: **cumuliform** or **stratiform**.

Cumuliform clouds are the billowy-type clouds having considerable vertical development, which enhances the growth rate of precipitation. They are formed in unstable conditions, and they produce showery precipitation made up of large water droplets. *See* Figure 6-8.

Stratiform clouds are the flat, more evenly based clouds formed in stable conditions. They produce steady, continuous light rain and drizzle made up of much smaller raindrops. *See* Figure 6-9.

Steady precipitation (in contrast to showery) preceding a front is an indication of stratiform clouds with little or no turbulence.

Clouds are divided into four families according to their height range: low, middle, high, and clouds with extensive vertical development. *See* Figure 6-10.

The first three families—low, middle, and high—are further classified according to the way they are formed. Clouds formed by vertical currents (unstable) are cumulus (heap) and are billowy in appearance. Clouds formed by the cooling of a stable layer are stratus (layered) and are flat and sheet-like in appearance. A further classification is the prefix "nimbo-" or suffix "-nimbus," which means raincloud.

**Answers**

| | | | | |
|---|---|---|---|---|
| 3405 [A] | 3408 [A] | 3412 [A] | 3413 [A] | 3414 [C] |

**Figure 6-8.** Cumulus clouds

**Figure 6-9.** Stratiform clouds

**Figure 6-10.** Cloud families

High clouds, called **cirrus**, are composed mainly of ice crystals; therefore, they are least likely to contribute to structural icing (since it requires water droplets).

The base of a cloud (AGL) that is formed by vertical currents (cumuliform clouds) can be roughly calculated by dividing the difference between the surface temperature and dew point by 4.4 and multiplying the remainder by 1,000. The convergence of the temperature and the dew point lapse rate is 4.4°F per 1,000 feet.

**Problem:** What is the approximate base of the cumulus clouds if the surface air temperature is 70°F and the dew point is 61°F?

**Solution:**

Use the following steps:

1.   70°F   (Temperature)
    − 61°F   (Dew point)
    ———
      9°F

2.  9 ÷ 4.4 = 2.05 or 2

3.  2 x 1,000 = 2,000 feet (base of cloud, AGL)

ALL

**3406.** Moist, stable air flowing upslope can be expected to

A—produce stratus type clouds.
B—cause showers and thunderstorms.
C—develop convective turbulence.

*When stable air is forced upward the air tends to retain horizontal flow and any cloudiness is flat and stratified. (I25) — AC 00-6A, Chapter 6*

ALL

**3407.** If an unstable air mass is forced upward, what type clouds can be expected?

A—Stratus clouds with little vertical development.
B—Stratus clouds with considerable associated turbulence.
C—Clouds with considerable vertical development and associated turbulence.

*When unstable air is forced upward, the disturbance grows. Any resulting cloudiness shows extensive vertical development. (I25) — AC 00-6A, Chapter 6*

ALL

**3424.** Steady precipitation preceding a front is an indication of

A—stratiform clouds with moderate turbulence.
B—cumuliform clouds with little or no turbulence.
C—stratiform clouds with little or no turbulence.

*Precipitation from stratiform clouds is usually steady and there is little or no turbulence. (I27) — AC 00-6A, Chapter 8*

ALL

**3433.** The conditions necessary for the formation of cumulonimbus clouds are a lifting action and

A—unstable air containing an excess of condensation nuclei.
B—unstable, moist air.
C—either stable or unstable air.

*For a cumulonimbus cloud or thunderstorm to form, the air must have:*

1.  *Sufficient water vapor,*

2.  *An unstable lapse rate, and*

3.  *An initial upward boost (lifting) to start the storm process in motion.*

*(I30) — AC 00-6A, Chapter 11*

**Answers**

3406 [A]     3407 [C]     3424 [C]     3433 [B]

ALL
**3409.** What is the approximate base of the cumulus clouds if the surface air temperature at 1,000 feet MSL is 70°F and the dewpoint is 48°F?

A—4,000 feet MSL.
B—5,000 feet MSL.
C—6,000 feet MSL.

*When lifted, unsaturated air cools at approximately 5.4°F per 1,000 feet. The dew point cools at approximately 1°F per 1,000 feet. Therefore, the convergence of the temperature and dew point lapse rates is 4.4°F per 1,000 feet. The base of a cloud (AGL) that is formed by vertical currents can be roughly calculated by dividing the difference between the surface temperature and the dew point by 4.4 and multiplying the remainder by 1,000.*

*1.  70°F  surface temperature*
    *− 48°F  dew point*
    *―――*
    *22°F*

*2.  22 ÷ 4.4 = 5*

*3.  5 x 1,000 = 5,000 feet AGL*

*4.  5,000  feet AGL*
    *+ 1,000  feet field elevation*
    *―――*
    *6,000  feet MSL*

*(I25) — AC 00-6A, Chapter 6*


ALL
**3410.** At approximately what altitude above the surface would the pilot expect the base of cumuliform clouds if the surface air temperature is 82°F and the dewpoint is 38°F?

A—9,000 feet AGL.
B—10,000 feet AGL.
C—11,000 feet AGL.

*When lifted, unsaturated air cools at approximately 5.4°F per 1,000 feet. The dew point cools at approximately 1°F per 1,000 feet. Therefore, the convergence of the temperature and dew point lapse rates is 4.4°F per 1,000 feet. The base of a cloud (AGL) that is formed by vertical currents can be roughly calculated by dividing the difference between the surface temperature and the dew point by 4.4 and multiplying the remainder by 1,000.*

*1.  82°F  surface temperature*
    *− 38°F  dew point*
    *―――*
    *44°F*

*2.  44 ÷ 4.4 = 10*

*3.  10 x 1,000 = 10,000 feet AGL*

*(I25) — AC 00-6A, Chapter 6*


ALL
**3415.** The suffix "nimbus," used in naming clouds, means

A—a cloud with extensive vertical development.
B—a rain cloud.
C—a middle cloud containing ice pellets.

*The prefix "nimbo-" or suffix "-nimbus" means rain cloud. (I26) — AC 00-6A, Chapter 7*


ALL
**3416.** Clouds are divided into four families according to their

A—outward shape.
B—height range.
C—composition.

*For identification purposes, clouds are divided into four families: high clouds, middle clouds, low clouds, and clouds with extensive vertical development. (I26) — AC 00-6A, Chapter 7*


**Answers**

| 3409 | [C] | 3410 | [B] | 3415 | [B] | 3416 | [B] |

# Turbulence

Cumulus clouds are formed by convective currents (heating from below); therefore, a pilot can expect turbulence below or inside cumulus clouds, especially towering cumulus clouds. The greatest turbulence could be expected inside cumulonimbus clouds.

If severe turbulence is encountered either inside or outside of clouds, the airplane's airspeed should be reduced to maneuvering speed and the pilot should attempt to maintain a level flight attitude because the amount of excess load that can be imposed on the wing will be decreased. Any attempt to maintain a constant altitude will greatly increase the stresses that are applied to the aircraft.

ALL
**3419.** What clouds have the greatest turbulence?

A—Towering cumulus.
B—Cumulonimbus.
C—Nimbostratus.

*Cumulonimbus are the ultimate manifestation of instability. They are vertically-developed clouds of large dimensions with dense boiling tops, often crowned with thick veils of dense cirrus (the anvil). Nearly the entire spectrum of flying hazards are contained in these clouds including violent turbulence. (I26) — AC 00-6A, Chapter 7*

ALL
**3417.** An almond or lens-shaped cloud which appears stationary, but which may contain winds of 50 knots or more, is referred to as

A—an inactive frontal cloud.
B—a funnel cloud.
C—a lenticular cloud.

*Crests of standing waves may be marked by stationary, lens-shaped clouds known as standing lenticular clouds. (I26) — AC 00-6A, Chapter 7*

ALL
**3418.** Crests of standing mountain waves may be marked by stationary, lens-shaped clouds known as

A—mammatocumulus clouds.
B—standing lenticular clouds.
C—roll clouds.

*Crests of standing waves may be marked by stationary, lens-shaped clouds known as standing lenticular clouds. (I26) — AC 00-6A, Chapter 7*

ALL
**3420.** What cloud types would indicate convective turbulence?

A—Cirrus clouds.
B—Nimbostratus clouds.
C—Towering cumulus clouds.

*Towering cumulus signifies a relatively deep layer of unstable air. They show considerable vertical development and have billowing cauliflower tops. Showers can result from these clouds. Expect very strong turbulence, and perhaps some clear icing above the freezing level. (I26) — AC 00-6A, Chapter 7*

ALL
**3425.** Possible mountain wave turbulence could be anticipated when winds of 40 knots or greater blow

A—across a mountain ridge, and the air is stable.
B—down a mountain valley, and the air is unstable.
C—parallel to a mountain peak, and the air is stable.

*Always anticipate possible mountain wave turbulence when strong winds of 40 knots or greater blow across a mountain or ridge and the air is stable. (I28) — AC 00-6A, Chapter 9*

**Answers**

3419 [B]   3417 [C]   3418 [B]   3420 [C]   3425 [A]

**ALL**
**3442.** Upon encountering severe turbulence, which flight condition should the pilot attempt to maintain?

A—Constant altitude and airspeed.
B—Constant angle of attack.
C—Level flight attitude.

*The primary concern is to avoid undue stress on the airframe. This can best be done by attempting to maintain a constant attitude while keeping the airspeed below design maneuvering speed (V$_A$). (I30) — AC 00-6A, Chapter 11*

Answer (A) is incorrect because attempting to maintain a constant altitude or airspeed may result in overstressing the aircraft. Answer (B) is incorrect because a constant angle of attack would be impossible to maintain with the wind shear and shifts encountered in severe turbulence.

# Thunderstorms

Thunderstorms present many hazards to flying. Three conditions necessary to the formation of a thunderstorm are:

1. Sufficient water vapor;

2. An unstable lapse rate; and

3. An initial upward boost (lifting).

The initial upward boost can be caused by heating from below, frontal lifting, or by mechanical lifting (wind blowing air upslope on a mountain).

There are three stages of a thunderstorm: the cumulus, mature, and dissipating stages. *See* Figure 6-11.

The **cumulus stage** is characterized by continuous updrafts, and these updrafts create low-pressure areas. Thunderstorms reach their greatest intensity during the **mature stage**, which is characterized by updrafts and downdrafts inside the cloud. Precipitation inside the cloud aids in the development of these downdrafts, and the start of rain from the base of the cloud signals the beginning of the mature stage. The precipitation that evaporates before it reaches the ground is called **virga**. The **dissipating stage** of a thunderstorm is characterized predominantly by downdrafts.

**Figure 6-11.** Stages of thunderstorms

**Lightning** is always associated with a thunderstorm.

**Hail** is formed inside thunderstorms by the constant freezing, melting, and refreezing of water as it is carried about by the up- and downdrafts.

A pilot should always expect the hazardous and invisible atmospheric phenomena called **wind shear turbulence** when operating anywhere near a thunderstorm (within 20 NM).

Thunderstorms that generally produce the most intense hazard to aircraft are called **squall-line thunderstorms**. These non-frontal, narrow bands of thunderstorms often develop ahead of a cold front.

**Embedded thunderstorms** are those that are obscured by massive cloud layers and cannot be seen.

**Answers**
3442   [C]

ALL
**3434.** What feature is normally associated with the cumulus stage of a thunderstorm?

A—Roll cloud.
B—Continuous updraft.
C—Frequent lightning.

*The key feature of the cumulus stage is an updraft. Precipitation beginning to fall from the cloudbase is the signal that a downdraft has developed also and a cell has entered the mature stage. (I30) — AC 00-6A, Chapter 11*

Answer (A) is incorrect because a roll cloud is associated with a mountain wave. Answer (C) is incorrect because frequent lightning may be present in any stage.

ALL
**3435.** Which weather phenomenon signals the beginning of the mature stage of a thunderstorm?

A—The appearance of an anvil top.
B—Precipitation beginning to fall.
C—Maximum growth rate of the clouds.

*The key feature of the cumulus stage is an updraft. Precipitation beginning to fall from the cloudbase is the signal that a downdraft has developed also and the cell has entered the mature stage. (I30) — AC 00-6A, Chapter 11*

Answer (A) is incorrect because the appearance of an anvil top is characteristic of the dissipating stage. Answer (C) is incorrect because the maximum growth rate of the clouds is during the mature stage of a thunderstorm, but it does not signal the beginning of that stage.

ALL
**3436.** What conditions are necessary for the formation of thunderstorms?

A—High humidity, lifting force, and unstable conditions.
B—High humidity, high temperature, and cumulus clouds.
C—Lifting force, moist air, and extensive cloud cover.

*For a cumulonimbus cloud or thunderstorm to form, the air must have:*

1. *Sufficient water vapor,*

2. *An unstable lapse rate, and*

3. *An initial upward boost (lifting) to start the storm process in motion.*

*(I30) — AC 00-6A, Chapter 11*

ALL
**3437.** During the life cycle of a thunderstorm, which stage is characterized predominately by downdrafts?

A—Cumulus.
B—Dissipating.
C—Mature.

*Downdrafts characterize the dissipating stage of the thunderstorm cell and the storm dies rapidly. (I30) — AC 00-6A, Chapter 11*

Answer (A) is incorrect because updrafts occur during the cumulus stage. Answer (C) is incorrect because both updrafts and downdrafts occur during the mature stage.

ALL
**3438.** Thunderstorms reach their greatest intensity during the

A—mature stage.
B—downdraft stage.
C—cumulus stage.

*All thunderstorm hazards reach their greatest intensity during the mature stage. (I30) — AC 00-6A, Chapter 11*

ALL
**3439.** Thunderstorms which generally produce the most intense hazard to aircraft are

A—squall line thunderstorms.
B—steady-state thunderstorms.
C—warm front thunderstorms.

*A squall line is a non-frontal, narrow band of active thunderstorms. The line may be too long to easily detour and too wide and severe to penetrate. It often contains severe steady-state thunderstorms and presents the single, most intense weather hazard to aircraft. (I30) — AC 00-6A, Chapter 11*

ALL
**3440.** A nonfrontal, narrow band of active thunderstorms that often develop ahead of a cold front is known as a

A—prefrontal system.
B—squall line.
C—dry line.

*A squall line is a nonfrontal, narrow band of active thunderstorms. The line may be too long to easily detour and too wide and severe to penetrate. It often contains severe steady-state thunderstorms and presents the single, most intense weather hazard to aircraft. (I30) — AC 00-6A, Chapter 11*

**Answers**

| 3434 | [B] | 3435 | [B] | 3436 | [A] | 3437 | [B] | 3438 | [A] | 3439 | [A] |
| 3440 | [B] | | | | | | | | | | |

**ALL**
**3441.** If there is thunderstorm activity in the vicinity of an airport at which you plan to land, which hazardous atmospheric phenomenon might be expected on the landing approach?

A—Precipitation static.
B—Wind-shear turbulence.
C—Steady rain.

*Wind shear is an invisible hazard associated with all thunderstorms. Shear turbulence has been encountered 20 miles laterally from a severe storm. (I30) — AC 00-6A, Chapter 11*

Answer (A) is incorrect because precipitation static is not considered a hazardous atmospheric phenomenon. Answer (C) is incorrect because showery precipitation is a characteristic of thunderstorm activity.

**ALL**
**3452.** Which weather phenomenon is always associated with a thunderstorm?

A—Lightning.
B—Heavy rain.
C—Hail.

*A thunderstorm is, in general, a local storm invariably produced by a cumulonimbus cloud, and is always accompanied by lightning and thunder. (I36) — AC 00-6A, Chapter 11*

**GLI**
**3449.** Which is considered to be the most hazardous condition when soaring in the vicinity of thunderstorms?

A—Static electricity.
B—Lightning.
C—Wind shear and turbulence.

*During the mature stage of a thunderstorm, updrafts and downdrafts in close proximity create strong vertical shears and a very turbulent environment. A lightning strike can puncture the skin of an aircraft and damage communication and navigation equipment. (I35) — AC 00-6A, Chapter 11*

# Wind Shear

Wind shear is defined as a change in wind direction and/or speed over a very short distance in the atmosphere. This can occur at any level of the atmosphere and can be detected by the pilot as a sudden change in airspeed.

**Low-level** (low-altitude) **wind shear** can be expected during strong temperature inversions, on all sides of a thunderstorm and directly below the cell. A pilot can expect a wind shear zone in a temperature inversion whenever the wind speed at 2,000 feet to 4,000 feet above the surface is at least 25 knots.

Low-level wind shear can also be found near frontal activity because winds can be significantly different in the two air masses which meet to form the front.

In warm front conditions, the most critical period is before the front passes. Warm front shear may exist below 5,000 feet for about 6 hours before surface passage of the front. The wind shear associated with a warm front is usually more extreme than that found in cold fronts.

The shear associated with cold fronts is usually found behind the front. If the front is moving at 30 knots or more, the shear zone will be 5,000 feet above the surface 3 hours after frontal passage.

Basically, there are two potentially hazardous shear situations—the loss of a tailwind or the loss of a headwind.

A tailwind may shear to either a calm or headwind component. The airspeed initially increases, the aircraft pitches up, and altitude increases. Lower than normal power would be required initially, followed by a further decrease as the shear is encountered, and then an increase as the glide slope is regained. *See* Figure 6-12 on the next page.

**Answers**
3441  [B]     3452  [A]     3449  [C]

A headwind may shear to a calm or tailwind component. Initially, the airspeed decreases, the aircraft pitches down, and altitude decreases. *See* Figure 6-13.

Some airports can report boundary winds as well as the wind at the tower. When a tower reports a boundary wind which is significantly different from the airport wind, there is a possibility of hazardous wind shear.

**Figure 6-12.** Tailwind shearing to headwind or calm

**Figure 6-13.** Headwind shearing to tailwind or calm

ALL
**3426.** Where does wind shear occur?

A—Only at higher altitudes.
B—Only at lower altitudes.
C—At all altitudes, in all directions.

*Wind shear may be associated with either a wind shift or a wind speed gradient at any level in the atmosphere. (I28) — AC 00-6A, Chapter 9*

ALL
**3427.** When may hazardous wind shear be expected?

A—When stable air crosses a mountain barrier where it tends to flow in layers forming lenticular clouds.
B—In areas of low-level temperature inversion, frontal zones, and clear air turbulence.
C—Following frontal passage when stratocumulus clouds form indicating mechanical mixing.

*Hazardous wind shear can occur near the ground with either thunderstorms or a strong temperature inversion. (I28) — AC 00-6A, Chapter 9*

Answer (A) is incorrect because turbulence can be expected when stable air crosses a mountain barrier. Answer (C) is incorrect because turbulence can be expected following frontal passage when stratocumulus clouds form, indicating mechanical mixing.

ALL
**3428.** A pilot can expect a wind-shear zone in a temperature inversion whenever the windspeed at 2,000 to 4,000 feet above the surface is at least

A—10 knots.
B—15 knots.
C—25 knots.

*An increase in temperature with altitude is defined as a temperature inversion. A pilot can be relatively certain of a shear zone in the inversion if the pilot knows the wind at 2,000 to 4,000 feet is 25 knots or more. (I28) — AC 00-6A, Chapter 9*

**Answers**

| 3426 [C] | 3427 [B] | 3428 [C] |
| --- | --- | --- |

# Icing

**Structural icing** occurs on an aircraft whenever supercooled condensed droplets of water make contact with any part of the aircraft that is also at a temperature below freezing. An in-flight condition necessary for structural icing to form is visible moisture (clouds or raindrops).

Icing in precipitation (rain) is of concern to the VFR pilot because it can occur outside of clouds. Aircraft structural ice will most likely have the highest accumulation in freezing rain which indicates warmer temperature at a higher altitude. *See* Figure 6-14. The effects of structural icing on an aircraft may be seen in Figure 6-15.

The presence of ice pellets at the surface is evidence that there is freezing rain at a higher altitude, while wet snow indicates that the temperature at your altitude is above freezing. A situation conducive to any icing would be flying in the vicinity of a front.

**Clear – Hard and Glossy**
Temperature 0° to -15°C
Large water droplets
Cumuliform clouds

**Rime – Brittle and Frost-like**
Temperature 0° to -10°C
Small water droplets
Stratiform clouds

**Figure 6-14.** Clear and rime ice

Lift lessens

Drag increases

Thrust falls off

Weight grows
Stalling speed increases

**Effects of icing are cumulative**

**Figure 6-15.** Effects of structural icing

**ALL**
**3402.** The presence of ice pellets at the surface is evidence that there

A—are thunderstorms in the area.
B—has been cold frontal passage.
C—is a temperature inversion with freezing rain at a higher altitude.

*Ice pellets always indicate freezing rain at higher altitude. (I24) — AC 00-6A, Chapter 5*

AIR, GLI, RTC
**3429.** One in-flight condition necessary for structural icing to form is

A—small temperature/dewpoint spread.
B—stratiform clouds.
C—visible moisture.

*Two conditions are necessary for structural icing in flight:*

*1. The aircraft must be flying through visible water such as rain or cloud droplets, and*

*2. The temperature at the point where the moisture strikes the aircraft must be 0°C (32°F) or colder.*

*(I28) — AC 00-6A, Chapter 9*

AIR, GLI, RTC
**3430.** In which environment is aircraft structural ice most likely to have the highest accumulation rate?

A—Cumulus clouds with below freezing temperatures.
B—Freezing drizzle.
C—Freezing rain.

*A condition favorable for rapid accumulation of clear icing is freezing rain below a frontal surface. (I29) — AC 00-6A, Chapter 10*

*Answers (A) and (B) are incorrect because although cumulus clouds with below-freezing temperatures and freezing drizzle are conducive to structural icing, they will not have as high an accumulation rate as freezing rain.*

**Answers**

| | | | | | |
|---|---|---|---|---|---|
| 3402 | [C] | 3429 | [C] | 3430 | [C] |

# Fog

Fog is a surface-based cloud (restricting visibility) composed of either water droplets or ice crystals. Fog may form by cooling the air to its dew point or by adding moisture to the air near the ground. A small temperature/dew point spread is essential to the formation of fog. An abundance of condensation nuclei from combustion products makes fog prevalent in industrial areas.

Fog is classified by the way it is formed.

**Radiation fog (ground fog)** is formed when terrestrial radiation cools the ground, which in turn cools the air in contact with it. When the air is cooled to its dew point (or within a few degrees), fog will form. This fog will form most readily in warm, moist air over low, flatland areas on clear, calm (no wind) nights.

**Advection fog (sea fog)** is formed when warm, moist air moves (wind is required) over colder ground or water (e.g., an air mass moving inland from the coast in winter).

**Upslope fog** is formed when moist, stable air is cooled to its dew point as it moves (wind is required) up sloping terrain. Cooling will be at the dry adiabatic lapse rate of approximately 3°C per 1,000 feet.

**Precipitation (rain or drizzle)-induced fog** is most commonly associated with frontal activity and is formed by relatively warm drizzle or rain falling through cooler air. Evaporation from the precipitation saturates the cool air and fog forms. This fog is especially critical because it occurs in the proximity of precipitation and other possible hazards such as icing, turbulence, and thunderstorms.

**Steam fog** forms in the winter when cold, dry air passes from land areas over comparatively warm ocean waters. Low-level turbulence can occur and icing can become hazardous in a steam fog.

ALL
**3443.** What situation is most conducive to the formation of radiation fog?

A—Warm, moist air over low, flatland areas on clear, calm nights.
B—Moist, tropical air moving over cold, offshore water.
C—The movement of cold air over much warmer water.

*Conditions favorable for radiation fog are clear sky, little or no wind, and small temperature/dew point spread (high relative humidity). Radiation fog is restricted to land because water surfaces cool little from nighttime radiation. (I31) — AC 00-6A, Chapter 12*

*Answers (B) and (C) are incorrect because radiation fog will not form over water since water surfaces cool little from nighttime radiation.*

ALL
**3445.** In which situation is advection fog most likely to form?

A—A warm, moist air mass on the windward side of mountains.
B—An air mass moving inland from the coast in winter.
C—A light breeze blowing colder air out to sea.

*Advection fog forms when moist air moves over colder ground or water. It is most common along coastal areas. This fog frequently forms offshore as a result of cold water, then is carried inland by the wind. (I31) — AC 00-6A, Chapter 12*

*Answer (A) is incorrect because a warm, moist air mass on the windward side of mountains will form upslope fog and/or rain. Answer (C) is incorrect because a light breeze blowing colder air out to sea will form steam fog.*

ALL
**3446.** What types of fog depend upon wind in order to exist?

A—Radiation fog and ice fog.
B—Steam fog and ground fog.
C—Advection fog and upslope fog.

*Advection fog forms when moist air moves over colder ground or water. It is most common along coastal areas, but often develops deep in continental areas. Advection fog deepens as wind speed increases up to about 15 knots. Wind much stronger than 15 knots lifts the fog into a layer of low stratus or stratocumulus. Upslope fog forms as a result of moist, stable air being cooled adiabatically as it moves up sloping terrain. Once upslope wind ceases, the fog dissipates. (I31) — AC 00-6A, Chapter 12*

*Answers (A) and (B) are incorrect because radiation, ice, and ground fog do not depend upon wind in order to exist.*

**Answers**

3443 [A]    3445 [B]    3446 [C]

**ALL**
**3447.** Low-level turbulence can occur and icing can become hazardous in which type of fog?

A—Rain-induced fog.
B—Upslope fog.
C—Steam fog.

*Steam fog forms in the winter when cold, dry air passes from land areas over comparatively warm ocean waters. Low-level turbulence can occur and icing can become hazardous in a steam fog. (I33) — AC 00-6A, Chapter 14*

# Frost

Frost is described as ice deposits formed by sublimation on a surface when the temperature of the collecting surface is at or below the dew point of the adjacent air and the dew point is below freezing.

Frost causes early airflow separation on an airfoil resulting in a loss of lift. Therefore, all frost should be removed from the lifting surfaces of an airplane before flight or it may prevent the airplane from becoming airborne.

**ALL**
**3401.** Which conditions result in the formation of frost?

A—The temperature of the collecting surface is at or below freezing when small droplets of moisture fall on the surface.
B—The temperature of the collecting surface is at or below the dewpoint of the adjacent air and the dewpoint is below freezing.
C—The temperature of the surrounding air is at or below freezing when small drops of moisture fall on the collecting surface.

*Frost forms in much the same way as dew. The difference is that the dew point of surrounding air must be colder than freezing. (I24) — AC 00-6A, Chapter 5*

*Answers (A) and (C) are incorrect because ice will form in these situations.*

**AIR, GLI**
**3206.** How will frost on the wings of an airplane affect takeoff performance?

A—Frost will disrupt the smooth flow of air over the wing, adversely affecting its lifting capability.
B—Frost will change the camber of the wing, increasing its lifting capability.
C—Frost will cause the airplane to become airborne with a higher angle of attack, decreasing the stall speed.

*The roughness of the surface of frost spoils the smooth flow of air, thus causing a slowing of the airflow. This slowing of the air causes early air flow separation over the affected airfoil, resulting in a loss of lift. Even a small amount of frost on airfoils may prevent an aircraft from becoming airborne at normal takeoff speed. (H300) — AC 61-23C, Chapter 1*

*Answer (B) is incorrect because frost will not change the shape of the wing. Answer (C) is incorrect because frost on the wings of an airplane will increase the stall speed.*

**AIR, GLI, RTC**
**3431.** Why is frost considered hazardous to flight?

A—Frost changes the basic aerodynamic shape of the airfoils, thereby decreasing lift.
B—Frost slows the airflow over the airfoils, thereby increasing control effectiveness.
C—Frost spoils the smooth flow of air over the wings, thereby decreasing lifting capability.

*The roughness of the surface of frost spoils the smooth flow of air, thus causing a slowing of the airflow. This slowing of the air causes early air flow separation over the affected airfoil, resulting in a loss of lift. Even a small amount of frost on airfoils may prevent an aircraft from becoming airborne at normal takeoff speed. (I29) — AC 00-6A, Chapter 10*

*Answer (A) is incorrect because frost does not change the basic aerodynamic shape of the airfoil. Answer (B) is incorrect because frost does not have an effect on the control effectiveness.*

**Answers**
3447 [C]      3401 [B]      3206 [A]      3431 [C]

AIR

**3432.** How does frost affect the lifting surfaces of an airplane on takeoff?

A—Frost may prevent the airplane from becoming airborne at normal takeoff speed.

B—Frost will change the camber of the wing, increasing lift during takeoff.

C—Frost may cause the airplane to become airborne with a lower angle of attack at a lower indicated airspeed.

*The roughness of the surface of frost spoils the smooth flow of air, thus causing a slowing of the airflow. This slowing of the air causes early air flow separation over the affected airfoil, resulting in a loss of lift. Even a small amount of frost on airfoils may prevent an aircraft from becoming airborne at normal takeoff speed. (I29) — AC 00-6A, Chapter 10*

Answer (B) is incorrect because frost does not change the basic aerodynamic shape of the airfoil. Answer (C) is incorrect because frost may prevent the aircraft from becoming airborne at normal takeoff speed and will not lower the angle of attack.

**Answers**

3432    [A]

# Chapter 7
# Weather Services

# Aviation Routine Weather Report (METAR)

An international weather reporting code is used for weather reports (METAR) and forecasts (TAFs) worldwide. The reports follow the format shown in Figure 7-1.

For aviation purposes, the ceiling is the lowest broken or overcast layer, or vertical visibility into an obscuration.

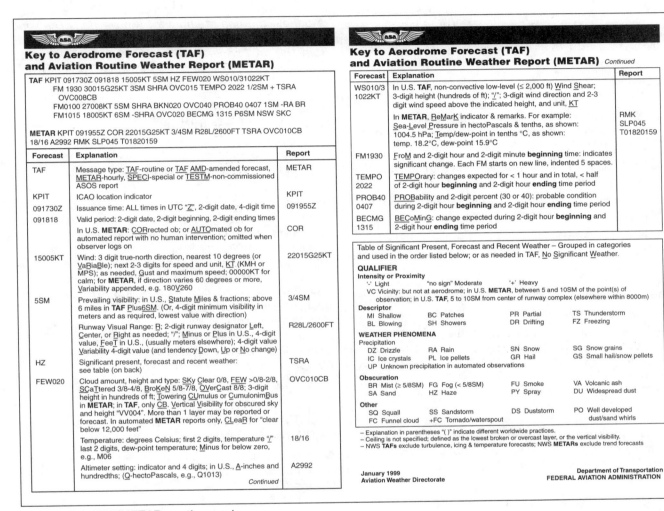

**Figure 7-1.** TAF/METAR weather card

**ALL**
**3462.** (Refer to Figure 12.) Which of the reporting stations have VFR weather?

A—All.
B—KINK, KBOI, and KJFK.
C—KINK, KBOI, and KLAX.

*IFR conditions are a ceiling less than 1,000 feet and/or visibility less than 3 miles.*

*KINK: Visibility is 15 statute miles and the sky is clear: VFR.*

*KBOI: Visibility is 30 statute miles and sky is scattered at 15,000 feet: VFR.*

*KLAX: Visibility is 6 statute miles with mist and the sky is scattered at 700 feet (SCT does not constitute a ceiling): VFR.*

*KMDW: Visibility is 1-1/2 statute miles with rain and the ceiling is overcast at 700 feet: IFR.*

*KJFK: Visibility is 1/2 statute mile with fog and the ceiling is overcast at 500 feet: IFR.*

*(I55) — AC 00-45E, Chapter 2*

**ALL**
**3463.** For aviation purposes, ceiling is defined as the height above the Earth's surface of the

A—lowest reported obscuration and the highest layer of clouds reported as overcast.
B—lowest broken or overcast layer or vertical visibility into an obscuration.
C—lowest layer of clouds reported as scattered, broken, or thin.

*For aviation purposes, the ceiling is the lowest broken or overcast layer, or vertical visibility into an obscuration. (I55) — AC 00-45E, Chapter 2*

**ALL**
**3464.** (Refer to Figure 12.) The wind direction and velocity at KJFK is from

A—180° true at 4 knots.
B—180° magnetic at 4 knots.
C—040° true at 18 knots.

*The wind is reported as a five-digit group (six digits if speed is over 99 knots). The first three digits is the direction the wind is blowing from in tens of degrees relative to true north, or "VRB" if the direction is variable. The next two digits is the speed in knots, or if over 99 knots, the next three digits. If the wind is gusty, it is reported as a "G" after the speed followed by the highest gust reported. The abbreviation "KT" is appended to denote the use of knots for wind speed. The wind group for KJFK is 18004KT which means the wind is from 180° at 4 knots. (I55) — AC 00-45E, Chapter 2*

**ALL**
**3465.** (Refer to Figure 12). What are the wind conditions at Wink, Texas (KINK)?

A—Calm.
B—110° at 12 knots, gusts 18 knots.
C—111° at 2 knots, gusts 18 knots.

*The wind is reported as a five-digit group (six digits if speed is over 99 knots). The first three digits is the direction the wind is blowing from in tens of degrees relative to true north, or "VRB" if the direction is variable. The next two digits is the speed in knots, or if over 99 knots, the next three digits. If the wind is gusty, it is reported as a "G" after the speed followed by the highest gust reported. The abbreviation "KT" is appended to denote the use of knots for wind speed. The wind group for KINK is 11012G18KT which means the wind is from 110° at 12 knots, with gusts to 18 knots. (I55) — AC 00-45E, Chapter 2*

**ALL**
**3466.** (Refer to Figure 12). The remarks section for KMDW has RAB35 listed. This entry means

A—blowing mist has reduced the visibility to 1-1/2 SM.
B—rain began at 1835Z.
C—the barometer has risen .35" Hg.

*The entry RAB35 means that rain began 35 minutes past the hour. (I55) — AC 00-45E, Chapter 2*

Answer (A) is incorrect because mist is reported as BR. Answer (C) is incorrect because there is no format for reporting a change in altimeter in a METAR.

**Answers**

3462　[C]　　　3463　[B]　　　3464　[A]　　　3465　[B]　　　3466　[B]

ALL

**3467.** (Refer to Figure 12.) What are the current conditions depicted for Chicago Midway Airport (KMDW)?

A—Sky 700 feet overcast, visibility 1-1/2 SM, rain

B—Sky 7000 feet overcast, visibility 1-1/2 SM, heavy rain

C—Sky 700 feet overcast, visibility 11, occasionally 2 SM, with rain.

*The current conditions at KMDW are 1-1/2 SM visibility (1-1/2SM) with rain (RA), ceiling overcast at 700 feet (OVC007). (I55) — AC 00-45E, Chapter 2*

# Pilot Weather Reports (PIREPs) (UA)

Aircraft in flight are the only means of directly observing cloud tops, icing, and turbulence; therefore, no observation is more timely than one made from the cockpit. While the FAA encourages pilots to report inflight weather, a report of any unforecast weather is required by regulation. A **PIREP** (identified by the letters "UA") is usually transmitted in a prescribed format. *See* Figure 7-2.

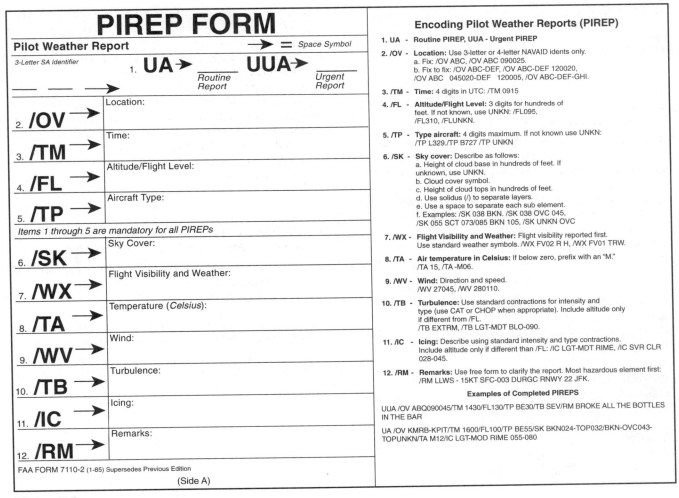

**Figure 7-2**

UA/OV KOKC-KTUL/TM 1800/FL120/TP BE90//SK BKN018-TOP055/OVC072-TOP089/CLR ABV/
TA M7/WV 08021/TB LGT 055-072/IC LGT-MOD RIME 072-089.

*Decodes as follows:*

Pilot report, Oklahoma City to Tulsa at 1800Z at 12,000 feet.

Type of aircraft is a Beech King Air 90.

The first cloud layer has a base of 1,800 feet broken, with tops at 5,500 feet.

The second cloud layer base is 7,200 feet overcast with tops at 8,900 feet.

It is clear above.

Outside air temperature is -7° Celsius.

The wind is 080° at 21 knots.

There is light turbulence between 5,500 feet and 7,200 feet.

There is light to moderate rime icing reported between 7,200 feet and 8,900 feet.

ALL
**3472.** (Refer to Figure 14.) The base and tops of the overcast layer reported by a pilot are

A—1,800 feet MSL and 5,500 feet MSL.
B—5,500 feet AGL and 7,200 feet MSL.
C—7,200 feet MSL and 8,900 feet MSL.

*Cloud layers in a PIREP are found after the "SK" heading. Height of the cloud base is given in hundreds of feet, then the cloud cover symbol (SCT, BKN, etc.) is given, followed by the height of cloud tops in hundreds of feet. A diagonal slash is used to separate cloud layers.*

*The base of the broken (BKN) layer was reported to be 1,800 feet and tops at 5,500 feet (BKN018-TOP055).*

*The question is asking for the overcast (OVC) layer that has a reported base at 7,200 feet and tops at 8,900 feet. All cloud heights in a PIREP are MSL (OVC072-TOP089). (I56) — AC 00-45E, Chapter 3*

ALL
**3473.** (Refer to Figure 14.) The wind and temperature at 12,000 feet MSL as reported by a pilot are

A—090° at 21 MPH and -9°F.
B—090° at 21 knots and -9°C.
C—080° at 21 knots and -7°C.

*Winds are given after the "WV" heading. Wind direction is listed first, followed by wind speed in knots. WV 08021/ means wind from 080° at 21 knots. Air temperature is given in 2 digits, (in degrees Celsius), after the "TA" heading. If below zero, it will be prefixed with an "M." Therefore, /TA M7/ means that the outside air temperature is -7°C. (I56) — AC 00-45E, Chapter 3*

ALL
**3474.** (Refer to Figure 14.) If the terrain elevation is 1,295 feet MSL, what is the height above ground level of the base of the ceiling?

A—505 feet AGL.
B—1,295 feet AGL.
C—6,586 feet AGL.

*Cloud layers in a PIREP are found after the "SK" heading. Height of the cloud base is given in hundreds of feet, then the cloud cover symbol (SCT, BKN, etc.) is given, followed by the height of the cloud tops in hundreds of feet. All cloud heights in a PIREP are MSL.*

*The first cloud layer was reported by a pilot to have bases at 1,800 feet and tops at 5,500 feet with broken (BKN) cloud cover (a broken cloud layer does constitute a ceiling).*

*If the field elevation is 1,295 feet MSL and the base of the first cloud layer (BKN) is 1,800 feet MSL, then the base of the ceiling is 505 feet AGL.*

```
  1,800  MSL
– 1,295  MSL
─────────────
    505  AGL
```

*(I56) — AC 00-45E, Chapter 3*

**Answers**

**ALL
3475.** (Refer to Figure 14.) The intensity of the turbulence reported at a specific altitude is

A—moderate from 5,500 feet to 7,200 feet.
B—moderate at 5,500 feet and at 7,200 feet.
C—light from 5,500 feet to 7,200 feet.

*Turbulence in a PIREP is found after the "TB" heading. /TB LGT 055-072/ means light turbulence between 5,500 feet MSL and 7,200 feet MSL. (I56) — AC 00-45E, Chapter 3*

**ALL
3476.** (Refer to Figure 14.) The intensity and type of icing reported by a pilot is

A—light to moderate.
B—light to moderate rime.
C—light to moderate clear.

*The intensity and type of icing is listed in a PIREP after the "IC" heading. /IC LGT-MOD RIME 072-089 means light (LGT) to moderate (MOD) rime icing from 7,200 feet MSL to 8,900 feet MSL. (I56) — AC 00-45E, Chapter 3*

# Terminal Aerodrome Forecast (TAF)

A Terminal Aerodrome Forecast (TAF) is a concise statement of the expected meteorological conditions at an airport during a specified period (usually 24 hours). TAFs use the same code used in the METAR weather reports (*See* Figure 7-1, page 7-3).

TAFs are issued in the following format:

TYPE / LOCATION / ISSUANCE TIME / VALID TIME / FORECAST

*Note:* The "/" above are for separation purposes and do not appear in the actual TAFs.

**ALL
3479.** (Refer to Figure 15.) What is the valid period for the TAF for KMEM?

A—1800Z to 1800Z.
B—1200Z to 1800Z.
C—1200Z to 1200Z.

*The valid period is the four-digit group of the forecast in UTC, usually a 24-hour period. FAA Figure 15 uses a six-digit group, and includes the date. The valid period for KMEM is a 24-hour period from 1800Z to 1800Z on the 12th of the month (121818). (I57) — AC 00-45E, Chapter 4*

**ALL
3480.** (Refer to Figure 15.) In the TAF for KMEM, what does "SHRA" stand for?

A—Rain showers.
B—A shift in wind direction is expected.
C—A significant change in precipitation is possible.

*"SH" stands for showers, and "RA" stands for rain. (I57) — AC 00-45E, Chapter 4*

Answers (B) and (C) are incorrect because a permanent change in existing conditions during the valid period of the TAF is indicated by the change groups FMHH (FroM) and BECMG (BECoMinG) HHhh.

**3481.** (Refer to Figure 15.) Between 1000Z and 1200Z the visibility at KMEM is forecast to be

A—1/2 statute mile.
B—3 statute miles.
C—6 statute miles.

*Between 1000Z and 1200Z, the visibility at KMEM is forecast to be 3 statute miles (BECMG 1012...3SM). (I57) — AC 00-45E, Chapter 4*

**3482.** (Refer to Figure 15.) What is the forecast wind for KMEM from 1600Z until the end of the forecast?

A—No significant wind.
B—Variable in direction at 4 knots.
C—Variable in direction at 6 knots.

*From 1600Z until the end of the forecast, wind will be variable in direction at 6 knots (VRB06KT). (I57) — AC 00-45E, Chapter 4*

**3483.** (Refer to Figure 15.) In the TAF from KOKC, the "FM (FROM) Group" is forecast for the hours from 1600Z to 2200Z with the wind from

A—160° at 10 knots.
B—180° at 10 knots, becoming 200° at 13 knots.
C—180° at 10 knots.

*The FROM group is forecast for the hours from 1600 (FM1600) to 2200Z (BECMG 2224) with the wind from 180° at 10 knots (18010KT). (I57) — AC 00-45E, Chapter 4*

*Answer (A) is incorrect because 18010 indicates the wind will be from 180. Answer (B) is incorrect because "BECMG" indicates another change group; the wind will change from 200 at 13 knots between 2200 and 2400Z.*

**3484.** (Refer to Figure 15.) In the TAF from KOKC, the clear sky becomes

A—overcast at 2,000 feet during the forecast period between 2200Z and 2400Z.
B—overcast at 200 feet with a 40% probability of becoming overcast at 600 feet during the forecast period between 2200Z and 2400Z.
C—overcast at 200 feet with the probability of becoming overcast at 400 feet during the forecast period between 2200Z and 2400Z.

*Between 2200Z and 2400Z (BECMG 2224), the sky will be overcast at 2,000 feet (OVC020). (I57) — AC 00-45E, Chapter 4*

**3485.** (Refer to Figure 15.) During the time period from 0600Z to 0800Z, what visibility is forecast for KOKC?

A—Greater than 6 statute miles.
B—Not forecasted.
C—Possibly 6 statute miles.

*During the period from 0600Z to 0800Z (0608), the visibilities are forecast to be greater than 6 statute miles (P6SM). (I57) — AC 00-45E, Chapter 4*

**3486.** (Refer to Figure 15.) The only cloud type forecast in TAF reports is

A—nimbostratus.
B—cumulonimbus.
C—scattered cumulus.

*Cumulonimbus clouds are the only cloud types forecast in TAFs. (I57) — AC 00-45E, Chapter 4*

**Answers**

| | | | | | |
|---|---|---|---|---|---|
| 3481 [B] | 3482 [C] | 3483 [C] | 3484 [A] | 3485 [A] | 3486 [B] |

# Aviation Area Forecast (FA)

The aviation Area Forecast is a forecast of general weather conditions over an area the size of several states. It is used to determine forecast en route weather and to interpolate conditions at airports which do not have TAFs issued.

The Area Forecast is issued 3 times a day, and is comprised of four sections: a communications and product header section, a precautionary statement section, and two weather sections; a SYNOPSIS section and a VFR CLOUDS/WX section.

ALL
**3478.** From which primary source should information be obtained regarding expected weather at the estimated time of arrival if your destination has no Terminal Forecast?

A—Low-Level Prognostic Chart.
B—Weather Depiction Chart.
C—Area Forecast.

*An Area Forecast (FA) is used to determine forecast enroute weather and to interpolate conditions at airports which do not have Terminal Forecasts (FT) issued. (I57) — AC 00-45E, Chapter 4*

ALL
**3487.** To best determine general forecast weather conditions over several states, the pilot should refer to

A—Aviation Area Forecasts.
B—Weather Depiction Charts.
C—Satellite Maps.

*An Area Forecast (FA) is a forecast of general conditions over an area the size of several states. (I57) — AC 00-45E, Chapter 4*

ALL
**3488.** (Refer to Figure 16.) What is the outlook for the southern half of Indiana after 0700Z?

A—VFR.
B—Scattered clouds at 3,000 feet AGL.
C—Scattered clouds at 10,000 feet.

*The Area Forecast for the southern half of Indiana (bottom of Figure 16) is forecasting scattered clouds at 3,000 feet AGL, another scattered cloud deck at 10,000 feet, with an outlook for VFR conditions. (I57) — AC 00-45E, Chapter 4*

ALL
**3489.** To determine the freezing level and areas of probable icing aloft, the pilot should refer to the

A—Inflight Aviation Weather Advisories.
B—Weather Depiction Chart.
C—Area Forecast.

*Freezing levels and probable icing aloft are found in AIRMETs and SIGMETs. Hazardous weather is not included in the area forecast (FA), but is included in the Inflight Aviation Weather Advisories. (I57) — AC 00-45E, Chapter 4*

**Answers**

| | | | |
|---|---|---|---|
| 3478 [C] | 3487 [A] | 3488 [A] | 3489 [A] |

ALL
**3490.** The section of the Area Forecast entitled "VFR CLDS/ WX" contains a general description of

A—cloudiness and weather significant to flight operations broken down by states or other geographical areas.
B—forecast sky cover, cloud tops, visibility, and obstructions to vision along specific routes.
C—clouds and weather which cover an area greater than 3,000 square miles and is significant to VFR flight operations.

*The "VFR CLDS/WX" section may be broken down by states or well-known geographical areas. The specific forecast section gives a general description of clouds and weather that cover an area greater than 3,000 square miles and are significant to VFR flight operations. (I57) — AC 00-45E, Chapter 4*

ALL
**3491.** (Refer to Figure 16.) What sky condition and visibility are forecast for upper Michigan in the eastern portions after 2300Z?

A—Ceiling 100 feet overcast and 3 to 5 statute miles visibility.
B—Ceiling 1,000 feet overcast and 3 to 5 nautical miles visibility.
C—Ceiling 1,000 feet overcast and 3 to 5 statute miles visibility.

*In the eastern portion of upper Michigan after 2300Z, the ceiling is forecast to be overcast at 1,000 feet MSL, with visibilities between 3–5 statute miles in light rain and mist. (I57) — AC 00-45E, Chapter 4*

ALL
**3492.** (Refer to Figure 16.) The Chicago FA forecast section is valid until the twenty-fifth at

A—1945Z.
B—0800Z.
C—1400Z.

*The Chicago FA forecast section is valid until the 25th day of the month at 0800Z. (I57) — AC 00-45E, Chapter 4*

Answer (A) is incorrect because 1945Z is the time the forecast was written. Answer (C) is incorrect because 1400Z is the time through which the synopsis and outlook are valid.

ALL
**3493.** (Refer to Figure 16.) What sky condition and type obstructions to vision are forecast for upper Michigan in the western portions from 0200Z until 0500Z?

A—Ceiling becoming 1,000 feet overcast with visibility 3 to 5 statute miles in mist.
B—Ceiling becoming 100 feet overcast with visibility 3 to 5 statue miles in mist.
C—Ceiling becoming 1,000 feet overcast with visibility 3 to 5 nautical miles in mist.

*In the western portions of upper Michigan, ceilings are forecast to be overcast at 1,000 feet with visibility between 3–5 statute miles in mist. (I57) — AC 00-45E, Chapter 4*

---

**Answers**

3490 [C]        3491 [C]        3492 [B]        3493 [A]

# Winds and Temperatures Aloft Forecast (FD)

The Winds and Temperatures Aloft Forecast (FD) shows wind direction, wind velocity, and the temperature that is forecast to exist at specified levels. No winds are forecast for a level within 1,500 feet of the surface, and no temperatures are forecast for the 3,000-foot level or for a level within 2,500 feet of the surface. The wind direction is shown in tens of degrees with reference to true north, and the velocity is shown in knots. Temperatures are in degrees Celsius, and are negative above 24,000 feet.

Each 6-digit group includes wind and temperature. For example, the entry "2045-26" indicates wind from 200° true north at 45 knots, temperature -26°C.

A forecast wind from 160 at 115 knots with a temperature at 34°C at the 30,000-foot level would be encoded "661534," with 50 added to the wind direction and 100 subtracted from the velocity. A wind coded "7699" would indicate wind from 260 at 199 knots or more. "9900" indicates wind light and variable, speed less than 5 knots.

ALL
**3500.** (Refer to Figure 17.) What wind is forecast for STL at 9,000 feet?

A—230° true at 32 knots.
B—230° magnetic at 25 knots.
C—230° true at 25 knots.

*A six-digit group shows wind directions (in reference to true north) in the first two digits, wind speed (in knots) in the second two digits, and temperature (in Celsius) in the last two digits. In this case, 2332+02 means 230° at 32 knots, and the temperature is 2°C. (I57) — AC 00-45E, Chapter 4*

ALL
**3501.** (Refer to Figure 17.) What wind is forecast for STL at 12,000 feet?

A—230° true at 56 knots.
B—230° magnetic at 56 knots.
C—230° true at 39 knots.

*A six-digit group shows wind directions (in reference to true north) in the first two digits, wind speed (in knots) in the second two digits, and temperature (in Celsius) in the last two digits. In this case, 2339-04 means 230° at 39 knots, and the temperature is -4°C. (I57) — AC 00-45E, Chapter 4*

ALL
**3502.** (Refer to Figure 17.) Determine the wind and temperature aloft forecast for DEN at 9,000 feet.

A—230° magnetic at 53 knots, temperature 47 °C.
B—230° true at 53 knots, temperature -47 °C.
C—230° true at 21 knots, temperature -4 °C.

*A six-digit group shows wind directions (in reference to true north) in the first two digits, wind speed (in knots) in the second two digits, and temperature (in Celsius) in the last two digits. In this case, 2321-04 means 230° at 21 knots, and the temperature is -4°C. (I57) — AC 00-45E, Chapter 4*

ALL
**3503.** (Refer to Figure 17.) Determine the wind and temperature aloft forecast for MKC at 6,000 feet.

A—200° true at 6 knots, temperature +3 °C.
B—050° true at 7 knots, temperature missing.
C—200° magnetic at 6 knots, temperature +3 °C.

*A six-digit group shows wind directions (in reference to true north) in the first two digits, wind speed (in knots) in the second two digits, and temperature (in Celsius) in the last two digits. In this case, 2006+03 means 200° at 6 knots, and the temperature is 3°C. (I57) — AC 00-45E, Chapter 4*

**Answers**
3500 [A]　　　3501 [C]　　　3502 [C]　　　3503 [A]

ALL
**3504.** (Refer to Figure 17.) What wind is forecast for STL at 12,000 feet?

A—230° true at 106 knots.
B—230° magnetic at 39 knots.
C—230° true at 39 knots.

*A six-digit group shows wind directions (in reference to true north) in the first two digits, wind speed (in knots) in the second two digits, and temperature (in Celsius) in the last two digits. In this case, 2339-04 means 230° at 39 knots, and the temperature is -4°C. (I57) — AC 00-45E, Chapter 4*

ALL
**3505.** What values are used for Winds Aloft Forecasts?

A—Magnetic direction and knots.
B—Magnetic direction and miles per hour.
C—True direction and knots.

*A six-digit group shows wind directions (in reference to true north) in the first two digits, wind speed (in knots) in the second two digits, and temperature (in Celsius) in the last two digits. (I57) — AC 00-45E, Chapter 4*

ALL
**3506.** When the term "light and variable" is used in reference to a Winds Aloft Forecast, the coded group and windspeed is

A—0000 and less than 7 knots.
B—9900 and less than 5 knots.
C—9999 and less than 10 knots.

*When the forecast speed is less than 5 knots, the coded group is "9900" and reads "light and variable" on the Winds Aloft Forecast. (I57) — AC 00-45E, Chapter 4*

# Weather Depiction Chart

The Weather Depiction Chart, which shows conditions that existed at the valid time of the chart, allows the pilot to readily determine general weather conditions on which to base flight planning.

A legend in the lower right-hand corner of the chart describes the method of identifying areas of VFR, MVFR, and IFR conditions.

Total sky cover is depicted by shading of the station circle as shown in Figure 7-3. Cloud height is entered under the station circle in hundreds of feet above ground level. Symbols for weather and obstructions to vision are normally shown to the left of the station circle.

Visibility (in statute miles) is entered to the left of any weather symbol. If the visibility is greater than 6 miles it will be omitted. Figure 7-4 shows examples of plotted data.

| Symbol | Total Sky Cover |
| --- | --- |
| | Sky clear |
| | Less than 1/10 (FEW) |
| | 1/10 to 5/10 Inclusive (SCATTERED) |
| | 6/10 to 9/10 inclusive (BROKEN) |
| | 10/10 with breaks (BINOVC) |
| | 10/10 (OVERCAST) |
| | Sky obscured or partially obscured |

**Figure 7-3.** Total sky cover symbols

| Plotted | Interpreted |
|---|---|
| ◐ 8 | Few clouds, base 800 feet, visibility more than 6. |
| ̇∨ ◕ 12 | Broken sky cover, ceiling 1,200 feet, rain shower, visibility more than 6. |
| 5∞ ◑ | Thin overcast with breaks, visibility 5 in haze. |
| ▲ ◕ 30 | Scattered at 3,000 feet, clouds topping ridges, visibility more than 6. |
| 2= ○ | Sky clear, visibility 2, ground fog or fog. |
| 1/2 ⊢▶ ⊗ | Sky partially obscured, visibility 1/2, blowing snow, no cloud layers observed. |
| 2= ⊗ 200 | Sky partially obscured, visibility 2, fog, cloud layer at 20,000 feet. Assume sky is partially obscured since 20,000 feet cannot be vertical visibility into fog. It is questionable if 20,000 feet is lowest scattered layer or ceiling.* |
| 1/4 ★ ⊗ 5 | Sky obscured, ceiling 500, visibility 1/4, snow. |
| 1 ⚡ ● 12 | Overcast, ceiling 1,200 feet thunderstorm, rain shower, visibility 1. |
| Ⓜ | Data missing. |

* Note: Since a partial and a total obscuration (x) is entered as total sky cover, it can be difficult to determine if a height entry is a cloud layer above a partial obscuration or vertical visibility into a total obscuration. Check the SA.

**Figure 7-4.** Examples of plotted data on the weather depiction chart

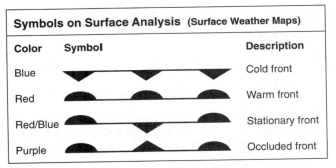

**Symbols on Surface Analysis** (Surface Weather Maps)

| Color | Symbol | Description |
|---|---|---|
| Blue | | Cold front |
| Red | | Warm front |
| Red/Blue | | Stationary front |
| Purple | | Occluded front |

**Question 3507**

ALL
**3508.** (Refer to Figure 18.) The IFR weather in northern Texas is due to

A—dust devils.
B—low ceilings.
C—intermittent rain.

*The IFR category observed weather is shown as a hatched area, outlined by a smooth line. The station circles reporting IFR conditions show the obstruction to vision as fog (=) which restricts visibility to 1-1/2 mile and a ceiling of 400 feet. (I58) — AC 00-45E, Chapter 5*

ALL
**3509.** (Refer to Figure 18.) Of what value is the Weather Depiction Chart to the pilot?

A—For determining general weather conditions on which to base flight planning.
B—For a forecast of cloud coverage, visibilities, and frontal activity.
C—For determining frontal trends and air mass characteristics.

ALL
**3507.** (Refer to Figure 18.) What is the status of the front that extends from Nebraska through the upper peninsula of Michigan?

A—Cold.
B—Warm.
C—Stationary.

*The front extending from Nebraska through the upper peninsula of Michigan is a cold front, indicated by the line with triangles on one side. (I58) — AC 00-45E, Chapter 5*

*The Weather Depiction Chart is computer-prepared from METAR reports to give a broad overview of observed flying category conditions as of the valid time of the chart. From it, you can determine general weather conditions more readily than any other source. Therefore, the Weather Depiction Chart is a choice place to begin the weather briefing and flight planning. (I59) — AC 00-45E, Chapter 6*

Answers (B) and (C) are incorrect because this chart does not include forecast or trend information.

**Answers**
3507 [A]  3508 [B]  3509 [A]

ALL

**3510.** (Refer to Figure 18.) The marginal weather in central Kentucky is due to low

A—visibility.
B—ceiling and visibility.
C—ceiling.

*The marginal weather in central Kentucky is due to low ceilings. Visibility is normally entered to the left of the weather symbols. Since it is omitted, we know the visibilities are greater than 6 miles. (I59) — AC 00-45E, Chapter 6*

ALL

**3511.** (Refer to Figure 18.) What weather phenomenon is causing IFR conditions in central Oklahoma?

A—Low visibility only.
B—Heavy rain showers.
C—Low ceilings and visibility.

*The contoured area with shading indicates IFR conditions due to ceilings less than 1,000 feet and/or visibilities less than 3 miles. (I59) — AC 00-45E, Chapter 6*

ALL

**3512.** (Refer to Figure 18.) According to the Weather Depiction Chart, the weather for a flight from southern Michigan to north Indiana is ceilings

A—1,000 to 3,000 feet and/or visibility 3 to 5 miles.
B—less than 1,000 feet and/or visibility less than 3 miles.
C—greater than 3, 000 feet and visibility greater than 5 miles.

*The lack of contours along this route indicates VFR areas with ceilings greater than 3,000 feet and visibility greater than 5 miles. (I59) AC 00-45E, Chapter 6*

# Radar Weather Reports

Radar Weather Reports (SDs) are of special interest to the pilot because they indicate the location of precipitation with type and intensity.

The Radar Summary Chart will yield a three-dimensional view of clouds and precipitation when used in conjunction with other charts and reports. Since radar detects only drops or ice particles of precipitation size, it does not detect clouds or fog. It is the only chart that shows lines and cells of hazardous thunderstorms.

Areas from which precipitation echoes were received are shown on the Radar Summary Chart, with echo intensity indicated by contours as shown in Figure 7-5. Echo heights are displayed in hundreds of feet MSL. Tops are entered above a short line, while any available bases are entered below a short line. Movement of an area of echoes is indicated by a shaft and barb combination with the shaft indicating the direction, and the barbs indicating the speed. A whole barb is 10 knots, a half barb is 5 knots, and a pennant is 50 knots. Individual cell movement is indicated by an arrow that shows the direction of movement with the speed in knots entered as a number. Severe weather watch areas are outlined by heavy dashed lines, usually in the form of a large rectangular box.

**Answers**

3510    [C]            3511    [C]            3512    [C]

| VIP Level | Echo Intensity | Precipitation Intensity | Rainfall Rate in/hr Stratiform | Rainfall Rate in/hr Convective |
|---|---|---|---|---|
| 1 | Weak | Light | Less than 0.1 | Less than 0.2 |
| 2 | Moderate | Moderate | 0.1 – 0.5 | 0.2 – 1.1 |
| 3 | Strong | Heavy | 0.5 – 1.0 | 1.1 – 2.2 |
| 4 | Very strong | Very heavy | 1.0 – 2.0 | 2.2 – 4.5 |
| 5 | Intense | Intense | 2.0 – 5.0 | 4.5 – 7.1 |
| 6 | Extreme | Extreme | More than 5.0 | More than 7.1 |

450
Highest precipitation top in area in hundreds of feet MSL (45,000 Feet MSL)

*The numbers representing the intensity level do not appear on the chart. Beginning from the first contour line, bordering the area, the intensity level is 1–2, second contour is 3–4, and the third contour is 5–6.

## Symbols Used on Charts

| Symbol | Meaning |
|---|---|
| R | Rain |
| RW | Rain shower |
| Hail | Hail |
| S | Snow |
| PL | Ice pellets |
| SW | Snow shower |
| L | Drizzle |
| T | Thunderstorm |
| ZR, ZL | Freezing precipitation |
| NE | No echoes observed |
| NA | Observations unavailbale |
| OM | Out for Maintenance |
| STC | STC ON – all precipitation may not be seen |
| ROBEPS | Radar Operating Below Performance Standards |
| RHINO | Range Height Indicator Not Operating |

| Symbol | Meaning |
|---|---|
| + | Intensity increasing or new echo |
| – | Intensity decreasing |
| No Symbol | No change in intensity |
| 35 | Cell movement to NE at 35 knots |
|  | Line or area movement to East at 20 knots |
| LM | Little movement |
| MA | Echoes mostly aloft |
| PA | Echoes partly aloft |

| Symbol | Meaning |
|---|---|
|  | Line of echoes |
| SLD | 8/10 or greater coverage in a line |
| WS999 | Severe thunderstorm watch |
| WT999 | Tornado watch |
| LEWP | Line echo wave pattern |
| HOOK | Hook echo |
| BWER | Bounded weak echo region |
| PCLL | Persistent cell |
| FNLN | Fine line |

**Figure 7-5**

ALL
**3513.** Radar weather reports are of special interest to pilots because they indicate

A—location of precipitation along with type, intensity, and cell movement of precipitation.
B—location of precipitation along with type, intensity, and trend.
C—large areas of low ceilings and fog.

*The radar weather report (SD) includes the type, intensity, and location of the echo top of the precipitation. The intensity trend of precipitation is no longer coded on the SD. (I60) — AC 00-45E, Chapter 3*

ALL
**3514.** What information is provided by the Radar Summary Chart that is not shown on other weather charts?

A—Lines and cells of hazardous thunderstorms.
B—Ceilings and precipitation between reporting stations.
C—Types of clouds between reporting stations.

*Radar detects objects of precipitation size or greater. Based on the amount of precipitation radar detects, it can determine if it is a thunderstorm. (I60) — AC 00-45E, Chapter 7*

Answers (B) and (C) are incorrect because it is not designed to detect ceilings and types of clouds.

**Answers**

3513    [A]          3514    [A]

ALL

**3515.** (Refer to Figure 19, area B.) What is the top for precipitation of the radar return?

A—24,000 feet AGL.
B—2,400 feet MSL.
C—24,000 feet MSL.

*The underlined 240 indicates the top for precipitation is 24,000 feet MSL. (I60) — AC 00-45E, Chapter 7*

ALL

**3516.** (Refer to Figure 19, area B.) What type of weather is occurring in the radar return?

A—Continuous rain.
B—Light to moderate rain showers.
C—Rain showers increasing in intensity.

*The radar return in area B shows the symbol "R" which means rain. (I60) — AC 00-45E, Chapter 7*

*Answers (B) and (C) are incorrect because rain showers are indicated with the symbol "RW."*

ALL

**3517.** (Refer to Figure 19, area D.) What is the direction and speed of movement of the cell?

A—North at 17 knots.
B—South at 17 knots.
C—North at 17 MPH.

*Individual cell movement is indicated by an arrow with the speed in knots entered as a number. The radar return at area D shows the cell movement toward the north at 17 knots. (I60) — AC 00-45E, Chapter 7*

ALL

**3518.** (Refer to Figure 19, area E.) The top of the precipitation of the cell is

A—16,000 feet MSL.
B—25,000 feet MSL.
C—16,000 feet AGL.

*The underlined 160 indicates the top for precipitation is 16,000 feet MSL. (I60) — AC 00-45E, Chapter 7*

*Answer (B) is incorrect because the underlined 250 has a line indicating these are the tops for area G. Answer (C) is incorrect because echo tops are given in hundreds of feet MSL.*

ALL

**3519.** What does the heavy dashed line that forms a large rectangular box on a radar summary chart refer to?

A—Severe weather watch area.
B—Areas of hail 1/4 inch in diameter.
C—Areas of heavy rain.

*The heavy dashed line that forms a large rectangular box on a radar summary chart indicates a severe weather watch area. (I60) — AC 00-45E, Chapter 7*

# Low-Level Significant Weather Prognostic Chart

The Low-Level Significant Weather Prognostic Chart (surface to 24,000 feet) portrays forecast weather which may influence flight planning, including information on those areas to avoid and/or altitudes of the freezing level and turbulence. The chart is a 24-hour forecast and it consists of four panels. The left-hand upper and lower panels forecast weather for the first 12 hours, while the right-hand upper and lower panels portray the forecast for the last 12 hours of the forecast period. A legend is in the center of the chart.

The chart uses standard weather symbols and significant weather prognostic symbols as shown in Figure 7-6. The upper two panels depict areas of IFR and MVFR (marginal VFR: ceiling 1,000 to 3,000 feet and/or visibility 3 to 5 miles inclusive) conditions, turbulence, and freezing levels. Figures above and below a short line show the expected base and top of the turbulent layer in hundreds of feet MSL. Absence of a figure below the line indicates turbulence from the surface upward. No figure above the line indicates turbulence extending above the upper limit of the chart.

The zigzag line shows where the freezing level is forecast to be at the surface and is labeled "32°" or "SFC." The freezing level aloft, shown by a small dashed line, is drawn at 4,000-foot intervals (4,000 feet MSL, 8,000 feet MSL, etc.)

The two lower panels outline areas of forecast precipitation and thunderstorms and the movement of fronts and pressure centers.

**Answers**

| | | | | | | | | | |
|---|---|---|---|---|---|---|---|---|---|
| 3515 | [C] | 3516 | [A] | 3517 | [A] | 3518 | [A] | 3519 | [A] |

| Symbol | Meaning | Symbol | Meaning | Depiction | Meaning |
|---|---|---|---|---|---|
| | Moderate Turbulence | | Rain Shower | | Showery precipitation (Thunderstorms/rain showers) covering half or more of the area. |
| | Severe Turbulence | | Snow Shower | | Continuous precipitation (rain) covering half or more of the area. |
| | Moderate Icing | | Thunderstorm | | Showery precipitation (snow showers) covering less than half of the area. |
| | Severe Icing | | Freezing Rain | | Intermittent precipitation (drizzle) covering less than half of the area. |
| • | Rain | | Tropical Storm | | Showery precipitation (rain showers) embedded in an area of continuous rain covering more than half of the area. |
| * | Snow | | Hurricane (typhoon) | | |
| , | Drizzle | | | | |

**Note:** Character of stable precipitation is the manner in which it occurs. It may be intermittent or continuous.

**Examples:**

| | Intermittent | Continuous |
|---|---|---|
| Rain | | |
| Drizzle | | |
| Snow | | |

**Figure 7-6**

ALL
**3520.** (Refer to Figure 20.) How are Significant Weather Prognostic Charts best used by a pilot?

A—For overall planning at all altitudes.
B—For determining areas to avoid (freezing levels and turbulence).
C—For analyzing current frontal activity and cloud coverage.

*While Significant Weather Prognostic Charts portray forecast weather which may influence flight planning, they are most useful in identifying the freezing level and areas of turbulence. (I64) — AC 00-45E, Chapter 8*

ALL
**3521.** (Refer to Figure 20.) Interpret the weather symbol depicted in Utah on the 12-hour Significant Weather Prognostic Chart.

A—Moderate turbulence, surface to 18,000 feet.
B—Base of clear air turbulence, 18,000 feet.
C—Thunderstorm tops at 18,000 feet.

*The symbol indicates moderate turbulence. The "180/" indicates the turbulent layer is from the surface to 18,000 feet. (I64) — AC 00-45E, Chapter 11*

**Answers**
3520 [B]    3521 [A]

**3522.** (Refer to Figure 20.) What weather is forecast for the Florida area just ahead of the stationary front during the first 12 hours?

A—Ceiling 1,000 to 3,000 feet and/or visibility 3 to 5 miles with intermittent precipitation.
B—Ceiling 1,000 to 3,000 feet and/or visibility 3 to 5 miles with continuous precipitation.
C—Ceiling less than 1,000 feet and/or visibility less than 3 miles with continuous precipitation.

*The two left panels are 12-hour progs. The upper left panel is the 12-hour prog of significant weather from the surface (SFC) to 400 millibars (24,000 feet). The Florida area is outlined in a scalloped line, indicating MVFR conditions of ceiling 1,000–3,000 feet inclusive and/or visibility 3–5 miles inclusive. The bottom left panel is the 12-hour surface prog. The shaded area with 3 circles indicates continuous rain. (I64) — AC 00-45E, Chapter 11*

**3523.** (Refer to Figure 20.) The enclosed shaded area associated with the low pressure system over northern Utah is forecast to have

A—continuous snow.
B—intermittent snow.
C—continuous snow showers.

*The double asterisks (\*\*) in the bottom left panel indicate continuous snow, as the arrow points them into the shaded area. (I64) — AC 00-45E, Chapter 11*

**3524.** (Refer to Figure 20.) At what altitude is the freezing level over the middle of Florida on the 12-hour Significant Weather Prognostic Chart?

A—4,000 feet.
B—12,000 feet.
C—8,000 feet.

*The dashed line indicates the freezing level above mean sea level. The "120" indicates the freezing level to be at 12,000 feet over the middle of Florida. (I64) — AC 00-45E, Chapter 11*

---

**Answers**

3522    [B]                3523    [A]                3524    [B]

# Inflight Weather Advisories (WA, WS, WST)

Inflight Weather Advisories advise enroute pilots of the possibility of encountering hazardous flying conditions that may not have been forecast at the time of the preflight weather briefing.

**AIRMETs (WA)** contain information on weather that may be hazardous to single engine, other light aircraft, and VFR pilots. The items covered are moderate icing or turbulence, sustained winds of 30 knots or more at the surface, widespread areas of IFR conditions, and extensive mountain obscurement.

**SIGMETs (WS)** advise of weather potentially hazardous to all aircraft. The items covered are severe icing, severe or extreme turbulence, and widespread sandstorms, dust storms or volcanic ash lowering visibility to less than 3 miles.

SIGMETs and AIRMETs are broadcast upon receipt and at 30-minute intervals (H + 15 and H + 45) during the first hour. If the advisory is still in effect after the first hour, an alert notice will be broadcast. Pilots may contact the nearest FSS to ascertain whether the advisory is pertinent to their flights.

**CONVECTIVE SIGMETs (WST)** cover weather developments such as tornadoes, lines of thunderstorms, and embedded thunderstorms, and they also imply severe or greater turbulence, severe icing, and low-level wind shear. When a SIGMET forecasts embedded thunderstorms, it indicates that the thunderstorms are obscured by massive cloud layers and cannot be seen. Convective SIGMET bulletins are issued hourly at H + 55. Unscheduled convective SIGMETs are broadcast upon receipt and at 15-minute intervals for the first hour (H + 15; H + 30; H + 45).

**ALL**
**3495.** What is indicated when a current CONVECTIVE SIGMET forecasts thunderstorms?

A—Moderate thunderstorms covering 30 percent of the area.
B—Moderate or severe turbulence.
C—Thunderstorms obscured by massive cloud layers.

*Convective SIGMETs include: severe thunderstorms, embedded thunderstorms, line of thunderstorms, thunderstorms greater than or equal to VIP (Digital Video Interrogator and Processor) level "A" affecting 40% or more of an area of 3,000 square miles. (I57) — AC 00-45E, Chapter 4*

**ALL**
**3496.** What information is contained in a CONVECTIVE SIGMET?

A—Tornadoes, embedded thunderstorms, and hail 3/4 inch or greater in diameter.
B—Severe icing, severe turbulence, or widespread dust storms lowering visibility to less than 3 miles.
C—Surface winds greater than 40 knots or thunderstorms equal to or greater than video integrator processor (VIP) level 4.

*Any convective SIGMET implies severe or greater turbulence, severe icing, and low-level wind shear. The forecast may be issued for any of the following:*

*Severe thunderstorms due to—*

*1. Surface winds greater than or equal to 50 knots, or*
*2. Hail at the surface greater than or equal to 3/4 inch in diameter, or*
*3. Tornadoes, embedded thunderstorms, lines of thunderstorms.*

*(I57) — AC 00-45E, Chapter 4*

**ALL**
**3497.** SIGMET's are issued as a warning of weather conditions hazardous to which aircraft?

A—Small aircraft only.
B—Large aircraft only.
C—All aircraft.

*A SIGMET advises of weather potentially hazardous to all aircraft. (I57) — AC 00-45E, Chapter 4*

**Answers**
3495 [C]     3496 [A]     3497 [C]

ALL
**3498.** Which in-flight advisory would contain information on severe icing not associated with thunderstorms?

A—Convective SIGMET.
B—SIGMET.
C—AIRMET.

*A SIGMET advises of weather potentially hazardous to all aircraft other than convective activity. Some items included are severe icing, and severe or extreme turbulence. (I57) — AC 00-45E, Chapter 4*

ALL
**3499.** AIRMET's are advisories of significant weather phenomena but of lower intensities than SIGMET's and are intended for dissemination to

A—only IFR pilots.
B—All pilots.
C—only VFR pilots.

*AIRMETs are intended for dissemination to all pilots in the preflight and enroute phase of flight to enhance safety. (I57) — AC 00-45E, Chapter 4*

# Transcribed Weather Broadcast (TWEB)

A **TWEB** is the continuous broadcast of weather information on low/medium frequency NAVAIDs and on selected VORs. TWEBs contain information concerning sky cover, cloud tops, visibility, weather, and obstructions to vision in a route format.

ALL
**3453.** Individual forecasts for specific routes of flight can be obtained from which weather source?

A—Transcribed Weather Broadcasts (TWEB's).
B—Terminal Forecasts.
C—Area Forecasts.

*The Transcribed Weather Broadcast (TWEB) is similar to the area forecast except information is contained in a route format; whereas a terminal forecast is a description of the surface weather expected to occur at an airport. (I54) — AC 00-45E, Chapter 1*

ALL
**3454.** Transcribed Weather Broadcasts (TWEB's) may be monitored by tuning the appropriate radio receiver to certain

A—airport advisory frequencies.
B—VOR and NDB frequencies.
C—ATIS frequencies.

*Transcribed Weather Broadcasts (TWEBs) are recorded on tapes and broadcast continuously over selected low-frequency navigational aids and/or VORs. (I54) — AC 00-45E, Chapter 1*

ALL
**3494.** To obtain a continuous transcribed weather briefing, including winds aloft and route forecasts for a cross-country flight, a pilot should monitor a

A—Transcribed Weather Broadcast (TWEB) on an NDB or a VOR facility.
B—VHF radio receiver tuned to an Automatic Terminal Information Service (ATIS) frequency.
C—regularly scheduled weather broadcast on a VOR frequency.

*A Transcribed Weather Broadcast (TWEB) contains route forecasts and winds aloft recorded on tapes and broadcast continuously over selected low-frequency navigational aids and/or VORs. (I57) — AC 00-45E, Chapter 4*

**Answers**

| | | | | |
|---|---|---|---|---|
| 3498 [B] | 3499 [B] | 3453 [A] | 3454 [B] | 3494 [A] |

# Enroute Flight Advisory Service (EFAS)

**EFAS** provides enroute aircraft with weather advisories pertinent to the type of flight, route to be flown, and the altitude. The service is normally available throughout the conterminous United States from 6 a.m. to 10 p.m. local time. Aircraft flying between 5,000 feet AGL and 18,000 feet AGL can obtain the service by calling "Flight Watch" on radio frequency 122.0 MHz.

ALL
**3617.** What service should a pilot normally expect from an En Route Flight Advisory Service (EFAS) station?

A—Actual weather information and thunderstorm activity along the route.
B—Preferential routing and radar vectoring to circumnavigate severe weather.
C—Severe weather information, changes to flight plans, and receipt of routine position reports.

*EFAS is a service specifically designed to provide enroute aircraft with timely and meaningful weather advisories pertinent to the type of flight intended, route of flight, and altitude. EFAS is also used for exchange of PIREPs which are especially important in rural areas. (J25) — AIM ¶7-1-4*

# Obtaining a Telephone Weather Briefing

When telephoning a weather briefing facility for preflight weather information, pilots should:

• Identify themselves as pilots;
• State whether they intend to fly VFR or IFR;
• State the intended route, destination, and type of aircraft;
• Request a standard briefing to get a "complete" weather briefing;
• Request an abbreviated briefing to supplement mass disseminated data or when only one or two items are needed; and
• Request an outlook briefing whenever the proposed departure time is 6 or more hours from the time of briefing.

ALL
**3455.** When telephoning a weather briefing facility for preflight weather information, pilots should state

A—whether they intend to fly VFR only.
B—that they possess a current pilot certificate.
C—the full name and address of the formation commander.

*When requesting a preflight weather briefing, identify yourself as a pilot or the tail number of the aircraft to be flown and provide the type of flight planned (e.g., VFR or IFR). (H320) — AC 61-23C, Chapter 5*

ALL
**3456.** To get a complete weather briefing for the planned flight, the pilot should request

A—a general briefing.
B—an abbreviated briefing.
C—a standard briefing.

*You should request a standard briefing any time you are planning a flight and you have not received a previous briefing or preliminary information through mass dissemination media, e.g., TWEB, PATWAS, VRS, etc. (I54) — AC 00-45E, Chapter 1*

**Answers**
3617    [A]          3455    [A]          3456    [C]

ALL

**3457.** Which type weather briefing should a pilot request, when departing within the hour, if no preliminary weather information has been received?

A—Outlook briefing.
B—Abbreviated briefing.
C—Standard briefing.

*You should request a standard briefing any time you are planning a flight and you have not received a previous briefing or preliminary information through mass dissemination media, e.g., TWEB, PATWAS, VRS, etc. (I54) — AC 00-45E, Chapter 1*

ALL

**3458.** Which type of weather briefing should a pilot request to supplement mass disseminated data?

A—An outlook briefing.
B—A supplemental briefing.
C—An abbreviated briefing.

*Request an abbreviated briefing when you need information to supplement mass disseminated data, update a previous briefing, or when you need only one or two specific items. (I54) — AC 00-45E, Chapter 1*

ALL

**3459.** To update a previous weather briefing, a pilot should request

A—an abbreviated briefing.
B—a standard briefing.
C—an outlook briefing.

*Request an abbreviated briefing when you need information to supplement mass disseminated data, update a previous briefing, or when you need only one or two specific items. (I54) — AC 00-45E, Chapter 1*

ALL

**3460.** A weather briefing that is provided when the information requested is 6 or more hours in advance of the proposed departure time is

A—an outlook briefing.
B—a forecast briefing.
C—a prognostic briefing.

*You should request an outlook briefing whenever your proposed time of departure is 6 or more hours from the time of the briefing. This type of briefing is provided for planning purposes only. You should obtain a standard or abbreviated briefing prior to departure in order to obtain such items as current conditions, updated forecasts, winds aloft and NOTAMs. (I54) — AC 00-45E, Chapter 1*

ALL

**3461.** When requesting weather information for the following morning, a pilot should request

A—an outlook briefing.
B—a standard briefing.
C—an abbreviated briefing.

*You should request an outlook briefing whenever your proposed time of departure is 6 or more hours from the time of the briefing. This type of briefing is provided for planning purposes only. You should obtain a standard or abbreviated briefing prior to departure in order to obtain such items as current conditions, updated forecasts, winds aloft and NOTAMs. (I54) — AC 00-45E, Chapter 1*

ALL

**3526.** What should pilots state initially when telephoning a weather briefing facility for preflight weather information?

A—The intended route of flight radio frequencies.
B—The address of the pilot in command.
C—The intended route of flight and destination.

*When requesting a briefing, pilots should identify themselves and provide as much information regarding the proposed flight as possible. (H320) — AC 61-23C, Chapter 5*

Answer (A) is incorrect because the pilot only needs to identify the route of flight. Answer (B) is incorrect because the caller only needs to provide an aircraft number or pilot's name.

**Answers**

| | | | | | |
|---|---|---|---|---|---|
| 3457 [C] | 3458 [C] | 3459 [A] | 3460 [A] | 3461 [A] | 3526 [C] |

ALL
**3527.** What should pilots state initially when telephoning a weather briefing facility for preflight weather information?

A—The intended route of flight radio frequencies.
B—The intended route of flight and destination.
C—The address of the pilot in command.

*When requesting a briefing, pilots should identify themselves and provide as much information regarding the proposed flight as possible. The information received will depend on the type of briefing requested. The following would be helpful to the briefer.*

1. *Type of flight, visual flight rule (VFR) or instrument operating rule (IFR)*
2. *Aircraft number or pilot's name*
3. *Aircraft type*
4. *Departure point*
5. *Route of flight*
6. *Destination*
7. *Flight altitude(s)*
8. *Estimated time of departure*
9. *Estimated time en route or estimated time of arrival*

*(H320) — AC 61-23C, Chapter 5*

ALL
**3528.** When telephoning a weather briefing facility for preflight weather information, pilots should state

A—the full name and address of the formation commander.
B—that they possess a current pilot certificate.
C—whether they intend to fly VFR only.

*When requesting a briefing, make known you are a pilot. Give clear and concise facts about your flight:*

1. *Type of flight: VFR or IFR*
2. *Aircraft identification or pilot's name*
3. *Aircraft type*
4. *Departure point*
5. *Route-of-flight*
6. *Destination*
7. *Altitude*
8. *Estimated time of departure*
9. *Estimated time en route or estimated time of arrival*

*(H320) — AC 61-23C, Chapter 5*

GLI
**3525.** In addition to the standard briefing, what additional information should be asked of the weather briefer in order to evaluate soaring conditions?

A—The upper soundings to determine the thermal index at all soaring levels.
B—Dry adiabatic rate of cooling to determine the height of cloud bases.
C—Moist adiabatic rate of cooling to determine the height of cloud tops.

*Since thermals depend on sinking cold air forcing warm air upward, strength of thermals depends on the temperature difference between the sinking air and the rising air—the greater the temperature difference, the stronger the thermals. To arrive at an approximation of this difference, a thermal index is computed. A thermal index may be computed for any level using upper soundings. (I62) — AC 00-45E, Chapter 9*

GLI
**3470.** (Refer to Figure 13.) What effect do the clouds mentioned in the weather briefing have on soaring conditions?

A—All thermals stop at the base of the clouds.
B—Thermals persist to the tops of the clouds at 25,000 feet.
C—The scattered clouds indicate thermals at least to the tops of the lower clouds.

*The telephone weather briefing indicates a few scattered clouds at 5,000 feet AGL, with higher scattered cirrus at 25,000 feet MSL. This briefing shows two different clouds bases and does not give cloud tops. Thermals are a product of instability. The height of thermals depends on the depth of the unstable layer, and their strength depends on the degree of instability. A cloud grows with a rising thermal and scattered cumulus clouds are positive signs of thermals. Whereas an abundant convective cloud cover reduces thermal activity, thermals will exist at least to the tops of the scattered clouds, especially if the outline is firm and sharp, indicating a growing cumulus. (I55) — AC 00-45E, Chapter 2*

**Answers**

| | | | |
|---|---|---|---|
| 3527 [B] | 3528 [C] | 3525 [A] | 3470 [C] |

GLI

**3471.** (Refer to Figure 13.) At what time will thermals begin to form?

A—Between 1300Z and 1500Z while the sky is clear.
B—By 1500Z (midmorning) when scattered clouds begin to form.
C—About 2000Z (early afternoon) when the wind begins to increase.

*The telephone weather briefing indicates there should be a few scattered clouds at 5,000 feet AGL by 15Z. The sky must be clear enough for the sun to warm the earth's surface in order for thermals to develop. (I55) — AC 00-45E, Chapter 2*

LTA

**3411.** What early morning weather observations indicate the possibility of good weather conditions for balloon flight most of the day?

A—Clear skies and surface winds, 10 knots or less.
B—Low moving, scattered cumulus clouds and surface winds, 5 knots or less.
C—Overcast with stratus clouds and surface winds, 5 knots or less.

*Stratiform clouds indicate no turbulence and 5 knots or less winds are well within safety parameters. (I25) — AC 00-6A, Chapter 6*

LTA

**3468.** (Refer to Figure 13.) According to the weather briefing, the most ideal time to launch balloons is

A—as soon as possible after 1300Z.
B—at 1500Z when the ground will be partially shaded.
C—at 2000Z when there is enough wind for cross-country.

*The telephone weather briefing given at 13Z indicates no clouds until 15Z, and no wind until after 20Z. The ideal time to launch balloons is as soon after 13Z as possible before the clouds and wind develop. (I55) — AC 00-45E, Chapter 2*

LTA

**3469.** (Refer to Figure 13.) According to the weather briefing, good balloon weather will begin to deteriorate

A—soon after 1300Z as the wind starts to increase.
B—about 1500Z when the lower scattered clouds begin to form.
C—at 2000Z due to sharp increase in wind conditions.

*The telephone weather briefing given at 13Z indicates only a few scattered clouds at 5,000 feet AGL, with higher scattered cirrus at 25,000 feet MSL to form by 15Z. After 20Z, however, the wind should pick up to about 15 knots from the south. The marked increase of wind at 20Z indicates deteriorating ballooning weather. (I55) — AC 00-45E, Chapter 2*

LTA

**3477.** Which weather reports and forecasts are most important for local area balloon operations?

A—Winds Aloft Forecasts and Radar Summary Charts.
B—Winds Aloft Forecasts and Surface Analysis Charts.
C—Winds Aloft Forecasts and Aviation Routine Weather Reports.

*Local information is provided by the Aviation Routine Weather Report (METAR). (I57) — AC 00-45E, Chapter 4*

Answer (A) is incorrect because it is a local flight. Answer (B) is incorrect because Surface Analysis Charts are a nationwide reference.

**Answers**

| | | | | |
|---|---|---|---|---|
| 3471 [A] | 3411 [C] | 3468 [A] | 3469 [C] | 3477 [C] |

# Chapter 8
# Aircraft Performance

# Weight and Balance

Even though an aircraft has been certificated for flight at a specified maximum gross weight, it may not be safe to take off with that load under all conditions. High altitude, high temperature, and high humidity are additional factors which may require limiting the load to some weight less than the maximum allowable.

In addition to considering the weight to be carried, the pilot must ensure that the load is arranged to keep the aircraft in balance. The balance point, or Center of Gravity (CG), is the point at which all of the weight of the airplane is considered to be concentrated. For an aircraft to be safe to fly, the center of gravity must fall between specified limits. To keep the CG within safe limits it may be necessary to move weight toward the nose of the aircraft (forward), which moves the CG forward, or toward the tail (aft) which moves the CG aft.

The **datum** is an imaginary vertical line from which locations in an aircraft are measured. The datum is established by the manufacturer and may vary in location between aircraft.

The **arm** is the horizontal distance measured in inches from the datum line to a point on the aircraft. If measured aft, toward the tail, the arm is given a positive (+) value; if measured forward, toward the nose, the arm is given a negative (-) value. *See* Figure 8-1.

The **moment** is the product of the weight of an object multiplied by its arm and is expressed in pound-inches (lbs-in). A formula that is used to find moment is usually expressed as follows:

Weight x Arm = Moment

The **moment index** is a moment divided by a constant such as 100 or 1,000. It is used to simplify computations where heavy items and long arms result in large, unmanageable numbers. This is usually expressed as Moment/100 or Mom/1,000, etc.

**Figure 8-1.** Positive and negative arm

The center of gravity (CG) is the point about which an aircraft will balance, and it is expressed in inches from datum. The center of gravity is found by dividing the total moment by the total weight, and the formula is usually expressed as follows:

$$\frac{\text{Total Moment}}{\text{Total Weight}} = \text{CG (inches aft of datum)}$$

The specified forward and aft points within which the CG must be located for safe flight are called the center of gravity limits. These limits are specified by the manufacturer. The distance between the forward and aft CG limits is called the center of gravity range.

The **empty weight** is obtained from appropriate charts. It includes the airframe, engine, all fixed equipment, and unusable fuel and oil. Some aircraft include all oil in the aircraft empty weight. The **useful load** includes the pilot, passengers, baggage, fuel and oil. The **takeoff weight** is the empty weight plus the useful load. The **landing weight** is the takeoff weight minus any fuel used.

**Standard weights** have been established for numerous items involved in weight and balance computations. These weights should not be used if actual weights are available. Some of the standard weights are:

| Item | Weight |
|---|---|
| General aviation crew and passenger | 170 lbs each |
| Gasoline | 6 lbs/U.S. gallon |
| Oil | 7.5 lbs/U.S. gallon |
| Water | 8.35 lbs/U.S. gallon |

AIR, RTC
**3661.** Which items are included in the empty weight of an aircraft?

A—Unusable fuel and undrainable oil.
B—Only the airframe, powerplant, and optional equipment.
C—Full fuel tanks and engine oil to capacity.

*Empty weight consists of the airframe, engines, and all items of operating equipment that have fixed locations and are permanently installed in the airplane. It includes optional and special equipment, fixed ballast, hydraulic fluid, unusable (residual) fuel, and undrainable (residual) oil. (H316) — AC 61-23C, Chapter 4*

Answer (B) is incorrect because empty weight also includes operating fluids and unusable fuel. Answer (C) is incorrect because empty weight does not include full fuel.

AIR, RTC
**3662.** An aircraft is loaded 110 pounds over maximum certificated gross weight. If fuel (gasoline) is drained to bring the aircraft weight within limits, how much fuel should be drained?

A—15.7 gallons.
B—16.2 gallons.
C—18.4 gallons.

1. Determine the total weight to be removed (110 pounds) and the weight per gallon of gasoline (6 pounds).
2. Calculate the amount of gasoline to be drained using the formula:

$$Gallons = \frac{Pounds}{Pounds/Gallon}$$

or:

$$\frac{110}{6} = 18.33 \text{ gallons}$$

*When "rounding" an answer, do so in the sense that will provide the greater flight safety. In this case, round to 18.4. (H316) — AC 61-23C, Chapter 4*

AIR, RTC
**3663.** If an aircraft is loaded 90 pounds over maximum certificated gross weight and fuel (gasoline) is drained to bring the aircraft weight within limits, how much fuel should be drained?

A—10 gallons.
B—12 gallons.
C—15 gallons.

1. Determine the total weight to be removed (90 pounds) and the weight per gallon of gasoline (6 pounds).
2. Calculate the amount of gasoline to be drained using the formula:

$$Gallons = \frac{Pounds}{Pounds/Gallon}$$

or:

$$\frac{90}{6} = 15 \text{ gallons}$$

*(H316) — AC 61-23C, Chapter 4*

**Answers**

3661 [A]    3662 [C]    3663 [C]

# Computing Weight and Balance Problems Using a Table

## Problem:

Determine if the airplane weight and balance is within limits.

Front seat occupants ................................. 340 lbs
Rear seat occupants ............................... 295 lbs
Fuel (main wing tanks) ............................. 44 gal
Baggage ................................................... 56 lbs

## Solution:

1. Determine the total weight. Using the information provided in the question, enter the items and the weights:

| Item | Weight (lbs) | Arm (in) | Moment (lbs-in) |
|---|---|---|---|
| Front seat occupants | 340 | | |
| Rear seat occupants | 295 | | |
| Fuel (main wing tanks) | 264 * | | |
| Baggage | 56 | | |
| Empty weight | + 2,015 ** | | |
| | 2,970 lbs | | |

*44 gal x 6 lbs/gal     **found in FAA Figure 33

2. Fill in the arms (found in FAA Figure 33) and calculate the moments. Moments are determined by multiplying in each row: weight x arm. Then divide that moment by 100 to keep the number a manageable size, and finally, total all moments.

| Item | Weight (lbs) | Arm (in) | Moment/100 (lbs-in) |
|---|---|---|---|
| Front seat occupants | 340 | 85 | 289.0 |
| Rear seat occupants | 295 | 121 | 357.0 |
| Fuel (main wing tanks) | 264 | 75 | 198.0 |
| Baggage | 56 | 140 | 78.4 |
| Empty weight | + 2,015 | | 1,554.0 |
| | 2,970 lbs | | 2,476.4 lbs-in |

3. Determine the balance conditions. Looking at FAA Figure 34, notice that the table stops at the maximum weight of 2,950. Even though the weight is off the scale, the Moment of 2,476.4 is between the minimum and maximum Moment limits given in the table. Therefore, we are 20 pounds overweight and within balance limits.

AIR
**3664.** GIVEN:

| | WEIGHT (LB) | ARM (IN) | MOMENT (LB-IN) |
|---|---|---|---|
| Empty weight | 1,495.0 | 101.4 | 151,593.0 |
| Pilot and passengers | 380.0 | 64.0 | — |
| Fuel (30 gal usable – no reserve) | — | 96.0 | — |

The CG is located how far aft of datum?

A—CG 92.44.
B—CG 94.01.
C—CG 119.8.

1.  Compute the total weight and moment using the formula:

    Weight x Arm = Moment

    or:

| Item | Weight | Arm | Moment |
|---|---|---|---|
| Empty weight | 1,495.0 | 101.4 | 151,593.0 |
| Pilot & passenger | 380.0 | 64.0 | 24,320.0 |
| Fuel (30 x 6) | 180.0 | 96.0 | 17,280.0 |
| Total | 2,055.0 lbs | | 193,193.0 |

2.  Compute the center of gravity using the formula:

$$CG = \frac{Total\ Moment}{Total\ Weight}$$

or:

$$CG = \frac{193,193}{2,055} = 94.01\ inches\ aft\ of\ datum$$

(H316) — AC 61-23C, Chapter 4

---

AIR
**3665.** (Refer to Figures 33 and 34.) Determine if the airplane weight and balance is within limits.

Front seat occupants .......................................... 340 lb
Rear seat occupants .......................................... 295 lb
Fuel (main wing tanks) ..................................... 44 gal
Baggage ............................................................. 56 lb

A—20 pounds overweight, CG aft of aft limits.
B—20 pounds overweight, CG within limits.
C—20 pounds overweight, CG forward of forward limits.

When multiplying a weight by its arm you must divide by 100 to get moment index (Moment/100). Moments listed in FAA Figures 33 and 34 are already divided by 100, and are therefore moment indexes.

1.  Calculate weight and moment index using the information from the question and from FAA Figures 33 and 34 and the formula:

    Weight x Arm ÷ 100 = Moment/Index

| Item | Weight | Arm | Moment/100 |
|---|---|---|---|
| Empty weight | 2,015 lbs | | 1,554.0 lbs-in |
| Front seat | 340 lbs | 85 | 289.0 lbs-in |
| Rear seat | 295 lbs | 121 | 357.0 lbs-in |
| Fuel (44 x 6) | 264 lbs | 75 | 198.0 lbs-in |
| Baggage | 56 lbs | 140 | 78.4 lbs-in |
| Total | 2,970 lbs | | 2,476.4 lbs-in |

2.  Consult the Moment Limits vs. Weight Table, FAA Figure 34. The aircraft weight is 2,970 pounds or 20 pounds in excess of the maximum weight on the chart. The moment of 2,476.4 lbs-in would be within limits if the chart went to 2,970 pounds gross weight.

(H316) — AC 61-23C, Chapter 4

---

AIR
**3666.** (Refer to Figures 33 and 34.) What is the maximum amount of baggage that can be carried when the airplane is loaded as follows?

Front seat occupants ......................................... 387 lb
Rear seat occupants ......................................... 293 lb
Fuel ................................................................... 35 gal

A—45 pounds.
B—63 pounds.
C—220 pounds.

1.  When multiplying a weight times its arm you must divide by 100 to get moment index. Calculate total weight and total moment index using the information from the question and from FAA Figures 33 and 34 and the formula:

    Weight x Arm ÷ 100 = Moment/Index

| Item | Weight | Arm | Moment/100 |
|---|---|---|---|
| Empty weight | 2,015 lbs | | 1,554.0 lbs-in |
| Front seat | 387 lbs | 85 | 329.0 lbs-in |
| Rear seat | 293 lbs | 121 | 354.5 lbs-in |
| Fuel (35 x 6) | 210 lbs | 75 | 157.5 lbs-in |
| Total | 2,905 lbs | | 2,395.0 lbs-in |

2.  The maximum takeoff weight is 2,950 pounds. Calculate what the allowed baggage weight would be:

    2,950 – 2,905 = 45 pounds

---

**Answers**

3664    [B]          3665    [B]          3666    [A]

3. Verify that the CG would remain within the allowable range with this much baggage by calculating the new weight and moment index.

| Item | Weight | Arm | Moment/100 |
|---|---|---|---|
| Original total | 2,905 lbs | | 2,395.0 lbs-in |
| Baggage | + 45 lbs | 140 | + 63.0 lbs-in |
| New Total | 2,950 lbs | | 2,458.0 lbs-in |

4. Consult the Moment Limit vs. Weight Table, FAA Figure 34. For a weight of 2,950 pounds, the range of allowable moments is 2,422 to 2,499. The new total moment index of 2,458.0 is acceptable.

*(H316) — AC 61-23C, Chapter 4*

---

AIR

**3667.** (Refer to Figures 33 and 34.) Calculate the weight and balance and determine if the CG and the weight of the airplane are within limits.

Front seat occupants .......................................... 350 lb
Rear seat occupants .......................................... 325 lb
Baggage ............................................................. 27 lb
Fuel .................................................................... 35 gal

A—CG 81.7, out of limits forward.
B—CG 83.4, within limits.
C—CG 84.1, within limits.

Use the following steps:

1. Calculate weight and moment index using the information from the problem and from FAA Figures 33 and 34 and the formula:

$$Weight \times Arm \div 100 = Moment/Index$$

| Item | Weight | Arm | Moment/100 |
|---|---|---|---|
| Empty weight | 2,015 lbs | | 1,554.0 lbs-in |
| Front seat | 350 lbs | 85 | 297.5 lbs-in |
| Rear seat | 325 lbs | 121 | 393.3 lbs-in |
| Baggage | 27 lbs | 140 | 37.8 lbs-in |
| Fuel (35 x 6) | 210 lbs | 75 | 157.5 lbs-in |
| Total | 2,927 lbs | | 2,440.1 lbs-in |

2. Calculate the position of CG using the formula:

$$CG = \frac{Total\ Mom\ Ind}{Total\ Weight} \times Reduction\ Factor$$

or:

$$CG = \frac{2,440.1}{2,927} \times 100 = 83.4\ inches\ aft\ of\ datum$$

*(H316) — AC 61-23C, Chapter 4*

---

AIR

**3668.** (Refer to Figures 33 and 34.) Determine if the airplane weight and balance is within limits.

Front seat occupants .......................................... 415 lb
Rear seat occupants .......................................... 110 lb
Fuel, main tanks ................................................ 44 gal
Fuel, aux. tanks ................................................. 19 gal
Baggage ............................................................. 32 lb

A—19 pounds overweight, CG within limits.
B—19 pounds overweight, CG out of limits forward.
C—Weight within limits, CG out of limits.

Use the following steps:

1. Calculate weight and moment index using the information from the problem and from FAA Figures 33 and 34, and the formula:

$$Weight \times Arm \div 100 = Moment/Index$$

| Item | Weight | Arm | Moment/100 |
|---|---|---|---|
| Empty weight | 2,015 lbs | | 1,554.0 lbs-in |
| Front seat | 415 lbs | 85 | 352.8 lbs-in |
| Rear seat | 110 lbs | 121 | 133.1 lbs-in |
| Fuel main 44 x 6 | 264 lbs | 75 | 198.0 lbs-in |
| Fuel aux. 19 x 6 | 114 lbs | 94 | 107.2 lbs-in |
| Baggage | 32 lbs | 140 | 44.8 lbs-in |
| Total | 2,950 lbs | | 2,389.9 lbs-in |

2. Calculate the CG using the formula:

$$CG = \frac{Total\ Mom\ Ind}{Total\ Weight} \times Reduction\ Factor$$

or:

$$CG = \frac{2,389.9}{2,950} \times 100 = 81.0\ inches\ aft\ of\ datum$$

3. Consult the Moment Limits vs. Weight Table (FAA Figure 34). A CG of 81 inches is 1.1 inches forward of the forward CG limit for a weight (allowed) of 2,950 pounds.

*(H316) — AC 61-23C, Chapter 4*

---

**Answers**

3667    [B]            3668    [C]

AIR
**3674.** (Refer to Figures 33 and 34.) Upon landing, the front passenger (180 pounds) departs the airplane. A rear passenger (204 pounds) moves to the front passenger position. What effect does this have on the CG if the airplane weighed 2,690 pounds and the MOM/100 was 2,260 just prior to the passenger transfer?

A—The CG moves forward approximately 3 inches.
B—The weight changes, but the CG is not affected.
C—The CG moves forward approximately 0.1 inch.

*Use the following steps:*

1. *Consider the effect on the total weight.*

   | Item | Weight |
   |------|--------|
   | Original weight | 2,690 pounds |
   | Deplaned passenger | – 180 pounds |
   | New Weight | 2,510 pounds |

2. *Consider the effect on the total moment index using the arms given in FAA Figure 33, and the formula:*

   *Weight x Arm ÷ 100 = Moment/Index*

   | Item | Weight | Arm | Moment/100 |
   |------|--------|-----|------------|
   | Original weight & Mom Ind | 2,690 | | 2,260.0 lbs-in |
   | Passenger exiting, front | -180 | 85 | -153.0 lbs-in |
   | Passenger exiting, rear | -204 | 121 | -246.8 lbs-in |
   | Passenger into front | + 204 | 85 | + 173.4 lbs-in |
   | New Total Weight & Moment | 2,510 | | 2,033.6 lbs-in |

3. *Determine both the original and new CG using the formula:*

   $$CG = \frac{Total\ Mom\ Ind}{Total\ Weight} \times Reduction\ Factor$$

   *or:*

   a. *Original CG =*

   $$\frac{2,260}{2,690} \times 100 = 84.0\ inches\ aft\ of\ datum$$

   b. *New CG =*

   $$\frac{2,033.6}{2,510} \times 100 = 81.0\ inches\ aft\ of\ datum$$

4. *Calculate the change in CG:*

   *84 – 81 = 3 inches (forward)*

*(H316) — AC 61-23C, Chapter 4*

AIR
**3675.** (Refer to Figures 33 and 34.) Which action can adjust the airplane's weight to maximum gross weight and the CG within limits for takeoff?

Front seat occupants ....................................... 425 lb
Rear seat occupants ........................................ 300 lb
Fuel, main tanks ............................................... 44 gal

A—Drain 12 gallons of fuel.
B—Drain 9 gallons of fuel.
C—Transfer 12 gallons of fuel from the main tanks to the auxiliary tanks.

*Use the following steps:*

1. *Calculate the original weights and moment index using the information from the problem and FAA Figures 33 and 34, and the formula:*

   *Weight x Arm ÷ 100 = Moment/Index*

   | Item | Weight | Arm | Moment/100 |
   |------|--------|-----|------------|
   | Empty weight | 2,015 lbs | | 1,554.0 lbs-in |
   | Front seat | 425 lbs | 85 | 361.3 lbs-in |
   | Rear seat | 300 lbs | 121 | 363.0 lbs-in |
   | Fuel (44 x 6) | 264 lbs | 75 | 198.0 lbs-in |
   | Total | 3,004 lbs | | 2,476.3 lbs-in |

2. *If the aircraft has a maximum allowable takeoff weight of 2,950 lbs, compute the weight to be removed to reach an acceptable takeoff weight.*

   *3,004 – 2,950 = 54 pounds*

3. *Compute the amount of fuel (in gallons) that totals 54 lbs:*

   *54 ÷ 6 = 9 gallons*

4. *Compute the revised weight and moment index:*

   | Item | Weight | Arm | Moment/100 |
   |------|--------|-----|------------|
   | Original totals | 3,004 lbs | | 2,476.3 lbs-in |
   | Fuel | – 54 lbs | 75 | – 40.5 lbs-in |
   | New Total | 2,950 lbs | | 2,435.8 lbs-in |

5. *Calculate the position of the CG using the formula:*

   $$CG = \frac{Total\ Mom\ Ind}{Total\ Weight} \times Reduction\ Factor$$

   *or:*

   $$CG = \frac{2,435.8}{2,950} \times 100 = 82.6\ inches\ aft\ of\ datum$$

6. *Consult the Moment Limits vs. Weight Chart. A CG position of 82.6 is within limits specified for a 2,950 lbs takeoff weight.*

*(H316) — AC 61-23C, Chapter 4*

**Answers**

3674    [A]                3675    [B]

AIR

**3676.** (Refer to Figures 33 and 34.) What effect does a 35-gallon fuel burn (main tanks) have on the weight and balance if the airplane weighed 2,890 pounds and the MOM/100 was 2,452 at takeoff?

A—Weight is reduced by 210 pounds and the CG is aft of limits.
B—Weight is reduced by 210 pounds and the CG is unaffected.
C—Weight is reduced to 2,680 pounds and the CG moves forward.

*Use the following steps:*

1. *Calculate the change in both weight and moment index caused by a burn of 35 gallons, using the information from FAA Figures 33 and 34.*

   *Weight x Arm ÷ 100 = Moment/Index*

   | Item | Weight | Arm | Moment |
   |------|--------|-----|--------|
   | Fuel (35 x 6) | 210 lbs | 75 | 158 lbs-in |

2. *Determine the effect of burn on total weight and moment index:*

   | Item | Weight | Arm | Moment/100 |
   |------|--------|-----|------------|
   | Original total | 2,890 lbs | | 2,452.0 lbs-in |
   | Fuel burn | – 210 lbs | 75 | – 158.0 lbs-in |
   | New Total | 2,680 lbs | | 2,294.0 lbs-in |

3. *Consult the Moment Limits vs. Weight Table (FAA Figure 34). The allowed range of moment indexes for a weight of 2,680 lbs is 2,123 to 2,287 lbs-in/100. Hence the new moment index exceeds the maximum allowed and the CG is aft of limits.*

(H316) — AC 61-23C, Chapter 4

AIR

**3677.** (Refer to Figures 33 and 34.) With the airplane loaded as follows, what action can be taken to balance the airplane?

Front seat occupants ......................................... 411 lb
Rear seat occupants ......................................... 100 lb
Main wing tanks ................................................ 44 gal

A—Fill the auxiliary wing tanks.
B—Add a 100-pound weight to the baggage compartment.
C—Transfer 10 gallons of fuel from the main tanks to the auxiliary tanks.

*Use the following steps:*

1. *Calculate the weights and moments using the information from the problem and FAA Figures 33 and 34, and the formula:*

   *Weight x Arm ÷ 100 = Moment/Index*

   | Item | Weight | Arm | Moment/100 |
   |------|--------|-----|------------|
   | Empty weight | 2,015 lbs | | 1,554.0 lbs-in |
   | Front seat | 411 lbs | 85 | 349.4 lbs-in |
   | Rear seat | 100 lbs | 121 | 121.0 lbs-in |
   | Fuel 44 x 6 | 264 lbs | 75 | 198.0 lbs-in |
   | Total | 2,790 lbs | | 2,222.4 lbs-in |

2. *Consulting the Moment Limits vs. Weight Table (FAA Figure 34), the allowed range of moments for 2,790 lbs is between 2,243 and 2,374 lbs-in/100.*

3. *Since the moment index is too small, add weight, and for maximum increase in moment index with minimum weight penalty, as far aft as practical. Add 100 lbs in the baggage compartment and recompute weight and moment index:*

   | Item | Weight | Arm | Moment/100 |
   |------|--------|-----|------------|
   | Original totals | 2,790 lbs | | 2,222.4 lbs-in |
   | Add weight | + 100 lbs | 140 | + 140.0 lbs-in |
   | New Totals | 2,890 lbs | | 2,362.4 lbs-in |

4. *Consult the Moment Limits vs. Weight Table. The allowed range of moments for 2,890 pounds is 2,354 to 2,452 lbs-in/100. The new moment is now within limits.*

(H316) — AC 61-23C, Chapter 4

**Answers**

3676   [A]             3677   [B]

# Computing Weight and Balance Problems Using a Graph

**Problem:**

Referring to FAA Figure 35, determine the maximum amount of baggage that may be loaded aboard the airplane for the CG to remain within the loading envelope.

| Item | Weight (lbs) | Moment/1,000 (lbs-in) |
|---|---|---|
| Empty weight | 1,350 | 51.5 |
| Pilot, Front Passenger | 250 | — |
| Rear Passengers | 400 | — |
| Baggage | — | — |
| Fuel 30 gal. | — | — |
| Oil 8 qt. | — | — |

**Solution:**

1. Determine the total weight. Using the information provided in the question, enter the items and the weights:

| Item | Weight (lbs) | Moment/1,000 (lbs-in) |
|---|---|---|
| Pilot, front passenger | 250 | |
| Rear passengers | 400 | |
| Fuel | 180 * | |
| Oil | 15 ** | |
| Baggage | — | |
| Empty weight | + 1,350 † | |
| | 2,195 lbs | |

*30 gal x 6 lbs/gal     **given in the note in the middle of FAA Figure 35     † given in problem

2. Determine the moments. Using FAA Figure 35, locate the moments for all the given weights:

| Item | Weight (lbs) | Moment/1,000 (lbs-in) |
|---|---|---|
| Pilot, front passenger | 250 | 9.3 |
| Rear passengers | 400 | 29.3 |
| Fuel | 180 | 8.7 |
| Oil | 15 | -0.2 * |
| Baggage | — | — |
| Empty weight | + 1,350 | 51.5 |
| | 2,195 lbs | 98.6 lbs-in |

*from note in center of FAA Figure 35

3. From the Center of Gravity Moment Envelope, bottom of FAA Figure 35, determine the maximum allowable gross weight of the aircraft, as indicated by the top of the "Normal Category" envelope (2,300 pounds). Comparing the total weight of this problem with the maximum allowable weight shows that 105 pounds of baggage could be carried:

```
  2,300
- 2,195
    105
```

4. From the Loading Graph, determine the Mom/1,000 of 105 pounds of baggage.

Add that amount to the previous total Mom/1,000:

| Item | Weight (lbs) | Moment/1,000 (lbs-in) |
|---|---|---|
| Totals | 2,195 | 98.6 |
| Baggage | + 105 | + 10.0 |
| New Totals | 2,300 lbs | 108.6 lbs-in |

5. Enter the Center of Gravity Moment Envelope Graph at the total Mom/1,000 (108.6) and the maximum allowable gross weight line at 2,300 pounds. The point of intersection falls within the "Normal Category" envelope and acceptable weight and balance conditions.

**3669.** (Refer to Figure 35.) What is the maximum amount of baggage that may be loaded aboard the airplane for the CG to remain within the moment envelope?

| | WEIGHT (LB) | MOM/1000 |
|---|---|---|
| Empty weight | 1,350 | 51.5 |
| Pilot and front passenger | 250 | — |
| Rear passengers | 400 | — |
| Baggage | — | — |
| Fuel, 30 gal | — | — |
| Oil, 8 qt | — | -0.2 |

A—105 pounds.
B—110 pounds.
C—120 pounds.

*Use the following steps:*

1. *Find total weight and moment index (except baggage) by using the loading graphs in FAA Figure 35. Note that the reduction factor is 1,000 in this problem. The standard weight for gasoline is 6 lbs/U.S. gallon, and for oil, 7.5 lbs/U.S. gallon.*

| Item | Weight | Moment/1,000 |
|---|---|---|
| B.E.W. | 1,350 lbs | 51.5 lbs-in |
| Pilot & Pax (a) | 250 lbs | 9.3 lbs-in |
| Rear Pax (b) | 400 lbs | 29.3 lbs-in |
| Fuel (30 x 6) (c) | 180 lbs | 8.7 lbs-in |
| Oil | 15 lbs | -0.2 lbs-in |
| Total | 2,195 lbs | 98.6 lbs-in |

2. *Calculate the maximum allowable weight for baggage:*

   *2,300 – 2,195 = 105 pounds*

3. *Add baggage and calculate the new totals for weight and moment index.*

| Weight | Moment/1,000 |
|---|---|
| 2,195 lbs | 98.6 lbs-in |
| + 105 lbs | 10.0 lbs-in |
| 2,300 lbs | 108.6 lbs-in |

4. *Plot the position of the point determined by 2,300 pounds and the moment of 108.6 lbs-in/1,000 on the center of gravity moment envelope graph. The point is in the normal category envelope.*

*(H316) — AC 61-23C, Chapter 4*

**3670.** (Refer to Figure 35.) Calculate the moment of the airplane and determine which category is applicable.

| | WEIGHT (LB) | MOM/1000 |
|---|---|---|
| Empty weight | 1,350 | 51.5 |
| Pilot and front passenger | 310 | — |
| Rear passengers | 96 | — |
| Fuel, 38 gal | — | — |
| Oil, 8 qt | — | -0.2 |

A—79.2, utility category.
B—80.8, utility category.
C—81.2, normal category.

*Use the following steps:*

1. *Find total weight and moment index by using the loading graph (FAA Figure 35). The standard weight for gasoline is 6 lbs/U.S. gallons and for oil, 7.5 lbs U.S. gallon.*

| Item | Weight | Moment/1,000 |
|---|---|---|
| B.E.W. | 1,350 lbs | 51.5 lbs-in |
| Pilot & Pax (a) | 310 lbs | 11.5 lbs-in |
| Rear Pax (b) | 96 lbs | 7.0 lbs-in |
| Fuel (38 x 6) (c) | 228 lbs | 11.0 lbs-in |
| Oil | 15 lbs | -0.2 lbs-in |
| Total | 1,999 lbs | 80.8 lbs-in |

2. *Plot the position of the point determined by 1,999 pounds and a moment of 80.8 lbs-in/1,000. The point is just inside the utility category envelope.*

*(H316) — AC 61-23C, Chapter 4*

**Answers**
3669  [A]          3670  [B]

AIR

**3671.** (Refer to Figure 35.) What is the maximum amount of fuel that may be aboard the airplane on takeoff if loaded as follows?

| | WEIGHT (LB) | MOM/1000 |
|---|---|---|
| Empty weight | 1,350 | 51.5 |
| Pilot and front passenger | 340 | — |
| Rear passengers | 310 | — |
| Baggage | 45 | — |
| Oil, 8 qt | — | — |

A—24 gallons.
B—32 gallons.
C—40 gallons.

1. Find the total weight and moment index (except fuel) by using the loading graph in FAA Figure 35.

| Item | Weight | Moment/1,000 |
|---|---|---|
| B.E.W. | 1,350 lbs | 51.5 lbs-in |
| Pilot & Pax (a) | 340 lbs | 12.6 lbs-in |
| Rear Pax (b) | 310 lbs | 22.6 lbs-in |
| Baggage (c) | 45 lbs | 4.2 lbs-in |
| Oil (d) | 15 lbs | -0.2 lbs-in |
| Total | 2,060 lbs | 90.7 lbs-in |

2. Calculate the additional fuel weight which can be added:

   $$2,300 - 2,060 = 240\ lbs$$

3. Calculate the number of gallons of fuel at 6 lbs/gallon:

   $$240 \div 6 = 40\ gallons$$

4. Calculate the added fuel moment index from the graph (40 gal fuel – 11.5 MOM/1,000).

5. Calculate the new total weight and moment index:

| Weight | Moment/1,000 |
|---|---|
| 2,060 lbs | 90.7 lbs-in |
| + 240 lbs | 11.5 lbs-in |
| 2,300 lbs | 102.2 lbs-in |

6. Plot the position of the point determined by 2,300 pounds and a moment index of 102.2 lbs-in/1,000. The point lies on the normal category envelope.

*(H316) — AC 61-23C, Chapter 4*

AIR

**3672.** (Refer to Figure 35.) Determine the moment with the following data:

| | WEIGHT (LB) | MOM/1000 |
|---|---|---|
| Empty weight | 1,350 | 51.5 |
| Pilot and front passenger | 340 | — |
| Fuel (std tanks) | Capacity | — |
| Oil, 8 qt | — | — |

A—69.9 pound-inches.
B—74.9 pound-inches.
C—77.6 pound-inches.

1. Find the total weight and moment index by using the loading graph from FAA Figure 35.

| Item | Weight | Moment/1,000 |
|---|---|---|
| B.E.W. | 1,350 lbs | 51.5 lbs-in |
| Pilot & Pax (a) | 340 lbs | 12.6 lbs-in |
| Fuel (Std. Tanks) (b) | 228 lbs | 11.0 lbs-in |
| Oil (c) | 15 lbs | -0.2 lbs-in |
| Total | 1,933 lbs | 74.9 lbs-in |

*(H316) — AC 61-23C, Chapter 4*

AIR

**3673.** (Refer to Figure 35.) Determine the aircraft loaded moment and the aircraft category.

| | WEIGHT (LB) | MOM/1000 |
|---|---|---|
| Empty weight | 1,350 | 51.5 |
| Pilot and front passenger | 380 | — |
| Fuel, 48 gal | 288 | — |
| Oil, 8 qt | — | — |

A—78.2, normal category.
B—79.2, normal category.
C—80.4, utility category.

*Use the following steps:*

1. Find the total weight and moment index by using the loading graph from FAA Figure 35.

| Item | Weight | Moment/1,000 |
|---|---|---|
| B.E.W. | 1,350 lbs | 51.5 lbs-in |
| Pilot & Pax (a) | 380 lbs | 14.0 lbs-in |
| Fuel (b) | 288 lbs | 13.8 lbs-in |
| Oil (c) | 15 lbs | -0.2 lbs-in |
| Total | 2,033 lbs | 79.1 lbs-in |

2. Plot the position of the point determined by 2,033 lbs. and a moment of 79.1 lbs-in/1,000. The point is within the normal category envelope.

*(H316) — AC 61-23C, Chapter 4*

**Answers**

3671　[C]　　　3672　[B]　　　3673　[B]

RTC
**3720.** (Refer to Figure 44.) What action, if any, should be taken for lateral balance if the helicopter is loaded as follows?

Gross weight ................................................. 1,800 lb
Pilot .................... 140 lb, 13.5 in. left of "0" MOM arm
Copilot .............. 180 lb, 13.5 in. right of "0" MOM arm

A—Add 10 pounds of weight to the pilot's side.
B—Decrease the gross weight 50 pounds.
C—No action is required.

*Use the following steps:*

1. *Compute the left and right moments using the formula:*

    *Weight x Arm = Moment*

    | Item | Weight | Arm | Moment |
    |------|--------|-----|--------|
    | Pilot | 140 lbs | 13.5 | 1,890 lbs-in (left) |
    | Copilot | 180 lbs | 13.5 | 2,430 lbs-in (right) |

2. *Find the offset to the left or right:*

    2,430.0 *lbs-in (right)*
    − 1,890.0 *lbs-in (left)*
    540.0 *lbs-in offset (right)*

3. *Enter the bottom of the Lateral Offset Moment Graph at 540 lbs-in right of the zero point. Proceed upward until intercepting the 1,800-pound gross weight line. The point of intercept lies inside the envelope.*

*(H76) — FAA-H-8083-21*

RTC
**3721.** (Refer to Figure 44.) What action should be taken for lateral balance if the helicopter is loaded as follows?

Gross weight ................................................. 1,800 lb
Pilot .................... 100 lb, 13.5 in. left of "0" MOM arm
Copilot .............. 200 lb, 13.5 in. right of "0" MOM arm

A—Add 50 pounds of weight to the pilot's side.
B—Decrease the gross weight 50 pounds.
C—No action is required.

*Use the following steps:*

1. *Compute the left and right moments using the formula:*

    *Weight x Arm = Moment*

    | Item | Weight | Arm | Moment |
    |------|--------|-----|--------|
    | Copilot | 200 lbs | 13.5 | 2,700 lbs-in (right) |
    | Pilot | 100 lbs | 13.5 | 1,350 lbs-in (left) |

2. *Find the offset to the right or left:*

    2,700.0 *lbs-in (right)*
    − 1,350.0 *lbs-in (left)*
    1,350.0 *lbs-in offset (right)*

3. *Enter the bottom of the Lateral Offset Moment Envelope Graph of FAA Figure 44 at 1,350 right of the zero point. Proceed upward until intercepting the 1,800-pound gross weight line. The point of intercept falls outside the envelope to the right.*

4. *Try adding 50 pounds to the pilot's side and do the same computations:*

    Copilot   200 x 13.5 = 2,700 *(right)*
    Pilot   150 x 13.5 = 2,025 *(left)*

    2,700 *(right)*
    − 2,025 *(left)*
    675 *(right)*

*Plot the new values on the lateral offset envelope graph of FAA Figure 44.*

*(H76) — FAA-H-8083-21*

RTC
**3722.** (Refer to Figure 42.) Determine the weight and balance of the helicopter.

| | WEIGHT (LB) | ARM (IN) | MOMENT (LB-IN) |
|---|---|---|---|
| Empty weight | 1,495.0 | — | 151,593.0 |
| Pilot and one passenger | 350.0 | 64.0 | — |
| Fuel (40 gal usable) | — | 96.0 | — |

A—Over gross weight limit, but within CG limit.
B—Within gross weight limit and at the aft CG limit.
C—Over gross weight limit and exceeds the aft CG limit.

*Use the following steps:*

1. *Calculate the weight and moment using the information given in the problem and the formula:*

    *Weight x Arm = Moment*

    *Note: The standard weight of gasoline is 6 lbs/U.S. gallon.*

    | Item | Weight | Arm | Moment |
    |------|--------|-----|--------|
    | Empty weight | 1,495 lbs | | 151,593.0 lbs-in |
    | Pilot & Pax | 350 lbs | 64 | 22,400.0 lbs-in |
    | Fuel 40 x 6 | 240 lbs | 96 | 23,040.0 lbs-in |
    | Total | 2,085 lbs | | 197,033.0 lbs-in |

    *Continued*

**Answers**
3720  [C]          3721  [A]          3722  [B]

2. Determine the position of the CG using the formula:

$$CG = \frac{Total\ Moment}{Total\ Weight}$$

or:

$$CG = \frac{197,033}{2,085} = 94.5\ inches\ aft\ of\ datum$$

3. Locate the point on FAA Figure 42 defined by a weight of 2,085 pounds and a CG of 94.5 inches, and find the aircraft within gross weight limit and at the aft CG limit.

(H76) — FAA-H-8083-21

---

RTC
**3723.** (Refer to Figure 43.) Determine if the helicopter's CG is within limits.

|  | WEIGHT (LB) | MOMENT (lb-in) |
|---|---|---|
| Empty weight (including oil) | 1,025 | 102,705 |
| Pilot and passenger | 345 | — |
| Fuel, 35 gal | — | — |

A—Out of limits forward.
B—Within limits.
C—Out of limits aft.

Use the following steps:

1. Calculate the weights and moments using the information from the problem and the Loading Chart of FAA Figure 43. Use the formula:

   Weight x Arm = Moment

   Note: The standard weight of gasoline is 6 lbs/U.S gallon.

| Item | Weight | Arm | Moment |
|---|---|---|---|
| Empty weight | 1,025 lbs | | 102,705.0 lbs-in |
| Pilot & Pax (a) | 345 lbs | 83.90 | 28,945.5 lbs-in |
| Fuel 35 x 6 (b) | 210 lbs | 107.0 | 22,470.0 lbs-in |
| Total | 1,580 lbs | | 154,120.5 lbs-in |

2. Determine the position of the CG using the formula:

$$CG = \frac{Total\ Moment}{Total\ Weight}$$

or:

$$CG = \frac{154,120.5}{1,580} = 97.54\ inches\ aft\ of\ datum$$

3. Plot the point determined by a weight of 1,580 pounds and a moment of 154,120.5 lbs-in on the CG limit graph of FAA Figure 43. The point is within the forward and aft limits.

(H76) — FAA-H-8083-21

RTC
**3724.** (Refer to Figure 43.) What effect does adding a 185-pound passenger have on the CG, if prior to boarding the passenger, the helicopter weighed 1,380 pounds and the moment is 136,647.5 pound-inches?

A—The CG is moved forward 1.78 inches.
B—The CG is moved aft 1.78 inches.
C—The CG is moved forward 2.36 inches.

Use the following steps:

1. Calculate the original position of the CG using the formula:

$$CG = \frac{Total\ Moment}{Total\ Weight}$$

or:

$$CG = \frac{136,647.5}{1,380} = 99.02\ inches\ aft\ of\ datum$$

2. Determine the revised weight and moment. The station for the passenger is 83.90 inches as shown on the Loading Chart of FAA Figure 43. Use the following formula:

   Weight x Arm = Moment

| Item | Weight | Arm | Moment |
|---|---|---|---|
| Original total | 1,380 lbs | | 136,647.5 lbs-in |
| Passenger | +185 lbs | 83.9 | 15,521.5 lbs-in |
| New Total | 1,565 lbs | | 152,169.0 lbs-in |

3. Calculate the new CG:

$$CG = \frac{152,169}{1,565} = 97.23\ inches\ aft\ of\ datum$$

4. Compute the change in CG:

| Original CG | 99.02 | inches aft of datum |
|---|---|---|
| minus new CG | – 97.23 | inches aft of datum |
| Movement | 1.79 | inches (forward) |

(H76) — FAA-H-8083-21

---

RTC
**3725.** How is the CG of the helicopter affected after a fuel burn of 20 gallons?

Gross weight prior to fuel burn ...................... 2,050 lb
Moment ................................................. 195,365 lb-in
Fuel arm ........................................................ 96.9 in

A—CG shifts forward 1.0 inch.
B—CG shifts forward 0.1 inch.
C—CG shifts aft 1.0 inch.

---

**Answers**

| 3723 | [B] | 3724 | [A] | 3725 | [B] |
|---|---|---|---|---|---|

Use the following steps:

1. Calculate the original position of the CG using the formula:

$$CG = \frac{Total\ Moment}{Total\ Weight}$$

or:

$$CG = \frac{195,365}{2,050} = 95.3\ inches\ aft\ of\ datum$$

2. Determine the revised weight and moment. The station for the fuel is 96.9 inches as shown on the question which contradicts FAA Figure 43. Use the following formula:

Weight x Arm = Moment

| Item | Weight | Arm | Moment | |
|------|--------|-----|--------|---|
| Original total | 2,050 lbs | | 195,365 | lbs-in |
| Fuel burn | – 120 lbs | 96.9 | 11,628 | lbs-in |
| New Total | 1,930 lbs | | 183,737 | lbs-in |

3. Calculate the new CG:

$$CG = \frac{183,737}{1,930} = 95.2\ inches\ aft\ of\ datum$$

4. Compute the change in CG:

| | | |
|---|---|---|
| Original CG | 95.3 | inches aft of datum |
| minus new CG | – 95.2 | inches aft of datum |
| Movement | .1 | inch (forward) |

(H76) — FAA-H-8083-21

---

RTC
**3726.** (Refer to Figure 43.) How is the CG of the helicopter affected when all of the auxiliary fuel is burned off?

Gross weight prior to fuel burn ........................ 1,660 lb
Moment .............................................. 159,898.5 lb-in

A—CG moves aft 0.12 inch.
B—CG moves forward 0.78 inch.
C—CG moves forward 1.07 inches.

Use the following steps:

1. Calculate the original position of the CG using the formula:

$$CG = \frac{Total\ Moment}{Total\ Weight}$$

or:

$$CG = \frac{159,858.5}{1,660} = 96.3\ inches\ aft\ of\ datum$$

2. Determine the revised weight and moment. The auxiliary fuel burn is 19 gallons (the dotted line goes from 44 to 25). 19 x 6 = 114 lbs. The station for the fuel is 107 inches as shown on the Loading Chart of FAA Figure 43. Use the following formula:

Weight x Arm = Moment

| Item | Weight | Arm | Moment | |
|------|--------|-----|--------|---|
| Original total | 1,660 lbs | | 159,858.5 | lbs-in |
| Fuel burn | – 114 lbs | 107 | –12,198 | lbs-in |
| New Total | 1,546 lbs | | 147,660.5 | lbs-in |

3. Calculate the new CG:

147,660.5 ÷ 1,546 = 95.51 inches aft of datum

4. Compute the change in CG:

| | | |
|---|---|---|
| Original CG | 96.30 | inches aft of datum |
| minus new CG | – 95.51 | inches aft of datum |
| Movement | .79 | inches (forward) |

(H76) — FAA-H-8083-21

---

RTC
**3728.** (Refer to Figure 44.) Determine if the helicopter weight and balance is within limits.

| | WEIGHT (LB) | ARM (IN) | MOMENT (100) |
|---|---|---|---|
| Empty weight | 1,495.0 | 101.4 | 1,515.93 |
| Oil, 8 qt | — | 100.5 | — |
| Fuel, 40 gal | — | 96.0 | — |
| Pilot and copilot | 300.0 | 64.0 | — |

A—CG 95.2 inches, within limits.
B—CG 95.3 inches, weight and CG out of limits.
C—CG 95.4 inches, within limits.

Use the following steps:

1. Calculate the weights and moment indexes using the information from the problem and the formula:

Weight x Arm ÷ Reduction Factor = Moment/Index

Note: The standard weight for gasoline is 6 lbs/U.S. gallon and for oil, 7.5 lbs/U.S. gallon.

| Item | Weight | Arm | Moment/100 | |
|------|--------|-----|------------|---|
| Empty weight | 1,495 lbs | 101.4 | 1,515.93 | lbs-in |
| Oil, 8 qts (2 x 7.5) | 15 lbs | 100.5 | 15.08 | lbs-in |
| Fuel (40 x 6) | 240 lbs | 96.0 | 230.40 | lbs-in |
| Pilots | 300 lbs | 64.0 | 192 | lbs-in |
| Total | 2,050 lbs | | 1,953.41 | lbs-in |

*Continued*

---

**Answers**

3726    [B]                    3728    [B]

2. Determine the position of the CG using the formula:

$$CG = \frac{Total\ Mom/Ind}{Total\ Weight} \times Reduction\ Factor$$

or:

$$\frac{1,953.41}{2,050} \times 100 = 95.29\ inches\ aft\ of\ datum$$

3. Plot the point determined by a weight of 2,050 pounds and a CG of 95.29 inches on the longitudinal CG envelope of FAA Figure 44. The point is outside the allowable limits.

(H76) — FAA-H-8083-21

---

RTC
**3727.** (Refer to Figure 44.) Calculate the weight and balance of the helicopter, and determine if the CG is within limits.

| | WEIGHT (LB) | ARM (IN) | MOMENT (100) |
|---|---|---|---|
| Empty weight | 1,495.0 | 101.4 | 1,515.93 |
| Oil, 8 qt | — | 100.5 | — |
| Fuel, 40 gal | — | 96.0 | — |
| Pilot | 160.0 | 64.0 | — |

A—CG 90.48 inches, out of limits forward.
B—CG 95.32 inches, within limits.
C—CG 97.58 inches, within limits.

This problem uses a reduction factor so we arrive at moment index instead of moment.

Use the following steps:

1. Calculate the weights and moment indexes using the information from the problem and the formula:

Weight x Arm ÷ Reduction Factor = Moment Index

Note: The standard weight for gasoline is 6 lbs/U.S. gallon and for oil, 7.5 lbs/U.S. gallon.

| Item | Weight | Arm | Moment/100 |
|---|---|---|---|
| Empty weight | 1,495 lbs | 101.4 | 1,515.93 lbs-in |
| Oil, 8 qts (2 x 7.5) | 15 lbs | 100.5 | 15.08 lbs-in |
| Fuel (40 x 6) | 240 lbs | 96.0 | 230.40 lbs-in |
| Pilot | 160 lbs | 64.0 | 102.40 lbs-in |
| Total | 1,910 lbs | | 1,863.81 lbs-in |

2. Determine the position of the CG using the formula:

$$CG = \frac{Total\ Mom/Ind}{Total\ Weight} \times Reduction\ Factor$$

or:

$$\frac{1,863.81}{1,910} \times 100 = 97.58\ inches\ aft\ of\ datum$$

3. Plot the point determined by a weight of 1,910 pounds and a CG of 97.58 inches on the longitudinal CG envelope of FAA Figure 44. The point is within the allowable limits.

(H76) — FAA-H-8083-21

---

RTC
**3729.** (Refer to Figures 45 and 46.) What is the new CG of the gyroplane after a 10-gallon fuel burn if the original weight was 1,450 pounds and the MOM/1000 was 108 pound-inches?

A—Out of limits forward.
B—Out of limits aft.
C—Within limits near the forward limit.

Use the following steps:

1. Determine the change in load moment resulting from 10 gallons of fuel burned by entering the Loading Chart at the 10 gallon point on the fuel line, drawing a line downward and reading the moment for 10 gallons of fuel (5.3 x 1,000 lbs-in).

2. Calculate the new weight and moment:

| Item | Weight | Moment/1,000 |
|---|---|---|
| Original total | 1,450.0 lbs | 108.0 lbs-in |
| Fuel (10 x 6) | – 60.0 lbs | – 5.3 lbs-in |
| New Total | 1,390.0 lbs | 102.7 lbs-in |

3. Plot the point determined by 1,390 and 102.7 lbs-in/ 1,000 on the center of gravity moment envelope graph. The point is outside (to the left or forward) of the center of gravity moment envelope.

(H719) — FAA-H-8083-21, Chapter 7

---

**Answers**

3727 [C]          3729 [A]

RTC
**3730.** (Refer to Figures 45 and 46.) What is the condition of the weight and balance of the gyroplane as loaded?

| | WEIGHT (LB) | MOMENT (1000) |
|---|---|---|
| Empty weight | 1,074 | 85.6 |
| Oil, 6 qt | — | 1.0 |
| Pilot and passenger | 247 | — |
| Fuel, 12 gal | — | — |
| Baggage | 95 | — |

A—Within limits.
B—Overweight.
C—Out of limits aft.

*Use the following steps:*

1. *Calculate the total weight and moments using the information in the problem and FAA Figure 46. The standard weight for oil is 7.5 lbs/U.S. gallon, and for gasoline it is 6 lbs/U.S. gallon.*

| Item | Weight | Moment/1,000 |
|---|---|---|
| Empty weight | 1,074 lbs | 85.6 lbs-in |
| Oil, 6 qts (1.5 X 7.5) | 11 lbs | 1.0 lbs-in |
| Pilot and Pax (seat aft) | 247 lbs | 14.1 lbs-in |
| Fuel (12 x 6) | 72 lbs | 6.3 lbs-in |
| Baggage | 95 lbs | 5.7 lbs-in |
| Total | 1,499 lbs | 112.7 lbs-in |

2. *Plot the point determined by 1,499 pounds and 112.7 x 1,000 lbs-in on FAA Figure 45. The point is within the envelope (Answer A).*

3. *Now, consider the effect of pilot and passenger in the forward position. The moment would now be 13.3 x 1,000 lbs-in and the resulting total moment would be reduced to 111.9 x 1,000 lbs-in. When plotted on the Center of Gravity Moment Envelope Graph SEAT FWD, the weight-moment is slightly outside the envelope. Note that the manufacturer uses an aft position in presenting sample weight and balance calculations for this aircraft.*

*(H719) — FAA-H-8083-21, Chapter 7*

RTC
**3731.** (Refer to Figures 45 and 46.) Approximately how much baggage, if any, may be carried in the gyroplane, without exceeding weight and balance limits?

| | WEIGHT (LB) | MOMENT (1000) |
|---|---|---|
| Empty weight | 1,074 | 85.6 |
| Oil, 6 qt | — | 1.0 |
| Fuel, Full | — | — |
| Pilot (FWD) | 224 | — |

A—None, overweight.
B—70 pounds.
C—100 pounds.

*Use the following steps:*

1. *Calculate the total weight and moment using the information in the problem and the Loading Chart. The standard weight for oil is 7.5 pounds per gallon and for gasoline is 6.0 pounds per gallon.*

| Item | Weight | Moment/1,000 |
|---|---|---|
| Empty weight | 1,074 lbs | 85.6 lbs-in |
| Oil, 6 qts. (1.5 x 7.5) | 11 lbs | 1.0 lbs-in |
| Pilot (a) | 224 lbs | 12.1 lbs-in |
| Fuel (full) (b) | 120 lbs | 11.6 lbs-in |
| Totals | 1,429 lbs | 110.3 lbs-in |

2. *Consider adding enough baggage to approach the maximum takeoff weight 1,500 pounds.*

   *1,500 − 1,429 = 71 or about 70 pounds*
   *(Answer B)*

   *(This remains within the weight limit.)*

3. *Determine the moment of the 70 pounds of added baggage (4.2 x 1,000 lbs-in).*

4. *Compute the new weight and moment.*

| Item | Weight | Moment |
|---|---|---|
| Original Total | 1,429 | 110.3 |
| Baggage | + 70 | + 4.2 |
| New Total | 1,499 | 114.5 |

5. *Plot the point determined by 1,499.3 lbs and 114.5 x 1,000 lbs-in on the Center of Gravity Moment Envelope Graph of FAA Figure 45. The point is within the envelope.*

*(H719) — FAA-H-8083-21, Chapter 7*

**Answers**
3730  [A]          3731  [B]

GLI

**3861.** (Refer to Figure 54.) Calculate the weight and balance of the glider, and determine if the CG is within limits.

Pilot (fwd seat) ................................................. 160 lb
Passenger (aft seat) ......................................... 185 lb

A—CG 71.65 inches aft of datum – out of limits forward.
B—CG 79.67 inches aft of datum – within limits.
C—CG 83.43 inches aft of datum – within limits.

*Use the following steps:*

1. Calculate the total weight and moment using the information in the question and in FAA Figure 54, and the formula:

$$Weight \times Arm = Moment$$

| Item | Weight | Arm | Moment |
|---|---|---|---|
| Empty weight | 610 | 96.47 | 58,846.7 lbs-in |
| Pilot (fwd seat) | 160 | 43.80 | 7,008.0 lbs-in |
| Passenger (aft seat) | 185 | 74.70 | 13,819.5 lbs-in |
| Totals | 955 | | 79,674.2 lbs-in |

2. Calculate the position of the CG using the formula:

$$CG = \frac{Total\ Moment}{Total\ Weight}$$

or:

$$CG = \frac{79,674.2}{955} = 83.43\ inches\ aft\ of\ datum$$

3. Compare the calculated value to the allowed range for the position of the CG, 78.20 to 86.10. The calculated position is within the allowed range of both maximum weight and CG.

*(N21) — Soaring Flight Manual*

GLI

**3862.** (Refer to Figure 54.) How is the CG affected if radio and oxygen equipment weighing 35 pounds is added at station 43.8? The glider weighs 945 pounds with a moment of 78,000.2 pound-inches prior to adding the equipment.

A—CG shifts forward 0.79 inch – out of limits forward.
B—CG shifts forward 1.38 inches – within limits.
C—CG shifts aft 1.38 inches – out of limits aft.

*Use the following steps:*

1. Calculate the weight and moment of the equipment to be added using the formula:

$$Weight \times Arm = Moment$$

| Item | Weight | Arm | Moment |
|---|---|---|---|
| Added equip. | 35 lbs | 43.8 | 1,533.0 lbs-in |

2. Calculate the new total weight and moment.

| Item | Weight | Moment |
|---|---|---|
| Old | 945 | 78,000.2 lbs-in |
| Added | 35 | 1,533.0 lbs-in |
| New Total | 980 | 79,533.2 lbs-in |

3. Calculate the old and new positions of the center of gravity using the formula:

$$CG = \frac{Total\ Moment}{Total\ Weight}$$

Original CG =

$$\frac{78,000.2}{945} = 82.54\ inches\ aft\ of\ datum$$

$$New\ CG = \frac{79,533.2}{980} = 81.16\ inches\ aft\ of\ datum$$

4. Compute change and direction of change of the CG.

Original CG    82.54
New CG    − 81.16
1.38 inches closer to datum (forward)

5. Compare the calculated values of weight and CG position to the allowed range shown in FAA Figure 54. The allowed CG range is 78.20 to 86.10 and the calculated value is within these limits.

*(N21) — Soaring Flight Manual*

GLI
**3863.** (Refer to Figure 54.) What is the CG of the glider if the pilot and passenger each weigh 215 pounds?

A—74.69 inches aft of datum – out of limits forward.
B—81.08 inches aft of datum – within limits.
C—81.08 inches aft of datum – over maximum gross weight.

*Use the following steps:*

1. *Calculate the total weight and moment using the information in the question and in FAA Figure 54, and the formula:*

    *Weight x Arm = Moment*

| Item | Weight | Arm | Moment |
|---|---|---|---|
| Empty weight | 610 | 96.47 | 58,846.7 lbs-in |
| Pilot (fwd seat) | 215 | 43.80 | 9,417.0 lbs-in |
| Passenger (aft seat) | 215 | 74.70 | 16,060.5 lbs-in |
| Totals | 1,040 | | 84,324.2 lbs-in |

2. *Calculate the position of the CG using the formula:*

$$CG = \frac{Total\ Moment}{Total\ Weight}$$

    *or:*

$$CG = \frac{84,324.2}{1,040} = 81.08\ inches\ aft\ of\ datum$$

3. *Compare the calculated value to the allowed range for the position of the CG, 78.20 to 86.10. The calculated position is within the allowed range of both maximum weight and CG.*

*(N21) — Soaring Flight Manual*

---

LTA
**3887.** What constitutes the payload of a balloon?

A—Total gross weight.
B—Total weight of passengers, cargo, and fuel.
C—Weight of the aircraft and equipment.

*Payload is the total weight of passengers, cargo, and fuel an aircraft can legally carry on a given flight, excluding weight of the aircraft and equipment. (O220) — Balloon Ground School*

LTA
**3888.** (Refer to Figure 57.) The gross weight of the balloon is 1,350 pounds and the outside air temperature (OAT) is +51°F. The maximum height would be

A—5,000 feet.
B—8,000 feet.
C—10,000 feet.

*Use the following steps:*

1. *Locate the gross weight, 1,350 pounds, on the bottom of the graph in FAA Figure 57.*

2. *From that point, draw a line upward through the graph.*

3. *Locate the OAT +51°F on the left side of the graph.*

4. *From that point, draw a line to the right through the graph.*

5. *Note the point of intersection of the two lines, which in this case falls on the 10,000-foot curve.*

*(O220) — Balloon Ground School*

---

LTA
**3889.** (Refer to Figure 57.) The gross weight of the balloon is 1,200 pounds and the maximum height the pilot needs to attain is 5,000 feet. The maximum temperature to achieve this performance is

A—+37°F.
B—+70°F.
C—+97°F.

*Use the following steps:*

1. *Locate the gross weight, 1,200 pounds, on the bottom of the graph in FAA Figure 57.*

2. *From that point, draw a line upward to the 5,000-foot pressure altitude line.*

3. *From there, draw a line to the left to the air temperature scale and read the maximum temperature, 100°F.*

*(O220) — Balloon Ground School*

---

**Answers**

| | | | |
|---|---|---|---|
| 3863 [B] | 3887 [B] | 3888 [C] | 3889 [C] |

**LTA**
**3890.** (Refer to Figure 58.) Determine the maximum payload for a balloon flying at 2,500 feet at an ambient temperature of 91°F.

A—420 pounds.
B—465 pounds.
C—505 pounds.

*Payload is the total weight of passengers, cargo and fuel an aircraft can legally carry on a given flight, excluding weight of the aircraft and equipment. Using FAA Figure 58, perform the following steps:*

1. *Enter the chart at an ambient temperature of 91°F. From that point, proceed upward to the 2,500-foot pressure altitude point (halfway between sea level and 5,000 feet).*

2. *From the point of intersection, proceed to the left to determine the gross weight for 2,500 feet (840 pounds).*

3. *Note that the empty weight is 335 pounds. Compute the payload using the formula:*

   *Payload = Gross Weight – Empty Weight*
   *Payload = 840 lbs – 335 lbs*
   *Payload = 505 lbs*

*(O220) — Balloon Ground School*

---

**LTA**
**3893.** (Refer to Figure 58.) Determine the maximum weight allowable for pilot and passenger for a flight at approximately 1,000 feet with a temperature of 68°F. Launch with 20 gallons of propane.

A—580 pounds.
B—620 pounds.
C—720 pounds.

*Use FAA Figure 58, and the following steps:*

*(The standard weight of propane is 4.23 pounds per gallon.)*

1. *Enter the chart at the 68°F ambient temperature value. Move upward to a point about 1/5 of the distance between the sea level and 5,000-foot pressure altitude curves.*

2. *From that point, draw a line to the left and read the gross weight as 1,040 pounds.*

3. *Calculate the weight of 20 gallons of propane:*
   *20 x 4.23 = 85 pounds*

4. *Compute the available lift:*

| Item | Weight | |
|---|---|---|
| Gross weight | 1,040 | lbs |
| Empty weight | -335 | lbs |
| Fuel weight | -85 | lbs |
| Pilot and passengers | 620 | lbs |

*(O220) — Balloon Ground School*

---

**LTA**
**3894.** (Refer to Figure 58.) What is the maximum weight allowed for pilot and passengers for a flight at 5,000 feet with a standard temperature? Launch with 20 gallons of propane.

A—670 pounds.
B—760 pounds.
C—1,095 pounds.

*Use FAA Figure 58, and the following steps:*

*(The standard weight of propane is 4.23 pounds per gallon.)*

1. *Enter the chart where 5,000 feet and the standard temperature line intersect.*

2. *From that point, draw a line to the left and read the gross weight as 1,090 pounds.*

3. *Calculate the weight of 20 gallons of propane:*
   *20 x 4.23 = 85   pounds*

4. *Compute the available lift:*

| Item | Weight | |
|---|---|---|
| Gross weight | 1,090 | lbs |
| Empty weight | -335 | lbs |
| Fuel weight | -85 | lbs |
| Pilot and passengers | 670 | lbs |

*(O220) — Balloon Ground School*

---

**Answers**

3890   [C]          3893   [B]          3894   [A]

# Density Altitude and Aircraft Performance

Aircraft performance charts show a pilot what can be expected of an airplane (rate of climb, takeoff roll, etc.) under stipulated conditions. Prediction of performance is based upon a sea level temperature of +15°C (+59°F) and atmospheric pressure of 29.92" Hg (1013.2 mb). This combination of temperature and pressure is called a "standard day." When the air is at a "standard density," temperature and/or pressure deviations from standard will change the air density, or the density altitude, which affects aircraft performance. Performance charts allow the pilot to predict how an aircraft will perform.

Relative humidity also affects density altitude, but is not considered when the performance charts are formulated. A combination of high temperature, high humidity, and high altitude result in a density altitude higher than the pressure altitude which, in turn, results in reduced aircraft performance.

### Problem:

Using the Density Altitude Chart shown in FAA Figure 8, and the following conditions, determine the density altitude.

### Conditions:

Altimeter Setting .......................................... 30.35
Airport Temperature .................................. +25°F
Airport Elevation .................................. 3,894 feet

### Solution:

1. Determine the applicable altitude correction for the altimeter setting of 30.35" Hg. *See* FAA Figure 8. That setting is not shown on the chart, so it is necessary to interpolate between the correction factors shown for 30.30" Hg and 30.40" Hg. To interpolate, add the two factors and divide by 2:

   -348 + (-440) = -788

   -788 ÷ 2 = -394

   Since the result is a negative number, subtract that value from the given airport elevation:

   | 3,894 | feet |
   |---|---|
   | − 394 | feet |
   | 3,500 | feet |

2. Along the bottom of the chart, locate the given OAT (+25°F). From that point, proceed upward until intersecting the pressure altitude line that is equal to the corrected airport elevation (3,500 feet). From that point, proceed to the left and read the density altitude (2,000 feet).

   Note that high-density altitude reduces propeller efficiency as well as overall aircraft performance.

ALL
**3289.** If the outside air temperature (OAT) at a given altitude is warmer than standard, the density altitude is

A—equal to pressure altitude.
B—lower than pressure altitude.
C—higher than pressure altitude.

*If the temperature is above standard, the density altitude will be higher than pressure altitude. (H312) — AC 61-23C, Chapter 3*

AIR, LTA, RTC
**3246.** What effect does high density altitude, as compared to low density altitude, have on propeller efficiency and why?

A—Efficiency is increased due to less friction on the propeller blades.
B—Efficiency is reduced because the propeller exerts less force at high density altitudes than at low density altitudes.
C—Efficiency is reduced due to the increased force of the propeller in the thinner air.

*The propeller produces thrust in proportion to the mass of air being accelerated through the rotating blades. If the air is less dense, propeller efficiency is decreased. (H308) — AC 61-23C, Chapter 2*

AIR, RTC
**3290.** Which combination of atmospheric conditions will reduce aircraft takeoff and climb performance?

A—Low temperature, low relative humidity, and low density altitude.
B—High temperature, low relative humidity, and low density altitude.
C—High temperature, high relative humidity, and high density altitude.

*An increase in air temperature or humidity, or a decrease in air pressure (which results in a higher density altitude), will significantly decrease both power output and propeller efficiency. (H317) — AC 61-23C, Chapter 4*

Answer (A) is incorrect because all of these conditions improve performance. Answer (B) is incorrect because low humidity and low density altitude improve performance.

AIR, RTC
**3291.** What effect does high density altitude have on aircraft performance?

A—It increases engine performance.
B—It reduces climb performance.
C—It increases takeoff performance.

*An increase in air temperature or humidity, or a decrease in air pressure (which results in a higher density altitude), will significantly decrease both power output and propeller efficiency. (H317) — AC 61-23C, Chapter 4*

AIR, RTC
**3292.** (Refer to Figure 8.) What is the effect of a temperature increase from 25 to 50°F on the density altitude if the pressure altitude remains at 5,000 feet?

A—1,200-foot increase.
B—1,400-foot increase.
C—1,650-foot increase.

*Referencing FAA Figure 8, use the following steps:*

1. *Enter the density altitude chart at 25°F. Proceed upward to intersect the 5,000-foot pressure altitude line. From the point of intersection, move left to the edge of the chart and read a density altitude of 3,850 feet.*

2. *Enter the density altitude chart at 50°F. Proceed upward to the 5,000-foot pressure altitude line. From the point of intersection, move left to the edge of the chart and read a density altitude of 5,500 feet.*

3. *Determine the change in density altitude:*

   *5,500 – 3,850 = 1,650 feet (increase)*

*(H317) — AC 61-23C, Chapter 4*

AIR, RTC
**3293.** (Refer to Figure 8.) Determine the pressure altitude with an indicated altitude of 1,380 feet MSL with an altimeter setting of 28.22 at standard temperature.

A—2,991 feet MSL.
B—2,913 feet MSL.
C—3,010 feet MSL.

*Referencing FAA Figure 8, use the following steps:*

1. *Since the altimeter setting that is given is not shown in FAA Figure 8, interpolation is necessary. Locate the settings immediately above and below the given value of 28.22" Hg:*

**Answers**

| 3289 | [C] | 3246 | [B] | 3290 | [C] | 3291 | [B] | 3292 | [C] | 3293 | [A] |

| Altimeter Setting | Conversion Factor |
|---|---|
| 28.2 | 1,630 feet |
| 28.3 | 1,533 feet |

2. Determine the difference in the two conversion factors:

$$1,630 - 1,533 = 97 \text{ feet}$$

3. Determine the amount of the difference to be subtracted from the 28.20" Hg conversion factor (2/10 of 97).

$$97.0 \times .2 = 19.4$$

4. Subtract the amount of difference from the amount shown for the 28.20" Hg conversion factor:

$$1,630.0 - 19.4 = 1,610.6$$

5. Add the correction factor to the indicated altitude to find the pressure altitude:

```
  1,610.6
+ 1,380.0
─────────
  2,990.6 feet MSL (pressure altitude)
```

(H317) — AC 61-23C, Chapter 4

---

ALL
**3294.** (Refer to Figure 8.) Determine the density altitude for these conditions:

Altimeter setting ...................................................29.25
Runway temperature .........................................+81°F
Airport elevation .................................... 5,250 ft MSL

A—4,600 feet MSL.
B—5,877 feet MSL.
C—8,500 feet MSL.

Referencing FAA Figure 8, use the following steps:

1. Since the altimeter setting that is given is not shown in FAA Figure 8, interpolation is necessary. Locate the settings immediately above and below the given value of 29.25" Hg:

| Altimeter Setting | Conversion Factor |
|---|---|
| 29.20 | 673 feet |
| 29.30 | 579 feet |

2. Determine the difference between the two conversion factors:

$$673 - 579 = 94 \text{ feet}$$

3. Determine the amount of difference to be added to the 29.30" Hg conversion factor:

$$94 \times .5 = 47 \text{ feet}$$

4. Add the amount of difference to the amount shown for the 29.30" Hg conversion factor:

$$579 + 47 = 626 \text{ feet}$$

5. Add the correction factor to the airport elevation to find pressure altitude:

```
  5,250
+   626
───────
  5,876 feet MSL (pressure altitude)
```

6. Determine the density altitude by entering the chart at +81°F; move upward to the 5,876 pressure altitude line; from the point of intersection, move to the left and read a density altitude of 8,500 feet.

(H317) — AC 61-23C, Chapter 4

---

ALL
**3295.** (Refer to Figure 8.) Determine the pressure altitude at an airport that is 3,563 feet MSL with an altimeter setting of 29.96.

A—3,527 feet MSL.
B—3,556 feet MSL.
C—3,639 feet MSL.

Referencing FAA Figure 8, use the following steps:

1. Since the altimeter setting that is given is not shown in FAA Figure 8, interpolation is necessary. Locate the settings immediately above and below the given value of 29.96" Hg:

| Altimeter Setting | Conversion Factor |
|---|---|
| 29.92 | 0 feet |
| 30.00 | -73 feet |

2. Determine the difference between the two conversion factors:

$$0 - 73 = -73 \text{ feet}$$

The setting 29.96 is halfway between the two values, so:

$$-73 \div 2 = -36.5 \text{ feet}$$

3. Determine the amount of difference to be subtracted from the 30.00" Hg conversion factor.

4. Subtract the correction factor from the airport elevation to find pressure altitude:

```
  3,563.0
-    36.5
─────────
  3,526.5 feet MSL (pressure altitude)
```

(H317) — AC 61-23C, Chapter 4

---

**Answers**

3294    [C]          3295    [A]

AIR, RTC

**3296.** (Refer to Figure 8.) What is the effect of a temperature increase from 30 to 50°F on the density altitude if the pressure altitude remains at 3,000 feet MSL?

A—900-foot increase.
B—1,100-foot decrease.
C—1,300-foot increase.

*Referencing FAA Figure 8, use the following steps:*

1. *Enter the density altitude chart at 30°F. Proceed upward to the 3,000-foot pressure altitude line. From the point of intersection, move left to the edge of the chart and read a density altitude of 1,650 feet.*

2. *Enter the density altitude chart at 50°F. Proceed upward to the 3,000-foot pressure altitude line. From the point of intersection, move left to the edge of the chart and read a density altitude of 3,000 feet.*

3. *Find the difference between the two values:*

   *3,000 – 1,650 = 1,350 foot (increase)*

*(H317) — AC 61-23C, Chapter 4*

---

AIR, RTC

**3297.** (Refer to Figure 8.) Determine the pressure altitude at an airport that is 1,386 feet MSL with an altimeter setting of 29.97.

A—1,341 feet MSL.
B—1,451 feet MSL.
C—1,562 feet MSL.

*Referencing FAA Figure 8, use the following steps:*

1. *Since the altimeter setting that is given is not shown in FAA Figure 8, interpolation is necessary. Locate the settings immediately above and below the given value of 29.97" Hg:*

   | Altimeter Setting | Conversion Factor |
   |---|---|
   | 29.92 | 0 feet |
   | 30.00 | -73 feet |

2. *Determine the difference between the two conversion factors:*

   *0 – 73 = -73 feet*

3. *Determine the amount of the difference to be subtracted from the 29.92" Hg conversion factor:*

   *(-73 ÷ 8) x 5 = -45.6 or 46 feet*

4. *Subtract the conversion factor from the airport elevation to determine the pressure altitude:*

   *1,386*
   *– 46*
   *1,340 feet MSL (pressure altitude)*

*(H317) — AC 61-23C, Chapter 4*

---

ALL

**3298.** (Refer to Figure 8.) Determine the density altitude for these conditions:

Altimeter setting ................................................. 30.35
Runway temperature ......................................... +25°F
Airport elevation ..................................... 3,894 ft MSL

A—2,000 feet MSL.
B—2,900 feet MSL.
C—3,500 feet MSL.

*Referencing FAA Figure 8, use the following steps:*

1. *Since the altimeter setting that is given is not shown in FAA Figure 8, interpolation is necessary. Locate the settings immediately above and below the given value of 30.35" Hg:*

   | Altimeter Setting | Conversion Factor |
   |---|---|
   | 30.30 | -348 feet |
   | 30.40 | -440 feet |

2. *Determine the difference between the two factors:*

   *-440 + 348 = -92 feet*

3. *Determine amount of difference to be added to the 30.30" Hg conversion factor:*

   *-92.0 x .5 = -46.0 feet*

4. *Add the amount of difference to the amount shown for the 30.30" Hg conversion factor:*

   *-348 + (-46) = -394 feet*

5. *Subtract the correction factor from the airport elevation to find pressure altitude:*

   *3,894*
   *– 394*
   *3,500 feet MSL (pressure altitude)*

6. *Determine the density altitude by entering the chart at +25°F; proceed upward to the 3,500-foot pressure altitude line; from the point of intersection move to the left edge of the chart and read a density altitude of 2,000 feet.*

*(H317) — AC 61-23C, Chapter 4*

---

**Answers**

3296 [C]          3297 [A]          3298 [A]

**ALL**
**3299.** (Refer to Figure 8.) What is the effect of a temperature decrease and a pressure altitude increase on the density altitude from 90°F and 1,250 feet pressure altitude to 55°F and 1,750 feet pressure altitude?

A—1,700-foot increase.
B—1,300-foot decrease.
C—1,700-foot decrease.

*Referencing FAA Figure 8, use the following steps:*

1. *Determine the density altitude when the temperature is +90°F and the pressure altitude is 1,250 feet. Enter the density altitude chart at +90°F and proceed upward to the 1,250-foot pressure altitude line. From the point of intersection move to the left edge of the chart and read a density altitude of 3,600 feet.*

2. *Determine the density altitude when the temperature is +55°F and the pressure altitude is 1,750 feet. Enter the density altitude chart at +55°F and proceed upward to the 1,750-foot pressure altitude line. From the point of intersection move to the left edge of the chart. Read a density altitude of 1,900 feet.*

3. *Determine the change in density altitude:*

*3,600 – 1,900 = 1,700 foot (decrease)*

*(H317) — AC 61-23C, Chapter 4*

**AIR, RTC**
**3300.** What effect, if any, does high humidity have on aircraft performance?

A—It increases performance.
B—It decreases performance.
C—It has no effect on performance.

*An increase in air temperature or humidity, or a decrease in air pressure (which results in a higher density altitude) will significantly decrease both power output and propeller efficiency. If an air mass is humid, there is more water in it, therefore, less oxygen. (H317) — AC 61-23C, Chapter 4*

**ALL**
**3386.** What are the standard temperature and pressure values for sea level?

A—15°C and 29.92" Hg.
B—59°C and 1013.2 millibars.
C—59°F and 29.92 millibars.

*Standard sea level pressure is 29.92 inches of mercury. Standard sea level temperature is 15°C. (I21) — AC 61-23C, Chapter 15*

**ALL**
**3394.** Which factor would tend to increase the density altitude at a given airport?

A—An increase in barometric pressure.
B—An increase in ambient temperature.
C—A decrease in relative humidity.

*On a hot day, the air becomes "thinner" or lighter, and its density is equivalent to a higher altitude in the standard atmosphere, thus the term "high density altitude." (I22) — AC 00-6A, Chapter 3*

*Answer (A) is incorrect because barometric pressure increases do not directly affect density altitude changes. Answer (C) is incorrect because a decrease in relative humidity does not affect density altitude changes.*

**LTA**
**3891.** (Refer to Figure 58.) What is the maximum altitude for the balloon if the gross weight is 1,100 pounds and standard temperature exists at all altitudes?

A—1,000 feet.
B—4,000 feet.
C—5,500 feet.

*Use FAA Figure 58, and the following steps:*

1. *Enter the graph at the 1,100-pound gross weight point and proceed to the right to intercept the standard temperature curve.*

2. *Note that the intercept is between sea level and the 5,000-foot limit lines, and is much closer to the 5,000-foot line (4,000 feet).*

*(O220) — Balloon Ground School*

**Answers**
3299 [C]    3300 [B]    3386 [A]    3394 [B]    3891 [B]

LTA

**3892.** (Refer to Figure 58.) What is the maximum altitude for the balloon if the gross weight is 1,000 pounds and standard temperature exists at all altitudes?

A—4,000 feet.
B—5,500 feet.
C—11,000 feet.

*Use FAA Figure 58, and the following steps:*

1. *Enter the graph at the 1,000-pound gross weight point and proceed to the right to intercept the standard temperature curve.*

2. *Note that the intercept is just over 10,000 feet (11,000 feet).*

*(O220) — Balloon Ground School*

RTC

**3702.** (Refer to Figure 40.) Determine the total takeoff distance required for a gyroplane to clear a 50-foot obstacle if the temperature is 95°F and the pressure altitude is 1,700 feet.

A—1,825 feet.
B—1,910 feet.
C—2,030 feet.

*Use the following steps:*

1. *Locate the 1,700-foot pressure altitude on the Take-Off Distance Graph (right).*

2. *Draw a horizontal line from the 1,700-foot position to the 95°F OAT point.*

3. *Draw a vertical line downward from the point of intersection to the total Take-Off Distance Scale. Note the distance 2,030 feet.*

*(H317) — AC 61-23C, Chapter 4*

# Takeoff Distance

The Takeoff Distance Graph, FAA Figure 41, allows the pilot to determine the ground roll required for takeoff under various conditions. It also shows the total distance required for a takeoff and climb to clear a 50-foot obstacle.

## Problem:

Using the Takeoff Distance Graph shown in FAA Figure 41, determine the approximate ground roll distance for takeoff and the total distance for a takeoff to clear a 50-foot obstacle under the following conditions:

Outside air temperature (OAT) .................... 90°F
Pressure altitude ................................ 2,000 feet
Takeoff weight ...................................... 2,500 lbs
Headwind component ............................ 20 knots

## Solution:

1. Locate the OAT, 90°F, on the graph.

2. From that point, draw a line upward to the line representing the pressure altitude of 2,000 feet.

3. From the point of intersection, draw a line to the right to the reference line.

4. From that point, proceed downward and to the right (remaining proportionally between the existing guide lines) to the vertical line representing 2,500 pounds.

5. From there, draw a line to the right to the second reference line.

6. Then proceed down and to the right (remaining proportionally between the existing guide lines) to the line representing the 20-knot headwind component line.

7. From there, draw a line to the right to the third reference line.

8. Finally, move to the right and read approximate ground roll for takeoff of 650 feet.

**Answers**

3892    [C]                3702    [C]

AIR
**3705.** (Refer to Figure 41.) Determine the total distance required for takeoff to clear a 50-foot obstacle.

OAT ........................................................................ Std
Pressure altitude ............................................. 4,000 ft
Takeoff weight ................................................. 2,800 lb
Headwind component ......................................... Calm

A—1,500 feet.
B—1,750 feet.
C—2,000 feet.

Use the following steps:

1.  Locate the ISA curve on FAA Figure 41.

2.  Note the intersection of the ISA curve with the pressure altitude, 4,000 feet.

3.  From that point, draw a line to the right to the first reference line.

4.  From there, proceed downward and to the right (remaining proportionally between the existing lines) to the vertical line representing 2,800 pounds.

5.  Then proceed to the right to the second reference line.

6.  In this case the reference line is also the vertical line representing the 0 MPH wind component.

7.  From that point, continue to the right to the third vertical reference line.

8.  From there, proceed upward and to the right (remaining proportionally between the existing lines) to the vertical line representing the obstacle height, 50 feet.

9.  Read the distance (approximately 1,750 feet).

(H317) — AC 61-23C, Chapter 4

AIR
**3706.** (Refer to Figure 41.) Determine the total distance required for takeoff to clear a 50-foot obstacle.

OAT ........................................................................ Std
Pressure altitude ......................................... Sea level
Takeoff weight ................................................. 2,700 lb
Headwind component ......................................... Calm

A—1,000 feet.
B—1,400 feet.
C—1,700 feet.

Use the following steps:

1.  Locate the OAT, 59°F, on FAA Figure 41.

2.  From that point, draw a line upward to the line representing the pressure altitude, 0 feet (SL).

3.  From that point, draw a line to the right to the first reference line.

4.  From there, proceed downward and to the right (remaining proportionally between the existing lines) to the vertical line representing 2,700 pounds.

5.  Then draw a line to the right to the second reference line.

6.  In this case, the reference line is also the vertical line representing the 0-knot wind component.

7.  From that point, continue a horizontal line to the third vertical reference line.

8.  Finally, proceed upward and to the right (remaining proportionally between the existing lines) to the vertical line representing the obstacle height, 50 feet and read the distance (approximately 1,400 feet).

(H317) — AC 61-23C, Chapter 4

AIR
**3707.** (Refer to Figure 41.) Determine the approximate ground roll distance required for takeoff.

OAT ..................................................................... 100°F
Pressure altitude ............................................. 2,000 ft
Takeoff weight ................................................. 2,750 lb
Headwind component ......................................... Calm

A—1,150 feet.
B—1,300 feet.
C—1,800 feet.

Use the following steps:

1.  Locate the OAT, 100°F, on FAA Figure 41.

2.  From that point, draw a line upward to the line representing the pressure altitude, 2,000 feet.

3.  From that point, draw a line to the right to the first reference line.

4.  From there, proceed downward and to the right (remaining proportionally between the existing lines) to the vertical line representing 2,750 pounds.

5.  Then draw a line to the right to the second reference line.

6.  In this case, the reference line is also the vertical line representing the 0-knot wind component.

*Continued*

**Answers**
3705  [B]        3706  [B]        3707  [A]

7. Then draw a horizontal line to the third vertical reference line.

8. In this case, the reference line is also the vertical line representing the obstacle height, 0 feet.

9. From that point, draw a horizontal line to the right and read the distance (approximately 1,150 feet).

*(H317) — AC 61-23C, Chapter 4*

---

AIR
**3708.** (Refer to Figure 41.) Determine the approximate ground roll distance required for takeoff.

OAT ................................................................ 95°F
Pressure altitude ............................................. 2,000 ft
Takeoff weight ................................................. 2,500 lb
Headwind component ....................................... 20 kts

A—650 feet.
B—850 feet.
C—1,000 feet.

*Use the following steps:*

1. *Locate the OAT, 95°F, on FAA Figure 41.*

2. *From that point, draw a line upward to the line representing the pressure altitude of 2,000 feet.*

3. *Form the point of intersection, draw a line to the right to the reference line and stop.*

4. *From that point, proceed downward and to the right (remaining proportionally between the existing guide lines) to the vertical line representing 2,500 pounds.*

5. *From there, draw a line to the right to the second reference line.*

6. *Then proceed down and to the right (remaining proportionally between the existing guide lines) to the line representing the 20-knot headwind component line.*

7. *From that point, draw a line to the right to the third reference line.*

8. *From there, move to the right and read an approximate ground roll for takeoff (650 feet).*

*(H317) — AC 61-23C, Chapter 4*

---

RTC
**3703.** (Refer to Figure 40.) Determine the total takeoff distance required for a gyroplane to clear a 50-foot obstacle if the temperature is standard at sea level pressure altitude.

A—950 feet.
B—1,090 feet.
C—1,200 feet.

1. *On the sea level line of FAA Figure 40 locate the intersection of the +59°F point.*

2. *Read landing distance of 1,200 feet.*

*(H317) — AC 61-23C, Chapter 4*

---

RTC
**3704.** (Refer to Figure 40.) Approximately how much additional takeoff distance will be required for a gyroplane to clear a 50-foot obstacle if the temperature increases from 75 to 90°F at a pressure altitude of 2,300 feet?

A—160 feet.
B—200 feet.
C—2,020 feet.

*Use the following steps:*

1. *Locate the 2,300-foot pressure altitude on FAA Figure 40.*

2. *Draw a horizontal line from the 2,300-foot position to the 75°F and the 90°F OAT points.*

3. *From these points, draw vertical lines downward to the takeoff distance scale and note the distances (2,025 and 2,185, respectively).*

4. *The difference is the increase in takeoff distance.*

    *2,185 – 2,025 = 160 feet*

*(H317) — AC 61-23C, Chapter 4*

---

**Answers**

3708   [A]                3703   [C]                3704   [A]

RTC
**3732.** (Refer to Figure 47.) What is the best rate-of-climb speed for the helicopter?

A—24 MPH.
B—40 MPH.
C—57 MPH.

*Use the following steps:*

1. *Locate the recommended takeoff profile on FAA Figure 47.*

2. *Note that the best rate-of-climb speed at sea level is designated by the arrow pointing to the vertical line.*

3. *Interpret the diagram. The vertical line is most closely aligned with an IAS of about 57 MPH.*

*(H720) — FAA-H-8083-21, Chapter 8*

# Cruise Power Setting Table

The Cruise Power Setting Table (FAA Figure 36) may be used to forecast fuel flow and true airspeed and, therefore allow a pilot to determine the amount of fuel required and the estimated time en route.

## Problem:

Using the Cruise Power Setting Table shown in FAA Figure 36, determine the expected fuel consumption for a 1,000-statute-mile flight under the following conditions:

Pressure altitude ................................. 8,000 feet
Temperature.................................................. -19°C
Manifold pressure ................................. 19.5" Hg
Wind .............................................................. Calm

## Solution:

1. Find the fuel flow and TAS. Enter the chart at the 8,000-foot pressure altitude line and proceed to the right and identify the chart which represents an indicated outside air temperature (IOAT) of -19°C at 8,000 feet (the chart for ISA -20°C). Continue reading to the right, noting the manifold pressure of 19.5" Hg, the fuel flow per engine will be 6.6 pounds per square inch or 11.5 gallons per hour (GPH), and the TAS will be 157 knots or 181 miles per hour (MPH).

2. Calculate the time flown. Using a flight computer, calculate the time en route:

    1,000 SM at 181 MPH = 5.52 hours

3. Calculate the fuel consumption. Using a flight computer, calculate the fuel burned in this time:

    5.52 hours x 11.5 GPH = 63.48 gallons consumed

**Answers**
3732   [C]

**AIR**

**3678.** (Refer to Figure 36.) Approximately what true airspeed should a pilot expect with 65 percent maximum continuous power at 9,500 feet with a temperature of 36°F below standard?

A—178 MPH.
B—181 MPH.
C—183 MPH.

*Use the following steps:*

1. *Locate -36°F (ISA -20°C) on FAA Figure 36. Notice that the stated altitude of 9,500 feet does not appear on the chart so it is necessary to interpolate.*

2. *Read across the 8,000-foot pressure altitude line and determine the TAS (181 MPH).*

3. *Read across the 10,000-foot pressure altitude line and determine the TAS (184 MPH).*

4. *Interpolate between the values for 8,000 feet and 10,000 feet to determine a TAS for 9,500 feet.*

   a.     184   *MPH (10,000 feet)*
        − 181   *MPH (8,000 feet)*
           3   *MPH difference in speed*

   b.  10,000 *feet*       10,000 *feet*
      − 8,000 *feet*     − 9,500 *feet*
       2,000 *feet difference*    500 *feet difference*

   c.  *.25 x 3 MPH = .75 MPH*

   d.  184.00 *MPH*
       − .75 *MPH*
     183.25 *MPH or 183 MPH*

*(H317) — AC 61-23C, Chapter 4*

---

**AIR**

**3679.** (Refer to Figure 36.) What is the expected fuel consumption for a 1,000-nautical mile flight under the following conditions?

Pressure altitude .............................................8,000 ft
Temperature.........................................................22°C
Manifold pressure...........................................20.8" Hg
Wind ..................................................................... Calm

A—60.2 gallons.
B—70.1 gallons.
C—73.2 gallons.

*Use the following steps:*

1. *Locate the pressure altitude of 8,000 feet on FAA Figure 36. Read to the right and identify the chart which presents an indicated outside temperature of 22°C at 8,000 feet (the chart for ISA +20°C).*

2. *On this chart, read across the 8,000-foot line, 22°C, 20.8" Hg manifold pressure line. The fuel flow is 11.5 GPH and the TAS is 164 knots.*

3. *Using a flight computer, calculate the time en route:*

    *Distance is 1,000 NM*
    *TAS is 164 knots, with no wind*

   *Therefore, the time en route is 6 hours, 6 minutes.*

4. *Using a flight computer, calculate the fuel consumption:*

    *Time en route is 6 hours, 6 minutes*
    *Fuel burn is 11.5 GPH*

   *Therefore, the fuel consumption is 70.1 gallons.*

*(H317) — AC 61-23C, page 96*

---

**AIR**

**3680.** (Refer to Figure 36.) What is the expected fuel consumption for a 500-nautical mile flight under the following conditions?

Pressure altitude .............................................4,000 ft
Temperature.......................................................+29°C
Manifold pressure...........................................21.3" Hg
Wind ..................................................................... Calm

A—31.4 gallons.
B—36.1 gallons.
C—40.1 gallons.

*Use the following steps:*

1. *Locate the pressure altitude of 4,000 feet on FAA Figure 36. Read to the right and identify the chart which presents an indicated outside temperature of +29°C at 4,000 feet (in this case, the chart for ISA +20°C).*

2. *On this chart, read across the 4,000-foot line, +29°C, 21.3" Hg manifold pressure line. The fuel flow is 11.5 GPH and the TAS is 159 knots.*

3. *Using a flight computer, calculate the time en route:*

    *Distance is 500 NM*
    *TAS is 159 knots, with no wind*

   *Therefore, the time en route is 3 hours, 9 minutes.*

---

**Answers**

3678   [C]           3679   [B]           3680   [B]

4. *Using a flight computer, calculate the fuel consumption:*

> *Time en route is 3 hours, 9 minutes*
> *Fuel burn is 11.5 GPH*

*Therefore, the fuel consumption is 36.2 gallons.*

*(H317) — AC 61-23C, Chapter 4*

---

AIR
**3681.** (Refer to Figure 36.) What fuel flow should a pilot expect at 11,000 feet on a standard day with 65 percent maximum continuous power?

A— 10.6 gallons per hour.
B— 11.2 gallons per hour.
C— 11.8 gallons per hour.

*Use the following steps:*

1. *Locate the Standard Day (ISA) Chart on FAA Figure 36. Notice that the stated altitude, 11,000 feet, does not appear on the chart, so it is necessary to interpolate.*

2. *Read across the 10,000-foot pressure altitude line and determine the fuel flow at that altitude (11.5 GPH).*

3. *Read across the 12,000-foot pressure altitude line and determine the fuel flow at that altitude (10.9 GPH).*

4. *To determine the flow at 11,000 feet, add the two flows and divide by two.*

$$Fuel\ Flow = \frac{(11.5+10.9)}{2} = \frac{22.4}{2} = 11.2\ gallons\ per\ hr$$

*(H317) — AC 61-23C, Chapter 4*

AIR
**3682.** (Refer to Figure 36.) Determine the approximate manifold pressure setting with 2,450 RPM to achieve 65 percent maximum continuous power at 6,500 feet with a temperature of 36°F higher than standard.

A— 19.8" Hg.
B— 20.8" Hg.
C— 21.0" Hg.

*Use the following steps:*

1. *Locate the +36°F (ISA + 20°C) Chart on FAA Figure 36. Notice that the stated altitude of 6,500 feet does not appear on the chart, so it is necessary to interpolate.*

2. *Read across the 6,000-foot pressure altitude line and determine the manifold pressure at that altitude (21.0" Hg).*

3. *Read across the 8,000-foot pressure altitude line and determine the manifold pressure at that altitude (20.8" Hg).*

4. *The altitude, 6,500 feet, is closer to the 6,000-foot value of 21.0" Hg. (In this instance, the FAA apparently did not interpolate.)*

*(H317) — AC 61-23C, Chapter 4*

---

**Answers**

3681    [B]          3682    [C]

# Landing Distance Graphs and Tables

Some landing distance graphs such as the one shown in FAA Figure 38, are used in the same manner as the takeoff distance graph.

Another type of landing distance table is shown in FAA Figure 39.

## Problem:

Using the Landing Distance Table shown in FAA Figure 39, determine the total distance required to land over a 50-foot obstacle.

Pressure altitude ................................. 5,000 feet
Headwind ................................................. 8 knots
Temperature ................................................. 41°F
Runway ......................................... Hard surface

## Solution:

Enter FAA Figure 39 at 5,000 feet and 41°F to find 1,195 feet is required to clear a 50-foot obstacle. Note #1 states an additional correction is necessary for the headwind, 10% for each 4 knots. This would mean 20% for 8 knots. 20% of 1,195 feet is 239 feet, resulting in 956 feet — total distance required to land:

1,195 x .20 = 239 feet

1,195 − 239 = 956 feet

AIR
**3689.** (Refer to Figure 38.) Determine the total distance required to land.

OAT ........................................................ 32°F
Pressure altitude ............................................. 8,000 ft
Weight ........................................................ 2,600 lb
Headwind component ....................................... 20 kts
Obstacle ......................................................... 50 ft

A—850 feet.
B—1,400 feet.
C—1,750 feet.

*Use the following steps:*

1. *Enter FAA Figure 38 at the point where the vertical 32°F temperature line intersects the 8,000-foot pressure altitude line.*

2. *From there, proceed to the right to the first vertical reference line.*

3. *From that point, proceed down and to the right (remaining proportionally between the existing lines) to the vertical line representing 2,600 pounds.*

4. *Then, proceed to the right to the second vertical reference line.*

5. *Then, proceed down and to the right (remaining proportionally between the existing headwind lines) to the vertical line representing 20 knots.*

6. *From that point, proceed to the right to the third reference line.*

7. *Finally, proceed up and to the right (remaining proportionally between the existing lines) to the 50-foot obstacle line at the end of the graph and read the landing distance (approximately 1,400 feet).*

*(H317) — AC 61-23C, Chapter 4*

AIR
**3690.** (Refer to Figure 38.) Determine the total distance required to land.

OAT ................................................................ Std
Pressure altitude ........................................... 10,000 ft
Weight .......................................................... 2,400 lb
Wind component ............................................... Calm
Obstacle ........................................................... 50 ft

A—750 feet.
B—1,925 feet.
C—1,450 feet.

**Answers**

3689 [B]        3690 [B]

Use the following steps:

1. Enter the graph at the point where the ISA line intercepts the 10,000-foot pressure altitude line.

2. From that point, proceed to the right to the first vertical reference line.

3. From there, proceed down to the right (remaining proportionally between the existing lines), to the vertical line representing 2,400 pounds.

4. Then proceed to the right to the second vertical reference line.

5. Since the wind is calm, continue to the right to the third vertical reference line.

6. From there, proceed upward and to the right (remaining proportionally between the existing lines) to the vertical line representing the required 50-foot obstacle height. Read the landing distance from the vertical scale (approximately 1,900 feet).

*(H317) — AC 61-23C, Chapter 4*

---

AIR
**3691.** (Refer to Figure 38.) Determine the total distance required to land.

OAT ........................................................... 90°F
Pressure altitude ...................................... 3,000 ft
Weight ....................................................... 2,900 lb
Headwind component .............................. 10 kts
Obstacle .................................................... 50 ft

A—1,450 feet.
B—1,550 feet.
C—1,725 feet.

Use the following steps:

1. Enter FAA Figure 38 at the point where the vertical 90°F temperature line intersects the 3,000-foot pressure altitude line. (The point must be visualized midway between the 2,000- and 4,000-foot pressure altitude lines.)

2. From that point, proceed to the right to the first vertical reference line.

3. From there, proceed downward and to the right (remaining proportionally between the existing lines), to the vertical line representing 2,900 pounds.

4. Then proceed to the right to the second vertical reference line.

5. Since there is a 10-knot headwind, proceed downward and to the right (remaining proportionally between the existing lines) to the vertical line representing 10 knots.

6. From that point, proceed to the right to the third vertical reference line.

7. From there, proceed upward and to the right (remaining proportionally between the existing lines) to the vertical line representing the required 50-foot obstacle height. Read the landing distance from the vertical scale (approximately 1,725 feet).

*(H317) — AC 61-23C, Chapter 4*

---

AIR
**3692.** (Refer to Figure 38.) Determine the approximate total distance required to land over a 50-foot obstacle.

OAT ........................................................... 90°F
Pressure altitude ...................................... 4,000 ft
Weight ....................................................... 2,800 lb
Headwind component .............................. 10 kts

A—1,525 feet.
B—1,775 feet.
C—1,950 feet.

Use the following steps:

1. Enter FAA Figure 38 at the point where the vertical 90°F temperature line intersects the 4,000-foot pressure altitude line.

2. From that point, proceed to the right to the first vertical reference line.

3. From there, proceed downward and to the right (remaining proportionally between the existing lines), to the vertical line representing 2,800 pounds.

4. Then proceed to the right to the intersection with the second vertical reference line.

5. Since there is a 10-knot headwind component, proceed downward and to the right (remaining proportionally between the existing lines) to the vertical line representing 10 knots.

6. From that point, proceed to the right to the third vertical reference line.

7. Proceed upward to the right following the diagonal line for the 50-foot obstacle and then continue to read the landing distance (approximately 1,775 feet).

*(H317) — AC 61-23C, Chapter 4*

---

**Answers**
3691 [C]          3692 [B]

AIR
**3693.** (Refer to Figure 39.) Determine the approximate landing ground roll distance.

Pressure altitude .......................................... Sea level
Headwind ......................................................... 4 kts
Temperature ...................................................... Std

A—356 feet.
B—401 feet.
C—490 feet.

*Use the following steps:*

1. *Locate the sea level portion of FAA Figure 39.*

2. *Read the landing ground roll distance (445 feet).*

3. *Note 1 requires that the distances shown be decreased by 10% for each 4 knots of headwind.*

        445 x .10 = 44.5 feet
        445.0 – 44.5 = 400.5 or 401 feet

*(H317) — AC 61-23C, Chapter 4*

---

AIR
**3694.** (Refer to Figure 39.) Determine the total distance required to land over a 50-foot obstacle.

Pressure altitude ........................................... 7,500 ft
Headwind ......................................................... 8 kts
Temperature ...................................................... 32°F
Runway .................................................. Hard surface

A—1,004 feet.
B—1,205 feet.
C—1,506 feet.

*Use the following steps:*

1. *Locate the portion of FAA Figure 39 that is applicable to a pressure altitude of 7,500 feet. The standard temperature at 7,500 feet is approximately 32°F, based on a temperature lapse rate of 3.5°F/1,000 feet.*

2. *Determine from the table that the basic distance to clear a 50-foot obstacle is 1,255 feet.*

3. *Apply Note 1 to account for an 8-knot headwind (a 20% decrease in distance):*

        1,255 x .20 = 251 feet
        1,255 – 251 = 1,004 feet

*(H317) — AC 61-23C, Chapter 4*

---

AIR
**3695.** (Refer to Figure 39.) Determine the total distance required to land over a 50-foot obstacle.

Pressure altitude ........................................... 5,000 ft
Headwind ......................................................... 8 kts
Temperature ...................................................... 41°F
Runway .................................................. Hard surface

A—837 feet.
B—956 feet.
C—1,076 feet.

*Use the following steps:*

1. *Locate the table applicable to a pressure altitude of 5,000 feet and ambient temperature of 41°F on FAA Figure 39.*

2. *Read the total distance required to clear a 50-foot obstacle (1,195 feet).*

3. *Apply Note 1 to account for an 8-knot headwind (a 20% decrease in distance):*

        1,195 x .20 = 239 feet
        1,195 – 239 = 956 feet

*(H317) — AC 61-23C, Chapter 4*

---

AIR
**3696.** (Refer to Figure 39.) Determine the approximate landing ground roll distance.

Pressure altitude ........................................... 5,000 ft
Headwind ........................................................ Calm
Temperature ..................................................... 101°F

A—495 feet.
B—545 feet.
C—445 feet.

*Use the following steps:*

1. *Locate the table which applies to a pressure altitude of 5,000 feet on FAA Figure 39.*

2. *Read the ground roll of 495 feet.*

3. *Apply Note 2 to account for the temperature difference between 101°F ambient and the 41°F value on which the table is based.*

        495 x .10 = 49.5 feet
        495 + 49.5 = 544.5 feet

*(H317) — AC 61-23C, Chapter 4*

**Answers**

3693  [B]        3694  [A]        3695  [B]        3696  [B]

AIR

**3697.** (Refer to Figure 39.) Determine the total distance required to land over a 50-foot obstacle.

Pressure altitude .............................................. 3,750 ft
Headwind ............................................................ 12 kts
Temperature ....................................................... Std

A—794 feet.
B—836 feet.
C—816 feet.

*Use the following steps:*

1. *Locate the 2,500-foot and 5,000-foot tables.*

2. *Interpolate (3,750 is midway between 2,500 feet and 5,000 feet) to obtain a landing distance:*

    *(1,135 + 1,195) ÷ 2 = 1,165 feet ground roll*

3. *Apply Note 1 to account for the 12-knot headwind.*

    *12 ÷ 4 = 3*
    *3.00 x .10 = .30*
    *1,165 x .30 = 349.5*
    *1,165 – 349.5 = 815.5 feet*

*(H317) — AC 61-23C, Chapter 4*

---

ALL

**3698.** (Refer to Figure 39.) Determine the approximate landing ground roll distance.

Pressure altitude .............................................. 1,250 ft
Headwind .............................................................. 8 kts
Temperature ....................................................... Std

A—275 feet.
B—366 feet.
C—470 feet.

*Use the following steps:*

1. *Locate the tables for sea level and 2,500 feet. Note that 1,250 feet is midway between sea level and 2,500 feet.*

2. *Interpolate between charts for 2,500 feet pressure altitude and sea level to find ground roll:*

    *(445 + 470) ÷ 2 = 457.5 ground roll*

3. *Apply Note 1 to account for the 8-knot headwind (a 20% decrease in distance):*

    *457.5 x .20 = 91.5 feet*
    *457.5 – 91.5 = 366 feet*

*(H317) — AC 61-23C, Chapter 4*

RTC

**3699.** (Refer to Figure 40.) Determine the total landing distance to clear a 50-foot obstacle in a gyroplane. The outside air temperature (OAT) is 75°F and the pressure altitude at the airport is 2,500 feet.

A—521 feet.
B—525 feet.
C—529 feet.

*Use the following steps:*

1. *Locate the horizontal line corresponding to 2,500 feet pressure altitude on FAA Figure 40.*

2. *Draw vertical lines through the points of intersection of the 2,500-foot pressure altitude line with the 75°F point. Note the landing distance of 525 feet.*

*(H317) — AC 61-23C, Chapter 4*

---

RTC

**3700.** (Refer to Figure 40.) Approximately how much additional landing distance will be required for a gyroplane to clear a 50-foot obstacle with an increase in temperature from 40 to 60°F at 3,200 feet pressure altitude?

A—4 feet.
B—8 feet.
C—12 feet.

*Use the following steps:*

1. *Locate the 3,200-foot pressure altitude point on FAA Figure 40.*

2. *Select any two adjacent temperature lines (which are separated by 20°F increments). Note the points of intersection of each line with the 3,200-foot pressure altitude.*

3. *Read downward from each of the two intersections to the distance scale.*

4. *Note the difference between the two distances (4 feet).*

*(H317) — AC 61-23C, Chapter 4*

---

**Answers**

3697  [C]       3698  [B]       3699  [B]       3700  [A]

RTC
**3701.** (Refer to Figure 40.) Determine the total landing distance to clear a 50-foot obstacle in a gyroplane. The outside air temperature (OAT) is 80°F and the pressure altitude is 3,500 feet.

A—521 feet.
B—526 feet.
C—531 feet.

*Use the following steps:*

1. *Locate the horizontal line corresponding to 3,500 feet pressure altitude on FAA Figure 40.*

2. *Draw vertical lines through the points of intersection of the 3,500-foot pressure altitude line with the 80°F point. Note the landing distance of 531 feet.*

*(H317) — AC 61-23C, Chapter 4*

GLI
**3864.** (Refer to Figure 55.) How many feet will the glider sink in 1 statute mile at 53 MPH in still air?

A—144 feet.
B—171 feet.
C—211 feet.

*Use the following steps:*

1. *Read the L/D ratio (which is numerically the same as the glide ratio) for a speed of 53 MPH from the graph (30.9:1).*

2. *Using the glide ratio of 30.9 feet forward for each foot of vertical sink, calculate the sink encountered in one statute mile (5,280 feet):*

$$\frac{Distance}{L/D\ Ratio} = Vertical\ Sink$$

$$\frac{5,280}{30.9} = 171\ feet\ vertical\ sink$$

*(N21) — Soaring Flight Manual*

GLI
**3865.** (Refer to Figure 55.) At what speed will the glider attain a sink rate of 5 feet per second in still air?

A—75 MPH.
B—79 MPH.
C—84 MPH.

*Use the following steps:*

1. *Locate the sinking speed (V$_S$) curve and its associated scale (on the right side) of FAA Figure 55.*

2. *Read to the left from the 5 FPS position to the sinking speed curved scale.*

3. *Read downward from the point of intersection to the horizontal velocity (V) scale. Interpreting the horizontal scale gives a speed of 79 MPH forward.*

*(N21) — Soaring Flight Manual*

GLI
**3866.** (Refer to Figure 55.) How many feet will the glider descend at minimum sink speed for 1 statute mile in still air?

A—132 feet.
B—170 feet.
C—180 feet.

*Use the following steps:*

1. *Locate the minimum sink speed (2.2 FPS at 44 MPH) on FAA Figure 55.*

2. *Determine the L/D (glide ratio) at 44 MPH by reading up from 44 MPH (on the V$_S$ coordinate) to the intersection with the L/D curve. Read from that intersection to the left (L/D) coordinate. At 44 MPH the L/D ratio is 29.3:1.*

3. *Using the glide ratio of 29.3 feet forward for each foot of vertical sink, calculate the sink encountered in 5,280 feet (one statue mile):*

$$\frac{Distance}{L/D\ Ratio} = Vertical\ Sink$$

$$\frac{5,280}{29.3} = 180\ feet\ vertical\ sink$$

*(N21) — Soaring Flight Manual*

**Answers**

3701   [C]         3864   [B]         3865   [B]         3866   [C]

GLI
**3867.** (Refer to Figure 55.) At what speed will the glider gain the most distance while descending 1,000 feet in still air?

A—44 MPH.
B—53 MPH.
C—83 MPH.

*The L/D ratio is numerically the same as the glide ratio. Hence, the best forward distance attained per foot of descent will be at the velocity which gives the maximum L/D. (N21) — Soaring Flight Manual*

GLI
**3868.** (Refer to Figure 55.) What approximate lift/drag ratio will the glider attain at 68 MPH in still air?

A—10.5:1.
B—21.7:1.
C—28.5:1.

*Use the following steps:*

1. *Locate 68 MPH on the V coordinate (at the bottom) on FAA Figure 55.*

2. *Read upward from the 68 MPH point to the intersection with the L/D curve.*

3. *Read to the left, from the point of intersection, to the L/D scale and read L/D, 28.5:1.*

*(N21) — Soaring Flight Manual*

# Headwind and Crosswind Component Graph

In general, taking off into a wind improves aircraft performance, and reduces the length of runway required to become airborne. The stronger the wind, the better the aircraft performs. Crosswinds, however, may make the aircraft difficult or impossible to control. The aircraft manufacturer determines the safe limit for taking off or landing with a crosswind and establishes the maximum allowable crosswind component. The graph shown in FAA Figure 37 is used to determine what extent a wind of a given direction and speed is felt as a headwind and/or crosswind.

### Problem:

The wind is reported to be from 085° at 30 knots, and you plan to land on Runway 11. What will the headwind and crosswind components be?

### Solution:

1. Determine the angular difference between the wind direction and the runway:

    110°  runway
    – 085°  wind
    ————————
     25°  difference

2. Find the intersection of the 25°-angle radial line and the 30-knot wind speed arc on the graph shown in FAA Figure 37. From the intersection move straight down to the bottom of the chart and read that the crosswind component equals 13 knots. From the point of intersection move horizontally left and read that the headwind component equals 27 knots.

**Answers**
3867    [B]          3868    [C]

AIR
**3683.** (Refer to Figure 37.) What is the headwind component for a landing on Runway 18 if the tower reports the wind as 220° at 30 knots?

A—19 knots.
B—23 knots.
C—26 knots.

*Use the following steps:*

1. Determine the relative wind angle (WA) from the difference between the runway heading (RH) and the wind direction (WD):

   WA = WD – RH
   WA = 220° – 180°
   WA = 40°

2. Locate the arc corresponding to a 30-knot wind on FAA Figure 37.

3. Find the point of intersection of the 40° line with the 30-knot wind speed arc.

4. Draw a line to the left from the intersection to the headwind component scale and read the resulting velocity of 23 knots.

(H317) — AC 61-23C, Chapter 4

---

AIR
**3684.** (Refer to Figure 37.) Determine the maximum wind velocity for a 45° crosswind if the maximum crosswind component for the airplane is 25 knots.

A—25 knots.
B—29 knots.
C—35 knots.

*Use the following steps:*

1. Locate the 45° wind angle in FAA Figure 37.

2. Locate the vertical line representing a 25-knot crosswind component and its point of intersection with the 45° wind angle line.

3. Interpret the intersection point as lying on an arc midway between the 30- and 40-knot wind velocity arcs, or 35 knots.

(H317) — AC 61-23C, Chapter 4

AIR
**3685.** (Refer to Figure 37.) What is the maximum wind velocity for a 30° crosswind if the maximum crosswind component for the airplane is 12 knots?

A—16 knots.
B—20 knots.
C—24 knots.

*Use the following steps:*

1. Locate the 30° wind angle line on FAA Figure 37.

2. Locate the vertical line representing the maximum crosswind component of 12 knots and its point of intersection with the 30° wind angle line.

3. Interpret the point of intersection as lying on an arc slightly less than midway between the 20- and 30-knot wind velocity arcs or about 24 knots.

(H317) — AC 61-23C, Chapter 4

---

AIR
**3686.** (Refer to Figure 37.) With a reported wind of north at 20 knots, which runway (6, 29, or 32) is acceptable for use for an airplane with a 13-knot maximum crosswind component?

A—Runway 6.
B—Runway 29.
C—Runway 32.

*Use the following steps:*

1. Locate the 20-knot wind velocity arc on FAA Figure 37.

2. Draw a line upward from the 13-knot crosswind component (maximum crosswind).

3. Note that in this case, acceptable crosswind components will result anytime the relative wind angle is equal to or less than about 40° (the intersection of the 13-knot vertical line and the 20-knot wind arc).

4. Calculate the relative wind angle between the north wind (0°) and the runway headings:

| RWY | Relative Angle | Landing |
|-----|----------------|---------|
| 6   | 60°            | Upwind  |
| 29  | 70°            | Upwind  |
| 32  | 40°            | Upwind  |

Only runway 32 provides a crosswind component that would be in acceptable limits for the airplane specified.
(H317) — AC 61-23C, Chapter 4

---

**Answers**

3683 [B]       3684 [C]       3685 [C]       3686 [C]

AIR

**3687.** (Refer to Figure 37.) With a reported wind of south at 20 knots, which runway (10, 14, or 24) is appropriate for an airplane with a 13-knot maximum crosswind component?

A—Runway 10.
B—Runway 14.
C—Runway 24.

*Use the following steps:*

1. *Locate the 20-knot wind velocity arc on FAA Figure 37.*

2. *Draw a line upward from the 13-knot crosswind component (maximum crosswind).*

3. *Note that in this case, acceptable crosswind components will result anytime the relative wind angle is equal to or less than 43° (the intersection of the 13-knot vertical line and the 20-knot wind arc).*

4. *Calculate the relative wind angle between the south wind (180°) and the runway headings:*

| RWY | Relative Angle | Landing |
|-----|----------------|----------|
| 6 | 60° | Downwind |
| 14 | 40° | Upwind |
| 24 | 60° | Upwind |
| 32 | 40° | Downwind |

*While both runways 14 and 32 would limit the crosswind component to an acceptable velocity, only runway 14 provides a safer upwind landing. (H317) — AC 61-23C, Chapter 4*

ALL

**3688.** (Refer to Figure 37.) What is the crosswind component for a landing on Runway 18 if the tower reports the wind as 220° at 30 knots?

A—19 knots.
B—23 knots.
C—30 knots.

*Use the following steps:*

1. *Determine the relative wind angle (WA) from the difference between the runway heading (RH) and the wind direction (WD).*

$$WA = WD - RH$$
$$WA = 220° - 180°$$
$$WA = 40°$$

2. *Locate the arc corresponding to a 30-knot wind velocity.*

3. *Find the point of intersection of the 40° line with the 30-knot wind speed arc.*

4. *Draw a line downward from the intersection to the crosswind component scale and read the resulting velocity of 19 knots.*

*(H317) — AC 61-23C, Chapter 4*

*Answer (B) is incorrect because this is the headwind component. Answer (C) is incorrect because this is the wind speed.*

**Answers**

3687   [B]          3688   [A]

# Chapter 9
# Enroute Flight

# Pilotage

Air navigation is the art of directing an aircraft along a desired course and being able to determine its geographical position at any time. Such navigation may be accomplished by pilotage, dead reckoning, or using radio navigational aids.

**Pilotage** is the use of visible landmarks to maintain a desired course, and is the basic form of navigation for the beginning pilot operating under Visual Flight Rules (VFR). Visible landmarks which can be identified on aeronautical charts allow the pilot to proceed from one check point to the next.

The aeronautical charts most commonly used by VFR pilots are the **VFR Sectional Aeronautical Chart**, the **VFR Terminal Area Chart**, and the **World Aeronautical Chart**. All three charts include aeronautical information such as airports, airways, special use airspace, and other pertinent data.

The scale of the VFR Sectional Aeronautical Chart is 1:500,000 (1 inch = 6.86 NM). Designed for visual navigation of slow speed aircraft in VFR conditions, this chart portrays terrain relief and checkpoints such as populated places, roads, railroads, and other distinctive landmarks. These charts have the best detail and are revised every 6 months.

Information found on the VFR Terminal Area Chart is similar to that found on the VFR Sectional Chart, but the scale on this chart is 1:250,000 (1 inch = 3.43 NM). These charts are for a specific city with Class B airspace. They show much detail, but have small coverage.

The World Aeronautical Chart has a scale of 1:1,000,000, which is more convenient for use in navigation by moderate speed aircraft. It depicts cities, railroads, and distinctive landmarks, etc. These charts have less detail and are revised no more than once a year.

To identify a point on the surface of the earth, a geographic coordinate, or "grid" system was devised. By reference to meridians of **longitude** and parallels of **latitude**, any position may be accurately located when using the grid system.

Equidistant from the poles is an imaginary circle called the **equator**. The lines running east and west, parallel to the equator are called parallels of latitude, and are used to measure angular distance north or south of the equator. From the equator to either pole is 90°, with 0° being at the equator; while 90° north latitude describes the location of the North Pole. *See* Figure 9-1.

Lines called meridians of longitude are drawn from pole to pole at right angles to the equator. The **prime meridian**, used as the zero degree line, passes through Greenwich, England. From this line, measurements are made in degrees both easterly and westerly up to 180°.

Any specific geographical point can be located by reference to its longitude and latitude. For example, Washington, DC is approximately 39° north of the equator and 77° west of the prime meridian and would be stated as 39°N 77°W. Note that latitude is stated first.

In order to describe a location more precisely, each degree (°) is subdivided into 60 minutes (') and each minute further divided into 60 seconds ("), although seconds are not shown. Thus, the location of the airport at Elk City, Oklahoma is described as being at 35°25'55"N 99°23'15"W (35 degrees, 25 minutes, 55 seconds north latitude; 99 degrees, 23 minutes, 15 seconds west longitude). Degrees of west longitude increase from east to west. Degrees of north latitude increase from south to north.

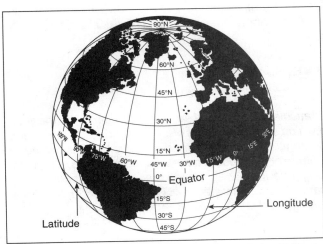

**Figure 9-1.** Meridians of longitude and parallels of latitude

ALL
**3530.** (Refer to Figure 21, area 3.) Determine the approximate latitude and longitude of Currituck County Airport.

A—36°24'N – 76°01'W.
B—36°48'N – 76°01'W.
C—47°24'N – 75°58'W.

*Graticules on Sectional Aeronautical Charts are the lines dividing each 30 minutes of latitude and each 30 minutes of longitude. Each tick mark represents one minute of latitude or longitude. Latitude increases northward, west longitude increases going westward. The approximate latitude and longitude of Currituck County Airport is 36°24'N, 76°01'W. (H340) — AC 61-23C, Chapter 8*

ALL
**3535.** (Refer to Figure 22, area 2.) Which airport is located at approximately 47°39'30"N latitude and 100°53'00"W longitude?

A—Linrud.
B—Crooked Lake.
C—Johnson.

*Graticules on Sectional Aeronautical Charts are the lines dividing each 30 minutes of latitude and each 30 minutes of longitude. Each tick mark represents one minute of latitude or longitude. Latitude increases northward, west longitude increases going westward. The Crooked Lake airport is located at approximately 47°39'30"N latitude and 100°53'00"W longitude. (H340) — AC 61-23C, Chapter 8*

ALL
**3536.** (Refer to Figure 22, area 3.) Which airport is located at approximately 47°21'N latitude and 101°01'W longitude?

A—Underwood.
B—Evenson.
C—Washburn.

*Graticules on Sectional Aeronautical Charts are the lines dividing each 30 minutes of latitude and each 30 minutes of longitude. Each tick mark represents one minute of latitude or longitude. Latitude increases northward, west longitude increases going westward. Washburn is located at approximately 47°21'N latitude and 101°01'W longitude. (H340) — AC 61-23C, Chapter 8*

ALL
**3543.** (Refer to Figure 23, area 3.) Determine the approximate latitude and longitude of Shoshone County Airport.

A—47°02'N – 116°11'W.
B—47°33'N – 116°11'W.
C—47°32'N – 116°41'W

*Graticules on Sectional Aeronautical Charts are the lines dividing each 30 minutes of latitude and each 30 minutes of longitude. Each tick mark represents one minute of latitude or longitude. Latitude increases northward, west longitude increases going westward. The approximate latitude and longitude of Shoshone County Airport is 47°33'N, 116°11'W. (H340) — AC 61-23C, Chapter 8*

ALL
**3567.** (Refer to Figure 27, area 2.) What is the approximate latitude and longitude of Cooperstown Airport?

A—47°25'N – 98°06'W.
B—47°25'N – 99°54'W.
C—47°55'N – 98°06'W.

*Graticules on Sectional Aeronautical Charts are the lines dividing each 30 minutes of latitude and each 30 minutes of longitude. Each tick mark represents one minute of latitude or longitude. Latitude increases northward, west longitude increases going westward. Cooperstown airport is approximately at 47°25'N latitude, and 98°06'W longitude. (H340) — AC 61-23C, Chapter 8*

**Answers**

| | | | | |
|---|---|---|---|---|
| 3530 [A] | 3535 [B] | 3536 [C] | 3543 [B] | 3567 [A] |

# Time

Time is measured in relation to the rotation of the earth. A day is defined as the time required for the earth to make one complete revolution of 360°. Since the day is divided into 24 hours, it follows that the earth revolves at the rate of 15° each hour. Thus, longitude may be expressed as either 90° or 6 hours west of Greenwich.

Twenty-four time zones have been established. Each time zone is 15° of longitude in width, with the first zone centered on the meridian of Greenwich. Each zone uses the local time of its central meridian as shown in FAA Figure 28.

For example, when the sun is above the 90th meridian, it is noon central standard time (CST). At the same time it is 6 p.m. Greenwich, 11 a.m. mountain standard time (MST), and 1 p.m. eastern standard time (EST). When daylight saving time (DST) is in effect, the sun is over the 75th meridian at noon CST.

Most aviation operations time is expressed in terms of the 24-hour clock, (for example, 8 a.m. is expressed as 0800; 2 p.m. is 1400; 11 p.m. is 2300) and may be either local or **Coordinated Universal Time (UTC)**. UTC is the time at the prime meridian and is represented in aviation operations by the letter "Z," referred to as "**Zulu time**." For example, 1500Z would be read as "one five zero zero Zulu."

In the United States, conversion from local time to UTC is made in accordance with the table in the lower left corner of FAA Figure 28.

**Problem:** An aircraft departs an airport in the Pacific standard time zone at 1030 PST for a 4-hour flight to an airport located in the central standard time zone. The landing should be at what coordinated universal time (UTC)?

**Solution:** Use the conversion table in FAA Figure 28 and the following steps:

1. Convert 1030 PST to UTC:

    1030   PST (takeoff time)
    + 0800  (conversion)
    _____
    1830   (UTC)

2. Add the flight time.

    1830   (UTC)
    + 0400  (flight time)
    _____
    2230   UTC (time the aircraft should land)

ALL
**3571.** (Refer to Figure 28.) An aircraft departs an airport in the eastern daylight time zone at 0945 EDT for a 2-hour flight to an airport located in the central daylight time zone. The landing should be at what coordinated universal time?

A—1345Z.
B—1445Z.
C—1545Z.

*Use the following steps:*

1. *Convert the EDT takeoff time to UTC:*

> 0945    *EDT takeoff time*
> + 0400    *conversion*
> ————————
> 1345 Z   *UTC (also called "ZULU" time)*

2. *Add the flight time to the ZULU time of takeoff:*

> 1345 Z   *takeoff time*
> + 0200
> ————————
> 1545 Z   *time of landing*

*(H340) — AC 61-23C, Chapter 8*

ALL
**3572.** (Refer to Figure 28.) An aircraft departs an airport in the central standard time zone at 0930 CST for a 2-hour flight to an airport located in the mountain standard time zone. The landing should be at what time?

A—0930 MST.
B—1030 MST.
C—1130 MST.

*Use the following steps:*

1. *Change the CST takeoff time to UTC:*

> 0930    *CST takeoff time*
> + 0600    *conversion*
> ————————
> 1530 Z   *UTC (also called "ZULU" time)*

2. *Add the flight time to the time of takeoff:*

> 1530 Z   *takeoff time*
> + 0200    *flight time*
> ————————
> 1730 Z   *time of landing*

3. *Convert UTC to MST:*

> 1730 Z   *UTC*
> – 0700    *conversion*
> ————————
> 1030     *MST time of landing*

*(H340) — AC 61-23C, Chapter 8*

ALL
**3573.** (Refer to Figure 28.) An aircraft departs an airport in the central standard time zone at 0845 CST for a 2-hour flight to an airport located in the mountain standard time zone. The landing should be at what coordinated universal time?

A—1345Z.
B—1445Z.
C—1645Z.

*Use the following steps:*

1. *Convert the CST takeoff time to UTC:*

> 0845    *CST takeoff time*
> + 0600    *conversion*
> ————————
> 1445 Z   *UTC (also called "ZULU" time)*

2. *Add the flight time to the ZULU time of takeoff:*

> 1445 Z   *takeoff time*
> + 0200    *flight time*
> ————————
> 1645 Z   *the time of landing*

*(H340) — AC 61-23C, Chapter 8*

ALL
**3574.** (Refer to Figure 28.) An aircraft departs an airport in the mountain standard time zone at 1615 MST for a 2-hour 15-minute flight to an airport located in the Pacific standard time zone. The estimated time of arrival at the destination airport should be

A—1630 PST.
B—1730 PST.
C—1830 PST.

*Use the following steps:*

1. *Convert the MST takeoff time to UTC:*

> 1615    *MST takeoff time*
> + 0700    *conversion*
> ————————
> 2315 Z   *UTC (also called "ZULU" time)*

2. *Add the flight time to the ZULU time of takeoff:*

> 2315 Z   *takeoff time*
> + 0215    *flight time*
> ————————
> 0130 Z   *time of landing*

3. *Convert UTC to PST:*

> 0130 Z   *UTC*
> – 0800    *conversion*
> ————————
> 1730     *PST time of landing*

*(H340) — AC 61-23C, Chapter 8*

---

**Answers**

3571  [C]        3572  [B]        3573  [C]        3574  [B]

ALL
**3575.** (Refer to Figure 28.) An aircraft departs an airport in the Pacific standard time zone at 1030 PST for a 4-hour flight to an airport located in the central standard time zone. The landing should be at what coordinated universal time?

A— 2030Z.
B— 2130Z.
C— 2230Z.

*Use the following steps:*

1. *Convert the PST takeoff time to UTC:*

> 1030     *PST takeoff time*
> + 0800    *conversion*
> 1830 Z   *UTC (also called "ZULU" time)*

2. *Add the flight time to the ZULU takeoff time:*

> 1830 Z   *takeoff time*
> + 0400   *flight time*
> 2230 Z   *time of landing*

*(H340) — AC 61-23C, Chapter 8*

ALL
**3576.** (Refer to Figure 28.) An aircraft departs an airport in the mountain standard time zone at 1515 MST for a 2-hour 30-minute flight to an airport located in the Pacific standard time zone. What is the estimated time of arrival at the destination airport?

A— 1645 PST.
B— 1745 PST.
C— 1845 PST.

*Use the following steps:*

1. *Convert the MST takeoff time to UTC:*

> 1515     *MST takeoff time*
> + 0700    *conversion*
> 2215 Z   *UTC (also called "ZULU" time)*

2. *Add the flight time to the ZULU takeoff time:*

> 2215 Z   *takeoff time*
> + 0230   *flight time*
> 2445 Z   *(0045)Z time of landing*

3. *Convert UTC to PST:*

> 2445 Z   *(0045)Z*
> – 0800   *conversion*
> 1645     *PST time of landing*

*(H340) — AC 61-23C, Chapter 8*

# Topography

A VFR Sectional Aeronautical Chart is a pictorial representation of a portion of the Earth's surface upon which lines and symbols in a variety of colors represent features and/or details that can be seen on the Earth's surface. Contour lines, shaded relief, color tints, obstruction symbols, and maximum elevation figures are all used to show topographical information. Explanations and examples may be found in the chart legend. Pilots should become familiar with all of the information provided in each Sectional Chart Legend, found in FAA Legend 1.

ALL
**3637.** (Refer to Figure 24, area 3.) What is the height of the lighted obstacle approximately 6 nautical miles southwest of Savannah International?

A— 1,500 feet MSL.
B— 1,531 feet AGL.
C— 1,549 feet MSL.

*Reference FAA Legend 1. The top number, printed in bold, is the height of the obstruction above mean sea level. The second number, printed in parentheses, is the height of the obstruction above ground level. The obstruction is shown as 1,549 feet MSL and 1,534 feet AGL. (J37) — Sectional Chart Legend*

**Answers**

3575   [C]         3576   [A]         3637   [C]

ALL
**3638.** (Refer to Figure 24, area 3.) The top of the group obstruction approximately 11 nautical miles from the Savannah VORTAC on the 340° radial is

A—400 feet AGL.
B—455 feet MSL.
C—432 feet MSL.

*Reference FAA Legend 1. The bold number (455) indicates the height of the obstruction above mean sea level. (J37) — Sectional Chart Legend*

ALL
**3639.** (Refer to Figure 25, area 1.) What minimum altitude is necessary to vertically clear the obstacle on the northeast side of Airpark East Airport by 500 feet?

A—1,010 feet MSL.
B—1,273 feet MSL.
C—1,283 feet MSL.

*The elevation of the top of the obstacle is shown as 773 feet above mean sea level (MSL). Add the 500-foot vertical clearance specified by the question to the height (MSL) of the obstacle:*

$$
\begin{array}{r}
773 \text{ feet MSL} \\
+\ 500 \\
\hline
1,273 \text{ feet MSL minimum altitude}
\end{array}
$$

*(J37) — Sectional Chart Legend*

ALL
**3640.** (Refer to Figure 25, area 2.) What minimum altitude is necessary to vertically clear the obstacle on the southeast side of Winnsboro Airport by 500 feet?

A—823 feet MSL.
B—1,013 feet MSL.
C—1,403 feet MSL.

*The elevation of the top of the obstacle is shown as 903 feet above mean sea level (MSL). Add the 500-foot vertical clearance specified by the question to the height (MSL) of the obstacle:*

$$
\begin{array}{r}
903 \text{ feet MSL} \\
+\ 500 \\
\hline
1,403 \text{ feet MSL}
\end{array}
$$

*(J37) — Sectional Chart Legend*

AIR
**3642.** (Refer to Figure 26, area 8.) What minimum altitude is required to fly over the Cedar Hill TV towers in the congested area south of NAS Dallas?

A—2,555 feet MSL.
B—3,449 feet MSL.
C—3,349 feet MSL.

*The height of the tower is 2,449 MSL. A 1,000-foot clearance is required between obstructions and aircraft over a congested area.*

$$
\begin{array}{r}
2,449 \text{ MSL} \\
+\ 1,000 \\
\hline
3,449 \text{ MSL}
\end{array}
$$

*(J37) — 14 CFR §91.119(b)*

ALL
**3631.** (Refer to Figure 21, area 5.) The CAUTION box denotes what hazard to aircraft?

A—Unmarked balloon on cable to 3,000 feet MSL.
B—Unmarked balloon on cable to 3,000 feet AGL.
C—Unmarked blimp hangers at 300 feet MSL.

*Reference FAA Legend 1. The boxed caution reads, "CAUTION: UNMARKED BALLOON ON CABLE TO 3,000 MSL." (J37) — Sectional Chart Legend*

ALL
**3632.** (Refer to Figure 21, area 2.) The flag symbol at Lake Drummond represents a

A—compulsory reporting point for Norfolk Class C airspace.
B—compulsory reporting point for Hampton Roads Airport.
C—visual checkpoint used to identify position for initial callup to Norfolk Approach Control.

*Reference FAA Legend 1. The flag symbol represents a visual checkpoint used to identify position for initial callup to Norfolk Approach Control. (J37) — Sectional Chart Legend*

ALL
**3633.** (Refer to Figure 21, area 2.) The elevation of the Chesapeake Municipal Airport is

A—20 feet.
B—36 feet.
C—360 feet.

**Answers**

| | | | | | |
|---|---|---|---|---|---|
| 3638 [B] | 3639 [B] | 3640 [C] | 3642 [B] | 3631 [A] | 3632 [C] |
| 3633 [A] | | | | | |

*Reference FAA Legend 1. The airport elevation is noted in the airport information, beneath the airport symbol. The elevation of Chesapeake Municipal Airport is 20 feet. (J37) — Sectional Chart Legend*

**ALL**
**3634.** (Refer to Figure 22.) The terrain elevation of the light tan area between Minot (area 1) and Audubon Lake (area 2) varies from

A—sea level to 2,000 feet MSL.
B—2,000 feet to 2,500 feet MSL.
C—2,000 feet to 2,700 feet MSL.

*Reference FAA Legend 1. The contour line which borders the tan area is labeled 2,000 feet. There are no higher contour levels depicted inside the tan area. (J37) — Sectional Chart Legend*

Answer (A) is incorrect because the light tan area indicates terrain between 2,000–3,000 feet MSL. Answer (C) is incorrect because contour intervals are 500 feet, not 700.

**ALL**
**3635.** (Refer to Figure 22.) Which public use airports depicted are indicated as having fuel?

A—Minot Intl. (area 1) and Garrison (area 2).
B—Minot Intl. (area 1) and Mercer County Regional Airport (area 3).
C—Mercer County Regional Airport (area 3) and Garrison (area 2).

*Reference FAA Legend 1. Minot and Mercer County Regional Airport are depicted as having fuel, as indicated by the ticks around the basic airport symbol. (J37) — Sectional Chart Legend*

**ALL**
**3636.** (Refer to Figure 24.) The flag symbols at Statesboro Bullock County Airport, Claxton-Evans County Airport, and Ridgeland Airport are

A—outer boundaries of Savannah Class C airspace.
B—airports with special traffic patterns.
C—visual checkpoints to identify position for initial callup prior to entering Savannah Class C airspace.

*Reference FAA Legend 1. "Visual check point" is the name for the flag symbol. (J37) — Sectional Chart Legend*

**LTA**
**3644.** (Refer to Figure 21, area 4.) A balloon launched at the town of Edenton drifts northeasterly along the railroad. What minimum altitude must it maintain to clear all of the obstacles in the vicinity of Hertford by at least 500 feet?

A—805 feet MSL.
B—1,000 feet MSL.
C—1,015 feet MSL.

*Use the following steps:*

1. *Locate the towns of Edenton and Hertford.*
2. *Note the highest obstruction in the vicinity of Hertford (515 feet MSL).*
3. *Calculate the minimum altitude (MSL) by adding the required 500-foot clearance to the obstacle height.*

$$\begin{array}{r} 515 \text{ feet} \\ + 500 \text{ feet} \\ \hline 1,015 \text{ feet MSL} \end{array}$$

*(J37) — Sectional Chart Legend*

**LTA**
**3645.** (Refer to Figure 22, area 1.) A balloon launched at Flying S Ranch Airport drifts southward towards the lighted obstacle. If the altimeter was set to the current altimeter setting upon launch, what should it indicate if the balloon is to clear the obstacle at 500 feet above the top?

A—1,531 feet AGL.
B—1,809 feet AGL.
C—3,649 feet AGL.

*Use the following steps:*

1. *Locate the Flying S and lighted obstacle.*
2. *Calculate the height of the obstacle above the Flying S field elevation:*

$$\begin{array}{r} 3,149 \text{ feet top of obstacle (MSL)} \\ - 1,840 \text{ feet Flying S elevation (MSL)} \\ \hline 1,309 \text{ feet difference in elevation} \end{array}$$

3. *Add the required clearance to obtain the altimeter indication:*

$$\begin{array}{r} 500 \text{ feet required clearance} \\ + 1,309 \text{ feet difference in elevation} \\ \hline 1,809 \text{ feet altimeter indication} \end{array}$$

*(J37) — Sectional Chart Legend*

**Answers**

| | | | | |
|---|---|---|---|---|
| 3634 [B] | 3635 [B] | 3636 [C] | 3644 [C] | 3645 [B] |

LTA

**3646.** (Refer to Figure 23, area 1.) A balloon, launched at CX Airport located near the east end of Lake Pend Oreille, drifts south-southwest. What is the approximate elevation of the highest terrain for 20 miles along its path?

A—2,000 – 4,000 feet MSL.
B—4,000 – 6,000 feet MSL.
C—6,000 – 7,000 feet MSL.

*On Sectional Aeronautical Charts, color tints are used to depict bands of elevation. These colors range from light green for the lowest elevations to brown for the higher elevations. Note the terrain height of 6,405 feet MSL within the tan shading south-southwest of CX airport. (J37) — Sectional Chart Legend*

# Dead Reckoning

Dead reckoning is the method used for determining position with a heading indicator and calculations based on speed, elapsed time, and wind effect from a known position. The instruments used for dead reckoning navigation include the outside air temperature gauge, the airspeed indicator, the altimeter, the clock, and the magnetic compass system or slaved gyro system. These instruments provide information concerning direction, airspeed, altitude, and time, and must be correctly interpreted for successful navigation.

## Plotting Courses

A course is the direction of flight measured in degrees clockwise from north. Meridians of longitude run from the south pole to the north pole. This alignment is called true north. When a course is plotted on a chart in relation to the lines of longitude and/or latitude it is called a **true course (TC)**, and will be expressed in three digits. North may be either 360° or 000°; east is 090°; south is 180°; and west is 270°. Any attempt to project lines of latitude and longitude onto a flat surface such as a chart results in a certain amount of distortion. When plotting a course on a sectional aeronautical chart, this distortion may be minimized by measuring true course in reference to the meridian nearest to the halfway point between the departure point and the destination.

A common type of plotter that is used to plot a course is shown in Figure 9-2. This plotter is a semi-circular protractor with a straight edge attached to it. The straight edge has distance scales that match various charts and these scales may depict both statute and nautical miles. A small hole at the base of the protractor portion indicates the center of the arc of the angular scale. Two complete scales cover the outer edge of the protractor, and they are graduated in degrees. An inner scale measures the angle from the vertical.

To determine true course (TC), use the plotter in the following manner:

1. Using the straight edge of the plotter as a guide, draw a line from the point of departure to the destination.

2. Place the top straight edge of the plotter parallel to the plotted course and move the plotter along the course line as necessary to place the small center hole over a meridian as near to the halfway point of the course as possible. *See* Figure 9-2a.

3. The true course is the angle measured between the meridian and the course line. *See* Figure 9-2b. The outer scale is used to read all angles between north through east to south, and the inner scale is used to read all angles between south through west to north. In Figure 9-2 the true course from point (a) to point (b) is 115° as read at point (c).

**Answers**

3646 [C]

**Figure 9-2.** Placing the plotter on the course line

4. Course lines which fall within 30° of true north or south can be more easily measured by sliding the plotter along the course line until the hole falls over a horizontal latitude line; use the partial protractor scale for these measurements.

## Magnetic Variation

The north pole where all meridians converge is **true north**. The north pole which attracts the needle of a compass is **magnetic north**. These two poles are not in the same place. At any point where magnetic north and true north are in line with each other, the compass needle points both to magnetic north, and coincidentally, true north. The line along which this occurs is known as the **agonic line**. When positioned west of the agonic line, a compass will point right (east) of true north. When positioned east of the agonic line, a compass will point left (west) of true north. This angular difference between true north and magnetic north is called **magnetic variation (VAR)**. West of the agonic line, variation is "easterly." East of the agonic line, variation is "westerly."

The amount and direction of variation is depicted on sectional charts as dashed magenta colored lines connecting points of equal variation, called isogonic lines.

A course measured on a sectional chart is a true course: it is measured from a meridian, which runs from the south pole to the north pole. Since a magnetic compass is used to maintain a course while flying, this true course must now be converted to a **magnetic course (MC)**. This conversion is made by either adding or subtracting the variation. To convert a true course to a magnetic course, subtract easterly variation, and add westerly variation: "East is least, west is best."

TC ± VAR = MC

ALL
**3531.** (Refer to Figure 21.) Determine the magnetic course from First Flight Airport (area 5) to Hampton Roads Airport (area 2).

A—141°.
B—321°.
C—331°.

*Use the following steps:*

1. Plot the course from First Flight Airport to Hampton Roads Airport.

2. Measure the true course angle at the approximate midpoint of the route. The true course is 321°.

3. Note that the variation is 10°W as shown on the isogonic line.

4. Using the formula:

   MC = TC ± VAR
   MC = 321° + 10°W
   MC = 331°

*(H346) — AC 61-23C, Chapter 8*

ALL
**3556.** (Refer to Figure 25). Determine the magnetic course from Airpark East Airport (area 1) to Winnsboro Airport (area 2). Magnetic variation is 6°30'E.

A—075°.
B—082°.
C—091°.

*Use the following steps:*

1. Plot the course from Airpark East Airport to Winnsboro Airport.

2. Measure the true course angle at the approximate midpoint of the route (082°).

3. Calculate the magnetic course by subtracting the magnetic variation (6° 30') from the true course (082°).

   MC = TC ± VAR
   MC = 082° – 6°30'E
   MC = 75°30' (075° is the closest answer)

*(H346) — AC 61-23C, Chapter 8*

ALL
**3568.** (Refer to Figure 27.) Determine the magnetic course from Breckheimer (Pvt) Airport (area 1) to Jamestown Airport (area 4).

A—180°.
B—188°.
C—360°.

*Use the following steps:*

1. Plot the course from Breckheimer (Pvt) Airport to Jamestown Airport.

2. Measure the true course angle at the approximate midpoint of the route (189°).

3. Note that the variation is 7° East as shown on the dashed isogonic line.

4. Using the formula:

   MC = TC ± VAR
   MC = 189 – 7° East
   MC = 182°

*(H346) — AC 61-23C, Chapter 8*

**Answers**

3531 [C]        3556 [A]        3568 [A]

## Magnetic Deviation

The magnetic compass is affected by influences within the aircraft such as electrical circuits, radios, engines, magnetized metal parts, etc., which cause the compass needle to be deflected from its normal reading. This deflection is known as **deviation (DEV)**, and it must be applied to convert a magnetic course to a **compass course (CC)** to make it usable in flight.

Deviation, which is different for each aircraft, may also vary for different courses in the same airplane. To let the pilot know the appropriate correction, a correction card is mounted near the compass.

To determine the actual compass reading to be followed during flight, it is necessary to apply the corrections for both variation and deviation:

True Course ± Variation = Magnetic Course ± Deviation = Compass Course

or,

TC ± VAR = MC ± DEV = CC.

# Wind and Its Effects

An additional computation, common to both pilotage and dead reckoning, is necessary to compensate for the effect of wind.

Wind direction is reported as the direction from which the wind blows, i.e., wind blowing from the west to the east is a west wind. Wind speed is the rate of motion without regard to direction. In the United States, wind speed is usually expressed in knots. Wind velocity includes both direction and speed of the wind; for example, a west wind of 25 knots.

Downwind movement is with the wind; upwind movement is against the wind. Moving air exerts a force in the direction of its motion on any object within it. Objects that are free to move in air will move in a downwind direction at the speed of the wind.

If a powered aircraft is flying in a 20-knot wind, it will move 20 nautical miles downwind in 1 hour in addition to its forward movement through the air. The path of an aircraft over the earth is determined both by the motion of the aircraft through the air and by the motion of the air over the earth's surface. Direction and movement through the air is governed both by the direction that the aircraft nose is pointing and by aircraft speed.

The sideward displacement of an aircraft caused by wind is called drift. Drift can be determined by measuring the angle between the heading (the direction in which the nose is pointing) and the track (the actual path of the aircraft over the earth). *See* Figure 9-3.

For example, Figure 9-3 shows an aircraft which departs point A on a heading of 360° and flies for 1 hour in a wind of 270° at 20 knots. Under

**Figure 9-3.** Drift

**Figure 9-4.** Different effects of wind on track and ground speed

a no-wind condition the aircraft would arrive at point B at the end of 1 hour. However, this example has a wind of 20 knots, and the aircraft moves with the wind; so at the end of 1 hour, the aircraft is at point C, 20 nautical miles downwind from B. From A to B is the intended path of the aircraft, from B to C is the motion of the body of air, and from A to C is the actual path of the aircraft over the earth (the track).

A given wind will cause a different drift on each aircraft heading and it will also affect the distance traveled over the ground in a given time. With a given wind, the ground speed varies with each different aircraft heading. Figure 9-4 illustrates how a wind of 270° at 20 knots would affect the ground speed and track of an aircraft on various headings. In this particular illustration, on a heading of 360°, drift would be to the right; on a heading of 180°, drift would be to the left. With a 90° crosswind and no heading correction applied, there would be little effect on ground speed. On a heading of 090°, no

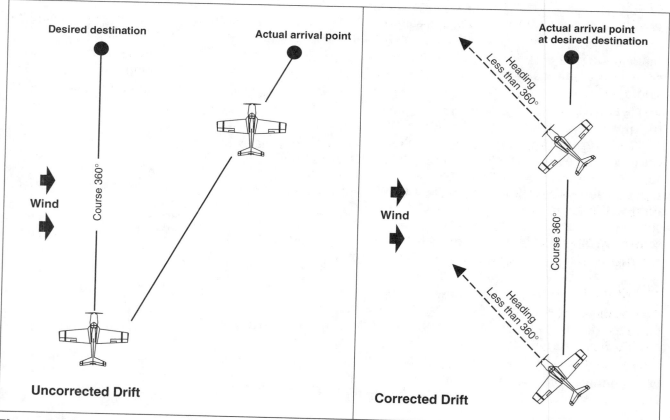

**Figure 9-5.** Compensating for wind drift

left or right drift would be experienced; instead, the ground speed would be increased by the tailwind. On a 270° heading, the ground speed would be reduced by the headwind.

By determining the amount of drift, a pilot can counteract the effect of wind and make the track of the aircraft coincide with the desired course. For example, if the wind is from the left, the correction would be made by pointing the aircraft to the left a certain number of degrees, thereby compensating for wind drift. This is the Wind Correction Angle (WCA), and it is expressed as degrees left or right of the course. *See* Figure 9-5.

Any course, true, magnetic, or compass, becomes a heading when it is corrected for wind. *See* Figure 9-6.

| Course | | | | Heading |
|---|---|---|---|---|
| True | ± | WCA | = | True |
| ± | | | | ± |
| Variation | | | | Variation |
| = | | | | = |
| Magnetic | ± | WCA | = | Magnetic |
| ± | | | | ± |
| Deviation | | | | Deviation |
| = | | | | = |
| Compass | ± | WCA | = | Compass |

**Figure 9-6**

# The Flight Computer (E6-B)

*Note:* ASA's CX-2 Pathfinder is an electronic flight computer and can be used in place of the E6-B. This aviation computer can solve all flight planning problems, as well as perform standard mathematical calculations.

### Finding Wind Correction Angle (WCA) and Ground Speed

The Wind Correction Angle (WCA) required to change a course to a heading can be found by using the wind face of the E6-B. Ground speed can also be determined as a part of this procedure.

The wind face of the E6-B consists of a transparent, rotatable plotting disk mounted in a frame as shown in Figure 9-7 on the next page. A compass rose is located around the plotting disk (Figure 9-7a). A correction scale on the top of the frame is graduated in degrees left and right of the true index (Figure 9-7b), and it is used for calculating drift correction. A small reference circle, called a grommet, is located at the center of the plotting disk (Figure 9-7c).

A sliding grid (Figure 9-7d) inserted behind the plotting disk is used for wind computations. The slide has converging lines (track or drift lines) which indicate degrees left or right of center (Figure 9-7e). Concentric arcs (speed circles) on the slide are used for calculations of speed (Figure 9-7f). The wind correction angle and ground speed may be found when true course, true airspeed, wind speed and wind direction (relative to true north) are known.

**Problem:** Using a flight computer and the following conditions, find the wind correction angle (WCA), the true heading (TH), and the ground speed (GS).

### Conditions:

True course (TC) ............................................. 090°
True airspeed (TAS) ............................. 120 knots
True wind direction ....................................... 160°
Wind speed ............................................. 30 knots

## Solution:

1. Using the wind face side of the E6-B, set the true wind direction (160°) under the true index (Figure 9-8a).

2. Plot the wind speed above the grommet 30 units (wind speed) and place a wind dot within a circle at this point (Figure 9-8b).

3. Rotate the plotting disk and set the true course (090°) under the true index (Figure 9-9a).

4. Adjust the sliding grid so that the TAS arc (120 knots) is at the wind dot (Figure 9-9b). Note the wind dot is 14° right of centerline (Figure 9-9c), so the WCA = 14°R.

5. Under the grommet, read the ground speed (GS) of 106 knots (Figure 9-9d).

**Figure 9-7.** Wind face of E6-B computer

**Figure 9-8.** Plotting wind speed and wind direction

6. Determine the true heading by applying the formula:

   TC + WCA = TH

In this case the wind correction is to the right, so it will be added to the true course:

$$
\begin{array}{r}
090° \text{ (TC)} \\
+ 14° \text{ (WCA)} \\
\hline
104° \text{ (TH)}
\end{array}
$$

## Flight Computer Calculator Face

Opposite the windface of the flight computer is a circular slide rule or calculator face. The outer scale, called the miles scale, is stationary (Figure 9-10a). The inner circle rotates and is called the minutes scale (Figure 9-10b).

The numbers on the computer scale represent multiples of 10, of the values shown. For example, the number 24 on either scale may be 0.24, 2.4, 24, 240, etc. On the inner scale, minutes may be converted to hours by reference to the adjacent hours scale. In Figure 9-10c, for example, 4 hours is found adjacent to 24, meaning 240 minutes.

Relative values must be kept in mind. For example, the numbers 21 and 22 are separated by divisions, each space representing 2 units. Thus, the second division past 21 will be read as 21.4, 214, or 2,140. Between 80 and 90 are 10 divisions, each space representing 1 unit. Thus, the second division past 80 will be read as 8.2, 82 or 820.

There are three index marks on the miles (outer) scale which are used for converting statute miles (SM), nautical miles (NM) and kilometers (KM). The E6-B computer has a scale for converting statute miles, nautical miles, and kilometers. Place the known figure on the inner scale under "naut," "stat," or

**Figure 9-9.** Determining the wind correction angle and ground speed

**Figure 9-10.** Slide rule (calculator) face

"KM," as appropriate, and read the equivalent value under the other indexes. For example, to convert 85 statute miles to kilometers and nautical miles, place 85 on the inner scale under the "stat" index. Under the "KM" index, read 137; under the "naut" index read 74.

Each scale has a 10-index used as a reference mark for multiplication and division. The 10-index on the inner scale can also be used as a rate index representing 1 hour. Also on the inner scale is a 60-index, representing 60 minutes and usually used for computation instead of the 10 or 1 hour index (Figure 9-10d) and a 36 or "seconds" index (3,600 seconds = 1 hour) (Figure 9-10e).

## Finding Time, Rate, and Distance

The flight computer will commonly be used to solve problems of time, rate, and distance. When two factors are known, the third can be found using the proportion:

$$\text{RATE (speed)} = \frac{\text{DISTANCE}}{\text{TIME}}$$

**Problem:** How far does an aircraft travel in 2 hours and 15 minutes at a ground speed of 138 knots?

**Solution:** Use the formula:

*Distance = Ground Speed x Time,* or use the flight computer in the following manner:

1. Place the 60 (speed) index (inner scale) under 138 (outer scale).
2. Over the time of 135 minutes or 2 hours +15 minutes (inner scale), read 310 NM (on the outer scale). *See* Figure 9-11.

**Figure 9-11.** Computing distance on the E6-B

**Figure 9-12.** Determining time required on the E6-B

**Problem:** How much time is required to fly 320 nautical miles at a ground speed of 174 knots?

**Solution:** Use the formula:

*Time = Distance ÷ Ground Speed,* or use the flight computer in the following manner:

1.  Set the 60 (speed) index under 174 (outer scale).
2.  Under 320 (outer scale), read 110 minutes or 1 hour 50 minutes (inner scale). *See* Figure 9-12.

**Problem:** What is the ground speed if it takes 40 minutes to fly 96 nautical miles?

**Solution:** Use the formula: *Ground Speed = Distance ÷ Time,* or use the flight computer in the following manner:

1.  Place 40 minutes (inner scale) under 96 (outer scale).
2.  Over the 60 (speed) index, read 144 knots (outer scale). *See* Figure 9-13.

**Problem:** If 50 minutes are required to fly 120 nautical miles, how many minutes are required to fly 86 nautical miles at the same rate?

**Solution:**

1.  Set 50 (inner scale) under 120 (outer scale).
2.  Under 86 (outer scale), read 36 minutes required (inner scale). *See* Figure 9-14.

**Figure 9-13.** Determining groundspeed on the E6-B

**Figure 9-14.** Determining time-rate-distance on the E6-B

## Calculating Fuel Consumption

Fuel consumption problems are solved in the same manner as Time-Rate-Distance problems.

**Problem:** If 18 gallons of fuel are consumed in 1 hour, how much fuel will be used in 2 hours 20 minutes?

**Solution:**

1.  Set the 60-index (inner scale) under 18 (outer scale).
2.  Over 2 hour 20 minute (inner scale), read 42 gallons (outer scale). *See* Figure 9-15.

**Problem:** What is the rate of fuel consumption if 30 gallons of fuel are consumed in 111 minutes?

**Solution:**

1.  Set 111 (inner scale) under 30 (outer scale).
2.  Over the 60-index (inner scale), read 16.2 gallons per hour (outer scale). *See* Figure 9-16.

**Problem:** Forty gallons of fuel have been consumed in 135 minutes (2 hours and 15 minutes) flying time. How much longer can the aircraft continue to fly if 25 gallons of available fuel remain and the rate of consumption remains the same?

**Solution:**

1.  Set 135 (inner scale) under 40 (outer scale).
2.  Under 25 (outer scale), read 84.5 minutes of fuel remaining. *See* Figure 9-17.

**Figure 9-15.** Determining total fuel consumed on the E6-B

**Figure 9-16.** Determining rate of consumption on the E6-B

# Finding True Airspeed and Density Altitude

The calculator (slide rule) side of the computer may also be used to determine true airspeed by correcting calibrated airspeed for temperature and pressure altitude. Density altitude is computed simultaneously.

**Problem:** Using a flight computer and the following conditions, find the true airspeed (TAS) and the density altitude (DA).

## Conditions:

True Air Temperature ................................ +10°C
Pressure Altitude (PA) ....................... 10,000 feet
Calibrated Airspeed (CAS) ................... 140 knots

## Solution:

1. Using the window marked "for airspeed and density altitude computations," place the true air temperature over the pressure altitude (Figure 9-18a).

2. In the density altitude window read the density altitude of 11,800 feet. (Figure 9-18b).

3. Over 140 knots CAS (inner scale) read the TAS of 167 knots (outer scale). *See* Figure 9-18c.

**Figure 9-17.** Determining flight time remaining on the E6-B

**Figure 9-18.** Determining true airspeed and density altitude on the E6-B

ALL

**3529.** (Refer to Figure 21.) En route to First Flight Airport (area 5), your flight passes over Hampton Roads Airport (area 2) at 1456 and then over Chesapeake Municipal at 1501. At what time should your flight arrive at First Flight?

A—1516.
B—1521.
C—1526.

Use the following steps:

1. Measure the distances from Hampton Roads to Chesapeake Municipal and from Chesapeake Municipal to First Flight:

   Hampton Roads to Chesapeake = 10 NM
   Chesapeake to First Flight = 50 NM

2. Calculate the elapsed time from Hampton Roads to Chesapeake Municipal:

   1501 − 1456 = 5 minutes elapsed time

3. Determine the time required to cover the remaining 50 NM from Chesapeake to First Flight with the ratio:

   $\frac{5}{10} = \frac{X}{50} = 25$ minutes

4. Add the time remaining to the actual time at Chesapeake to determine the estimated time of arrival (ETA).

   1501 + 25 = 1526 ETA

(H342) — AC 61-23C, Chapter 8

AIR, RTC

**3534.** (Refer to Figure 22.) What is the estimated time en route from Mercer County Regional Airport (area 3) to Minot International (area 1)? The wind is from 330° at 25 knots and the true airspeed is 100 knots. Add 3-1/2 minutes for departure and climb-out.

A—44 minutes.
B—48 minutes.
C—52 minutes.

Use the following steps:

1. Plot the course from Mercer Airport to Minot Airport.

2. Measure the true course angle at the approximate midpoint of the route. The true course (TC) is 011°.

3. Determine the ground speed using a flight computer:

   Wind direction is 330° (given in question)
   Wind speed is 25 knots (given in question)
   True course is 011° (found in Step 2)
   True airspeed is 100 knots (given in question)

   Therefore, the ground speed is 79.8 knots.

4. Measure the distance from Mercer Airport to Minot Airport (59 NM).

5. Calculate the time en route using a flight computer:

   Distance is 59 NM (found in Step 4)
   Ground speed is 80 knots (found in Step 3)

   Therefore, time en route is 44.5 minutes.

6. Add the allowance for departure and climbout (3.5 minutes) to the time en route (44.5 minutes) to obtain the estimated total time:

   44.5 + 3.5 = 48.0 minutes total time

(H346) — AC 61-23C, Chapter 8

AIR, RTC

**3540.** (Refer to Figure 23.) What is the estimated time en route from Sandpoint Airport (area 1) to St. Maries Airport (area 4)? The wind is from 215° at 25 knots and the true airspeed is 125 knots.

A—38 minutes.
B—30 minutes.
C—34 minutes.

Use the following steps:

1. Plot the course from Sandpoint Airport to St. Maries Airport.

2. Measure the true course angle at the approximate midpoint of the route (181°).

3. Determine the ground speed using a flight computer:

   Wind direction is 215° (given in question)
   Wind speed is 25 knots (given in question)
   True course is 181° (found in Step 2)
   True airspeed is 125 knots (given in question)

   Therefore, the ground speed is 103.5 knots.

4. Measure the distance from Sandpoint Airport to St. Maries Airport (58 NM).

5. Calculate the time en route using a flight computer:

   Distance is 58 NM (found in Step 4)
   Ground speed is 103.5 knots (found in Step 3)

   Therefore, the time en route is 33 minutes, 37 seconds.

(H346) — AC 61-23C, Chapter 8

**Answers**

3529 [C]        3534 [B]        3540 [C]

AIR, RTC

**3541.** (Refer to Figure 23.) Determine the estimated time en route for a flight from Priest River Airport (area 1) to Shoshone County Airport (area 3). The wind is from 030 at 12 knots and the true airspeed is 95 knots. Add 2 minutes for climb-out.

A—29 minutes.
B—27 minutes.
C—31 minutes.

Use the following steps:

1.  Plot the course from Priest River Airport to Shoshone County Airport.

2.  Measure the true course angle at the approximate midpoint of the route (144°).

3.  Determine the ground speed:

    Wind direction is 030° (given in question)
    Wind speed is 12 knots (given in question)
    True course is 144° (found in Step 2)
    True airspeed is 95 knots (given in question)

    Therefore, the ground speed is 99.2 knots.

4.  Measure the distance from Priest River Airport to Shoshone County Airport (49 NM).

5.  Calculate the time en route using a flight computer:

    Distance is 49 NM (found in Step 4)
    Ground speed is 99.2 knots (found in Step 3)

    Therefore, the time en route is 29 minutes, 38 seconds.

6.  Add the allowance for climbout (2 minutes) to the time en route (29.6 minutes) to obtain the estimated total time:

    29.6 + 2.0 = 31.6 minutes total time

(H346) — AC 61-23C, Chapter 8

AIR, RTC

**3542.** (Refer to Figure 23.) What is the estimated time en route for a flight from St. Maries Airport (area 4) to Priest River Airport (area 1)? The wind is from 300° at 14 knots and the true airspeed is 90 knots. Add 3 minutes for climb-out.

A—38 minutes.
B—43 minutes.
C—48 minutes.

Use the following steps:

1.  Plot the course from St. Maries Airport to Priest River Airport.

2.  Measure the true course angle at the approximate midpoint of the route (345°).

3.  Determine the ground speed using a flight computer:

    Wind direction is 300° (given in question)
    Wind speed is 14 knots (given in question)
    True course is 345° (found in Step 2)
    True airspeed is 90 knots (given in question)

    Therefore, the ground speed is 79.6 knots.

4.  Measure the distance from St. Maries Airport to Priest River Airport (53 NM).

5.  Calculate the time en route using a flight computer:

    Distance is 53 NM (found in Step 4)
    Ground speed is 79.6 knots (found in Step 3)

    Therefore, the time en route is 39 minutes, 57 seconds.

6.  Add the allowance for climbout (3 minutes) to the time en route (40 minutes) to obtain the estimated total time:

    40 + 3 = 43 minutes total time

(H346) — AC 61-23C, Chapter 8

**Answers**

3541  [C]          3542  [B]

AIR, RTC

**3548.** (Refer to Figure 24.) What is the estimated time en route for a flight from Allendale County Airport (area 1) to Claxton-Evans County Airport (area 2)? The wind is from 100° at 18 knots and the true airspeed is 115 knots. Add 2 minutes for climb-out.

A—33 minutes.
B—27 minutes.
C—30 minutes.

*Use the following steps:*

1. *Plot the course from Allendale County Airport to Claxton-Evans County Airport.*

2. *Measure the true course angle at the approximate midpoint of the route (212°).*

3. *Use a flight computer to determine the ground speed:*

   *Wind direction is 100° (given in question)*
   *Wind speed is 18 knots (given in question)*
   *True course is 212° (found in Step 2)*
   *True airspeed is 115 knots (given in question)*

   *Therefore, the ground speed is 120.5 knots.*

4. *Measure the distance between the departure and destination airports (55 NM).*

5. *Use a flight computer to calculate the time en route:*

   *Distance is 55 NM (found in Step 4)*
   *Ground speed is 120.5 knots (found in Step 3)*

   *Therefore, the time en route is 00:27:23 (27 minutes, 23 seconds).*

6. *Add the allowance for climbout (2 minutes) to the time en route (27:23) to obtain the estimated total time: 27:23 + 2 = 29:23 minutes total time.*

*(H346) — AC 61-23C, Chapter 8*


AIR, RTC

**3549.** (Refer to Figure 24.) What is the estimated time en route for a flight from Claxton-Evans County Airport (area 2) to Hampton Varnville Airport (area 1)? The wind is from 290° at 18 knots and the true airspeed is 85 knots. Add 2 minutes for climb-out.

A—35 minutes.
B—39 minutes.
C—44 minutes.

*Use the following steps:*

1. *Plot the true course from Claxton-Evans County Airport to Hampton Varnville Airport.*

2. *Measure the true course angle at the approximate midpoint of the route (044°).*

3. *Determine the ground speed, using a flight computer:*

   *Wind direction is 290° (given in question)*
   *Wind speed is 18 knots (given in question)*
   *True course is 044° (found in Step 2)*
   *True airspeed is 85 knots (given in question)*

   *Therefore, the ground speed is 90.7 knots.*

4. *Measure the distance from Claxton-Evans County Airport to Hampton Varnville County Airport (57 NM).*

5. *Calculate the time en route, using a flight computer:*

   *Distance is 57 NM (found in Step 4)*
   *Ground speed is 90.7 knots (found in Step 3)*

   *Therefore, the time en route is 37 minutes, 42 seconds.*

6. *Add the allowance for climbout (2 minutes) to the time en route (37 minutes) to obtain the estimated total time.*

   *37 + 2 = 39 minutes total time*

*(H346) — AC 61-23C, Chapter 8*


AIR, RTC

**3554.** (Refer to Figure 24.) While en route on Victor 185, a flight crosses the 248° radial of Allendale VOR at 0953 and then crosses the 216° radial of Allendale VOR at 1000. What is the estimated time of arrival at Savannah VORTAC?

A—1023.
B—1036.
C—1028.

*Use the following steps:*

1. *Locate the intersection of the 248° radial of Allendale VOR with V185 (MILEN intersection).*

2. *Locate the intersection of the 216° radial of Allendale VOR with V185 (DOVER intersection).*

3. *Measure the distance between the MILEN and DOVER intersections (10 NM).*

4. *Compute the time it takes to fly from MILEN intersection to DOVER intersection:*

   *1000 − 0953 = 7 minutes elapsed time*

5. *Use a flight computer to calculate the ground speed (85.7 knots).*

---

**Answers**

3548 [C]        3549 [B]        3554 [C]

6.   *Measure the distance remaining from DOVER intersection to Savannah VORTAC (40 NM).*

7.   *Use a flight computer to compute the time it takes to fly from DOVER intersection to Savannah VORTAC (40 NM at 85.7 knots) as 28 minutes.*

8.   *Compute the time of arrival (ETA) at Savannah VORTAC: 1000 + 0028 = 1028 ETA.*

*(H342) — AC 61-23C, Chapter 8*

AIR
**3562.** (Refer to Figure 26.) What is the estimated time en route for a flight from Denton Muni (area 1) to Addison (area 2)? The wind is from 200° at 20 knots, the true airspeed is 110 knots, and the magnetic variation is 7° east.

A—13 minutes.
B—16 minutes.
C—19 minutes.

*Use the following steps:*

1.   *Plot the course from Denton Muni (area 1) to Addison (area 2).*

2.   *Measure the true course angle at the approximate midpoint of the route (127.5°).*

3.   *Determine the ground speed, using a flight computer:*

   *Wind direction is 200° (given in question)*
   *Wind speed is 20 knots (given in question)*
   *True course is 127.5° (found in Step 2)*
   *True airspeed is 110 knots (given in question)*

   *Therefore, the ground speed is 102 knots.*

4.   *Measure the distance from Denton Muni to Addison as 22.5 NM. For maximum precision, draw lines over your checkpoints that are perpendicular to your course line.*

5.   *Calculate the time en route, using a flight computer:*

   *Distance is 22.5 NM (found in Step 4)*
   *Ground speed is 102 knots (found in Step 3)*

   *Therefore, the time en route is 13 minutes, 13 seconds.*

6.   *All your calculations used true course and true wind, so variation is not relevant to this problem.*

*(H346) — AC 61-23C, Chapter 8*

AIR
**3563.** (Refer to Figure 26.) Estimate the time en route from Addison (area 2) to Redbird (area 3). The wind is from 300° at 15 knots, the true airspeed is 120 knots, and the magnetic variation is 7° east.

A—8 minutes.
B—11 minutes.
C—14 minutes.

*Use the following steps:*

1.   *Plot the course from Addison to Redbird.*

2.   *Measure the true course angle at the approximate midpoint of the route (186°).*

3.   *Determine the ground speed, using a flight computer:*

   *Wind direction is 300° (given in question)*
   *Wind speed is 15 knots (given in question)*
   *True course is 186° (found in Step 2)*
   *True airspeed is 120 knots (given in question)*

   *Therefore, the ground speed is 126 knots.*

4.   *Measure the distance from Addison to Redbird as 17.3 NM. For maximum precision, draw lines over your checkpoints that are perpendicular to your course line.*

5.   *Calculate the time en route, using a flight computer:*

   *Distance is 17.3 NM (found in Step 4)*
   *Ground speed is 126 knots (found in Step 3)*

   *Therefore, the time en route is 8.1 minutes.*

6.   *All your calculations used true course and true wind, so variation is not relevant to this problem.*

*(H346) — AC 61-23C, Chapter 8*

---

**Answers**

3562   [A]          3563   [A]

AIR, RTC

**3538.** (Refer to Figure 22.) Determine the magnetic heading for a flight from Mercer County Regional Airport (area 3) to Minot International (area 1). The wind is from 330° at 25 knots, the true airspeed is 100 knots, and the magnetic variation is 10° east.

A—002°
B—012°.
C—352°.

*Use the following steps:*

1. Plot the course from Mercer County Regional Airport to Minot Airport.

2. Measure the true course angle at the approximate midpoint of the route. The true course (TC) is 011°.

3. Find the true heading using a flight computer:

   Wind direction is 330° (given in question)
   Wind speed is 25 knots (given in question)
   True course is 011° (found in Step 2)
   True airspeed is 100 knots (given in question)

   Therefore, the true heading is 002°.

4. Calculate the magnetic heading by subtracting the easterly variation (10°) from the true heading (002°).

   $MH = TH \pm VAR$

   $MH = 002° - 10°E$

   $MH = 352°$

*(H346) — AC 61-23C, Chapter 8*

AIR, RTC

**3545.** (Refer to Figure 23.) Determine the magnetic heading for a flight from Sandpoint Airport (area 1) to St. Maries Airport (area 4). The wind is from 215° at 25 knots and the true airspeed is 125 knots.

A—169°.
B—349°.
C—187°.

*Use the following steps:*

1. Plot the course from Sandpoint Airport to St. Maries Airport.

2. Measure the true course angle at the approximate midpoint of the route (181°).

3. Find true heading, using a flight computer:

   Wind direction is 215° (given in question)
   Wind speed is 25 knots (given in question)
   True course is 181° (found in Step 2)
   True airspeed is 125 knots (given in question)

   Therefore, the true heading is 187°.

4. Calculate the magnetic heading by subtracting the easterly variation (18°) from the true heading (187°).

   $MH = TH \pm VAR$
   $MH = 187° - 18°E$
   $MH = 169°$

*(H346) — AC 61-23C, Chapter 8*

AIR, RTC

**3546.** (Refer to Figure 23.) What is the magnetic heading for a flight from Priest River Airport (area 1) to Shoshone County Airport (area 3)? The wind is from 030° at 12 knots and the true airspeed is 95 knots.

A—118°.
B—143°.
C—136°.

*Use the following steps:*

1. Plot the course from Priest River to Shoshone County Airport.

2. Measure the true course angle at the approximate midpoint of the route (143°).

3. Find the true heading using a flight computer:

   Wind direction is 030° (given in question)
   Wind speed is 12 knots (given in question)
   True course is 143° (found in Step 2)
   True airspeed is 95 knots (given in question)

   Therefore, the true heading is 136°.

4. Calculate the magnetic heading by subtracting the easterly variation (18°E, as shown on the dashed isogonic line) from the true heading (136°).

   $MH = TH \pm VAR$
   $MH = 136° - 18°E$
   $MH = 118°$

*(H346) — AC 61-23C, Chapter 8*

**Answers**

3538   [C]          3545   [A]          3546   [A]

AIR, RTC
**3547.** (Refer to Figure 23.) Determine the magnetic heading for a flight from St. Maries Airport (area 4) to Priest River Airport (area 1). The wind is from 340° at 10 knots, and the true airspeed is 90 knots.

A—345°.
B—320°.
C—327°.

*Use the following steps:*

1. *Plot the course from St. Maries Airport to Priest River Airport.*

2. *Measure the true course angle at the approximate midpoint of the route (345°).*

3. *Use a flight computer to find true heading:*

    *Wind direction is 340° (given in question)*
    *Wind speed is 10 knots (given in question)*
    *True course is 345° (found in Step 2)*
    *True airspeed is 90 knots (given in question)*

   *Therefore, the true heading is 344°.*

4. *Calculate the magnetic heading by subtracting the easterly variation (18°E, as shown on the dashed isogonic line) from the true heading (344°).*

    *MH = TH ± VAR*
    *MH = 344° − 18°E*
    *MH = 326°*

*(H346) — AC 61-23C, Chapter 8*

AIR
**3565.** (Refer to Figure 26.) Determine the magnetic heading for a flight from Fort Worth Meacham (area 4) to Denton Muni (area 1). The wind is from 330° at 25 knots, the true airspeed is 110 knots, and the magnetic variation is 7° east.

A—003°.
B—017°.
C—023°.

*Use the following steps:*

1. *Plot a course from Meacham to Denton, and measure the course (021°).*

2. *Using the wind obtained, calculate a correction angle. This angle will be the difference between the course bearing and the heading required to maintain that course. Wind correction angle is 10° to the left.*

3. *Add course bearing and wind correction angle to obtain true heading.*

    *021 + -010 = 011° (true heading)*

4. *Find the magnetic heading by adding the variation to the true heading.*

    *011 + -7 = 004° (magnetic heading)*

*(H346) — AC 61-23C, Chapter 8*

AIR, RTC
**3550.** (Refer to Figure 24.) Determine the magnetic heading for a flight from Allendale County Airport (area 1) to Claxton-Evans County Airport (area 2). The wind is from 090° at 16 knots and the true airspeed is 90 knots.

A—208°.
B—230°.
C—212°.

*Use the following steps:*

1. *Plot the course from Allendale County Airport to Claxton-Evans County Airport.*

2. *Measure the true course angle at the approximate midpoint of the route (212°).*

3. *Find true heading, using a flight computer:*

    *Wind direction is 090° (given in question)*
    *Wind speed is 16 knots (given in question)*
    *True course is 212° (found in Step 2)*
    *True airspeed is 90 knots (given in question)*

   *Therefore, the true heading is 203°.*

4. *Calculate the magnetic heading by adding the westerly variation (5°W, as shown on the dashed isogonic line) from the true heading (203°).*

    *MH = TH ± VAR*
    *MH = 203° + 5°W*
    *MH = 208°*

*(H346) — AC 61-23C, Chapter 8*

**Answers**

3547  [C]          3565  [A]          3550  [A]

AIR

**3551.** (Refer to Figures 24 and 59.) Determine the compass heading for a flight from Claxton-Evans County Airport (area 2) to Hampton Varnville Airport (area 1). The wind is from 280° at 08 knots, and the true airspeed is 85 knots.

A—033°.
B—042°.
C—038°.

*Use the following steps:*

1. *Plot the course from Claxton-Evans County Airport to Hampton Varnville Airport.*

2. *Measure the true course angle at the approximate midpoint of the route (044°).*

3. *Use a flight computer to find the true heading:*

   *Wind direction is 280° (given in question)*
   *Wind speed is 8 knots (given in question)*
   *True course is 044° (found in Step 2)*
   *True airspeed is 85 knots (given in question)*

   *Therefore, the true heading is 40°.*

4. *Calculate the magnetic heading by adding the westerly variation (5°W) to the true heading (40°).*

   $MH = TH \pm VAR$
   $MH = 40° + 5°W$
   $MH = 045°$

5. *Note the compass deviation card in Figure 59 indicates that in order to fly a magnetic course of 030°, the pilot must steer a compass heading of 027° or a 3° compass deviation. To fly a magnetic course of 060°, the pilot must steer a compass heading of 056° or a 4° compass deviation. Interpolate between these to find the compass correction for 045° (3.5°). Calculate the compass heading (CH) by subtracting the compass deviation (3.5°) from the magnetic heading (045°).*

   $CH = MH \pm DEV$
   $CH = 045° - 3.5°$
   $CH = 41.5°$

*(H346) — AC 61-23C, Chapter 8*

GLI

**3564.** (Refer to Figure 26.) Determine the magnetic heading for a flight from Redbird (area 3) to Fort Worth Meacham (area 4). The wind is from 030° at 10 knots, the true airspeed is 35 knots, and the magnetic variation is 7° east.

A—266°.
B—298°.
C—312°.

*Use the following steps:*

1. *Plot a course from Redbird to Meacham, and measure the course (289°).*

2. *Using the wind obtained, calculate a correction angle. This angle will be the difference between the course bearing and the heading required to maintain that course. Wind correction angle is 16° to the right.*

3. *Add course bearing and wind correction angle to obtain true heading.*

   289°   course bearing
   + 16°   wind correction angle
   ─────
   305°   true heading

4. *Find the magnetic heading by adding the variation to the true heading.*

   305°   true heading
   − 007°   variation (E)
   ─────
   298°   magnetic heading

*(H346) — AC 61-23C, Chapter 8*

GLI

**3648.** (Refer to Figure 27.) If a glider is launched over Barnes County Airport (area 6) with sufficient altitude to glide to Jamestown Airport (area 4), how long will it take for the flight at an average of 40 MPH groundspeed?

A—20 minutes.
B—27 minutes.
C—48 minutes.

*Use the following steps:*

1. *Draw a direct course line between Barnes County Airport and Jamestown Airport and determine the distance (31 SM).*

2. *Calculate the time required to cover 31 SM at 40 MPH ground speed using the formula:*

   *Time = Distance ÷ Speed = 31 ÷ 40 =*
   *0.75 hours = 46.5 minutes*

*(N27) — Soaring Flight Manual*

**Answers**

3551    [B]              3564    [B]              3648    [C]

GLI
**3649.** (Refer to Figure 25, area 1.) A glider is launched over Caddo Mills Airport with sufficient altitude to glide to Airpark East Airport, south of Caddo Mills. How long will it take for the flight at an average of 35 MPH groundspeed?

A—27 minutes.
B—25 minutes.
C—31 minutes.

Use the following steps:

1. Draw a direct course line between Caddo Mills Airport and Airpark East Airport and determine the distance (15 SM).

2. Calculate the time required to cover 15 SM at 35 MPH ground speed using the formula:

Time = Distance ÷ Speed = 15 ÷ 35
= .429 hours = 25.7 minutes

(N27) — Soaring Flight Manual

GLI
**3650.** (Refer to Figure 27, areas 5 and 6.) What minimum altitude should be used for a go-ahead point at Eckelson in order to arrive at Barnes County Airport at 1,000 feet AGL if the glide ratio is 22:1 in no wind conditions? Use the recommended safety factor.

A—5,959 feet MSL.
B—7,960 feet MSL.
C—9,359 feet MSL.

Use the following steps:

1. A safety margin is provided to allow for any performance degradation. Use one-half the published L/D ratio for planning purposes. In this case use 11 to 1 (no wind).

2. Determine the distance from Eckelson to Barnes County Airport (14.5 SM).

3. If 1 SM = 5,280 feet, calculate the total sink in 14.5 SM at a glide ratio of 11:1.

5,280 ÷11= 480 feet sink per SM
480.0 x 14.5 = 6,960.0 feet total sink

4. Calculate the arrival altitude (MSL) by adding 1,000 feet AGL to the Barnes County elevation of 1,400 feet.

1,400 Barnes County elevation
+ 1,000 arrival (AGL)
2,400 arrival (MSL)

5. Determine the go-ahead minimum by adding total sink to the required arrival altitude.

6,960 feet total sink
+ 2,400 feet MSL arrival altitude
9,360 feet MSL go-ahead minimum altitude

(N34) — Soaring Flight Manual

LTA
**3537.** (Refer to Figure 22.) An airship crosses over Minot VORTAC (area 1) at 1056 and over the creek 8 nautical miles south-southeast on Victor 15 at 1108. What should be the approximate position on Victor 15 at 1211?

A—Over Lake Nettie National Wildlife Refuge.
B—Crossing the road east of Underwood.
C—Over the powerlines east of Washburn Airport.

This is a time/speed/distance problem.

1. The distance is 8 NM (given in the question).

2. The time is:
11:08 – 10:56 = 12 minutes

3. Use: $\frac{Distance}{Time}$ x 60 = Ground speed

$\frac{8\ NM}{12\ min.}$ x 60 = 40 knots

4. Calculate the distance traveled on the next leg at this speed by 12:11.
12:11 – 11:08 = :63 minutes

5. Use: $\frac{Speed}{60}$ x Time = Distance

$\frac{40\ kts}{60\ min.}$ x 63 min. = 42 NM

6. Locate the 8 NM creek and measure an additional 42 NM along V15. You are east of Underwood; it is west of your position. The legs were 8 NM and 42 NM, total 50 NM.

(H342) — AC 61-23C, Chapter 8

**Answers**
3649 [B]        3650 [C]        3537 [B]

LTA
**3544.** (Refer to Figure 23, area 2.) If a balloon is launched at Ranch Aero (Pvt) Airport with a reported wind from 220° at 5 knots, what should be its approximate position after 2 hours of flight?

A—Near Hackney (Pvt) Airport.
B—Crossing the railroad southwest of Granite Airport.
C—3-1/2 miles southwest of Rathdrum.

*A balloon moves with the wind, so the problem asks: where do you end up if your ground speed is 5 knots and you are flying a true course of 220° for two hours?*

1. *Calculate the distance that will be traveled at this speed during the time given.*

    *Speed x Time = Distance*
    *5 NM x 2 hours = 10 NM total distance*

2. *Draw your true course line from Ranch Aero, from 220°, and measure 10 NM up the line from Ranch Aero to find you are near Hackney (Pvt) Airport.*

*(H341) — AC 61-23C, Chapter 8*

LTA
**3555.** (Refer to Figure 25.) Estimate the time en route from Majors Airport (area 1) to Winnsboro Airport (area 2). The wind is from 340° at 12 knots and the true airspeed is 36 knots.

A—55 minutes.
B—59 minutes.
C—63 minutes.

*Use the following steps:*

1. *Plot the course from Majors Airport to Winnsboro Airport.*

2. *Measure the true course angle at the approximate midpoint of the route (100°).*

3. *Determine the ground speed, using a flight computer:*

    *Wind direction is 340° (given in question)*
    *Wind speed is 12 knots (given in question)*
    *True course is 100° (found in Step 2)*
    *True airspeed is 36 knots (given in question)*

    *Therefore, the ground speed is 40.5 knots.*

4. *Measure the distance from Majors Airport to Winnsboro Airport, (41 NM).*

5. *Calculate the time en route, using a flight computer:*

    *Distance is 41 NM (found in Step 4)*
    *Ground speed is 40.5 knots (found in Step 3)*

    *Therefore, the time en route is 1 hour (60 minutes), 44 seconds.*

*(H346) — AC 61-23C, Chapter 8*

LTA
**3557.** (Refer to Figure 25.) An airship passes over the Quitman VOR-DME (area 2) at 0940 and then over the intersection of the powerline and Victor 114 at 0948. Approximately what time should the flight arrive over the Bonham VORTAC (area 3)?

A—1138.
B—1109.
C—1117.

*Use the following steps:*

1. *Locate the Quitman VOR-DME (area 2) and Bonham VORTAC (area 3).*

2. *Measure the distance from Quitman VOR-DME to the intersection of the powerline with V114 (4 NM).*

3. *Calculate the ground speed of the airship:*

    *Speed = Distance ÷ Time*
    *Speed = 4 NM ÷ (0948 – 0940)*
    *Speed = 4 NM ÷ 8 minutes*
    *Speed = 30 knots*

4. *Measure the distance remaining from the "intersection" to Bonham VORTAC (55 NM).*

5. *Calculate the time required to travel 55 NM at a constant 30 knot ground speed.*

    *Time = Distance ÷ Speed*
    *Time = 55 NM ÷ 30 knots*
    *Time = 1 hour 50 minutes*

6. *Compute the arrival time by adding the estimated enroute time to the time of passing the intersection:*

    *0150   time en route*
    *+ 0948   time passing intersection*
    *———*
    *1138*

*(H342) — AC 61-23C, Chapter 8*

**Answers**

3544    [A]                3555    [B]                3557    [A]

LTA
**3558.** (Refer to Figure 25.) Determine the magnetic heading for a flight from Majors Airport (area 1) to Winnsboro Airport (area 2). The wind is from 340° at 12 knots, the true airspeed is 36 knots, and the magnetic variation is 6°30'E.

A—078°.
B—091°.
C—101°.

1. Plot the course from Majors Airport to Winnsboro Airport.

2. Measure the true course angle at the approximate midpoint of the route (100°).

3. Find true heading, using a flight computer:

   Wind direction is 340° (given in question)
   Wind speed is 12 knots (given in question)
   True course is 100° (found in Step 2)
   True airspeed is 36 knots (given in question)

   Therefore, the true heading is 083°.

4. Calculate the magnetic heading by subtracting the easterly variation (6°30'E) from the true heading (084°).

   MH = TH ± VAR
   MH = 084° – 6°30'E
   MH = 78°

(H346) — AC 61-23C, Chapter 8

LTA
**3569.** (Refer to Figure 27, area 5.) A balloon drifts over the town of Eckelson on a magnetic course of 282° at 10 MPH. If wind conditions remain constant, where will the balloon be after 2 hours 30 minutes?

A—4.5 miles north-northwest of Hoggarth Airport (Pvt).
B—Over Buchanan.
C—Over Hoggarth Airport (Pvt).

Use the following steps:

1. Calculate the distance traveled at 10 MPH during 2-1/2 hours.

   Distance = Speed x Time
   Distance = 10 MPH x 2.5 H = 25 SM

2. Locate Eckelson in FAA Figure 27.

3. Note that the magnetic variation near Eckelson, as shown on the dashed isogonic line, is 7°E.

4. Calculate the true course from the magnetic course:

   TC ± VAR = MC
   TC – 7° = 282°
   TC = 289°

5. Plot a true course of 289° from Eckelson extending 25 statute miles. The balloon would be over Buchanan.

(H342) — AC 61-23C, Chapter 8

**Answers**
3558 [A]     3569 [B]

# Airspace

**Figure 9-19**

Controlled airspace, that is, airspace within which some or all aircraft may be subject to air traffic control, consists of those areas designated as Class A, Class B, Class C, Class D, and Class E airspace.

Much of the controlled airspace begins at either 700 feet or 1,200 feet above the ground. The lateral limits and floors of Class E airspace of 700 feet are defined by a magenta vignette; while the lateral limits and floors of 1,200 feet are defined by a blue vignette if it abuts uncontrolled airspace. Floors other than 700 feet or 1,200 feet are indicated by a number indicating the floor.

**Class A** — Class A airspace extends from 18,000 feet MSL up to and including FL600 and is not depicted on VFR sectional charts. No flight under visual flight rules (VFR), including VFR-On-Top, is authorized in Class A airspace.

**Class B** — Class B airspace consists of controlled airspace extending upward from the surface or higher to specified altitudes. Each Class B airspace sector, outlined in blue on the sectional aeronautical chart, is labeled with its delimiting altitudes. On the Terminal Area Chart, each Class B airspace sector is, again, outlined in blue and is labeled with its delimiting arcs, radials, and altitudes. Each Class B airspace location will contain at least one primary airport. An ATC clearance is required prior to operating within Class B airspace. A pilot landing or taking off from one of a group of 12 specific, busy airports must hold at least a Private Pilot Certificate. At other airports, a student pilot may not operate an aircraft on a solo flight within Class B airspace or to, from, or at an airport located within Class B airspace unless both ground and flight instruction has been received from an authorized instructor to operate within that Class B airspace or at that airport, and the flight and ground instruction has been received within that Class B airspace or at the specific airport for which the solo flight is authorized. The student's logbook must be endorsed within the preceding 90 days by the instructor who gave the flight training and the endorsement must specify that the student has been found competent to conduct solo flight operations in that Class B airspace or at that specific airport. Each airplane operating within Class B airspace must be equipped with a two-way radio with appropriate ATC frequencies, and a 4096 code transponder with Mode C automatic altitude-reporting capability.

**Class C** — All Class C airspace has the same dimensions with minor site variations. They are composed of two circles both centered on the primary airport. The inner circle (now called surface area) has a radius of 5 nautical miles and extends from the surface up to 4,000 feet above the airport. The outer circle (now called shelf area) has a radius of 10 nautical miles and extends vertically from 1,200 feet AGL up to 4,000 feet above the primary airport. In addition to the Class C airspace proper, there is an outer area with a radius of 20 nautical miles and vertical coverage from the lower limits of the radio/radar coverage up to the top of the approach control facility's delegated airspace. Within the outer area, pilots are encouraged to participate but it is not a VFR requirement. Class C airspace service to aircraft proceeding to a satellite airport will be terminated at a sufficient distance to allow time to change to the appropriate tower or advisory frequency. Aircraft departing satellite airports within Class C airspace shall establish two-way communication with ATC as soon as practicable after takeoff. On aeronautical charts, Class C airspace is depicted by solid magenta lines.

**Class D** — Class D airspace extends upward from the surface to approximately 2,500 feet AGL (the actual height is as needed). Class D airspace may include one or more airports and is normally 4 nautical miles in radius. The actual size and shape is depicted by a blue dashed line and numbers showing the top. When the ceiling of Class D airspace is less than 1,000 feet and/or the visibility is less than 3 statute miles, pilots wishing to take off or land must hold an instrument rating, must have filed an instrument flight plan, and must have received an appropriate clearance from ATC. In addition, the aircraft must be equipped for instrument flight. At some locations, a pilot who does not hold an instrument rating may be authorized to take off or land when the weather is less than that required for visual flight rules. When special VFR flight is prohibited, it will be depicted by "No SVFR" above the airport information on the chart.

**Class E** — Magenta shading identifies Class E airspace starting at 700 feet AGL, and no shading (or blue if next to Class G airspace) identifies Class E airspace starting at 1,200 feet AGL. It may also start at other altitudes. All airspace from 14,500 feet to 17,999 feet is Class E airspace. It also includes the surface area of some airports with an instrument approach but no control tower.

An **airway** is a corridor of controlled airspace extending from 1,200 feet above the surface (or as designated) up to and including 17,999 feet MSL, and 4 nautical miles either side of the centerline. The airway is indicated by a centerline, shown in blue.

**Class G** — Class G airspace is airspace within which Air Traffic Control (ATC) has neither the authority nor responsibility to exercise any control over air traffic. Class G airspace typically extends from the surface to the base of the overlying controlled (Class E) airspace which is normally 700 or 1,200 feet AGL. In some areas of the western U.S. and Alaska, Class G airspace may extend from the surface to 14,500 feet MSL. An exception to this rule occurs when 14,500 feet MSL is lower than 1,500 feet AGL.

**Prohibited Areas** are blocks of airspace within which the flight of aircraft is prohibited.

**Restricted Areas** denote the presence of unusual, often invisible, hazards to aircraft such as artillery firing, aerial gunnery, or guided missiles. Penetration of Restricted Areas without authorization of the using or controlling agency may be extremely hazardous to the aircraft and its occupants.

**Warning Areas** contain the same hazardous activities as those found in Restricted Areas, but are located in international airspace. Prohibited, restricted, or warning areas are depicted as shown in FAA Legend 1.

**Military Operations Areas (MOAs)** consist of airspace established for the purpose of separating certain military training activities from instrument flight rules (IFR) traffic. Pilots operating under VFR should exercise extreme caution while flying within an active MOA. Any Flight Service Station (FSS) within 100 miles of the area will provide information concerning MOA hours of operation. Prior to entering an active MOA, pilots should contact the controlling agency for traffic advisories.

*Continued*

**Alert Areas** may contain a high volume of pilot training activities or an unusual type of aerial activity, neither of which is hazardous to aircraft. Pilots of participating aircraft as well as pilots transiting the area are equally responsible for collision avoidance.

An **Airport Advisory Area** is the area within 10 statute miles of an airport where a control tower is not in operation but where a Flight Service Station (FSS) is located. The FSS provides advisory service to aircraft arriving and departing. It is not mandatory for pilots to use the advisory service, but it is strongly recommended that they do so.

Aircraft are requested to remain at least 2,000 feet above the surface of National Parks, National Monuments, Wilderness and Primitive Areas, and National Wildlife Refuges.

**Military Training Routes (MTRs)** have been developed for use by the military for the purpose of conducting low-altitude, high-speed training. Generally, MTRs are established below 10,000 feet MSL for operations at speeds in excess of 250 knots.

**IFR Military Training Routes (IR)** operations are conducted in accordance with instrument flight rules (IFRs), regardless of weather conditions. **VFR Military Training Routes (VR)** operations are conducted in accordance with visual flight rules (VFRs). IR and VR at and below 1,500 feet AGL (with no segment above 1,500) will be identified by four digit numbers, e.g., VR1351, IR1007. IR and VR above and below 1,500 feet AGL (segments of these routes may be below 1,500) will be identified by three digit numbers, e.g., IR341, VR426.

AIR, GLI
**3130.** In which type of airspace are VFR flights prohibited?

A—Class A.
B—Class B.
C—Class C.

*No person may operate an aircraft within Class A airspace unless that aircraft is operated under IFR at a specific flight level assigned by ATC. (B08) — 14 CFR §91.135(a)(1)*

ALL
**3599.** (Refer to Figure 26, area 4.) The floor of Class B airspace overlying Hicks Airport (T67) north-northwest of Fort Worth Meacham Field is

A—at the surface.
B—3,200 feet MSL.
C—4,000 feet MSL.

*The thick blue lines on the sectional chart indicate the boundaries of the overlying Class B airspace. Within each segment, the floor and ceiling are denoted by one number over a second number or the letters SFC. The floor of the Class B airspace is 4,000 feet MSL. (J08) — AIM ¶3-2-3*

ALL
**3600.** (Refer to Figure 26, area 2.) The floor of Class B airspace at Addison Airport is

A—at the surface.
B—3,000 feet MSL.
C—3,100 feet MSL.

*The thick blue lines on the sectional chart indicate the boundaries of the overlying Class B airspace. Within each segment, the floor and ceiling are denoted by one number over a second number or the letters SFC. The floor of the Class B airspace is 3,000 feet MSL. (J08) — AIM ¶3-2-3*

ALL
**3126.** What minimum pilot certification is required for operation within Class B airspace?

A—Commercial Pilot Certificate.
B—Private Pilot Certificate or Student Pilot Certificate with appropriate logbook endorsements.
C—Private Pilot Certificate with an instrument rating.

**Answers**

| 3130 | [A] | 3599 | [C] | 3600 | [B] | 3126 | [B] |

*It is generally true that no person may operate a civil aircraft within Class B airspace unless the pilot-in-command holds at least a Private Pilot Certificate or is a student pilot that has the proper logbook endorsements. However, there are certain Class B airports which never permit students, even if they have the proper endorsements. (B08) — 14 CFR §91.131(b)(1), (2)*

Answer (A) is incorrect because Private pilots may operate in Class B airspace. Answer (C) is incorrect because only some airports restrict student pilots, and none require an instrument rating.

**3127.** What minimum pilot certification is required for operation within Class B airspace?

A—Private Pilot Certificate or Student Pilot Certificate with appropriate logbook endorsements.
B—Commercial Pilot Certificate.
C—Private Pilot Certificate with an instrument rating.

*It is generally true that no person may operate a civil aircraft within Class B airspace unless the pilot-in-command holds at least a Private Pilot Certificate or a student pilot has the proper logbook endorsements. However, there are some Class B airports which never permit students, even if they have the proper endorsements. (B08) — 14 CFR §61.95, §91.131(b)(1), (2)*

Answers (B) and (C) are incorrect because only some airports require a private pilot license and none require a commercial license or instrument rating.

**3128.** What minimum radio equipment is required for VFR operation within Class B airspace?

A—Two-way radio communications equipment and a 4096-code transponder.
B—Two-way radio communications equipment, a 4096-code transponder, and an encoding altimeter.
C—Two-way radio communications equipment, a 4096-code transponder, an encoding altimeter, and a VOR or TACAN receiver.

*Unless otherwise authorized by ATC, no person may operate an aircraft within Class B airspace unless that aircraft is equipped with an operable two-way radio capable of communications with ATC, a transponder with applicable altitude reporting equipment, and an encoding altimeter. (B08) — 14 CFR §91.131(c), (d)*

**3628.** (Refer to Figure 26.) At which airports is fixed-wing Special VFR not authorized?

A—Fort Worth Meacham and Fort Worth Spinks.
B—Dallas-Fort Worth International and Dallas Love Field.
C—Addison and Redbird.

*Special VFR operations by fixed-wing aircraft are prohibited in some Class B, C, and D airspaces due to the volume of IFR traffic. These airspaces are depicted by the notation "No SVFR" over the airport information. (J37) — AIM ¶4-4-5*

**3117.** A blue segmented circle on a Sectional Chart depicts which class airspace?

A—Class B.
B—Class C.
C—Class D.

*A blue segmented circle on a sectional chart depicts Class D airspace which means a control tower is in operation. (B08) — 14 CFR §1.1*

Answer (A) is incorrect because Class B airspace is depicted by a solid blue line. Answer (B) is incorrect because Class C airspace is depicted by a solid magenta line.

**3118.** Airspace at an airport with a part-time control tower is classified as Class D airspace only

A—when the weather minimums are below basic VFR.
B—when the associated control tower is in operation.
C—when the associated Flight Service Station is in operation.

*Class D airspace means a control tower is in operation. If the tower closes, it reverts to Class E airspace. (B08) — 14 CFR §1.1*

Answer (A) is incorrect because weather minimums have nothing to do with airspace classifications. Answer (C) is incorrect because an FSS has nothing to do with the class of airspace.

ALL

**3787.** The lateral dimensions of Class D airspace are based on

A—the number of airports that lie within the Class D airspace.
B—5 statute miles from the geographical center of the primary airport.
C—the instrument procedures for which the controlled airspace is established.

*The dimensions of Class D airspace are as needed for each individual circumstance. The airspace may include extensions necessary for IFR arrival and departure paths. (J10) — AIM ¶3-2-5*

ALL

**3788.** A non-tower satellite airport, within the same Class D airspace as that designated for the primary airport, requires radio communications be established and maintained with the

A—satellite airport's UNICOM.
B—associated Flight Service Station.
C—primary airport's control tower.

*Radio communications must be established and maintained with the primary control tower even when operating to and from a non-tower airport located within the lateral limits of Class D airspace. On takeoff from a satellite airport, communication must be established as soon as practicable after takeoff. (J10) — AIM ¶3-2-5*

ALL

**3124.** Two-way radio communication must be established with the Air Traffic Control facility having jurisdiction over the area prior to entering which class airspace?

A—Class C.
B—Class E.
C—Class G.

*Two-way radio communication must be established with the ATC facility having jurisdiction over the Class C airspace prior to entry and thereafter as instructed by ATC. (B08) — 14 CFR §91.130*

Answers (B) and (C) are incorrect because airports within Class E and G airspace only require two-way radio communication when a control tower is present.

ALL

**3799.** Which initial action should a pilot take prior to entering Class C airspace?

A—Contact approach control on the appropriate frequency.
B—Contact the tower and request permission to enter.
C—Contact the FSS for traffic advisories.

*Radio contact is required to operate in Class C airspace, but permission is not required. (J11) — AIM ¶3-2-4*

ALL

**3779.** The vertical limit of Class C airspace above the primary airport is normally

A—1,200 feet AGL.
B—3,000 feet AGL.
C—4,000 feet AGL.

*Class C airspace consists of two circles, both centered on the primary/Class C airspace airport. The surface area has a radius of 5 NM. The shelf area usually has a radius of 10 NM. The airspace of the surface area usually extends from the surface of the Class C airspace airport up to 4,000 feet above that airport. The airspace area between the 5 and 10 NM rings usually begins at a height of 1,200 feet AGL and extends to the same altitude cap as the inner circle. These dimensions may be varied to meet individual situations. (J08) — AIM ¶3-2-4*

ALL

**3780.** The normal radius of the outer area of Class C airspace is

A—5 nautical miles.
B—15 nautical miles.
C—20 nautical miles.

*The normal radius of the outer area will be 20 NM. (J08) — AIM ¶3-2-4*

ALL

**3781.** All operations within Class C airspace must be in

A—accordance with instrument flight rules.
B—compliance with ATC clearances and instructions.
C—an aircraft equipped with a 4096-code transponder with Mode C encoding capability.

**Answers**

| 3787 | [C] | 3788 | [C] | 3124 | [A] | 3799 | [A] | 3779 | [C] | 3780 | [C] |
| 3781 | [C] | | | | | | | | | | |

Aircraft operating in Class C airspace must have a Mode C transponder. (J08) — AIM ¶3-2-4

*Answer (A) is incorrect because visual flight rules are also used within Class C airspace. Answer (B) is incorrect because an ATC clearance is not required to operate within Class C airspace.*

ALL
**3782.** Under what condition may an aircraft operate from a satellite airport within Class C airspace?

A—The pilot must file a flight plan prior to departure.
B—The pilot must monitor ATC until clear of the Class C airspace.
C—The pilot must contact ATC as soon as practicable after takeoff.

*For aircraft departing a satellite airport, two-way radio communication must be established as soon as practicable and thereafter maintained with ATC while within the area. (J08) — AIM ¶3-2-4*

*Answers (A) and (B) are incorrect because Class C airspace does not require flight plans, and a pilot must maintain contact with ATC in Class C airspace.*

ALL
**3626.** (Refer to Figure 24, area 3.) What is the floor of the Savannah Class C airspace at the outer circle?

A—1,300 feet AGL.
B—1,300 feet MSL.
C—1,700 feet MSL.

*Within the outer magenta circle of Savannah Class C airspace, there is a number 41 directly above the number 13. These depict the floor and ceiling of the Class C airspace; the floor being 1,300 feet MSL and the ceiling being 4,100 feet MSL. (J37) — AIM ¶3-2-4*

ALL
**3627.** (Refer to Figure 21, area 1.) What minimum radio equipment is required to land and take off at Norfolk International?

A—Mode C transponder and omnireceiver.
B—Mode C transponder and two-way radio.
C—Mode C transponder, omnireceiver, and DME.

*Norfolk International is in Class C airspace. To operate within Class C airspace, an aircraft must have (1) two-way communications capability and (2) a Mode C transponder. (J37) — AIM ¶3-2-4*

ALL
**3125.** What minimum radio equipment is required for operation within Class C airspace?

A—Two-way radio communications equipment and a 4096-code transponder.
B—Two-way radio communications equipment, a 4096-code transponder, and DME.
C—Two-way radio communications equipment, a 4096-code transponder, and an encoding altimeter.

*Class C requires two-way radio communications equipment, a transponder, and an encoding altimeter. (B08) — 14 CFR §91.130(c),(d),(f) and §91.215(b)(4)*

ALL
**3069.** Normal VFR operations in Class D airspace with an operating control tower require the ceiling and visibility to be at least

A—1,000 feet and 1 mile.
B—1,000 feet and 3 miles.
C—2,500 feet and 3 miles.

*Except as provided in 14 CFR §91.157, no person may operate an aircraft, under VFR, within the lateral boundaries of the surface areas of Class B, Class C, Class D, or Class E airspace designated for an airport when the ceiling is less than 1,000 feet. The flight visibility and cloud clearance for VFR operations in Class D airspace is 3 statute miles visibility, and 500 feet below, 1,000 feet above, 2,000 feet horizontal from all clouds. (A60) — 14 CFR §91.155(a),(c)*

ALL
**3119.** Unless otherwise authorized, two-way radio communications with Air Traffic Control are required for landings or takeoffs

A—at all tower controlled airports regardless of weather conditions.
B—at all tower controlled airports only when weather conditions are less than VFR.
C—at all tower controlled airports within Class D airspace only when weather conditions are less than VFR.

*No person may operate an aircraft to, from, or on an airport having a control tower operated by the United States unless two-way radio communications are maintained between that aircraft and the control tower. (B08) — 14 CFR §91.126, §91.127, and §91.129(b)*

**Answers**
3782 [C]    3626 [B]    3627 [B]    3125 [C]    3069 [B]    3119 [A]

ALL
**3625.** (Refer to Figure 26, area 4.) The airspace directly overlying Fort Worth Meacham is

A—Class B airspace to 10,000 feet MSL.
B—Class C airspace to 5,000 feet MSL.
C—Class D airspace to 3,200 feet MSL.

*A blue segmented circle depicts Class D airspace which extends from the surface to 3,200 feet MSL, in this case as shown by the blue number 32 surrounded by the blue segmented box. (J37) — AIM ¶3-2-5*

Answer (A) is incorrect because although Class B airspace does overlie Fort Worth Meacham to 10,000 feet MSL, its base is 4,000 feet MSL. Answer (B) is incorrect because Class C airspace does not exist around Fort Worth Meacham.

ALL
**3067.** The width of a Federal Airway from either side of the centerline is

A—4 nautical miles.
B—6 nautical miles.
C—8 nautical miles.

*Federal airways are part of Class B, C, D, or E airspace. They are eight miles wide, four miles either side of centerline. They usually begin at 1,200 AGL and continue up to but not including 18,000 feet MSL, or FL180. (A60) — 14 CFR §71.5(b)(1)*

ALL
**3068.** Unless otherwise specified, Federal Airways include that Class E airspace extending upward from

A—700 feet above the surface up to and including 17,999 feet MSL.
B—1,200 feet above the surface up to and including 17,999 feet MSL.
C—the surface up to and including 18,000 feet MSL.

*Federal airways are part of Class B, C, D, or E airspace. They are eight miles wide, four miles either side of centerline. They usually begin at 1,200 AGL and continue up to but not including 18,000 feet MSL, or FL180. (A60) — 14 CFR §71.5(c)(1)*

ALL
**3629.** (Refer to Figure 23, area 3.) The vertical limits of that portion of Class E airspace designated as a Federal Airway over Magee Airport are

A—700 feet MSL to 12,500 feet MSL.
B—7,500 feet MSL to 17,999 feet MSL.
C—1,200 feet AGL to 17,999 feet MSL.

*The VOR and L/MF Airway System consists of airways designated from 1,200 feet above the surface (in some instances higher) up to, but not including, 18,000 feet MSL. (J37) — AIM ¶3-2-6*

ALL
**3622.** (Refer to Figure 27, area 1.) Identify the airspace over Lowe Airport.

A—Class G airspace – surface up to but not including 18,000 feet MSL.
B—Class G airspace – surface up to but not including 1,200 feet AGL, Class E airspace – 1,200 feet AGL up to but not including 18,000 feet MSL.
C—Class G airspace – surface up to but not including 700 feet MSL, Class E airspace – 700 feet to 14,500 feet MSL.

*The blue circle in the bottom left corner of Figure 27 indicates Lowe airport lies in Class G airspace from the surface to 1,200 feet AGL, and Class E airspace from 1,200 feet AGL to 18,000 feet MSL. The blue shading of the Victor airways (east of the Mississippi) indicates Class E airspace from 1,200 feet AGL. (J37) — AIM 3-2-1*

ALL
**3623.** (Refer to Figure 27, area 6.) The airspace overlying and within 5 miles of Barnes County Airport is

A—Class D airspace from the surface to the floor of the overlying Class E airspace.
B—Class E airspace from the surface to 1,200 feet MSL.
C—Class G airspace from the surface to 700 feet AGL.

*The Barnes County Airport is depicted inside the magenta shading, which is controlled airspace from 700 feet AGL up to but not including 18,000 feet. Therefore, the airspace below 700 feet AGL is Class G. (J37) — AIM ¶3-2-1*

**Answers**

| 3625 [C] | 3067 [A] | 3068 [B] | 3629 [C] | 3622 [B] | 3623 [C] |
|---|---|---|---|---|---|

ALL
**3624.** (Refer to Figure 26, area 7.) The airspace overlying McKinney (TKI) is controlled from the surface to

A—2,500 feet MSL.
B—2,900 feet MSL.
C—700 feet AGL.

*The [29] indicates the Class D airspace around McKinney (TKI) goes from the surface to 2,900 feet MSL. (J37) — AIM ¶3-2-1*

ALL
**3601.** (Refer to Figure 21, area 4.) What hazards to aircraft may exist in restricted areas such as R-5302B?

A—Military training activities that necessitate acrobatic or abrupt flight maneuvers.
B—Unusual, often invisible, hazards such as aerial gunnery or guided missiles.
C—High volume of pilot training or an unusual type of aerial activity.

*Restricted areas denote the presence of unusual, often invisible, hazards to aircraft such as artillery firing, aerial gunnery, or guided missiles. Penetration of restricted areas without authorization of the using or controlling agency may be extremely hazardous to the aircraft and its occupants. (J09) — AIM 3-4-4*

Answer (A) is incorrect because this defines a military operations area. Answer (C) is incorrect because this defines an alert area.

ALL
**3602.** (Refer to Figure 27.) What hazards to aircraft may exist in areas such as Devils Lake East MOA?

A—Unusual, often invisible, hazards to aircraft such as artillery firing, aerial gunnery, or guided missiles.
B—High volume of pilot training or an unusual type of aerial activity.
C—Military training activities that necessitate acrobatic or abrupt flight maneuvers.

*A Military Operations Area (MOA) contains military training activities such as aerobatics, and calls for extreme caution. (J09) — AIM ¶3-4-5*

ALL
**3783.** Under what condition, if any, may pilots fly through a restricted area?

A—When flying on airways with an ATC clearance.
B—With the controlling agency's authorization.
C—Regulations do not allow this.

*Restricted areas can be penetrated but only with the permission of the controlling agency. No person may operate an aircraft within a restricted area contrary to the restrictions imposed unless he/she has the permission of the using or controlling agency as appropriate. Penetration of restricted areas without authorization from the using or controlling agency may be fatal to the aircraft and its occupants. (J09) — AIM ¶3-4-3*

ALL
**3785.** What action should a pilot take when operating under VFR in a Military Operations Area (MOA)?

A—Obtain a clearance from the controlling agency prior to entering the MOA.
B—Operate only on the airways that transverse the MOA.
C—Exercise extreme caution when military activity is being conducted.

*Pilots operating under VFR should exercise extreme caution while flying within a MOA when military activity is being conducted. No clearance is necessary to enter a MOA. (J09) — AIM ¶3-4-5*

ALL
**3786.** Responsibility for collision avoidance in an alert area rests with

A—the controlling agency.
B—all pilots.
C—Air Traffic Control.

*All activity within an Alert Area shall be conducted in accordance with FAA regulations, without waiver, and pilots of participating aircraft, as well as pilots transiting the area, shall be equally responsible for collision avoidance. (J09) — AIM ¶3-4-6*

---

**Answers**

| 3624 [B] | 3601 [B] | 3602 [C] | 3783 [B] | 3785 [C] | 3786 [B] |
|---|---|---|---|---|---|

LTA
**3784.** A balloon flight through a restricted area is

A—permitted at certain times, but only with prior permission by the appropriate authority.
B—permitted anytime, but caution should be exercised because of high-speed military aircraft.
C—never permitted.

*Restricted areas can be penetrated but only with the permission of the controlling agency. No person may operate an aircraft within a restricted area contrary to the restrictions imposed unless he/she has the permission of the using or controlling agency as appropriate. Penetration of restricted areas without authorization from the using or controlling agency may be fatal to the aircraft and its occupants. (J09) — AIM ¶3-4-3*

ALL
**3603.** (Refer to Figure 22.) What type military flight operations should a pilot expect along IR 644?

A—IFR training flights above 1,500 feet AGL at speeds in excess of 250 knots.
B—VFR training flights above 1,500 feet AGL at speeds less than 250 knots.
C—Instrument training flights below 1,500 feet AGL at speeds in excess of 150 knots.

*IR644 begins at the lower left (eastbound) and turns northeast as a thin gray line. IR644 has three digits, which mean: generally above 1,500 feet AGL (but some segments below), operations under IFR, and (as with all MTRs) may be over 250 knots. (J10) — AIM ¶3-5-2*

ALL
**3618.** (Refer to Figure 27, area 3.) When flying over Arrowwood National Wildlife Refuge, a pilot should fly no lower than

A—2,000 feet AGL.
B—2,500 feet AGL.
C—3,000 feet AGL.

*All aircraft are requested to maintain a minimum altitude of 2,000 feet above the surface of national parks, monuments, seashores, lakeshores, recreation areas, and scenic riverways administered by the National Park Service, National Wildlife Refuges, Big Game Refuges, Game Ranges and Wildlife Ranges administered by the U.S. Fish and Wildlife Service, and Wilderness and Primitive areas administered by the U.S. Forest Service. (J28) — AIM ¶7-4-6*

ALL
**3789.** Prior to entering an Airport Advisory Area, a pilot should

A—monitor ATIS for weather and traffic advisories.
B—contact approach control for vectors to the traffic pattern.
C—contact the local FSS for airport and traffic advisories.

*An Airport Advisory Area is the area within 10 statute miles of an airport where a control tower is not operating, but where a FSS is located. At such locations, the FSS provides advisory service to arriving and departing aircraft. It is not mandatory that pilots participate in the Airport Advisory Service Program, but it is strongly recommended. (J10) — AIM ¶3-5-1*

ALL
**3831.** Pilots flying over a national wildlife refuge are requested to fly no lower than _____.

A—1,000 feet AGL.
B—2,000 feet AGL.
C—3,000 feet AGL.

*All aircraft are requested to maintain a minimum altitude of 2,000 feet above the surface of the following: national parks, monuments, seashores, lakeshores, recreation areas and scenic riverways administered by the National Park Service, National Wildlife Refuges, Big Game Refuges, Game Ranges and Wildlife Ranges administered by the U.S. Fish and Wildlife Service, and Wilderness and Primitive areas administered by the U.S. Forest Service. (J28) — AIM ¶7-4-6*

**Answers**

3784 [A]        3603 [A]        3618 [A]        3789 [C]        3831 [B]

# Chapter 10
# Navigation

# VHF Omnidirectional Range (VOR)

The **VHF Omnidirectional Range (VOR)** is the backbone of the National Airway System, and this radio aid to navigation (**NAVAID**) provides guidance to pilots operating under visual flight rules as well as those flying instruments.

On sectional aeronautical charts, VOR locations are shown by blue symbols centered in a blue compass rose which is oriented to Magnetic North. A blue identification box adjacent to the VOR symbol lists the name and frequency of the facility, its three-letter identifier and Morse Code equivalent, and other information as appropriate. For example: a small solid blue square in the bottom right hand corner indicates Hazardous Inflight Weather Advisory Service (HIWAS) are available. *See* the "Radio Aids to Navigation and Communications Box" information in FAA Legend 1.

Some VORs have a voice identification alternating with the Morse Code identifier. Absence of the identifier indicates the facility is unreliable or undergoing routine maintenance; in either case, it should not be used for navigation. Some VORs also transmit a T-E-S-T code when undergoing maintenance.

The VOR station continuously transmits navigation signals, providing 360 magnetic courses to or radials from the station. Courses are TO the station and radials are FROM the station.

TACAN, a military system which provides directional guidance, also informs the pilot of the aircraft's distance from the TACAN Station. When a VOR and a TACAN are co-located, the facility is called a VORTAC. Civil pilots may receive both azimuth and distance information from a VORTAC.

At some VOR sites, additional equipment has been installed to provide pilots with distance information. Such an installation is termed a VOR/DME (for "distance measuring equipment").

ALL
**3643.** (Refer to Figure 26, area 5.) The navigation facility at Dallas-Ft. Worth International (DFW) is a

A—VOR.
B—VORTAC.
C—VOR/DME.

*Reference FAA Legend 1. There is a VOR/DME at DFW. (J37) — Sectional Chart Legend*

# VOR Orientation

Cockpit display of VOR information is by means of an indicator as shown in Figure 10-1.

The **Omni Bearing Selector (OBS)** is an azimuth dial which can be rotated to select a course or to determine which radial the aircraft is on. The **TO/FROM indicator** shows whether flying the selected course would take the aircraft to or from the VOR station. A TO indication shows the radial selected is on the far side of the VOR station, while a FROM indication means the aircraft and the selected course are on the same side.

The **Course Deviation Indicator (CDI)**, when centered, indicates the aircraft is on the selected course, or, when not centered, whether that course is to the left or right of the aircraft. For example,

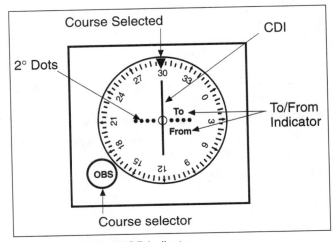

**Figure 10-1.** The VOR indicator

Figure 10-2 is indicating that a course of 030° would take the aircraft to the selected station, and to get on that course, the aircraft would have to fly to the left of 030°.

**Figure 10-2.** Interpreting the OBS and CDI indications

To determine position in relation to one or more VOR stations, first tune and identify the selected station. Next, rotate the OBS until the CDI centers with a FROM indication. The OBS reading is the magnetic course from the VOR station to the aircraft. With reference to Figure 10-3, the line of position is established on the 265° radial of the XYZ VOR.

Repeat the procedure using a second VOR. The aircraft is located at the point where the two lines of position cross. *See* Figure 10-4.

**Figure 10-3.** Aircraft on the 265° radial of a VOR

ALL
**3552.** (Refer to Figure 24.) What is the approximate position of the aircraft if the VOR receivers indicate the 320° radial of Savannah VORTAC (area 3) and the 184° radial of Allendale VOR (area 1)?

A—Town of Guyton.
B—Town of Springfield.
C—3 miles east of Marlow.

1.  Plot the 320° radial (magnetic course FROM) of the Savannah VORTAC.

2.  Plot the 184° radial of the Allendale VOR.

3.  Note the intersection of the two plotted radials over the town of Springfield.

(H346) — AC 61-23C, Chapter 8

ALL
**3559.** (Refer to Figure 25.) What is the approximate position of the aircraft if the VOR receivers indicate the 245° radial of Sulphur Springs VOR-DME (area 5) and the 140° radial of Bonham VORTAC (area 3)?

A—Meadowview Airport.
B—Glenmar Airport.
C—Majors Airport.

Use the following steps:

1.  Plot the 245° radial (magnetic course FROM) of the Sulphur Springs VOR-DME.

2.  Plot the 140° radial (magnetic course FROM) of the Bonham VORTAC.

3.  Note the intersection of the two plotted radials over the Glenmar Airport (Pvt).

(H348) — AC 61-23C, Chapter 8

**Answers**

3552　[B]　　　　　3559　[B]

**Figure 10-4.** VOR orientation using two VORs

ALL
**3566.** (Refer to Figure 26, area 5.) The VOR is tuned to the Dallas/Fort Worth VORTAC. The omnibearing selector (OBS) is set on 253°, with a TO indication, and a right course deviation indicator (CDI) deflection. What is the aircraft's position from the VORTAC?

A—East-northeast.
B—North-northeast.
C—West-southwest.

*The course selected is 253° and the TO/FROM indicator has a TO flag, which means the aircraft is south of the course but north of the VOR. The CDI needle is deflected to the right, which means the aircraft is left (or east) of the course. Therefore, the aircraft must be to the east northeast of the station to satisfy the VOR indications. (H348) — AC 61-23C, Chapter 8*

ALL
**3577.** (Refer to Figure 29, illustration 1.) The VOR receiver has the indications shown. What is the aircraft's position relative to the station?

A—North.
B—East.
C—South.

*The course selected is 030° and the TO/FROM indicator is showing TO, which means the aircraft is south of the course. The CDI needle is deflected to the left, which means the aircraft is right of the course. (H348) — AC 61-23C, Chapter 8*

ALL
**3578.** (Refer to Figure 29, illustration 3.) The VOR receiver has the indications shown. What is the aircraft's position relative to the station?

A—East.
B—Southeast.
C—West.

*Observe from illustration #3 of FAA Figure 29, that there is no TO/FROM indication and the CDI is deflected left with an OBS set on 030°. The aircraft is somewhere along the perpendicular line (120/300°). The CDI left means the 030° radial is to the left, or west, of the aircraft position. Answer B is the only one placing the aircraft on the 120° radial, or southeast of the station. (H348) — AC 61-23C, Chapter 8*

**Answers**

3566 [A]          3577 [C]          3578 [B]

ALL
**3579.** (Refer to Figure 29, illustration 8.) The VOR receiver has the indications shown. What radial is the aircraft crossing?

A—030°.
B—210°.
C—300°.

The CDI is centered with the OBS set to 210° with a TO indication. Therefore, the aircraft is located on the 030° radial. (H348) — AC 61-23C, Chapter 8

# Course Determination

To determine the course to be flown to a VOR station on the sectional aeronautical chart, first draw a line from the starting point to the VOR symbol in the center of the compass rose. At the point where the course line crosses the compass rose, read the radial. The course to the station is the reciprocal of that radial. *See* Figure 10-5.

**Figure 10-5.** Determining course to a VOR station

AIR, RTC
**3539.** (Refer to Figure 22.) What course should be selected on the omnibearing selector (OBS) to make a direct flight from Mercer County Regional Airport (area 3) to the Minot VORTAC (area 1) with a TO indication?

A—001°.
B—359°.
C—179°.

*Use the following steps:*

1. *Plot a direct course from Mercer Airport to the Minot Airport VORTAC.*

2. *Note the radial (magnetic course FROM Minot VORTAC) on which the plotted course lies (179°).*

3. *Determine the course TO Minot VORTAC by finding the reciprocal:*

    *TO = FROM + 180°*
    *TO = 179° + 180°*
    *TO = 359°*

*(H348) — AC 61-23C, Chapter 8*

ALL
**3553.** (Refer to Figure 24.) On what course should the VOR receiver (OBS) be set to navigate direct from Hampton Varnville Airport (area 1) to Savannah VORTAC (area 3)?

A—003°.
B—183°.
C—200°.

1. *Plot the course direct from Hampton Varnville Airport to the Savannah VORTAC.*

2. *Note the radial (magnetic course from Savannah) on which the plotted course lies (003°).*

3. *Determine the course TO the VORTAC by finding the reciprocal:*

    *TO = FROM + 180°*
    *TO = 003° + 180°*
    *TO = 183°*

*(H348) — AC 61-23C, Chapter 8*

**Answers**

3579 [A]          3539 [B]          3553 [B]

ALL
**3560.** (Refer to Figure 25.) On what course should the VOR receiver (OBS) be set in order to navigate direct from Majors Airport (area 1) to Quitman VORTAC (area 2)?
A—101°.
B—108°.
C—281°.

Use the following steps:

1. Plot the course direct from Majors Airport to Quitman VORTAC.

2. Note the radial (magnetic course FROM) of Quitman VORTAC on which the plotted course lies (281°).

3. Determine the course TO the VORTAC by finding the reciprocal:

TO = FROM + 180°
TO = 281° + 180°
TO = 461° – 360° = 101°

(H348) — AC 61-23C, Chapter 8

ALL
**3533.** (Refer to Figure 21, area 3; and Figure 29.) The VOR is tuned to Elizabeth City VOR, and the aircraft is positioned over Shawboro. Which VOR indication is correct?
A—2.
B—5.
C—9.

1. Locate the Shawboro Airport and the Elizabeth City VOR in FAA Figure 21. Draw the radial (magnetic course FROM) of the Elizabeth City VOR on which Shawboro lies (030°).

2. When over Shawboro on the 030 radial, the CDI should be centered with a 030 FROM indication or a 210 TO indication (the reciprocal). Dials 2 and 8 satisfy these conditions. Only dial 2 is listed as an answer choice.

(H348) — AC 61-23C

ALL
**3561.** (Refer to Figure 25, and Figure 29.) The VOR is tuned to Bonham VORTAC (area 3), and the aircraft is positioned over the town of Sulphur Springs (area 5). Which VOR indication is correct?
A—1.
B—7.
C—8.

Use the following steps:

1. Locate and draw the magnetic course from Bonham VORTAC to Sulphur Springs (120°).

2. Notice that the OBS selections of all the dials in FAA Figure 29 are 030° or 210°, both of which are at 90° with respect to the 120° radial. Therefore, when over Sulphur Springs, the flag should indicate neither TO nor FROM and the course needle should have a full deflection either side.

3. Dials 3 and 7 of FAA Figure 29 are on the 120° radial. Both provide a correct indication, but on reciprocal headings. Dial 7 is the only correct answer provided.

(H348) — AC 61-23C, Chapter 8

ALL
**3570.** (Refer to Figure 27, areas 4 and 3; and Figure 29.) The VOR is tuned to Jamestown VOR, and the aircraft is positioned over Cooperstown Airport. Which VOR indication is correct?
A—9.
B—6.
C—2.

1. Locate the Cooperstown Airport and the Jamestown VOR in FAA Figure 27. Draw the radial (magnetic course FROM) of the Jamestown VOR on which Cooperstown Airport lies (030°).

2. When over Cooperstown Airport on the 030 radial, the CDI should be centered with a 030 FROM indication or a 210 TO indication (the reciprocal). Dials 2 and 8 satisfy these conditions. Only dial 2 is listed as an answer choice.

(H348) — AC 61-23C, Chapter 8

**Answers**
3560  [A]      3533  [A]      3561  [B]      3570  [C]

# VOR Airways

The routes established between VORs are depicted by blue-tinted bands showing the airway number following the letter "V," and are called "Victor airways." *See* Figure 10-6.

When approaching a VOR where airways converge, a pilot must exercise extreme vigilance for other aircraft. In addition, when climbing or descending VFR on an airway, it is considered good operating practice to execute gentle banks left and right for continuous visual scanning of the airspace.

ALL
**3532.** (Refer to Figure 21.) What is your approximate position on low altitude airway Victor 1, southwest of Norfolk (area 1), if the VOR receiver indicates you are on the 340° radial of Elizabeth City VOR (area 3)?

A—15 nautical miles from Norfolk VORTAC.
B—18 nautical miles from Norfolk VORTAC.
C—23 nautical miles from Norfolk VORTAC.

*Use the following steps:*

1. *Plot the 340° radial from the Elizabeth City VOR to the point of intersection with V1. Caution: the numerals "330" just inside the Elizabeth City compass rose (just to the left of the course line), refer to an obstruction height, not a VOR radial.*

2. *Measure the distance from Norfolk to the plotted intersection using the sectional scale of a plotter. The distance is 18 NM.*

*(H348) — AC 61-23C, Chapter 8*

**Figure 10-6**

AIR, RTC
**3814.** What procedure is recommended when climbing or descending VFR on an airway?

A—Execute gentle banks, left and right for continuous visual scanning of the airspace.
B—Advise the nearest FSS of the altitude changes.
C—Fly away from the centerline of the airway before changing altitude.

*During climbs and descents in flight conditions which permit visual detection of other traffic, pilots should execute gentle banks, left and right, at a frequency which permits continuous visual scanning of the airspace about them. (J14) — AIM ¶4-4-14*

# VOR Receiver Check Points

VOR receiver accuracy may be checked by means of a VOR Test Facility (VOT), ground check points, or airborne check points.

VOTs transmit only the 360° radial signal. Thus, when the OBS is set to 360°, the CDI will center with a FROM indication; while the reciprocal, 180°, will cause the CDI to center with a TO indication. An accuracy factor of plus or minus 4° is allowed when using a VOT facility.

ALL
**3598-1.** When the course deviation indicator (CDI) needle is centered during an omnireceiver check using a VOR test signal (VOT), the omnibearing selector (OBS) and the TO/FROM indicator should read

A—180° FROM, only if the pilot is due north of the VOT.
B—0° TO or 180° FROM, regardless of the pilot's position from the VOT.
C—0° FROM or 180° TO, regardless of the pilot's position from the VOT.

*To use the VOT service, tune in the VOT frequency on the VOR receiver. With the CDI centered, the OBS should read 0° with the TO/FROM indication showing "FROM" or the OBS should read 180° with the TO/FROM indication showing "TO." (J01) — AIM ¶1-1-4*

**Answers**
3532    [B]          3814    [A]          3598-1    [C]

# Automatic Direction Finder (ADF)

The **Automatic Direction Finder (ADF)** consists of a receiver that receives radio waves in the low- and medium-frequency bands and an instrument needle that points to the station. Some ADF indicators have a compass card that remains in a fixed position, while in others, the compass card turns as the aircraft turns. This is called a **Radio Magnetic Indicator (RMI)**.

An instrument with a fixed-compass card (fixed-scale) will always show zero degrees at the nose of the aircraft (Figure 10-7). The actual magnetic heading must be obtained from the magnetic compass or other heading indicator.

ADF indicators which have rotating compass cards (RMIs) allow the pilot to read the magnetic heading of the aircraft directly without referring to another instrument (Figure 10-8).

**Figure 10-7.** ADF indicator with a fixed scale

The ADF may be used to either home or track to a station. ADF **homing** is flying the aircraft on any heading required to keep the azimuth needle pointing directly in front of the aircraft until the station is reached. **Tracking** is following a straight geographic path by establishing a heading that will maintain the desired track over the ground regardless of wind effect.

On an indicator with a fixed card, the azimuth needle, pointing to the selected station indicates the angular difference between the aircraft heading and the direction to the station, measured clockwise from the nose of the aircraft. This angular difference is the **relative bearing (RB)** to the station, and may be read directly from a fixed-scale indicator. For example, in Figure 10-7, the relative bearing to the station is 135°.

**Figure 10-8.** ADF indicator with a rotating scale

If the indicator has a rotating scale, the number of degrees clockwise from the nose of the aircraft to the head of the needle must be determined. In Figure 10-8, the relative bearing is 025°.

The direction the aircraft should fly to arrive at the selected station is the **magnetic bearing (MB)**. The magnetic bearing to the station may be read directly from an indicator with a rotating scale. In Figure 10-8, the magnetic bearing to the selected station is 295°, as shown by the head of the needle; and the bearing from the station (115° in this example) may be read under the tail of the needle.

When the indicator has a fixed scale, computation is necessary to determine the magnetic bearing to the selected station. The ADF formula is:

Magnetic Heading (MH) + Relative Bearing (RB) = Magnetic Bearing to the Station (MB)

## Problem:

What is the magnetic bearing TO the station using the ADF in Figure 10-9?

## Solution:

1. MH (350°) + RB (315°) = MB (665°)

2. If the sum is greater than 360, subtract 360:

$$665°$$
$$-\ 360°$$
$$\overline{305°}$$

In this case, the magnetic bearing FROM the station would be 125°, which is the reciprocal of 305°.

ADF orientation and tracking procedures are used when intercepting a specific inbound or outbound magnetic bearing. With an aircraft on a magnetic heading of 270° and a relative bearing to the station of 290°, indications would appear as shown in Figure 10-10.

To intercept an inbound magnetic bearing with the indications shown in Figure 10-10, the following steps can be used:

**Figure 10-9.** ADF problem

1. If it is desired to intercept the 180° magnetic bearing to the station, turn to parallel the desired inbound bearing.

2. Note whether the station is to the right or left of the nose of the aircraft and determine the number of degrees of needle deflection. In this example, the ADF needle is pointing 20° to the right of the nose of the aircraft. Double the amount of needle deflection to find the interception angle: 40°.

3. Turn the aircraft toward the desired magnetic bearing the number of degrees determined (40°) for the interception angle.

4. If using an ADF with a fixed scale, maintain the intercept heading until the needle is deflected the same number of degrees from the nose of the aircraft as the angle of interception. At that time, the desired magnetic bearing to the station, 180°, has been intercepted. Turn inbound and track to the station.

5. If using an ADF with a rotating scale, maintain the intercept heading until the needle points to the desired magnetic bearing to the station of 180°. Turn inbound and track to the station.

**Figure 10-10.** ADF indications with fixed and rotary scales

ALL
**3580.** (Refer to Figure 30, illustration 1.) Determine the magnetic bearing TO the station.

A—030°.
B—180°.
C—210°.

*The head of the needle indicates the magnetic bearing TO the station, which is 210°. (H348) — AC 61-23C, Chapter 8*

ALL
**3581.** (Refer to Figure 30, illustration 2.) What magnetic bearing should the pilot use to fly TO the station?

A—010°.
B—145°.
C—190°.

*The nose of the needle indicates the magnetic bearing TO the station which is 190°. (H348) — AC 61-23C, Chapter 8*

ALL
**3582.** (Refer to Figure 30, illustration 2.) Determine the approximate heading to intercept the 180° bearing TO the station.

A—040°.
B—160°.
C—220°.

*To determine the intercept angle, turn to the inbound bearing and note degrees the needle is from the nose. Double this figure to get the intercept angle of 20°:*

*180° + 20° = 200°*

*The only possible answer is 220° since the other true headings would not intercept the 180° bearing to the station. (H348) — AC 61-23C, Chapter 8*

ALL
**3583.** (Refer to Figure 30, illustration 3.) What is the magnetic bearing FROM the station?

A—025°.
B—115°.
C—295°.

*The tail of the needle indicates the magnetic bearing FROM the station, which is 115°. (H348) — AC 61-23C, Chapter 8*

ALL
**3584.** (Refer to Figure 30.) Which ADF indication represents the aircraft tracking TO the station with a right crosswind?

A—1.
B—2.
C—4.

*FAA Figure 30 depicts ADF indications combined with aircraft heading information. In this case, the magnetic bearing TO can be read under the nose of the needle and the bearing FROM can be read directly under the tail of the needle. Use the following steps:*

*1. Note which dials, #3 and #4, of FAA Figure 30, show an aircraft proceeding toward the station.*

*2. A right crosswind (wind FROM the right) requires that the aircraft heading be to the right of the course to compensate for drift to the left. With the nose of the aircraft to the right of the course, the station appears to be left of the nose, as shown on dial #4.*

*(H348) — AC 61-23C, Chapter 8*

ALL
**3585.** (Refer to Figure 30, illustration 1.) What outbound bearing is the aircraft crossing?

A—030°.
B—150°.
C—180°.

*The tail of the needle indicates the magnetic bearing FROM the station, which is 030°. (H348) — AC 61-23C, Chapter 8*

**Answers**

| | | | | | |
|---|---|---|---|---|---|
| 3580 [C] | 3581 [C] | 3582 [C] | 3583 [B] | 3584 [C] | 3585 [A] |

ALL

**3586.** (Refer to Figure 30, illustration 1.) What is the relative bearing TO the station?

A—030°.
B—210°.
C—240°.

*FAA Figure 30 depicts ADF indications combined with aircraft heading information. In this case, the magnetic bearing TO can be read under the nose of the needle and the bearing FROM can be read directly under the tail of the needle. Use the following steps:*

1. *The aircraft magnetic heading is 330°.*

2. *The magnetic bearing TO the station is 210°.*

3. *Calculate the relative bearing (RB):*

   $$MB = MH + RB$$
   $$RB = 210° - 330° + 360°$$
   $$RB = 240°$$

*(H348) — AC 61-23C, Chapter 8*


ALL

**3587.** (Refer to Figure 30, illustration 2.) What is the relative bearing TO the station?

A—190°.
B—235°.
C—315°.

*FAA Figure 30 depicts ADF indications combined with aircraft heading information. In this case, the magnetic bearing TO can be read under the nose of the needle and the bearing FROM can be read directly under the tail of the needle. Use the following steps:*

1. *The aircraft magnetic heading is 315°.*

2. *The magnetic bearing TO the station is 190°.*

3. *Calculate the relative bearing (RB):*

   $$MB = MH + RB$$
   $$RB = 190° - 315° + 360°$$
   $$RB = 235°$$

*(H348) — AC 61-23C, Chapter 8*


ALL

**3588.** (Refer to Figure 30, illustration 4.) What is the relative bearing TO the station?

A—020°.
B—060°.
C—340°.

*FAA Figure 30 depicts ADF indications combined with aircraft heading information. In this case, the magnetic bearing TO can be read under the nose of the needle and the bearing FROM can be read directly under the tail of the needle. Use the following steps:*

1. *The aircraft magnetic heading is 220°.*

2. *The magnetic bearing TO the station is 200°.*

3. *Calculate the relative bearing (RB):*

   $$MB = MH + RB$$
   $$RB = 200° - 220° + 360°$$
   $$RB = 340°$$

*(H348) — AC 61-23C, Chapter 8*


ALL

**3589.** (Refer to Figure 31, illustration 1.) The relative bearing TO the station is

A—045°.
B—180°.
C—315°.

*On a fixed-scale (fixed-card) ADF, the nose of the aircraft is marked as 0°. The ADF indication is relative to aircraft heading, thus relative bearing may be read directly under the head of the needle, which is 315°. (H348) — AC 61-23C, Chapter 8*


ALL

**3590.** (Refer to Figure 31, illustration 2.) The relative bearing TO the station is

A—090°.
B—180°.
C—270°.

*On a fixed-scale (fixed-card) ADF, the nose of the aircraft is marked as 0°. The ADF indication is relative to aircraft heading, thus relative bearing may be read directly under the head of the needle, which is 090°. (H348) — AC 61-23C, Chapter 8*


**Answers**

| | | | | |
|---|---|---|---|---|
| 3586 [C] | 3587 [B] | 3588 [C] | 3589 [C] | 3590 [A] |

**ALL**
**3591.** (Refer to Figure 31, illustration 3.) The relative bearing TO the station is

A—090°.
B—180°.
C—270°.

*On a fixed-scale (fixed-card) ADF, the nose of the aircraft is marked as 0°. The ADF indication is relative to aircraft heading, thus relative bearing may be read directly under the head of the needle, which is 180°. (H348) — AC 61-23C, Chapter 8*

**ALL**
**3592.** (Refer to Figure 31, illustration 4.) On a magnetic heading of 320°, the magnetic bearing TO the station is

A—005°.
B—185°.
C—225°.

*Use the following steps:*

1. *On a fixed-scale ADF, the aircraft heading is marked as 0°. The ADF indication is relative to the aircraft heading, thus relative bearing (RB) may be read directly under the head of the needle (225°).*

2. *Calculate the magnetic bearing to the station at a magnetic heading of 320°:*

$$MB = RB + MH$$
$$MB = 225° + 320° = 545° - 360°$$
$$MB = 185°$$

*(H348) — AC 61-23C, Chapter 8*

**ALL**
**3593.** (Refer to Figure 31, illustration 5.) On a magnetic heading of 035°, the magnetic bearing TO the station is

A—035°.
B—180°.
C—215°.

*Use the following steps:*

1. *On a fixed-scale ADF, the aircraft heading is marked as 0°. The ADF indication is relative to the aircraft heading, thus relative bearing (RB) may be read directly under the head of the needle (000°).*

2. *Calculate the magnetic bearing to the station for a magnetic heading of 035°:*

$$MB = RB + MH$$
$$MB = 0° + 035°$$
$$MB = 035°$$

*(H348) — AC 61-23C, Chapter 8*

**ALL**
**3594.** (Refer to Figure 31, illustration 6.) On a magnetic heading of 120°, the magnetic bearing TO the station is

A—045°.
B—165°.
C—270°.

*Use the following steps:*

1. *On a fixed-scale ADF, the aircraft heading is marked as 0°. The ADF indication is relative to the aircraft heading, thus relative bearing (RB) may be read directly under the head of the needle (045°).*

2. *Calculate the magnetic bearing to the station for a magnetic heading of 120°:*

$$MB = RB + MH$$
$$MB = 045° + 120°$$
$$MB = 165°$$

*(H348) — AC 61-23C, Chapter 8*

**ALL**
**3595.** (Refer to Figure 31, illustration 6.) If the magnetic bearing TO the station is 240°, the magnetic heading is

A—045°.
B—105°.
C—195°.

*Use the following steps:*

1. *On a fixed-scale ADF, the aircraft heading is marked as 0°. The ADF indication is relative to the aircraft heading and thus, relative bearing (RB) may be read directly under the head of the needle (045°).*

2. *Note that the magnetic bearing TO the station is 240°. Calculate the magnetic heading using:*

$$MB = RB + MH$$
$$240° = 045° + MH$$
$$MH = 240° - 045° = 195°$$

*(H348) — AC 61-23C, Chapter 8*

**Answers**

| | | | | |
|---|---|---|---|---|
| 3591 [B] | 3592 [B] | 3593 [A] | 3594 [B] | 3595 [C] |

ALL
**3596.** (Refer to Figure 31, illustration 7.) If the magnetic bearing TO the station is 030°, the magnetic heading is

A—060°.
B—120°.
C—270°.

1.  On a fixed-scale ADF, the aircraft heading is marked as 0°. The ADF indication is relative to the aircraft heading, thus relative bearing (RB) may be read directly under the head of the needle (270°).

2.  Note that the magnetic bearing TO the station is 030°. Calculate the magnetic heading using:

$$MB = RB + MH$$
$$030° = 270° + MH$$
$$MH = 030° - 270° + 360°$$
$$MH = 120°$$

(H348) — AC 61-23C, Chapter 8

ALL
**3597.** (Refer to Figure 31, illustration 8.) If the magnetic bearing TO the station is 135°, the magnetic heading is

A—135°.
B—270°.
C—360°.

Use the following steps:

1.  On a fixed-scale ADF, the aircraft heading is marked as 0°. The ADF indication is relative to the aircraft heading, thus relative bearing (RB) may be read directly under the head of the needle (135°).

2.  Note that the magnetic bearing TO the station is 135°. Calculate the magnetic heading using:

$$MB = RB + MH$$
$$135° = 135° + MH$$
$$MH = 0° \text{ or } 360°$$

(H348) — AC 61-23C, Chapter 8

# Global Positioning System (GPS)

GPS is a United States satellite-based radio navigational, positioning, and time transfer system operated by the Department of Defense (DOD). The system provides highly accurate position and velocity information and precise time on a continuous global basis to an unlimited number of properly-equipped users. The GPS constellation of 24 satellites is designed so that a minimum of five are always observable by a user anywhere on earth. The GPS receiver uses data from a minimum of four satellites to yield a three dimensional position (latitude, longitude, and altitude) and time solution.

ALL
**3598-2.** How many satellites make up the Global Positioning System (GPS)?

A—25.
B—22.
C—24.

The GPS constellation of 24 satellites is designed so that a minimum of five are always observable by a user anywhere on earth. (J01) — AIM ¶1-1-21

ALL
**3598-3.** What is the minimum number of Global Positioning System (GPS) satellites that are observable by a user anywhere on earth?

A—6.
B—5.
C—4.

The GPS constellation of 24 satellites is designed so that a minimum of five are always observable by a user anywhere on earth. (J01) — AIM ¶1-1-21

ALL
**3598-4.** How many Global Positioning System (GPS) satellites are required to yield a three dimensional position (latitude, longitude, and altitude) and time solution?

A—5.
B—6.
C—4.

The GPS receiver uses data from a minimum of four satellites to yield a three-dimensional position (latitude, longitude, and altitude) and time solution. (J01) — AIM ¶1-1-21

**Answers**

| 3596 [B] | 3597 [C] | 3598-2 [C] | 3598-3 [B] | 3598-4 [C] |
|---|---|---|---|---|

# Chapter 11
# Communication Procedures

# Phraseology, Techniques, and Procedures

**Automatic Terminal Information Service (ATIS)** is a continuous broadcast of non-control information in selected high-activity terminal areas. To relieve frequency congestion, pilots are urged to listen to ATIS, and on initial contact, to advise controllers that the information has been received by repeating the alphabetical code word appended to the broadcast. For example: "information Sierra received." The phrase "have numbers" does not indicate receipt of the ATIS broadcast.

Enroute Flight Advisory Service (EFAS) provides aircraft with weather advisories pertinent to the route and altitude being flown. To obtain this service, pilots flying below FL180 should contact "flight watch" on frequency 122.0 MHz followed by the aircraft identification and the name of the nearest VOR to their position. Example:

"Cleveland flight watch, Cessna one two three four Kilo, Mansfield VOR, over."

When establishing initial contact with a facility, the following format should be used:

1. Name the facility being called. When calling a ground station, begin with the name of the facility followed by the type of facility being called. For example: When calling an FAA flight service station: "Seattle Radio"; or when calling an approach control: "Oklahoma City Approach."

2. Civil aircraft pilots should state the aircraft type, model or manufacturer's name followed by the digits/letters of the registration number using the Phonetic Alphabet. For example: when flying Easy N2959S, the proper phraseology for initial contact with Buffalo Approach Control is: "Buffalo Approach, Easy two niner five niner Sierra." (The prefix "N" is dropped when the manufacturer's name or model is stated.

3. The type of message or report follows.

4. The word "over," if required.

When transmitting an altitude to ATC (up to but not including 18,000 feet MSL), state the separate digits of the thousands, plus the hundreds. For example, 13,500 is "one three thousand five hundred" and 4,500 is "four thousand five hundred."

At airports with operating air traffic control towers (ATCT), approval must be obtained prior to moving an aircraft onto the movement area. Ground control frequencies are provided to reduce congestion on the tower frequency. They are used for issuance of taxi information, clearances and other necessary contacts. If instructed by ground control to "taxi to" a particular runway, the pilot may proceed via taxiways and across runways to, but not onto, the assigned runway.

Aircraft arriving at an airport where a control tower is in operation should not change to ground control frequency until directed to do so by ATC.

The key to operating at an airport without an operating control tower is selection of the correct **Common Traffic Advisory Frequency (CTAF)**. The CTAF is identified in appropriate aeronautical publications and on the sectional chart. If the airport has a part-time air traffic control tower (ATCT), the CTAF is usually a tower frequency. If a flight service station (FSS) is located on the airport, they will usually monitor that frequency and provide advisories when the tower is closed. Where there is no tower or FSS, UNICOM, (if available) is usually the CTAF. UNICOM is limited to the necessities of safe and expeditious operation of private aircraft pertaining to runways and wind conditions, types of fuel available, weather, and dispatching. Secondarily, communications may be transmitted concerning ground transportation, food, lodging and services available during transit. When no tower, FSS, or UNICOM is available, use MULTICOM frequency 122.9 for self-announce procedures. *See* Figure 11-1 on the next page.

| Facility at Airport | Frequency Use | Communication/Broadcast Procedures | | |
|---|---|---|---|---|
| | | *Outbound* | *Inbound* | *Practice Instrument Approach* |
| 1 UNICOM (No Tower or FSS) | Communicate with UNICOM station on published CTAF frequency (122.7, 122.8, 122.725, 122.975, or 123.0). If unable to contact UNICOM station, use self-announce procedures on CTAF. | Before taxiing and before taxiing on the runway for departure. | 10 miles out. Entering downwind, base, and final. Leaving the runway. | |
| 2 No Tower, FSS, or UNICOM | Self-announce on MULTICOM frequency 122.9. | Before taxiing and before taxiing on the runway for departure. | 10 miles out. Entering downwind, base, and final. Leaving the runway. | Departing final approach fix (name) or on final approach segment inbound. |
| 3 No Tower in operation, FSS open | Communicate with FSS on CTAF frequency. | Before taxiing and before taxiing on the runway for departure. | 10 miles out. Entering downwind, base, and final. Leaving the runway. | Approach completed/terminated. |
| 4 FSS closed (No Tower) | Self-announce on CTAF. | Before taxiing and before taxiing on the runway for departure. | 10 miles out. Entering downwind, base, and final. Leaving the runway. | |
| 5 Tower or FSS not in operation | Self-announce on CTAF. | Before taxiing and before taxiing on the runway for departure. | 10 miles out. Entering downwind, base, and final. Leaving the runway. | |

**Figure 11-1.** Summary of recommended communications procedures

ALL

**3613.** When flying HAWK N666CB, the proper phraseology for initial contact with McAlester AFSS is

A—"MC ALESTER RADIO, HAWK SIX SIX SIX CHARLIE BRAVO, RECEIVING ARDMORE VORTAC, OVER."

B—"MC ALESTER STATION, HAWK SIX SIX SIX CEE BEE, RECEIVING ARDMORE VORTAC, OVER."

C—"MC ALESTER FLIGHT SERVICE STATION, HAWK NOVEMBER SIX CHARLIE BRAVO, RECEIVING ARDMORE VORTAC, OVER."

*The term "initial radio contact," or "initial callup," means the first radio call you make to a given facility, or the first call to a different controller or FSS specialist within a facility. Use the following format:*

1. *Name of facility being called;*

2. *Your full aircraft identification as filed in the flight plan;*

3. *Type of message to follow or your request if it is short, and*

4. *The word "over," if required.*

   *Example: "New York Radio, Mooney Three One One Echo."*

*When the aircraft manufacturer's name or model is stated, the prefix "N" is dropped. The first two characters of the call sign may be dropped only after ATC calls you by your last three letters/numbers. (J12) — AIM ¶4-2-3*

ALL

**3614.** The correct method of stating 4,500 feet MSL to ATC is

A—"FOUR THOUSAND FIVE HUNDRED."
B—"FOUR POINT FIVE."
C—"FORTY-FIVE HUNDRED FEET MSL."

*Up to but not including 18,000 feet MSL, state the separate digits of the thousands, plus the hundreds, if appropriate. Example: "4,500 — four thousand, five hundred." (J12) — AIM ¶4-2-9*

**Answers**

3613   [A]          3614   [A]

ALL
**3615.** The correct method of stating 10,500 feet MSL to ATC is

A—"TEN THOUSAND, FIVE HUNDRED FEET."
B—"TEN POINT FIVE."
C—"ONE ZERO THOUSAND, FIVE HUNDRED."

*Up to but not including 18,000 feet MSL, state the separate digits of the thousands, plus the hundreds, if appropriate. Example: "10,500—one zero thousand, five hundred." (J12) — AIM ¶4-2-9*

ALL
**3616.** How should contact be established with an En Route Flight Advisory Service (EFAS) station, and what service would be expected?

A—Call EFAS on 122.2 for routine weather, current reports on hazardous weather, and altimeter settings.
B—Call flight assistance on 122.5 for advisory service pertaining to severe weather.
C—Call Flight Watch on 122.0 for information regarding actual weather and thunderstorm activity along proposed route.

*122.0 MHz is assigned nationwide as the Flight Watch which provides enroute aircraft with enroute weather reports along your route of flight. Flight Service Stations provide routine weather, current reports on hazardous weather, and altimeter settings that can be reached on 122.2, 122.4, 122.5, or 122.6. Discrete high-altitude frequencies are being implemented also. (J25) — AIM ¶7-1-4*

ALL
**3823.** Below FL180, en route weather advisories should be obtained from an FSS on

A—122.0 MHz.
B—122.1 MHz.
C—123.6 MHz.

*122.0 MHz is assigned nationwide as the Flight Watch frequency, which provides enroute aircraft with enroute weather reports along your route of flight. (J25) — AIM ¶7-1-3*

*Answers (B) and (C) are incorrect because 122.1 is the FSS frequency for remote communication outlets, and 123.6 is the FSS frequency for airport advisory service with an FSS on the field.*

ALL
**3604.** (Refer to Figure 21, area 3.) What is the recommended communications procedure for a landing at Currituck County Airport?

A—Transmit intentions on 122.9 MHz when 10 miles out and give position reports in the traffic pattern.
B—Contact Elizabeth City FSS for airport advisory service.
C—Contact New Bern FSS for area traffic information.

*Where there is no tower, FSS, or UNICOM station on the airport, use MULTICOM frequency 122.9 for self-announce procedures. Such airports will be identified in the appropriate aeronautical information publications. (J11) — AIM ¶4-1-9*

ALL
**3630.** (Refer to Figure 22.) On what frequency can a pilot receive Hazardous Inflight Weather Advisory Service (HIWAS) in the vicinity of area 1?

A—117.1 MHz.
B—118.0 MHz.
C—122.0 MHz.

*The reversed-out H in the upper-right corner indicates HIWAS on the VOR frequency. (J37) — AIM ¶7-1-8*

ALL
**3605.** (Refer to Figure 22, area 2.) The CTAF/MULTICOM frequency for Garrison Airport is

A—122.8 MHz.
B—122.9 MHz.
C—123.0 MHz.

*Where there is no tower, FSS, or UNICOM station on the airport, use MULTICOM frequency 122.9 for self-announce procedures. Such airports will be identified in the appropriate aeronautical information publications. (J11) — AIM ¶4-1-9*

**Answers**

| | | | | | |
|---|---|---|---|---|---|
| 3615 [C] | 3616 [C] | 3823 [A] | 3604 [A] | 3630 [A] | 3605 [B] |

ALL

**3606.** (Refer to Figure 23, area 2; and Figure 32.) At Coeur D'Alene, which frequency should be used as a Common Traffic Advisory Frequency (CTAF) to self-announce position and intentions?

A— 122.05 MHz.
B— 122.1/108.8 MHz.
C— 122.8 MHz.

*CTAF (Common Traffic Advisory Frequency) is a frequency designed for the purpose of carrying out airport advisory practices and/or position reporting at an uncontrolled airport (which may also occur during hours when a tower is closed). The CTAF may be a UNICOM, MULTICOM, FSS, or tower frequency and is identified in the appropriate aeronautical publications. A solid dot with the letter "C" inside indicates the Common Traffic Advisory Frequency. When the control tower operates part time and a UNICOM frequency is provided, use the UNICOM frequency. (J11) — AIM ¶4-1-9*

ALL

**3607.** (Refer to Figure 23, area 2; and Figure 32). At Coeur D'Alene, which frequency should be used as a Common Traffic Advisory Frequency (CTAF) to monitor airport traffic?

A— 122.05 MHz.
B— 135.075 MHz.
C— 122.8 MHz.

*CTAF (Common Traffic Advisory Frequency) is a frequency designed for the purpose of carrying out airport advisory practices and/or position reporting at an uncontrolled airport (which may also occur during hours when a tower is closed). The CTAF may be a UNICOM, MULTICOM, FSS, or tower frequency and is identified in the appropriate aeronautical publications. A solid dot with the letter "C" inside indicates Common Traffic Advisory Frequency. When the control tower operates part time and a UNICOM frequency is provided, use the UNICOM frequency. (J11) — AIM ¶4-1-9*

ALL

**3608.** (Refer to Figure 23, area 2; and Figure 32.) What is the correct UNICOM frequency to be used at Coeur D'Alene to request fuel?

A— 135.075 MHz.
B— 122.1/108.8 MHz.
C— 122.8 MHz.

*The sectional chart and Airport Facility Directory both list the UNICOM frequency as 122.8. This is the appropriate frequency to use to contact UNICOM. The UNICOM frequency is depicted in the airport information in the lower right-hand corner. (J11) — AIM ¶4-1-11*

ALL

**3609.** (Refer to Figure 26, area 3.) If Redbird Tower is not in operation, which frequency should be used as a Common Traffic Advisory Frequency (CTAF) to monitor airport traffic?

A— 120.3 MHz.
B— 122.95 MHz.
C— 126.35 MHz.

*A solid dot with the letter "C" inside indicates the Common Traffic Advisory Frequency. (J11) — AIM ¶4-1-9*

ALL

**3641.** (Refer to Figure 26, area 2.) The control tower frequency for Addison Airport is

A— 122.95 MHz.
B— 126.0 MHz.
C— 133.4 MHz.

*The correct answer is found in the explanatory box for Addison airport in area 2: 126.0 MHz. (J37) — Sectional Chart Legend*

ALL

**3610.** (Refer to Figure 27, area 2.) What is the recommended communication procedure when inbound to land at Cooperstown Airport?

A— Broadcast intentions when 10 miles out on the CTAF/MULTICOM frequency, 122.9 MHz.
B— Contact UNICOM when 10 miles out on 122.8 MHz.
C— Circle the airport in a left turn prior to entering traffic.

*MULTICOM frequency is always 122.9 MHz, and the correct procedure is to broadcast intentions when 10 miles from the airport. (J11) — AIM ¶4-1-9*

**Answers**

| 3606 [C] | 3607 [C] | 3608 [C] | 3609 [A] | 3641 [B] | 3610 [A] |

ALL

**3611.** (Refer to Figure 27, area 4.) The CTAF/UNICOM frequency at Jamestown Airport is

A—122.0 MHz.
B—123.0 MHz.
C—123.6 MHz.

*CTAF (Common Traffic Advisory Frequency) is a frequency designed for the purpose of carrying out airport advisory practices and/or position reporting at an uncontrolled airport (which may also occur during hours when a tower is closed). The CTAF may be a UNICOM, MULTICOM, FSS, or tower frequency and is identified in the appropriate aeronautical publications. A solid dot with the letter "C" inside indicates Common Traffic Advisory Frequency; it may be a UNICOM, MULTICOM, FSS, or tower frequency. (J11) — AIM ¶4-1-9*

ALL

**3612.** (Refer to Figure 27, area 6.) What is the CTAF/UNICOM frequency at Barnes County Airport?

A—122.0 MHz.
B—122.8 MHz.
C—123.6 MHz.

*CTAF (Common Traffic Advisory Frequency) is a frequency designed for the purpose of carrying out airport advisory practices and/or position reporting at an uncontrolled airport (which may also occur during hours when a tower is closed). The CTAF may be a UNICOM, MULTICOM, FSS, or tower frequency and is identified in the appropriate aeronautical publications. A solid dot with the letter "C" inside indicates Common Traffic Advisory Frequency. (J11) — AIM ¶4-1-9*

ALL

**3791.** Automatic Terminal Information Service (ATIS) is the continuous broadcast of recorded information concerning

A—pilots of radar-identified aircraft whose aircraft is in dangerous proximity to terrain or to an obstruction.
B—nonessential information to reduce frequency congestion.
C—noncontrol information in selected high-activity terminal areas.

*ATIS is the continuous broadcast of recorded noncontrol information in selected high-activity terminal areas. (J11) — AIM ¶4-1-13*

AIR, RTC

**3811.** After landing at a tower-controlled airport, when should the pilot contact ground control?

A—When advised by the tower to do so.
B—Prior to turning off the runway.
C—After reaching a taxiway that leads directly to the parking area.

*A pilot who has just landed should not change from tower to ground frequency until advised to do so by the controller. (J13) — AIM ¶4-3-14*

AIR, RTC

**3812.** If instructed by ground control to taxi to Runway 9, the pilot may proceed

A—via taxiways and across runways to, but not onto, Runway 9.
B—to the next intersecting runway where further clearance is required.
C—via taxiways and across runways to Runway 9, where an immediate takeoff may be made.

*When ATC clears an aircraft to "taxi to" an assigned takeoff runway, the absence of holding instructions authorizes the aircraft to "cross" all runways which the taxi route intersects except the assigned takeoff runway. It does not include authorization to "Taxi on to" or "cross" the assigned takeoff runway at any point. (J13) — AIM ¶4-3-18*

ALL

**3790.** Select the UNICOM frequencies normally assigned to stations at landing areas used exclusively as heliports.

A—122.75 and 123.65 MHz.
B—123.0 and 122.95 MHz.
C—123.05 and 123.075 MHz.

*Frequencies used solely for heliports are 123.050 and 123.075. (J11) — AIM ¶4-1-11*

# Airport Traffic Area Communications and Light Signals

Unless otherwise authorized, aircraft are required to maintain two-way radio communication with the airport traffic control towers (ATCT) when operating to, from, or on the controlled airport, regardless of the weather. If radio contact cannot be maintained, ATC will direct traffic by means of light gun signals as shown in Figure 11-2.

If the aircraft radios fail while inbound to a tower-controlled airport, the pilot should remain outside or above the airport traffic area until the direction and flow of traffic has been determined and then join the airport traffic pattern and watch the tower for light signals.

The general warning signal (alternating red and green) may be followed by any other signal. For example, while on final approach for landing, an alternating red and green light followed by a flashing red light is received from the control tower. Under these circumstances, the pilot should abandon the approach, realizing the airport is unsafe for landing.

| Color & Type of Signal | Movement of Vehicles, Equipment & Personnel | Aircraft on the Ground | Aircraft in Flight |
|---|---|---|---|
| Steady green | Cleared to cross, proceed or go | Cleared for takeoff | Cleared to land |
| Flashing green | Not applicable | Cleared for taxi | Return for landing (to be followed by steady green at the proper time) |
| Steady red | STOP | STOP | Give way to other aircraft and continue circling |
| Flashing red | Clear the taxiway/runway | Taxi clear of the runway in use | Airport unsafe, do not land |
| Flashing white | Return to starting point on airport | Return to starting point on airport | Not applicable |
| Alternating red and green | Exercise extreme caution | Exercise extreme caution | Exercise extreme caution |

**Figure 11-2**

ALL

**3111.** A steady green light signal directed from the control tower to an aircraft in flight is a signal that the pilot

A—is cleared to land.
B—should give way to other aircraft and continue circling.
C—should return for landing.

*A steady green light signal directed to an aircraft in flight means that the pilot is cleared to land. (B08) — 14 CFR §91.125*

Answer (B) is incorrect because this would be a steady red signal. Answer (C) is incorrect because this would be a flashing green signal.

AIR, RTC

**3112.** Which light signal from the control tower clears a pilot to taxi?

A—Flashing green.
B—Steady green.
C—Flashing white.

*A flashing green light signal clears a pilot to taxi. (B08) — 14 CFR §91.125*

Answer (B) is incorrect because this means cleared to takeoff/land. Answer (C) is incorrect because this means return to starting point on airport.

**Answers**

3111   [A]          3112   [A]

AIR, RTC

**3113.** If the control tower uses a light signal to direct a pilot to give way to other aircraft and continue circling, the light will be

A—flashing red.
B—steady red.
C—alternating red and green.

*A steady red signal directed to an aircraft in flight indicates the pilot should give way to other aircraft and continue circling. (B08) — 14 CFR §91.125*

Answer (A) is incorrect because this means the airport is unsafe. Answer (C) is incorrect because this means the pilot should exercise extreme caution.

AIR, RTC

**3114.** A flashing white light signal from the control tower to a taxiing aircraft is an indication to

A—taxi at a faster speed.
B—taxi only on taxiways and not cross runways.
C—return to the starting point on the airport.

*A flashing white light signal to a taxiing aircraft is an indication to return to the starting point on the airport. (B08) — 14 CFR §91.125*

Answers (A) and (B) are incorrect because there are no light signals for these instructions.

ALL

**3115.** An alternating red and green light signal directed from the control tower to an aircraft in flight is a signal to

A—hold position.
B—exercise extreme caution.
C—not land; the airport is unsafe.

*An alternating red and green light signal means to exercise extreme caution. (B08) — 14 CFR §91.125*

Answer (A) is incorrect because you can't hold position in flight. Answer (C) is incorrect because this would be a flashing red signal.

AIR, RTC

**3116.** While on final approach for landing, an alternating green and red light followed by a flashing red light is received from the control tower. Under these circumstances, the pilot should

A—discontinue the approach, fly the same traffic pattern and approach again, and land.
B—exercise extreme caution and abandon the approach, realizing the airport is unsafe for landing.
C—abandon the approach, circle the airport to the right, and expect a flashing white light when the airport is safe for landing.

*An alternating red and green light means to exercise extreme caution. A flashing red light means the airport is unsafe, do not land. (B08) — 14 CFR §91.125*

Answer (A) is incorrect because the flashing red light indicates the airport is unsafe for landing. Answer (C) is incorrect because a flashing white is not applicable in flight.

AIR, RTC

**3804.** If the aircraft's radio fails, what is the recommended procedure when landing at a controlled airport?

A—Observe the traffic flow, enter the pattern, and look for a light signal from the tower.
B—Enter a crosswind leg and rock the wings.
C—Flash the landing lights and cycle the landing gear while circling the airport.

*When a transmitter, receiver, or both have become inoperative, an aircraft should observe the traffic flow, enter the pattern, and look for a light signal from the tower, when landing at a controlled airport. (J12) — AIM ¶4-2-13*

Answers (B) and (C) are incorrect because entering on the crosswind is not required and rocking the wings is used to acknowledge light signals during the day. Flashing the lights is used to acknowledge light signals during night, and a fixed gear airplane would not be able to cycle the gear.

**Answers**

| 3113 | [B] | 3114 | [C] | 3115 | [B] | 3116 | [B] | 3804 | [A] |

# VHF Direction Finder

Many flight service stations have equipment which determines the direction to an aircraft, which is transmitting on a particular VHF frequency. Availability of this service at a particular airport is shown by the notation "VHF/DF" in the Airport/Facility Directory (A/FD). The only airborne equipment required to obtain VHF/DF service is an operating VHF transmitter and receiver.

ALL
**3759.** To use VHF/DF facilities for assistance in locating an aircraft's position, the aircraft must have a

A—VHF transmitter and receiver.
B—4096-code transponder.
C—VOR receiver and DME.

*The VHF/DF receiver display indicates the magnetic direction to the aircraft each time the aircraft transmits. The DF specialist will give the pilot headings to fly. Thus, the aircraft must be equipped with an operational VHF transmitter and receiver. Transponder and VOR are not necessary. (J01) — AIM ¶1-1-18*

ALL
**3843.** The letters VHF/DF appearing in the Airport/Facility Directory for a certain airport indicate that

A—this airport is designated as an airport of entry.
B—the Flight Service Station has equipment with which to determine your direction from the station.
C—this airport has a direct-line phone to the Flight Service Station.

*FAA facilities that provide VHF/Direction Finder (DF) service are identified in the Airport/Facility Directory. The VHF/DF receiver display indicates the magnetic direction of the aircraft from the ground station each time the aircraft transmits. (J34) — AIM ¶1-1-18*

# Radar Assistance to VFR Aircraft

Radar-equipped ATC facilities provide traffic advisories and limited vectoring (called "basic radar service") to VFR aircraft, provided the aircraft can communicate with the facility, is within radar coverage, and can be radar-identified.

Stage II service provides radar advisories and sequencing for VFR aircraft. Arriving aircraft should initiate contact with approach control. Approach control will assume Stage II service is requested, unless the pilot states that the service is not wanted. Pilots of departing VFR aircraft should request Stage II terminal radar advisory service from ground control on initial contact.

At some locations Stage III service has been established to provide separation between all participating VFR aircraft and all IFR aircraft in the terminal radar service area (TRSA). Unless the pilot states "negative Stage III" on initial contact with approach control, the service will be provided.

Traffic advisories given by a radar service will refer to the other aircraft by azimuth in terms of the 12-hour clock, with 12 o'clock being the direction of flight (track), not aircraft heading. Each hour is equal to 30°. For example, an aircraft heading 090° is advised of traffic at the 3 o'clock position. The pilot should look 90° to the right of the direction of flight, or to the south. In Figure 11-3, traffic information would be issued to the pilot of aircraft A as 12 o'clock. The actual position of the traffic as seen by the pilot of aircraft A would be 2 o'clock. Traffic information issued to aircraft B would also be given as 12 o'clock, but in this case, the pilot of B would see traffic at 10 o'clock.

**Figure 11-3.** Traffic advisory

These radar programs are not to be interpreted as relieving pilots of their responsibilities to see and avoid other traffic operating in basic VFR weather conditions, to maintain appropriate terrain and obstruction clearance, or to remain in weather conditions equal to or better than the minimum required by FAA regulations. Whenever compliance with an assigned route, heading, and/or altitude is likely to compromise pilot responsibilities respecting terrain, obstruction clearance, and weather minimums, the controller should be so advised and a revised clearance or instruction obtained.

ALL
**3792.** An ATC radar facility issues the following advisory to a pilot flying on a heading of 090°:

"TRAFFIC 3 O'CLOCK, 2 MILES, WESTBOUND..."

Where should the pilot look for this traffic?

A—East.
B—South.
C—West.

*Traffic information will be given in azimuth from the aircraft in terms of the 12-hour clock. Thus, each hour would constitute an angle of 30°. Picture a clock in your lap; 3 o'clock is to your right, 9 o'clock is to your left, 12 o'clock is straight ahead, and 6 o'clock is behind you. If an aircraft is proceeding on a heading of 090° (east), traffic located at the 3 o'clock position would be 90° right of the nose, south of the aircraft. (J11) — AIM ¶4-1-14*

ALL
**3793.** An ATC radar facility issues the following advisory to a pilot flying on a heading of 360°:

"TRAFFIC 10 O'CLOCK, 2 MILES, SOUTHBOUND..."

Where should the pilot look for this traffic?

A—Northwest.
B—Northeast.
C—Southwest.

*If an aircraft is proceeding on a heading of 360° (north), traffic located at the 10 o'clock position would be 60° (left) of the nose, or to the northwest. (J11) — AIM ¶4-1-14*

AIR
**3794.** An ATC radar facility issues the following advisory to a pilot during a local flight:

"TRAFFIC 2 O'CLOCK, 5 MILES, NORTHBOUND..."

Where should the pilot look for this traffic?

A—Between directly ahead and 90° to the left.
B—Between directly behind and 90° to the right.
C—Between directly ahead and 90° to the right.

*Traffic information issued to the pilot as "2 o'clock" would mean approximately 60° right. (J11) — AIM ¶4-1-14*

AIR
**3795.** An ATC radar facility issues the following advisory to a pilot flying north in a calm wind:

"TRAFFIC 9 O'CLOCK, 2 MILES, SOUTHBOUND..."

Where should the pilot look for this traffic?

A—South.
B—North.
C—West.

*An aircraft flying north in calm wind would be heading 360°. When advised of traffic at the 9 o'clock position, the pilot should look 90° left of the nose, to the west. (J11) — AIM ¶4-1-14*

AIR, RTC
**3796.** Basic radar service in the terminal radar program is best described as

A—traffic advisories and limited vectoring to VFR aircraft.
B—mandatory radar service provided by the Automated Radar Terminal System (ARTS) program.
C—wind-shear warning at participating airports.

*In addition to the use of radar for the control of IFR aircraft, all commissioned radar facilities provide traffic advisories and limited vectoring (on a workload-permitting basis) to VFR aircraft. Radar facilities are not responsible for weather information and the service is not mandatory. (J11) — AIM ¶4-1-17*

**Answers**
3792 [B]    3793 [A]    3794 [C]    3795 [C]    3796 [A]

AIR, RTC

**3797.** From whom should a departing VFR aircraft request Stage II Terminal Radar Advisory Service during ground operations?

A—Clearance delivery.
B—Tower, just before takeoff.
C—Ground control, on initial contact.

*Pilots of departing VFR aircraft are encouraged to request radar traffic information by notifying ground control on initial contact with their request and proposed direction of flight. Note: Stage I, II and III are obsolete terms. Radar service is now classified as basic service, TRSA service, Class C service, and Class B service. (J11) — AIM ¶4-1-17*

ALL

**3798.** Stage III Service in the terminal radar program provides

A—IFR separation (1,000 feet vertical and 3 miles lateral) between all aircraft.
B—warning to pilots when their aircraft are in unsafe proximity to terrain, obstructions, or other aircraft.
C—sequencing and separation for participating VFR aircraft.

*Stage III radar provides separation of participating VFR aircraft and all IFR aircraft operating within the airspace. Note: Stage I, II and III are obsolete terms. Radar service is now classified as basic service, TRSA service, Class C service, and Class B service. (J11) — AIM ¶4-1-17*

# Transponder

A transponder is an airborne radar beacon transmitter-receiver that automatically receives signals from a ground-based radar beacon transmitter-receiver (interrogator). The transponder selectively replies (with a specific code) only to those interrogations being received on the mode to which it is set. Civil Mode A transponders have 4,096 discrete four-digit codes. This return signal is displayed on a radarscope on the ground, and a controller can then identify and pinpoint the position of each aircraft (target) under his/her control.

Some transponders are also equipped with a Mode C automatic altitude-reporting capability. This system converts aircraft altitude (in 100-foot increments) to coded digital information which is transmitted back to the interrogating radar system. With Mode C, the controller has information on the aircraft's altitude as well as its position. The IDENT feature should not be activated unless requested by ATC. Mode C, which should be operated at all times unless ATC requests otherwise, is also required for all flights above 10,000 feet MSL.

The transponder code for VFR flight is 1200. When changing transponder codes, avoid inadvertent selection of codes 7500 (hijack), 7600 (lost communications), 7700 (emergency), and 7777 (military interceptor operations).

Operation in Class A, Class B, and Class C airspace requires a transponder with Mode A/C capability and 4,096 codes available.

If air traffic control advises that radar service is being terminated, the transponder should be set to code 1200.

**Answers**

3797    [C]            3798    [C]

ALL
**3165.** An operable 4096-code transponder with an encoding altimeter is required in which airspace?

A—Class A, Class B (and within 30 miles of the Class B primary airport), and Class C.
B—Class D and Class E (below 10,000 feet MSL).
C—Class D and Class G (below 10,000 feet MSL).

*Class A, B (and within 30 miles of the Class B primary airport), and C airspace require a Mode C transponder. (B11) — 14 CFR §91.215(b)(1),(3),(4)*

AIR, RTC
**3166.** With certain exceptions, all aircraft within 30 miles of a Class B primary airport from the surface upward to 10,000 feet MSL must be equipped with

A—an operable VOR or TACAN receiver and an ADF receiver.
B—instruments and equipment required for IFR operations.
C—an operable transponder having either Mode S or 4096-code capability with Mode C automatic altitude reporting capability.

*With certain exceptions, all aircraft need encoding transponders under the 30-mile veil of Class B airspace. (B11) — 14 CFR §91.215(b)*

*Answers (A) and (B) are incorrect because they apply to IFR flight.*

ALL
**3129.** An operable 4096-code transponder and Mode C encoding altimeter are required in

A—Class B airspace and within 30 miles of the Class B primary airport.
B—Class D airspace.
C—Class E airspace below 10,000 feet MSL.

*Encoding transponders are required within all Class B airspace and within 30 miles of the primary airport even if you are below a Class B airspace layer. (B08) — 14 CFR §91.131(a), §91.215*

*Answers (B) and (C) are incorrect because transponders are not required in Class D airspace, or below 10,000 feet unless in Class B or C airspace.*

AIR, RTC
**3800.** When making routine transponder code changes, pilots should avoid inadvertent selection of which codes?

A—0700, 1700, 7000.
B—1200, 1500, 7000.
C—7500, 7600, 7700.

*When making routine code changes, pilots should avoid selecting codes 7500, 7600 or 7700, thereby preventing false alarms at automated ground facilities. (J11) — AIM ¶4-1-19*

ALL
**3801.** When operating under VFR below 18,000 feet MSL, unless otherwise authorized, what transponder code should be selected?

A—1200.
B—7600.
C—7700.

*Unless otherwise instructed by an ATC facility, adjust the transponder to reply on Mode 3/A, code 1200, regardless of altitude. (J11) — AIM ¶4-1-19*

ALL
**3803.** If Air Traffic Control advises that radar service is terminated when the pilot is departing Class C airspace, the transponder should be set to code

A—0000.
B—1200.
C—4096.

*When VFR, unless otherwise instructed by an ATC facility, adjust transponder to reply code 1200 regardless of altitude. (J11) — AIM ¶4-1-19*

REC
**3802.** Unless otherwise authorized, if flying a transponder equipped aircraft, a recreational pilot should squawk which VFR code?

A—1200.
B—7600.
C—7700.

*It is especially important for recreational pilots, who are typically not communicating with ATC, to operate the transponder and encoder so radar controllers will know the aircraft's position and altitude. (J11) — AIM ¶4-1-19*

**Answers**

| | | | | |
|---|---|---|---|---|
| 3165 [A] | 3166 [C] | 3129 [A] | 3800 [C] | 3801 [A] | 3803 [B] |
| 3802 [A] | | | | |

# Emergency Locator Transmitter (ELT)

Emergency Locator Transmitters (ELT) have been developed as a means of locating downed aircraft. Transmitting on 121.5 and 243.0 MHz, the ELT will operate continuously for at least 48 hours.

To prevent false alarms, the ELT should be tested only during the first 5 minutes after any hour and only for one to three sweeps. False alarms can also be minimized by monitoring 121.5 MHz prior to engine shutdown at the end of each flight.

Non-rechargeable batteries used in ELTs must be replaced when 50% of their useful life has expired, or when the transmitter has been in use for more than 1 cumulative hour.

AIR
**3160.** When must batteries in an emergency locator transmitter (ELT) be replaced or recharged, if rechargeable?

A—After any inadvertent activation of the ELT.
B—When the ELT has been in use for more than 1 cumulative hour.
C—When the ELT can no longer be heard over the airplane's communication radio receiver.

*ELT batteries must be replaced after 1 hour of cumulative use or when 50% of their useful life has expired, whichever comes first. (B11) — 14 CFR §91.207(c)*

AIR
**3161.** When are non-rechargeable batteries of an emergency locator transmitter (ELT) required to be replaced?

A—Every 24 months.
B—When 50 percent of their useful life expires.
C—At the time of each 100-hour or annual inspection.

*ELT batteries must be replaced after 1 hour of cumulative use or when 50% of their useful life has expired, whichever comes first. (B11) — 14 CFR §91.207(c)(1),(2)*

ALL
**3819.** When activated, an emergency locator transmitter (ELT) transmits on

A—118.0 and 118.8 MHz.
B—121.5 and 243.0 MHz.
C—123.0 and 119.0 MHz.

*ELTs transmit an audio tone on 121.5 MHz and 243.0 MHz. (J22) — AIM ¶6-2-5*

AIR
**3820.** When must the battery in an emergency locator transmitter (ELT) be replaced (or recharged if the battery is rechargeable)?

A—After one-half the battery's useful life.
B—During each annual and 100-hour inspection.
C—Every 24 calendar months.

*ELT batteries must be replaced after 1 hour of cumulative use or when 50% of their useful life has expired, whichever comes first. (J22) — AIM ¶6-2-5*

AIR
**3821.** When may an emergency locator transmitter (ELT) be tested?

A—Anytime.
B—At 15 and 45 minutes past the hour.
C—During the first 5 minutes after the hour.

*An ELT test should be conducted only during the first 5 minutes after any hour and then only for three audible sweeps. (J22) — AIM ¶6-2-5*

AIR
**3822.** Which procedure is recommended to ensure that the emergency locator transmitter (ELT) has not been activated?

A—Turn off the aircraft ELT after landing.
B—Ask the airport tower if they are receiving an ELT signal.
C—Monitor 121.5 before engine shutdown.

*Immediately after hard landings and before parking, check radio frequency 121.5 MHz. (J22) — AIM ¶6-2-5*

---

**Answers**

| | | | | | |
|---|---|---|---|---|---|
| 3160 [B] | 3161 [B] | 3819 [B] | 3820 [A] | 3821 [C] | 3822 [C] |

# Cross-Reference A:
## Answer, Subject Matter Knowledge Code, Category & Page Number

**T**he FAA does not publish a category list for any exam; therefore, the category assigned below is based on historical data and the best judgement of our researchers.

**ALL**   All aircraft
**AIR**   Airplane
**GLI**   Glider
**LTA**   Lighter-Than-Air (applies to hot air balloon, gas balloon and airship)
**REC**   Recreational
**RTC**   Rotorcraft (applies to both helicopter and gyroplane)

It is important to answer every question assigned on your FAA Knowledge Test. If in their ongoing review, the FAA test authors decide a question has no correct answer, is no longer applicable, or is otherwise defective, your answer will be marked correct no matter which one you choose. You will not be given the automatic credit unless you have marked an answer. For those questions for which none of the answer choices provide an accurate response, we have noted [X] as the Answer.

| Question | Answer | SMK Code | Category | Page |
|---|---|---|---|---|
| 3001 | [B] | (A01) | ALL | 4-8 |
| 3002 | [B] | (A01) | ALL | 4-8 |
| 3003 | [A] | (A01) | ALL | 4-33 |
| 3004 | [A] | (A01) | ALL | 4-33 |
| 3005 | [C] | (A01) | ALL | 4-3 |
| 3006 | [A] | (A02) | ALL | 3-5 |
| 3007 | [A] | (A02) | AIR, GLI | 3-5 |
| 3008 | [A] | (A02) | AIR, GLI | 3-5 |
| 3009 | [C] | (A02) | AIR, GLI | 3-5 |
| 3010 | [A] | (A02) | AIR, GLI | 3-5 |
| 3011 | [C] | (A02) | AIR | 3-6 |
| 3012-1 | [A] | (A02) | AIR | 4-42 |
| 3012-2 | [B] | (A13) | ALL | 4-42 |
| 3012-3 | [C] | (A13) | ALL | 4-42 |
| 3013-1 | [C] | (A15) | ALL | 4-40 |
| 3013-2 | [B] | (A15) | ALL | 4-41 |
| 3013-3 | [B] | (A15) | ALL | 4-41 |
| 3014 | [A] | (A16) | ALL | 4-41 |
| 3015 | [B] | (A16) | ALL | 4-41 |
| 3016 | [C] | (A20) | ALL | 4-10 |
| 3017 | [C] | (A20) | ALL | 4-11 |
| 3018 | [B] | (A20) | ALL | 4-11 |
| 3019 | [C] | (A20) | ALL | 4-11 |
| 3020 | [B] | (A20) | AIR, RTC, REC, LTA | 4-9 |
| 3021 | [C] | (A20) | AIR, RTC, REC, LTA | 4-9 |
| 3022 | [C] | (A20) | AIR, RTC, REC, LTA | 4-9 |
| 3023 | [C] | (A20) | AIR, RTC, REC, LTA | 4-9 |
| 3024 | [B] | (A20) | AIR, RTC | 4-8 |
| 3025 | [A] | (A20) | AIR | 4-14 |
| 3026 | [C] | (A20) | AIR | 4-14 |
| 3027 | [C] | (A20) | AIR | 4-14 |
| 3028 | [C] | (A20) | ALL | 4-12 |
| 3029 | [C] | (A20) | ALL | 4-12 |
| 3030 | [A] | (A20) | ALL | 4-12 |
| 3031 | [C] | (A20) | ALL | 4-12 |
| 3032 | [C] | (A20) | AIR | 4-13 |
| 3033 | [B] | (A20) | AIR, RTC | 4-13 |
| 3034 | [A] | (A20) | ALL | 4-13 |
| 3035 | [A] | (A20) | ALL | 4-15 |
| 3036 | [B] | (A21) | AIR, GLI | 4-15 |
| 3037 | [C] | (A21) | AIR, GLI | 4-15 |
| 3038 | [B] | (A29) | REC | 4-11 |
| 3039 | [B] | (A20) | ALL | 4-10 |
| 3040 | [C] | (A20) | ALL | 4-13 |
| 3041 | [A] | (A20) | ALL | 4-13 |
| 3042 | [C] | (A20) | ALL | 4-13 |
| 3043 | [A] | (A29) | REC | 4-7 |
| 3044 | [B] | (A29) | REC | 4-4 |
| 3045 | [C] | (A29) | REC | 4-5 |
| 3046 | [A] | (A29) | REC | 4-5 |
| 3047 | [C] | (A29) | REC | 4-5 |
| 3048 | [B] | (A29) | REC | 4-5 |
| 3049 | [C] | (A29) | REC | 4-5 |
| 3050 | [C] | (A29) | REC | 4-5 |
| 3051 | [B] | (A29) | REC | 4-5 |
| 3052 | [A] | (A29) | REC | 4-6 |
| 3053 | [C] | (A29) | REC | 4-6 |
| 3054 | [C] | (A29) | REC | 4-6 |
| 3055 | [A] | (A29) | REC | 4-6 |
| 3056 | [B] | (A29) | REC | 4-6 |
| 3057 | [B] | (A29) | REC | 4-6 |
| 3058 | [C] | (A29) | REC | 4-7 |
| 3059 | [C] | (A29) | REC | 4-7 |
| 3060 | [C] | (A29) | REC | 4-7 |
| 3061 | [C] | (A29) | REC | 4-7 |
| 3062 | [C] | (A20) | GLI | 4-10 |

| Question | Answer | SMK Code | Category | Page |
|---|---|---|---|---|
| 3063 | [B] | (A20) | LTA | 4-10 |
| 3064 | [A] | (A23) | ALL | 4-4 |
| 3065 | [C] | (A23) | ALL | 4-4 |
| 3066 | [B] | (A23) | AIR, RTC | 4-4 |
| 3067 | [A] | (A60) | ALL | 9-38 |
| 3068 | [B] | (A60) | ALL | 9-38 |
| 3069 | [B] | (A60) | ALL | 9-37 |
| 3070 | [B] | (B07) | ALL | 4-16 |
| 3071 | [B] | (B07) | LTA | 4-16 |
| 3072 | [B] | (B07) | ALL | 4-16 |
| 3073 | [C] | (B07) | ALL | 4-16 |
| 3074 | [B] | (B07) | ALL | 4-16 |
| 3075 | [B] | (B07) | ALL | 4-37 |
| 3076 | [B] | (B07) | ALL | 4-34 |
| 3077 | [A] | (B07) | ALL | 4-20 |
| 3078 | [A] | (B07) | ALL | 4-20 |
| 3079 | [C] | (B07) | ALL | 4-20 |
| 3080 | [B] | (B07) | ALL | 4-17 |
| 3081 | [C] | (B07) | ALL | 4-17 |
| 3082 | [C] | (B07) | ALL | 4-18 |
| 3083 | [A] | (B07) | ALL | 4-19 |
| 3084 | [C] | (B07) | ALL | 4-19 |
| 3085 | [B] | (B07) | AIR, GLI, RTC, REC | 4-19 |
| 3086 | [A] | (B07) | AIR, GLI, RTC, REC | 4-19 |
| 3087 | [B] | (B07) | AIR, GLI, RTC, REC | 4-20 |
| 3088 | [C] | (B08) | ALL | 4-34 |
| 3089 | [B] | (B08) | ALL | 4-22 |
| 3090 | [B] | (B08) | ALL | 4-22 |
| 3091 | [C] | (B08) | ALL | 4-22 |
| 3092 | [A] | (B08) | ALL | 4-22 |
| 3093 | [B] | (B08) | ALL | 4-22 |
| 3094 | [C] | (B08) | AIR, GLI, REC | 4-22 |
| 3095 | [C] | (B08) | ALL | 4-22 |
| 3096 | [B] | (B08) | AIR | 4-22 |
| 3097 | [B] | (B08) | AIR, RTC | 4-35 |
| 3098 | [A] | (B08) | AIR, RTC | 4-35 |
| 3099 | [A] | (B08) | AIR, RTC | 4-36 |
| 3100 | [B] | (B08) | AIR, RTC | 4-36 |
| 3101 | [A] | (B08) | ALL | 4-26 |
| 3102 | [C] | (B08) | AIR, GLI, LTA, REC | 4-26 |
| 3103 | [B] | (B08) | AIR, GLI, LTA, REC | 4-26 |
| 3104 | [A] | (B08) | AIR, GLI, LTA, REC | 4-26 |
| 3105 | [B] | (B08) | ALL | 3-9 |
| 3106 | [A] | (B08) | ALL | 3-9 |
| 3107 | [B] | (B08) | ALL | 3-9 |
| 3108 | [B] | (B08) | ALL | 4-25 |
| 3109 | [A] | (B08) | ALL | 4-25 |
| 3110 | [B] | (B08) | ALL | 4-25 |
| 3111 | [A] | (B08) | ALL | 11-8 |
| 3112 | [A] | (B08) | AIR, RTC | 11-8 |
| 3113 | [B] | (B08) | AIR, RTC | 11-9 |
| 3114 | [C] | (B08) | AIR, RTC | 11-9 |
| 3115 | [B] | (B08) | ALL | 11-9 |
| 3116 | [B] | (B08) | AIR, RTC | 11-9 |
| 3117 | [C] | (B08) | ALL | 9-35 |
| 3118 | [B] | (B08) | ALL | 9-35 |
| 3119 | [A] | (B08) | ALL | 9-37 |
| 3120 | [B] | (B08) | AIR, RTC | 5-12 |
| 3121 | [B] | (B08) | AIR, RTC | 5-12 |
| 3122 | [B] | (B08) | RTC | 5-5 |
| 3123 | [C] | (B08) | ALL | 5-4 |
| 3124 | [A] | (B08) | ALL | 9-36 |
| 3125 | [C] | (B08) | ALL | 9-37 |
| 3126 | [B] | (B08) | ALL | 9-34 |
| 3127 | [A] | (B08) | ALL | 9-35 |
| 3128 | [B] | (B08) | ALL | 9-35 |
| 3129 | [A] | (B08) | ALL | 11-13 |
| 3130 | [A] | (B08) | AIR, GLI | 9-34 |
| 3131 | [B] | (B09) | AIR, REC | 4-18 |
| 3132 | [C] | (B09) | AIR | 4-18 |
| 3133 | [A] | (B09) | RTC | 4-18 |
| 3134 | [B] | (B09) | REC | 4-7 |
| 3135 | [B] | (B09) | REC | 4-7 |
| 3136 | [C] | (B09) | ALL | 4-27 |
| 3137 | [A] | (B09) | AIR, GLI, LTA | 4-27 |
| 3138 | [B] | (B09) | ALL | 4-27 |
| 3139 | [B] | (B09) | ALL | 4-28 |
| 3140 | [B] | (B09) | ALL | 4-28 |
| 3141 | [A] | (B09) | ALL | 4-28 |
| 3142 | [B] | (B09) | AIR, GLI, RTC, LTA | 4-28 |
| 3143 | [A] | (B09) | AIR, GLI, LTA, REC | 4-28 |
| 3144 | [A] | (B09) | AIR, GLI, LTA | 4-28 |
| 3145 | [C] | (B09) | ALL | 4-28 |
| 3146 | [C] | (B09) | ALL | 4-29 |
| 3147 | [B] | (B09) | ALL | 4-29 |
| 3148 | [C] | (B09) | AIR, GLI, RTC, LTA | 4-29 |
| 3149 | [B] | (B09) | AIR, GLI, RTC, LTA | 4-29 |
| 3150 | [B] | (B09) | AIR | 4-30 |
| 3151 | [A] | (B09) | AIR | 4-30 |
| 3152 | [C] | (B09) | RTC | 4-31 |
| 3153 | [C] | (B09) | AIR | 4-31 |
| 3154 | [B] | (B09) | AIR | 4-31 |
| 3155 | [C] | (B09) | AIR, RTC | 4-32 |
| 3156 | [C] | (B09) | AIR, RTC | 4-32 |
| 3157 | [B] | (B09) | AIR, RTC | 4-32 |
| 3158 | [B] | (B09) | AIR, RTC | 4-32 |
| 3159 | [C] | (B11) | ALL | 4-37 |
| 3160 | [B] | (B11) | AIR | 11-14 |
| 3161 | [B] | (B11) | AIR | 11-14 |
| 3162 | [C] | (B11) | ALL | 5-27 |
| 3163 | [C] | (B11) | ALL | 5-18 |
| 3164 | [C] | (B11) | ALL | 5-18 |
| 3165 | [A] | (B11) | ALL | 11-13 |
| 3166 | [C] | (B11) | AIR, RTC | 11-13 |
| 3167 | [B] | (B12) | AIR, GLI, REC | 4-23 |
| 3168 | [B] | (B12) | AIR, GLI, REC | 4-23 |
| 3169 | [B] | (B12) | AIR, GLI, REC | 4-23 |
| 3170 | [A] | (B12) | AIR, GLI, REC | 4-24 |

| Question | Answer | SMK Code | Category | Page |
|---|---|---|---|---|
| 3171 | [C] | (B12) | AIR, GLI, RTC, REC | 4-24 |
| 3172 | [A] | (B12) | AIR, GLI, RTC, REC | 4-24 |
| 3173 | [B] | (B12) | AIR, GLI, RTC, REC | 4-24 |
| 3174 | [A] | (B12) | GLI | 2-22 |
| 3175 | [B] | (B12) | GLI | 2-22 |
| 3176 | [C] | (B12) | GLI | 2-23 |
| 3177 | [B] | (B12) | GLI | 2-23 |
| 3178 | [B] | (B12) | AIR, GLI, RTC | 4-33 |
| 3179 | [B] | (B12) | ALL | 4-33 |
| 3180-1 | [B] | (B13) | ALL | 4-38 |
| 3180-2 | [C] | (B13) | ALL | 4-38 |
| 3181-1 | [A] | (B13) | ALL | 4-39 |
| 3181-2 | [A] | (B13) | ALL | 4-39 |
| 3181-3 | [A] | (B13) | ALL | 4-43 |
| 3182 | [B] | (B13) | ALL | 4-39 |
| 3183 | [B] | (B13) | ALL | 4-41 |
| 3184 | [B] | (B13) | ALL | 4-42 |
| 3185 | [C] | (B13) | ALL | 4-39 |
| 3186 | [C] | (B13) | ALL | 4-39 |
| 3187 | [C] | (B13) | ALL | 4-37 |
| 3188 | [A] | (B13) | ALL | 4-39 |
| 3189 | [B] | (B13) | AIR, RTC | 4-40 |
| 3190 | [B] | (B13) | AIR, RTC | 4-40 |
| 3191 | [C] | (B13) | ALL | 4-40 |
| 3192 | [C] | (B13) | ALL | 4-40 |
| 3193 | [A] | (B13) | ALL | 4-42 |
| 3194 | [A] | (G11) | ALL | 4-44 |
| 3195 | [C] | (G11) | ALL | 4-44 |
| 3196 | [B] | (G11) | ALL | 4-44 |
| 3197 | [A] | (G11) | ALL | 4-44 |
| 3198 | [B] | (G12) | ALL | 4-45 |
| 3199 | [C] | (G13) | ALL | 4-45 |
| 3200 | [C] | (G13) | ALL | 4-45 |
| 3201 | [A] | (H300) | ALL | 1-7 |
| 3202 | [A] | (H300) | AIR, GLI | 1-8 |
| 3203 | [B] | (H300) | ALL | 1-4 |
| 3204 | [A] | (H300) | ALL | 1-4 |
| 3205 | [A] | (H300) | AIR | 1-8 |
| 3206 | [A] | (H300) | AIR, GLI | 6-21 |
| 3207 | [A] | (H300) | AIR | 2-14 |
| 3208 | [B] | (H301) | AIR | 2-14 |
| 3209 | [B] | (H301) | AIR | 2-14 |
| 3210 | [B] | (H302) | AIR, GLI | 1-9 |
| 3211 | [A] | (H302) | AIR, GLI | 1-9 |
| 3212 | [B] | (H302) | AIR, GLI | 1-10 |
| 3213 | [A] | (H302) | AIR | 1-7 |
| 3214 | [C] | (H303) | AIR | 1-12 |
| 3215 | [C] | (H303) | AIR | 1-12 |
| 3216 | [B] | (H303) | AIR | 1-12 |
| 3217 | [B] | (H303) | AIR | 1-12 |
| 3218 | [B] | (H303) | AIR | 1-13 |
| 3219 | [C] | (H305) | AIR, GLI | 1-15 |
| 3220 | [A] | (H305) | AIR, GLI | 1-15 |
| 3221 | [B] | (H307) | AIR, RTC | 2-10 |
| 3222 | [C] | (H307) | AIR, RTC | 2-10 |
| 3223 | [A] | (H307) | AIR | 2-4 |
| 3224 | [B] | (H307) | AIR | 2-9 |
| 3225 | [B] | (H307) | AIR, RTC | 2-5 |
| 3226 | [B] | (H307) | AIR, RTC | 2-5 |
| 3227 | [A] | (H307) | AIR | 2-6 |
| 3228 | [A] | (H307) | AIR, RTC | 2-5 |
| 3229 | [C] | (H307) | AIR, RTC | 2-6 |
| 3230 | [A] | (H307) | AIR, RTC | 2-7 |
| 3231 | [C] | (H307) | AIR | 2-7 |
| 3232 | [B] | (H307) | AIR, RTC | 2-7 |
| 3233 | [B] | (H307) | AIR, RTC | 2-7 |
| 3234 | [A] | (H307) | AIR, RTC | 2-7 |
| 3235 | [C] | (H307) | AIR | 2-7 |
| 3236 | [A] | (H307) | AIR, RTC | 2-8 |
| 3237 | [C] | (H307) | AIR, RTC | 2-8 |
| 3238 | [C] | (H307) | AIR, RTC | 2-9 |
| 3239 | [B] | (H307) | AIR | 2-10 |
| 3240 | [B] | (H307) | AIR, RTC | 2-9 |
| 3241 | [A] | (H307) | AIR, RTC | 2-11 |
| 3242 | [A] | (H307) | AIR, RTC | 2-9 |
| 3243 | [C] | (H307) | AIR, RTC | 2-9 |
| 3244 | [C] | (H307) | AIR, RTC | 2-11 |
| 3245 | [A] | (H307) | AIR, RTC | 2-11 |
| 3246 | [B] | (H308) | AIR, LTA, RTC | 8-22 |
| 3247 | [B] | (H312) | AIR, GLI, RTC | 3-3 |
| 3248 | [C] | (H312) | ALL | 3-3 |
| 3249 | [C] | (H312) | ALL | 3-4 |
| 3250 | [C] | (H312) | ALL | 3-12 |
| 3251 | [C] | (H312) | ALL | 3-12 |
| 3252 | [A] | (H312) | ALL | 3-12 |
| 3253 | [B] | (H312) | ALL | 3-12 |
| 3254 | [C] | (H312) | ALL | 3-9 |
| 3255 | [A] | (H312) | ALL | 3-10 |
| 3256 | [A] | (H312) | ALL | 3-10 |
| 3257 | [B] | (H312) | ALL | 3-10 |
| 3258 | [B] | (H312) | ALL | 3-10 |
| 3259 | [B] | (H312) | ALL | 3-10 |
| 3260 | [B] | (H312) | ALL | 3-11 |
| 3261 | [C] | (H312) | ALL | 3-11 |
| 3262 | [C] | (H312) | AIR, GLI, RTC | 3-4 |
| 3263 | [C] | (H312) | AIR, GLI | 1-14 |
| 3264 | [C] | (H312) | ALL | 3-6 |
| 3265 | [A] | (H312) | AIR | 3-6 |
| 3266 | [C] | (H312) | AIR, GLI | 3-6 |
| 3267 | [C] | (H312) | AIR | 3-6 |
| 3268 | [C] | (H312) | ALL | 3-7 |
| 3269 | [C] | (H312) | ALL | 3-7 |
| 3270 | [B] | (H312) | AIR | 3-7 |
| 3271 | [C] | (H312) | AIR | 3-7 |
| 3272 | [C] | (H312) | AIR | 3-7 |
| 3273 | [B] | (H312) | AIR | 3-7 |
| 3274 | [C] | (H312) | AIR | 3-7 |
| 3275 | [A] | (H313) | AIR | 3-14 |

| Question | Answer | SMK Code | Category | Page | Question | Answer | SMK Code | Category | Page |
|----------|--------|----------|----------|------|----------|--------|----------|----------|------|
| 3276 | [C] | (H313) | AIR, RTC | 3-14 | 3330 | [A] | (H748) | RTC | 2-17 |
| 3277 | [C] | (H313) | AIR, RTC | 3-13 | 3331 | [C] | (H748) | RTC | 2-17 |
| 3278 | [C] | (H313) | ALL | 3-13 | 3332 | [B] | (H749) | RTC | 2-18 |
| 3279 | [C] | (H314) | ALL | 3-14 | 3333 | [C] | (H745) | RTC | 2-18 |
| 3280 | [B] | (H314) | AIR, GLI, RTC | 3-15 | 3334 | [A] | (H745) | RTC | 2-18 |
| 3281 | [C] | (H314) | AIR, GLI, RTC | 3-15 | 3335 | [C] | (H747) | RTC | 2-18 |
| 3282 | [C] | (H314) | ALL | 3-15 | 3336 | [B] | (H727) | RTC | 2-18 |
| 3283 | [C] | (H314) | ALL | 3-15 | 3337 | [C] | (H727) | RTC | 2-18 |
| 3284 | [B] | (H314) | ALL | 3-15 | 3338 | [B] | (H767) | RTC | 2-18 |
| 3285 | [B] | (H314) | GLI | 3-16 | 3339 | [B] | (H766) | RTC | 2-19 |
| 3286 | [A] | (H314) | AIR, GLI, RTC | 3-15 | 3340 | [C] | (N20) | GLI | 2-23 |
| 3287 | [B] | (H315) | AIR, GLI | 1-10 | 3341 | [B] | (N21) | GLI | 2-23 |
| 3288 | [A] | (H315) | AIR, GLI | 1-10 | 3342 | [B] | (N21) | GLI | 2-23 |
| 3289 | [C] | (H312) | ALL | 8-22 | 3343 | [B] | (N22) | GLI | 2-23 |
| 3290 | [C] | (H317) | AIR, RTC | 8-22 | 3344 | [C] | (N22) | GLI | 2-23 |
| 3291 | [B] | (H317) | AIR, RTC | 8-22 | 3345 | [B] | (N27) | GLI | 2-24 |
| 3292 | [C] | (H317) | AIR, RTC | 8-22 | 3346 | [A] | (N27) | GLI | 2-24 |
| 3293 | [A] | (H317) | AIR, RTC | 8-22 | 3347 | [B] | (N27) | GLI | 2-24 |
| 3294 | [C] | (H317) | ALL | 8-23 | 3348 | [C] | (N27) | GLI | 2-24 |
| 3295 | [A] | (H317) | ALL | 8-23 | 3349 | [B] | (N27) | GLI | 2-25 |
| 3296 | [C] | (H317) | AIR, RTC | 8-24 | 3350 | [A] | (N34) | GLI | 6-5 |
| 3297 | [A] | (H317) | AIR, RTC | 8-24 | 3351 | [C] | (O155) | LTA | 2-30 |
| 3298 | [A] | (H317) | ALL | 8-24 | 3352 | [C] | (O170) | LTA | 2-30 |
| 3299 | [C] | (H317) | ALL | 8-25 | 3353 | [B] | (O170) | LTA | 2-30 |
| 3300 | [B] | (H317) | AIR, RTC | 8-25 | 3354 | [A] | (O170) | LTA | 2-30 |
| 3301 | [A] | (H534) | AIR, GLI | 1-12 | 3355 | [A] | (O220) | LTA | 2-30 |
| 3302 | [C] | (H516) | AIR | 5-14 | 3356 | [C] | (O220) | LTA | 2-30 |
| 3303 | [A] | (H516) | AIR | 5-14 | 3357 | [A] | (O220) | LTA | 2-30 |
| 3304 | [A] | (H516) | AIR | 5-15 | 3358 | [B] | (O220) | LTA | 2-31 |
| 3305 | [A] | (H516) | AIR | 5-15 | 3359 | [A] | (O220) | LTA | 2-31 |
| 3306 | [A] | (H516) | AIR | 5-15 | 3360 | [A] | (O220) | LTA | 2-31 |
| 3307 | [C] | (H516) | AIR | 5-15 | 3361 | [C] | (O220) | LTA | 2-31 |
| 3308 | [B] | (H516) | AIR | 5-15 | 3362 | [C] | (O220) | LTA | 2-31 |
| 3309 | [C] | (H540) | AIR, GLI | 1-14 | 3363 | [B] | (O220) | LTA | 2-31 |
| 3310 | [A] | (H540) | AIR, GLI | 1-14 | 3364 | [A] | (O30) | LTA | 2-31 |
| 3311 | [C] | (H303) | AIR, GLI | 1-14 | 3365 | [C] | (O30) | LTA | 2-32 |
| 3312 | [A] | (H317) | AIR, GLI, RTC | 1-16 | 3366 | [C] | (O30) | LTA | 2-32 |
| 3313 | [A] | (H317) | AIR, GLI, RTC | 1-16 | 3367 | [C] | (O150) | LTA | 2-32 |
| 3314 | [B] | (H317) | AIR, GLI, RTC | 1-16 | 3368 | [C] | (P01) | LTA | 2-32 |
| 3315 | [B] | (H317) | ALL | 1-16 | 3369 | [B] | (P01) | LTA | 2-32 |
| 3316 | [A] | (H303) | AIR, GLI | 1-13 | 3370 | [C] | (P01) | LTA | 2-32 |
| 3317 | [A] | (H702) | RTC | 1-4 | 3371 | [C] | (P01) | LTA | 2-33 |
| 3318 | [A] | (H703) | RTC | 2-16 | 3372 | [A] | (P04) | LTA | 2-33 |
| 3319 | [B] | (H703) | RTC | 2-16 | 3373 | [A] | (P04) | LTA | 2-33 |
| 3320 | [C] | (H703) | RTC | 2-16 | 3374 | [A] | (P04) | LTA | 2-33 |
| 3321 | [A] | (H703) | RTC | 2-16 | 3375 | [A] | (P04) | LTA | 2-33 |
| 3322 | [B] | (H703) | RTC | 2-16 | 3376 | [C] | (P04) | LTA | 2-33 |
| 3323 | [C] | (H703) | RTC | 2-16 | 3377 | [C] | (P04) | LTA | 2-33 |
| 3324 | [C] | (H703) | RTC | 1-16 | 3378 | [C] | (P04) | LTA | 2-33 |
| 3325 | [B] | (H703) | RTC | 2-17 | 3379 | [B] | (P11) | LTA | 2-34 |
| 3326 | [C] | (H705) | RTC | 2-17 | 3380 | [C] | (P11) | LTA | 2-34 |
| 3327 | [B] | (H705) | RTC | 2-17 | 3381 | [C] | (I21) | ALL | 6-3 |
| 3328 | [A] | (H703) | RTC | 2-17 | 3382 | [A] | (I21) | ALL | 6-3 |
| 3329 | [B] | (H748) | RTC | 2-17 | 3383 | [C] | (I21) | ALL | 6-5 |

| Question | Answer | SMK Code | Category | Page | | Question | Answer | SMK Code | Category | Page |
|---|---|---|---|---|---|---|---|---|---|---|
| 3384 | [A] | (I21) | ALL | 6-6 | | 3438 | [A] | (I30) | ALL | 6-16 |
| 3385 | [A] | (I21) | ALL | 6-9 | | 3439 | [A] | (I30) | ALL | 6-16 |
| 3386 | [A] | (I21) | ALL | 8-25 | | 3440 | [B] | (I30) | ALL | 6-16 |
| 3387 | [C] | (I22) | AIR, GLI, RTC | 3-11 | | 3441 | [B] | (I30) | ALL | 6-17 |
| 3388 | [B] | (I22) | ALL | 3-11 | | 3442 | [C] | (I30) | ALL | 6-15 |
| 3389 | [C] | (I22) | ALL | 3-11 | | 3443 | [A] | (I31) | ALL | 6-20 |
| 3390 | [C] | (I22) | ALL | 3-12 | | 3444 | [C] | (I31) | ALL | 6-7 |
| 3391 | [B] | (I22) | ALL | 3-12 | | 3445 | [B] | (I31) | ALL | 6-20 |
| 3392 | [A] | (I22) | ALL | 3-10 | | 3446 | [C] | (I31) | ALL | 6-20 |
| 3393 | [C] | (I22) | ALL | 3-12 | | 3447 | [C] | (I33) | ALL | 6-21 |
| 3394 | [B] | (I22) | ALL | 8-25 | | 3448 | [C] | (I35) | GLI | 6-3 |
| 3395 | [B] | (I23) | ALL | 6-5 | | 3449 | [C] | (I35) | GLI | 6-17 |
| 3396 | [A] | (I23) | LTA | 2-34 | | 3450 | [C] | (I35) | ALL | 6-5 |
| 3397 | [C] | (I24) | ALL | 6-7 | | 3451 | [C] | (I35) | GLI | 6-9 |
| 3398 | [B] | (I24) | ALL | 6-7 | | 3452 | [A] | (I36) | ALL | 6-17 |
| 3399 | [A] | (I24) | ALL | 6-7 | | 3453 | [A] | (I54) | ALL | 7-20 |
| 3400 | [A] | (I24) | ALL | 6-7 | | 3454 | [B] | (I54) | ALL | 7-20 |
| 3401 | [B] | (I24) | ALL | 6-21 | | 3455 | [A] | (H320) | ALL | 7-21 |
| 3402 | [C] | (I24) | ALL | 6-19 | | 3456 | [C] | (I54) | ALL | 7-21 |
| 3403 | [B] | (I25) | ALL | 6-9 | | 3457 | [C] | (I54) | ALL | 7-22 |
| 3404 | [A] | (I25) | ALL | 6-9 | | 3458 | [C] | (I54) | ALL | 7-22 |
| 3405 | [A] | (I25) | ALL | 6-10 | | 3459 | [A] | (I54) | ALL | 7-22 |
| 3406 | [A] | (I25) | ALL | 6-12 | | 3460 | [A] | (I54) | ALL | 7-22 |
| 3407 | [C] | (I25) | ALL | 6-12 | | 3461 | [A] | (I54) | ALL | 7-22 |
| 3408 | [A] | (I25) | ALL | 6-10 | | 3462 | [C] | (I55) | ALL | 7-4 |
| 3409 | [C] | (I25) | ALL | 6-13 | | 3463 | [B] | (I55) | ALL | 7-4 |
| 3410 | [B] | (I25) | ALL | 6-13 | | 3464 | [A] | (I55) | ALL | 7-4 |
| 3411 | [C] | (I25) | LTA | 7-24 | | 3465 | [B] | (I55) | ALL | 7-4 |
| 3412 | [A] | (I25) | ALL | 6-10 | | 3466 | [B] | (I55) | ALL | 7-4 |
| 3413 | [A] | (I25) | ALL | 6-10 | | 3467 | [A] | (I55) | ALL | 7-5 |
| 3414 | [C] | (I25) | ALL | 6-10 | | 3468 | [A] | (I55) | LTA | 7-24 |
| 3415 | [B] | (I26) | ALL | 6-13 | | 3469 | [C] | (I55) | LTA | 7-24 |
| 3416 | [B] | (I26) | ALL | 6-13 | | 3470 | [C] | (I55) | GLI | 7-23 |
| 3417 | [C] | (I26) | ALL | 6-14 | | 3471 | [A] | (I55) | GLI | 7-24 |
| 3418 | [B] | (I26) | ALL | 6-14 | | 3472 | [C] | (I56) | ALL | 7-6 |
| 3419 | [B] | (I26) | ALL | 6-14 | | 3473 | [C] | (I56) | ALL | 7-6 |
| 3420 | [C] | (I26) | ALL | 6-14 | | 3474 | [A] | (I56) | ALL | 7-6 |
| 3421 | [C] | (I27) | ALL | 6-8 | | 3475 | [C] | (I56) | ALL | 7-7 |
| 3422 | [A] | (I27) | ALL | 6-8 | | 3476 | [B] | (I56) | ALL | 7-7 |
| 3423 | [A] | (I27) | ALL | 6-8 | | 3477 | [C] | (I57) | LTA | 7-24 |
| 3424 | [C] | (I27) | ALL | 6-12 | | 3478 | [C] | (I57) | ALL | 7-9 |
| 3425 | [A] | (I28) | ALL | 6-14 | | 3479 | [A] | (I57) | ALL | 7-7 |
| 3426 | [C] | (I28) | ALL | 6-18 | | 3480 | [A] | (I57) | ALL | 7-7 |
| 3427 | [B] | (I28) | ALL | 6-18 | | 3481 | [B] | (I57) | ALL | 7-8 |
| 3428 | [C] | (I28) | ALL | 6-18 | | 3482 | [C] | (I57) | ALL | 7-8 |
| 3429 | [C] | (I28) | AIR, GLI, RTC | 6-19 | | 3483 | [C] | (I57) | ALL | 7-8 |
| 3430 | [C] | (I29) | AIR, GLI, RTC | 6-19 | | 3484 | [A] | (I57) | ALL | 7-8 |
| 3431 | [C] | (I29) | AIR, GLI, RTC | 6-21 | | 3485 | [A] | (I57) | ALL | 7-8 |
| 3432 | [A] | (I29) | AIR | 6-22 | | 3486 | [B] | (I57) | ALL | 7-8 |
| 3433 | [B] | (I30) | ALL | 6-12 | | 3487 | [A] | (I57) | ALL | 7-9 |
| 3434 | [B] | (I30) | ALL | 6-16 | | 3488 | [A] | (I57) | ALL | 7-9 |
| 3435 | [B] | (I30) | ALL | 6-16 | | 3489 | [A] | (I57) | ALL | 7-9 |
| 3436 | [A] | (I30) | ALL | 6-16 | | 3490 | [C] | (I57) | ALL | 7-10 |
| 3437 | [B] | (I30) | ALL | 6-16 | | 3491 | [C] | (I57) | ALL | 7-10 |

| Question | Answer | SMK Code | Category | Page |
|---|---|---|---|---|
| 3492 | [B] | (I57) | ALL | 7-10 |
| 3493 | [A] | (I57) | ALL | 7-10 |
| 3494 | [A] | (I57) | ALL | 7-20 |
| 3495 | [C] | (I57) | ALL | 7-19 |
| 3496 | [A] | (I57) | ALL | 7-19 |
| 3497 | [C] | (I57) | ALL | 7-19 |
| 3498 | [B] | (I57) | ALL | 7-20 |
| 3499 | [B] | (I57) | ALL | 7-20 |
| 3500 | [A] | (I57) | ALL | 7-11 |
| 3501 | [C] | (I57) | ALL | 7-11 |
| 3502 | [C] | (I57) | ALL | 7-11 |
| 3503 | [A] | (I57) | ALL | 7-11 |
| 3504 | [C] | (I57) | ALL | 7-12 |
| 3505 | [C] | (I57) | ALL | 7-12 |
| 3506 | [B] | (I57) | ALL | 7-12 |
| 3507 | [A] | (I58) | ALL | 7-13 |
| 3508 | [B] | (I58) | ALL | 7-13 |
| 3509 | [A] | (I59) | ALL | 7-13 |
| 3510 | [C] | (I59) | ALL | 7-14 |
| 3511 | [C] | (I59) | ALL | 7-14 |
| 3512 | [C] | (I59) | ALL | 7-14 |
| 3513 | [A] | (I60) | ALL | 7-15 |
| 3514 | [A] | (I60) | ALL | 7-15 |
| 3515 | [C] | (I60) | ALL | 7-16 |
| 3516 | [A] | (I60) | ALL | 7-16 |
| 3517 | [A] | (I60) | ALL | 7-16 |
| 3518 | [A] | (I60) | ALL | 7-16 |
| 3519 | [A] | (I60) | ALL | 7-16 |
| 3520 | [B] | (I64) | ALL | 7-17 |
| 3521 | [A] | (I64) | ALL | 7-17 |
| 3522 | [B] | (I64) | ALL | 7-18 |
| 3523 | [A] | (I64) | ALL | 7-18 |
| 3524 | [B] | (I64) | ALL | 7-18 |
| 3525 | [A] | (I62) | GLI | 7-23 |
| 3526 | [C] | (H320) | ALL | 7-22 |
| 3527 | [B] | (H320) | ALL | 7-23 |
| 3528 | [C] | (H320) | ALL | 7-23 |
| 3529 | [C] | (H342) | ALL | 9-22 |
| 3530 | [A] | (H340) | ALL | 9-4 |
| 3531 | [C] | (H346) | ALL | 9-12 |
| 3532 | [B] | (H348) | ALL | 10-8 |
| 3533 | [A] | (H348) | ALL | 10-7 |
| 3534 | [B] | (H346) | AIR, RTC | 9-22 |
| 3535 | [B] | (H340) | ALL | 9-4 |
| 3536 | [C] | (H340) | ALL | 9-4 |
| 3537 | [B] | (H342) | LTA | 9-29 |
| 3538 | [C] | (H346) | AIR, RTC | 9-26 |
| 3539 | [B] | (H348) | AIR, RTC | 10-6 |
| 3540 | [C] | (H346) | AIR, RTC | 9-22 |
| 3541 | [C] | (H346) | AIR, RTC | 9-23 |
| 3542 | [B] | (H346) | AIR, RTC | 9-23 |
| 3543 | [B] | (H340) | ALL | 9-4 |
| 3544 | [A] | (H341) | LTA | 9-30 |
| 3545 | [A] | (H346) | AIR, RTC | 9-26 |

| Question | Answer | SMK Code | Category | Page |
|---|---|---|---|---|
| 3546 | [A] | (H346) | AIR, RTC | 9-26 |
| 3547 | [C] | (H346) | AIR, RTC | 9-27 |
| 3548 | [C] | (H346) | AIR, RTC | 9-24 |
| 3549 | [B] | (H346) | AIR, RTC | 9-24 |
| 3550 | [A] | (H346) | AIR, RTC | 9-27 |
| 3551 | [B] | (H346) | AIR | 9-28 |
| 3552 | [B] | (H346) | ALL | 10-4 |
| 3553 | [B] | (H348) | ALL | 10-6 |
| 3554 | [C] | (H342) | AIR, RTC | 9-24 |
| 3555 | [B] | (H346) | LTA | 9-30 |
| 3556 | [A] | (H346) | ALL | 9-12 |
| 3557 | [A] | (H342) | LTA | 9-30 |
| 3558 | [A] | (H346) | LTA | 9-31 |
| 3559 | [B] | (H348) | ALL | 10-4 |
| 3560 | [A] | (H348) | ALL | 10-7 |
| 3561 | [B] | (H348) | ALL | 10-7 |
| 3562 | [A] | (H346) | AIR | 9-25 |
| 3563 | [A] | (H346) | AIR | 9-25 |
| 3564 | [B] | (H346) | GLI | 9-28 |
| 3565 | [A] | (H346) | AIR | 9-27 |
| 3566 | [A] | (H348) | ALL | 10-5 |
| 3567 | [A] | (H340) | ALL | 9-4 |
| 3568 | [A] | (H346) | ALL | 9-12 |
| 3569 | [B] | (H342) | LTA | 9-31 |
| 3570 | [C] | (H348) | ALL | 10-7 |
| 3571 | [C] | (H340) | ALL | 9-6 |
| 3572 | [B] | (H340) | ALL | 9-6 |
| 3573 | [C] | (H340) | ALL | 9-6 |
| 3574 | [B] | (H340) | ALL | 9-6 |
| 3575 | [C] | (H340) | ALL | 9-7 |
| 3576 | [A] | (H340) | ALL | 9-7 |
| 3577 | [C] | (H348) | ALL | 10-5 |
| 3578 | [B] | (H348) | ALL | 10-5 |
| 3579 | [A] | (H348) | ALL | 10-6 |
| 3580 | [C] | (H348) | ALL | 10-11 |
| 3581 | [C] | (H348) | ALL | 10-11 |
| 3582 | [C] | (H348) | ALL | 10-11 |
| 3583 | [B] | (H348) | ALL | 10-11 |
| 3584 | [C] | (H348) | ALL | 10-11 |
| 3585 | [A] | (H348) | ALL | 10-11 |
| 3586 | [C] | (H348) | ALL | 10-12 |
| 3587 | [B] | (H348) | ALL | 10-12 |
| 3588 | [C] | (H348) | ALL | 10-12 |
| 3589 | [C] | (H348) | ALL | 10-12 |
| 3590 | [A] | (H348) | ALL | 10-12 |
| 3591 | [B] | (H348) | ALL | 10-13 |
| 3592 | [B] | (H348) | ALL | 10-13 |
| 3593 | [A] | (H348) | ALL | 10-13 |
| 3594 | [B] | (H348) | ALL | 10-13 |
| 3595 | [C] | (H348) | ALL | 10-13 |
| 3596 | [B] | (H348) | ALL | 10-14 |
| 3597 | [C] | (H348) | ALL | 10-14 |
| 3598-1 | [C] | (J01) | ALL | 10-8 |
| 3598-2 | [C] | (J01) | ALL | 10-14 |

| Question | Answer | SMK Code | Category | Page |
|----------|--------|----------|----------|------|
| 3598-3 | [B] | (J01) | ALL | 10-14 |
| 3598-4 | [C] | (J01) | ALL | 10-14 |
| 3599 | [C] | (J08) | ALL | 9-34 |
| 3600 | [B] | (J08) | ALL | 9-34 |
| 3601 | [B] | (J09) | ALL | 9-39 |
| 3602 | [C] | (J09) | ALL | 9-40 |
| 3603 | [A] | (J10) | ALL | 11-5 |
| 3604 | [A] | (J11) | ALL | 11-5 |
| 3605 | [B] | (J11) | ALL | 11-6 |
| 3606 | [C] | (J11) | ALL | 11-6 |
| 3607 | [C] | (J11) | ALL | 11-6 |
| 3608 | [C] | (J11) | ALL | 11-6 |
| 3609 | [A] | (J11) | ALL | 11-6 |
| 3610 | [A] | (J11) | ALL | 11-7 |
| 3611 | [B] | (J11) | ALL | 11-7 |
| 3612 | [B] | (J11) | ALL | 11-4 |
| 3613 | [A] | (J12) | ALL | 11-4 |
| 3614 | [A] | (J12) | ALL | 11-5 |
| 3615 | [C] | (J12) | ALL | 11-5 |
| 3616 | [C] | (J25) | ALL | 11-5 |
| 3617 | [A] | (J25) | ALL | 7-21 |
| 3618 | [A] | (J28) | ALL | 9-40 |
| 3619 | [B] | (J34) | ALL | 5-16 |
| 3620-1 | [C] | (J37) | ALL | 4-29 |
| 3620-2 | [A] | (J37) | ALL | 4-29 |
| 3621-1 | [C] | (J37) | ALL | 4-30 |
| 3621-2 | [C] | (J37) | ALL | 4-30 |
| 3622 | [B] | (J37) | ALL | 9-38 |
| 3623 | [C] | (J37) | ALL | 9-38 |
| 3624 | [B] | (J37) | ALL | 9-39 |
| 3625 | [C] | (J37) | ALL | 9-38 |
| 3626 | [B] | (J37) | ALL | 9-37 |
| 3627 | [B] | (J37) | ALL | 9-37 |
| 3628 | [B] | (J37) | ALL | 9-35 |
| 3629 | [C] | (J37) | ALL | 9-38 |
| 3630 | [A] | (J37) | ALL | 11-5 |
| 3631 | [A] | (J37) | ALL | 9-8 |
| 3632 | [C] | (J37) | ALL | 9-8 |
| 3633 | [A] | (J37) | ALL | 9-8 |
| 3634 | [B] | (J37) | ALL | 9-9 |
| 3635 | [B] | (J37) | ALL | 9-9 |
| 3636 | [C] | (J37) | ALL | 9-9 |
| 3637 | [C] | (J37) | ALL | 9-7 |
| 3638 | [B] | (J37) | ALL | 9-8 |
| 3639 | [B] | (J37) | ALL | 9-8 |
| 3640 | [C] | (J37) | ALL | 9-8 |
| 3641 | [B] | (J37) | ALL | 11-6 |
| 3642 | [B] | (J37) | AIR | 9-8 |
| 3643 | [C] | (J37) | ALL | 10-3 |
| 3644 | [C] | (J37) | LTA | 9-9 |
| 3645 | [B] | (J37) | LTA | 9-9 |
| 3646 | [C] | (J37) | LTA | 9-10 |
| 3647 | [A] | (N23) | GLI | 6-4 |
| 3648 | [C] | (N27) | GLI | 9-28 |
| 3649 | [B] | (N27) | GLI | 9-29 |
| 3650 | [C] | (N34) | GLI | 9-29 |
| 3651 | [A] | (H307) | AIR, RTC | 2-11 |
| 3652 | [A] | (H307) | AIR, RTC | 2-11 |
| 3653 | [A] | (H308) | AIR | 2-12 |
| 3654 | [B] | (H308) | AIR | 2-12 |
| 3655 | [B] | (H308) | AIR | 2-12 |
| 3656 | [A] | (H309) | AIR, RTC | 2-4 |
| 3657 | [B] | (H309) | AIR | 2-4 |
| 3658 | [A] | (H311) | ALL | 2-15 |
| 3659 | [B] | (H311) | ALL | 2-15 |
| 3660 | [B] | (H311) | ALL | 2-15 |
| 3661 | [A] | (H316) | AIR, RTC | 8-4 |
| 3662 | [C] | (H316) | AIR, RTC | 8-4 |
| 3663 | [C] | (H316) | AIR, RTC | 8-4 |
| 3664 | [B] | (H316) | AIR | 8-6 |
| 3665 | [B] | (H316) | AIR | 8-6 |
| 3666 | [A] | (H316) | AIR | 8-6 |
| 3667 | [B] | (H316) | AIR | 8-7 |
| 3668 | [C] | (H316) | AIR | 8-7 |
| 3669 | [A] | (H316) | AIR | 8-11 |
| 3670 | [B] | (H316) | AIR | 8-11 |
| 3671 | [C] | (H316) | AIR | 8-12 |
| 3672 | [B] | (H316) | AIR | 8-12 |
| 3673 | [B] | (H316) | AIR | 8-12 |
| 3674 | [A] | (H316) | AIR | 8-8 |
| 3675 | [B] | (H316) | AIR | 8-8 |
| 3676 | [A] | (H316) | AIR | 8-9 |
| 3677 | [B] | (H316) | AIR | 8-9 |
| 3678 | [C] | (H317) | AIR | 8-30 |
| 3679 | [B] | (H317) | AIR | 8-30 |
| 3680 | [B] | (H317) | AIR | 8-30 |
| 3681 | [B] | (H317) | AIR | 8-31 |
| 3682 | [C] | (H317) | AIR | 8-31 |
| 3683 | [B] | (H317) | AIR | 8-38 |
| 3684 | [C] | (H317) | AIR | 8-38 |
| 3685 | [C] | (H317) | AIR | 8-38 |
| 3686 | [C] | (H317) | AIR | 8-38 |
| 3687 | [B] | (H317) | AIR | 8-39 |
| 3688 | [A] | (H317) | ALL | 8-39 |
| 3689 | [B] | (H317) | AIR | 8-32 |
| 3690 | [B] | (H317) | AIR | 8-32 |
| 3691 | [C] | (H317) | AIR | 8-33 |
| 3692 | [B] | (H317) | AIR | 8-33 |
| 3693 | [B] | (H317) | AIR | 8-34 |
| 3694 | [A] | (H317) | AIR | 8-34 |
| 3695 | [B] | (H317) | AIR | 8-34 |
| 3696 | [B] | (H317) | AIR | 8-34 |
| 3697 | [C] | (H317) | AIR | 8-35 |
| 3698 | [B] | (H317) | ALL | 8-35 |
| 3699 | [B] | (H317) | RTC | 8-35 |
| 3700 | [A] | (H317) | RTC | 8-35 |
| 3701 | [C] | (H317) | RTC | 8-36 |
| 3702 | [C] | (H317) | RTC | 8-26 |

| Question | Answer | SMK Code | Category | Page | Question | Answer | SMK Code | Category | Page |
|---|---|---|---|---|---|---|---|---|---|
| 3703 | [C] | (H317) | RTC | 8-28 | 3756 | [B] | (I35) | GLI | 2-26 |
| 3704 | [A] | (H317) | RTC | 8-28 | 3757 | [B] | (I35) | GLI | 2-26 |
| 3705 | [B] | (H317) | AIR | 8-27 | 3758 | [A] | (I35) | GLI | 2-26 |
| 3706 | [B] | (H317) | AIR | 8-27 | 3759 | [A] | (J01) | ALL | 11-10 |
| 3707 | [A] | (H317) | AIR | 8-27 | 3760 | [B] | (J03) | AIR, RTC | 5-12 |
| 3708 | [A] | (H317) | AIR | 8-28 | 3761 | [A] | (J03) | AIR, RTC | 5-12 |
| 3709 | [B] | (M52) | ALL | 4-43 | 3762 | [C] | (J03) | AIR | 5-13 |
| 3710 | [B] | (H507) | ALL | 5-25 | 3763 | [B] | (J03) | AIR | 5-13 |
| 3711 | [A] | (H582) | AIR, RTC | 2-11 | 3764 | [C] | (J03) | AIR | 5-13 |
| 3712 | [B] | (H564) | AIR, RTC, LTA | 5-25 | 3765 | [B] | (J03) | AIR, RTC | 5-13 |
| 3713 | [A] | (H564) | AIR, RTC, LTA | 5-25 | 3766 | [B] | (J03) | AIR, RTC | 5-13 |
| 3714 | [C] | (H564) | AIR, RTC, LTA | 5-26 | 3767 | [B] | (J03) | AIR, RTC | 5-13 |
| 3715 | [A] | (H567) | AIR, RTC, LTA | 5-27 | 3768 | [C] | (J03) | AIR, RTC | 5-9 |
| 3716 | [A] | (H567) | AIR, RTC, LTA | 5-27 | 3769 | [B] | (J03) | ALL | 5-9 |
| 3717 | [C] | (H567) | AIR, RTC, LTA | 5-27 | 3770 | [A] | (J03) | AIR, RTC, LTA | 5-10 |
| 3718 | [B] | (H568) | AIR, RTC | 5-9 | 3771 | [B] | (J03) | AIR, RTC, LTA | 5-10 |
| 3719 | [C] | (H573) | AIR, RTC | 5-4 | 3772 | [B] | (J03) | AIR, RTC, LTA | 5-10 |
| 3720 | [C] | (H76) | RTC | 8-13 | 3773 | [B] | (J05) | AIR, RTC, LTA | 5-6 |
| 3721 | [A] | (H76) | RTC | 8-13 | 3774 | [B] | (J05) | AIR, GLI, RTC, REC | 5-6 |
| 3722 | [B] | (H76) | RTC | 8-13 | 3775 | [A] | (J05) | AIR, GLI, RTC, REC | 5-7 |
| 3723 | [B] | (H76) | RTC | 8-14 | 3776 | [C] | (J05) | AIR, GLI, RTC, REC | 5-7 |
| 3724 | [A] | (H76) | RTC | 8-14 | 3777 | [C] | (J05) | AIR, GLI, RTC, REC | 5-7 |
| 3725 | [B] | (H76) | RTC | 8-14 | 3778 | [C] | (J05) | ALL | 5-7 |
| 3726 | [B] | (H76) | RTC | 8-15 | 3779 | [C] | (J08) | ALL | 9-36 |
| 3727 | [C] | (H76) | RTC | 8-16 | 3780 | [C] | (J08) | ALL | 9-36 |
| 3728 | [B] | (H76) | RTC | 8-15 | 3781 | [C] | (J08) | ALL | 9-36 |
| 3729 | [A] | (H719) | RTC | 8-16 | 3782 | [C] | (J08) | ALL | 9-37 |
| 3730 | [A] | (H719) | RTC | 8-17 | 3783 | [B] | (J09) | ALL | 9-39 |
| 3731 | [B] | (H719) | RTC | 8-17 | 3784 | [A] | (J09) | LTA | 9-40 |
| 3732 | [C] | (H720) | RTC | 8-29 | 3785 | [C] | (J09) | ALL | 9-39 |
| 3733 | [B] | (H720) | RTC | 2-19 | 3786 | [B] | (J09) | ALL | 9-39 |
| 3734 | [B] | (H745) | RTC | 2-19 | 3787 | [C] | (J10) | ALL | 9-36 |
| 3735 | [C] | (H747) | RTC | 1-17 | 3788 | [C] | (J10) | ALL | 9-36 |
| 3736-1 | [C] | (H747) | RTC | 2-19 | 3789 | [C] | (J10) | ALL | 9-40 |
| 3736-2 | [A] | (H747) | RTC | 2-19 | 3790 | [C] | (J11) | ALL | 11-7 |
| 3737 | [A] | (H78) | RTC | 2-19 | 3791 | [C] | (J11) | ALL | 11-7 |
| 3738 | [B] | (H78) | RTC | 2-20 | 3792 | [B] | (J11) | ALL | 11-11 |
| 3739 | [C] | (H738) | RTC | 2-20 | 3793 | [A] | (J11) | ALL | 11-11 |
| 3740 | [A] | (H738) | RTC | 2-20 | 3794 | [C] | (J11) | AIR | 11-11 |
| 3741 | [C] | (H746) | RTC | 2-20 | 3795 | [C] | (J11) | AIR | 11-11 |
| 3742 | [B] | (H746) | RTC | 2-20 | 3796 | [A] | (J11) | AIR, RTC | 11-11 |
| 3743 | [C] | (H739) | RTC | 2-21 | 3797 | [C] | (J11) | AIR, RTC | 11-12 |
| 3744 | [C] | (H742) | RTC | 2-21 | 3798 | [C] | (J11) | ALL | 11-12 |
| 3745 | [B] | (H742) | RTC | 2-21 | 3799 | [A] | (J11) | ALL | 9-36 |
| 3746 | [B] | (H743) | RTC | 2-21 | 3800 | [C] | (J11) | AIR, RTC | 11-13 |
| 3747 | [A] | (H743) | RTC | 2-21 | 3801 | [A] | (J11) | ALL | 11-13 |
| 3748 | [C] | (H744) | RTC | 2-22 | 3802 | [A] | (J11) | REC | 11-13 |
| 3749 | [A] | (H743) | RTC | 2-22 | 3803 | [B] | (J11) | ALL | 11-13 |
| 3750 | [B] | (I35) | GLI | 2-25 | 3804 | [A] | (J12) | AIR, RTC | 11-9 |
| 3751 | [A] | (I35) | GLI | 2-25 | 3805 | [B] | (J13) | AIR, GLI, RTC, REC | 5-7 |
| 3752 | [C] | (I35) | GLI | 2-25 | 3806 | [A] | (J13) | AIR, GLI, RTC, REC | 5-7 |
| 3753 | [C] | (I35) | GLI | 2-25 | 3807 | [A] | (J13) | ALL | 5-4 |
| 3754 | [A] | (I35) | GLI | 2-25 | 3808 | [C] | (J13) | ALL | 5-4 |
| 3755 | [B] | (I35) | GLI | 2-25 | 3809 | [A] | (J13) | ALL | 5-4 |

| Question | Answer | SMK Code | Category | Page | Question | Answer | SMK Code | Category | Page |
|----------|--------|----------|----------|------|----------|--------|----------|----------|------|
| 3810 | [C] | (J13) | ALL | 5-5 | 3864 | [B] | (N21) | GLI | 8-36 |
| 3811 | [A] | (J13) | AIR, RTC | 11-7 | 3865 | [B] | (N21) | GLI | 8-36 |
| 3812 | [A] | (J13) | AIR, RTC | 11-7 | 3866 | [C] | (N21) | GLI | 8-37 |
| 3813 | [B] | (J14) | AIR, RTC | 4-31 | 3867 | [B] | (N21) | GLI | 8-37 |
| 3814 | [A] | (J14) | AIR, RTC | 10-8 | 3868 | [C] | (N21) | GLI | 8-37 |
| 3815 | [A] | (J15) | AIR, RTC | 4-35 | 3869 | [C] | (N30) | GLI | 2-27 |
| 3816 | [B] | (J15) | AIR, RTC | 4-35 | 3870 | [B] | (N30) | GLI | 2-27 |
| 3817 | [C] | (J15) | AIR, RTC | 4-35 | 3871 | [C] | (N30) | GLI | 2-27 |
| 3818 | [B] | (J15) | ALL | 4-35 | 3872 | [A] | (N30) | GLI | 2-27 |
| 3819 | [B] | (J22) | ALL | 11-14 | 3873 | [B] | (N30) | GLI | 2-27 |
| 3820 | [A] | (J22) | AIR | 11-14 | 3874 | [C] | (N30) | GLI | 2-27 |
| 3821 | [C] | (J22) | AIR | 11-14 | 3875 | [C] | (N30) | GLI | 2-28 |
| 3822 | [C] | (J22) | AIR | 11-14 | 3876 | [B] | (N30) | GLI | 2-28 |
| 3823 | [A] | (J25) | ALL | 11-5 | 3877 | [B] | (N30) | GLI | 2-28 |
| 3824 | [C] | (J27) | AIR, GLI, RTC | 1-18 | 3878 | [A] | (N30) | GLI | 2-28 |
| 3825 | [C] | (J27) | AIR, GLI, RTC | 1-18 | 3879 | [C] | (N30) | GLI | 2-28 |
| 3826 | [A] | (J27) | AIR, GLI, RTC | 1-18 | 3880 | [C] | (N32) | GLI | 2-28 |
| 3827 | [C] | (J27) | AIR | 1-19 | 3881 | [C] | (N32) | GLI | 2-29 |
| 3828 | [B] | (J27) | AIR, GLI, RTC | 1-19 | 3882 | [B] | (N32) | GLI | 2-29 |
| 3829 | [A] | (J27) | AIR, GLI, RTC | 1-19 | 3883 | [B] | (N32) | GLI | 2-29 |
| 3830 | [B] | (J27) | AIR, GLI, RTC | 1-19 | 3884 | [C] | (N34) | GLI | 2-29 |
| 3831 | [B] | (J28) | ALL | 9-40 | 3885 | [A] | (O220) | LTA | 2-34 |
| 3832 | [B] | (J31) | ALL | 5-18 | 3886 | [C] | (O220) | LTA | 2-34 |
| 3833 | [C] | (J31) | ALL | 5-26 | 3887 | [B] | (O220) | LTA | 8-19 |
| 3834 | [B] | (J31) | ALL | 5-26 | 3888 | [C] | (O220) | LTA | 8-19 |
| 3835 | [A] | (J31) | ALL | 5-26 | 3889 | [C] | (O220) | LTA | 8-19 |
| 3836 | [C] | (J31) | ALL | 5-26 | 3890 | [C] | (O220) | LTA | 8-20 |
| 3837 | [C] | (J33) | ALL | 4-25 | 3891 | [B] | (O220) | LTA | 8-25 |
| 3838 | [A] | (J34) | AIR, RTC | 5-16 | 3892 | [C] | (O220) | LTA | 8-26 |
| 3839 | [C] | (J34) | AIR, RTC | 5-16 | 3893 | [B] | (O220) | LTA | 8-20 |
| 3840 | [A] | (J34) | AIR, RTC, REC | 5-16 | 3894 | [A] | (O220) | LTA | 8-20 |
| 3841 | [B] | (J34) | ALL | 5-17 | 3895 | [A] | (O220) | LTA | 2-34 |
| 3842 | [B] | (J34) | ALL | 5-17 | 3896 | [C] | (O220) | LTA | 2-34 |
| 3843 | [B] | (J34) | ALL | 11-10 | 3897 | [B] | (O220) | LTA | 2-35 |
| 3844 | [A] | (J31) | ALL | 5-18 | 3898 | [A] | (O220) | LTA | 2-35 |
| 3845 | [A] | (J31) | ALL | 5-18 | 3899 | [C] | (O220) | LTA | 2-35 |
| 3846 | [A] | (J31) | ALL | 5-18 | 3900 | [C] | (O220) | LTA | 2-35 |
| 3847 | [B] | (J31) | ALL | 5-19 | 3901 | [B] | (O265) | LTA | 2-35 |
| 3848 | [A] | (J31) | ALL | 5-19 | 3902 | [C] | (O220) | LTA | 2-35 |
| 3849 | [C] | (J31) | ALL | 5-26 | 3903 | [B] | (O220) | LTA | 2-36 |
| 3850 | [B] | (J31) | ALL | 5-19 | 3904 | [C] | (O220) | LTA | 2-36 |
| 3851 | [A] | (J31) | ALL | 5-19 | 3905 | [C] | (O10) | LTA | 2-36 |
| 3852 | [B] | (J31) | ALL | 5-19 | 3906 | [A] | (O220) | LTA | 2-36 |
| 3853 | [A] | (J31) | ALL | 5-19 | 3907 | [B] | (O220) | LTA | 2-36 |
| 3854 | [A] | (M52) | ALL | 4-43 | 3908 | [B] | (O30) | LTA | 2-36 |
| 3855 | [B] | (M52) | ALL | 4-43 | 3909 | [B] | (O30) | LTA | 2-36 |
| 3856 | [C] | (M52) | ALL | 4-43 | 3910 | [B] | (O263) | LTA | 2-36 |
| 3857 | [A] | (N31) | GLI | 2-26 | 3911 | [A] | (P03) | LTA | 2-37 |
| 3858 | [C] | (N31) | GLI | 2-26 | 3912 | [C] | (P11) | LTA | 2-37 |
| 3859 | [C] | (N21) | GLI | 2-26 | 3913 | [B] | (P11) | LTA | 2-37 |
| 3860 | [B] | (N21) | GLI | 2-27 | 3914 | [A] | (P11) | LTA | 2-37 |
| 3861 | [C] | (N21) | GLI | 8-18 | 3915 | [C] | (P11) | LTA | 2-37 |
| 3862 | [B] | (N21) | GLI | 8-18 | 3916 | [Reserved] | | | |
| 3863 | [B] | (N21) | GLI | 8-19 | 3917 | [Reserved] | | | |

| Question | Answer | SMK Code | Category | Page |
|---|---|---|---|---|
| 3918 | [Reserved] | | | |
| 3919 | [Reserved] | | | |
| 3920 | [Reserved] | | | |
| 3921 | [Reserved] | | | |
| 3922 | [Reserved] | | | |
| 3923 | [Reserved] | | | |
| 3924 | [Reserved] | | | |
| 3925 | [Reserved] | | | |
| 3926 | [Reserved] | | | |
| 3927 | [Reserved] | | | |
| 3928 | [Reserved] | | | |
| 3929 | [Reserved] | | | |
| 3930 | [Reserved] | | | |
| 3931 | [A] | (L05) | ALL | 5-23 |
| 3932 | [C] | (L05) | ALL | 5-23 |
| 3933 | [C] | (L05) | ALL | 5-23 |
| 3934 | [C] | (L05) | ALL | 5-23 |
| 3935 | [B] | (L05) | ALL | 5-23 |
| 3936 | [C] | (L05) | ALL | 5-23 |
| 3937 | [C] | (L05) | ALL | 5-24 |
| 3938 | [C] | (L05) | ALL | 5-24 |
| 3939 | [A] | (L05) | ALL | 5-24 |
| 3940 | [A] | (L05) | ALL | 5-24 |

| Question | Answer | SMK Code | Category | Page |
|---|---|---|---|---|
| 3941 | [Reserved] | | | |
| 3942 | [Reserved] | | | |
| 3943 | [Reserved] | | | |
| 3944 | [Reserved] | | | |
| 3945 | [Reserved] | | | |
| 3946 | [Reserved] | | | |
| 3947 | [Reserved] | | | |
| 3948 | [Reserved] | | | |
| 3949 | [Reserved] | | | |
| 3950 | [Reserved] | | | |
| 3951 | [C] | (J13) | ALL | 5-8 |
| 3952 | [A] | (J13) | ALL | 5-8 |
| 3953 | [A] | (J13) | ALL | 5-8 |
| 3954 | [A] | (J13) | ALL | 5-8 |
| 3955 | [B] | (J13) | ALL | 5-8 |

# Cross-Reference B:
## Subject Matter Knowledge Code & Question Number

The subject matter knowledge codes establish the specific reference for the knowledge standard. When reviewing results of your knowledge test, you should compare the subject matter knowledge code(s) on your test report to the ones found below. All the questions on the Recreational and Private tests have been broken down into their subject matter knowledge codes and listed under the appropriate reference. This will be helpful for both review and preparation for the practical test. This list of Subject Matter Knowledge Codes is taken from Advisory Circular 60-25E.

## 14 CFR Part 1: Definitions and Abbreviations

A01 ......... General Definitions
3001, 3002, 3003, 3004, 3005

A02 ......... Abbreviations and Symbols
3006, 3007, 3008, 3009, 3010, 3011, 3012-1

## 14 CFR Part 39: Airworthiness Directives

A13 ......... General
3012-2, 3012-3

## 14 CFR Part 43: Maintenance, Preventive Maintenance, Rebuilding, and Alteration

A15 ......... General
3013-1, 3013-2, 3013-3

A16 ......... Appendixes
3014, 3015

## 14 CFR Part 61: Certification: Pilots, Flight Instructors, and Ground Instructors

A20 ......... General
3016, 3017, 3018, 3019, 3020, 3021, 3022, 3023, 3024, 3025, 3026, 3027, 3028, 3029, 3030, 3031, 3032, 3033, 3034, 3035, 3039, 3040, 3041, 3042, 3062, 3063

A21 ......... Aircraft Ratings and Pilot Authorizations
3036, 3037

A23 ......... Private Pilots
3064, 3065, 3066

A29 ......... Recreational Pilot
3038, 3043, 3044, 3045, 3046, 3047, 3048, 3049, 3050, 3051, 3052, 3053, 3054, 3055, 3056, 3057, 3058, 3059, 3060, 3061

# 14 CFR Part 71: Designation of Class A, B, C, D, and E Airspace Areas; Air Traffic Service Routes; and Reporting Points

**A60** ......... General: Class A Airspace
    **3067, 3068, 3069**

# 14 CFR Part 91: General Operating and Flight Rules

**B07** ......... General
    **3070, 3071, 3072, 3073, 3074, 3075, 3076, 3077, 3078, 3079, 3080, 3081, 3082, 3083, 3084, 3085, 3086, 3087**

**B08** ......... Flight Rules: General
    **3088, 3089, 3090, 3091, 3092, 3093, 3094, 3095, 3096, 3097, 3098, 3099, 3100, 3101, 3102, 3103, 3104, 3105, 3106, 3107, 3108, 3109, 3110, 3111, 3112, 3113, 3114, 3115, 3116, 3117, 3118, 3119, 3120, 3121, 3122, 3123, 3124, 3125, 3126, 3127, 3128, 3129, 3130**

**B09** ......... Visual Flight Rules
    **3131, 3132, 3133, 3134, 3135, 3136, 3137, 3138, 3139, 3140, 3141, 3142, 3143, 3144, 3145, 3146, 3147, 3148, 3149, 3150, 3151, 3152, 3153, 3154, 3155, 3156, 3157, 3158**

**B11** ......... Equipment, Instrument, and Certification Requirements
    **3159, 3160, 3161, 3162, 3163, 3164, 3165, 3166**

**B12** ......... Special Flight Operations
    **3167, 3168, 3169, 3170, 3171, 3172, 3173, 3174, 3175, 3176, 3177, 3178, 3179**

**B13** ......... Maintenance, Preventive Maintenance, and Alterations
    **3180-1, 3180-2, 3181-1, 3181-2, 3181-3, 3182, 3183, 3184, 3185, 3186, 3187, 3188, 3189, 3190, 3191, 3192, 3193**

# NTSB 830: Rules Pertaining to the Notification and Reporting of Aircraft Accidents or Incidents and Overdue Aircraft, and Preservation of Aircraft Wreckage, Mail, Cargo, and Records

**G11** ........ Initial Notification of Aircraft Accidents, Incidents, and Overdue Aircraft
    **3194, 3195, 3196, 3197**

**G12** ........ Preservation of Aircraft Wreckage, Mail, Cargo, and Records
    **3198**

**G13** ........ Reporting of Aircraft Accidents, Incidents, and Overdue Aircraft
    **3199, 3200**

# AC 61-13B: Basic Helicopter Handbook

**H76** ......... Weight and Balance
    **3720, 3721, 3722, 3723, 3724, 3725, 3726, 3727, 3728**

**H78** ......... Some Hazards of Helicopter Flight
    **3737, 3738**

# FAA-H-8083-21: Rotorcraft Flying Handbook

**H702**....... General Aerodynamics
   **3317**

**H703**....... Aerodynamics of Flight
   **3318, 3319, 3320, 3321, 3322, 3323, 3324, 3325, 3328**

**H705**....... Helicopter Flight Controls
   **3326, 3327**

**H719**....... Weight and Balance
   **3729, 3730, 3731**

**H720**....... Performance
   **3732, 3733**

**H727**....... Taxiing
   **3336, 3337**

**H738**....... Running/Rolling Takeoff
   **3739, 3740**

**H739**....... Rapid Deceleration (Quick Stop)
   **3743**

**H742**....... Slope Operations
   **3744, 3745**

**H743**....... Confined Area Operations
   **3746, 3747, 3749**

**H744**....... Pinnacle and Ridgeline Operations
   **3748**

**H745**....... Helicopter Emergencies
   **3333, 3334, 3734**

**H746**....... Autorotation
   **3741, 3742**

**H747**....... Height/Velocity Diagram
   **3335, 3735, 3736-1, 3736-2**

**H748**....... Retreating Blade Stall
   **3329, 3330, 3331**

**H749**....... Ground Resonance
   **3332**

# AC 61-23: Pilot's Handbook of Aeronautical Knowledge

**H300** ....... Forces Acting on the Airplane in Flight
**3201, 3202, 3203, 3204, 3205, 3206, 3207**

**H301** ....... Turning Tendency (Torque Effect)
**3208, 3209**

**H302** ....... Airplane Stability
**3210, 3211, 3212, 3213**

**H303** ....... Loads and Load Factors
**3214, 3215, 3216, 3217, 3218, 3311, 3316**

**H305** ....... Flight Control Systems
**3219, 3220**

**H307** ....... Engine Operation
**3221, 3222, 3223, 3224, 3225, 3226, 3227, 3228, 3229, 3230, 3231, 3232, 3233, 3234, 3235, 3236, 3237, 3238, 3239, 3240, 3241, 3242, 3243, 3244, 3245, 3651, 3652**

**H308** ....... Propeller
**3246, 3653, 3654, 3655**

**H309** ....... Starting the Engine
**3656, 3657**

**H311** ....... Aircraft Documents, Maintenance, and Inspection
**3658, 3659, 3660**

**H312** ....... The Pitot-Static System and Associated Instruments
**3247, 3248, 3249, 3250, 3251, 3252, 3253, 3254, 3255, 3256, 3257, 3258, 3259, 3260, 3261, 3262, 3263, 3264, 3265, 3266, 3267, 3268, 3269, 3270, 3271, 3272, 3273, 3274, 3289**

**H313** ....... Gyroscopic Flight Instruments
**3275, 3276, 3277, 3278**

**H314** ....... Magnetic Compass
**3279, 3280, 3281, 3282, 3283, 3284, 3285, 3286**

**H315** ....... Weight Control
**3287, 3288**

**H316** ....... Balance, Stability, and Center of Gravity
**3661, 3662, 3663, 3664, 3665, 3666, 3667, 3668, 3669, 3670, 3671, 3672, 3673, 3674, 3675, 3676, 3677**

**H317** ....... Airplane Performance
**3290, 3291, 3292, 3293, 3294, 3295, 3296, 3297, 3298, 3299, 3300, 3312, 3313, 3314, 3315, 3678, 3679, 3680, 3681, 3682, 3683, 3684, 3685, 3686, 3687, 3688, 3689, 3690, 3691, 3692, 3693, 3694, 3695, 3696, 3697, 3698, 3699, 3700, 3701, 3702, 3703, 3704, 3705, 3706, 3707, 3708**

**H320** ....... Weather Briefings
**3455, 3526, 3527, 3528**

**H340** ....... Latitude and Longitude
   **3530, 3535, 3536, 3543, 3567, 3571, 3572, 3573, 3574, 3575, 3576**

**H341** ....... Effect of Wind
   **3544**

**H342** ....... Basic Calculations
   **3529, 3537, 3554, 3557, 3569**

**H346** ....... Charting the Course
   **3531, 3534, 3538, 3540, 3541, 3542, 3545, 3546, 3547, 3548, 3549, 3550, 3551, 3552, 3555, 3556,
   3558, 3562, 3563, 3564, 3565, 3568**

**H348** ....... Radio Navigation
   **3532, 3533, 3539, 3553, 3559, 3560, 3561, 3566, 3570, 3577, 3578, 3579, 3580, 3581, 3582, 3583,
   3584, 3585, 3586, 3587, 3588, 3589, 3590, 3591, 3592, 3593, 3594, 3595, 3596, 3597**

## FAA-H-8083-3: Airplane Flying Handbook

**H507** ....... Collision Avoidance
   **3710**

**H516** ....... Taxiing
   **3302, 3303, 3304, 3305, 3306, 3307, 3308**

**H534** ....... Turns
   **3301**

**H540** ....... Spins
   **3309, 3310**

**H564** ....... Night Vision
   **3712, 3713, 3714**

**H567** ....... Airplane Equipment and Lighting
   **3715, 3716, 3717**

**H568** ....... Airport and Navigation Lighting Aids
   **3718**

**H573** ....... Approaches and Landings
   **3719**

**H582** ....... Systems and Equipment Malfunctions
   **3711**

## FAA-H-8083-21: Rotorcraft Flying Handbook

H766....... Gyroplane Flight Operations
**3339**

H767....... Gyroplane Emergencies
**3338**

## AC 00-6: Aviation Weather

I21 .......... Temperature
**3381, 3382, 3383, 3384, 3385, 3386**

I22 .......... Atmospheric Pressure and Altimetry
**3387, 3388, 3389, 3390, 3391, 3392, 3393, 3394**

I23 .......... Wind
**3395, 3396**

I24 .......... Moisture, Cloud Formation, and Precipitation
**3397, 3398, 3399, 3400, 3401, 3402**

I25 .......... Stable and Unstable Air
**3403, 3404, 3405, 3406, 3407, 3408, 3409, 3410, 3411, 3412, 3413, 3414**

I26 .......... Clouds
**3415, 3416, 3417, 3418, 3419, 3420**

I27 .......... Air Masses and Fronts
**3421, 3422, 3423, 3424**

I28 .......... Turbulence
**3425, 3426, 3427, 3428, 3429**

I29 .......... Icing
**3430, 3431, 3432**

I30 .......... Thunderstorms
**3433, 3434, 3435, 3436, 3437, 3438, 3439, 3440, 3441, 3442**

I31 .......... Common IFR Producers
**3443, 3444, 3445, 3446**

I33 .......... Arctic Weather
**3447**

I35 .......... Soaring Weather
**3448, 3449, 3450, 3451, 3750, 3751, 3752, 3753, 3754, 3755, 3756, 3757, 3758**

I36 .......... Glossary of Weather Terms
**3452**

# AC 00-45: Aviation Weather Services

**I54** .......... The Aviation Weather Service Program
**3453, 3454, 3456, 3457, 3458, 3459, 3460, 3461**

**I55** .......... Aviation Routine Weather Report (METAR)
**3462, 3463, 3464, 3465, 3466, 3467, 3468, 3469, 3470, 3471**

**I56** .......... Pilot and Radar Reports, Satellite Pictures, and Radiosonde Additional Data (RADATs)
**3472, 3473, 3474, 3475, 3476**

**I57** .......... Aviation Weather Forecasts
**3477, 3478, 3479, 3480, 3481, 3482, 3483, 3484, 3485, 3486, 3487, 3488, 3489, 3490, 3491, 3492, 3493, 3494, 3495, 3496, 3497, 3498, 3499, 3500, 3501, 3502, 3503, 3504, 3505, 3506**

**I58** .......... Surface Analysis Chart
**3507, 3508**

**I59** .......... Weather Depiction Chart
**3509, 3510, 3511, 3512**

**I60** .......... Radar Summary Chart
**3513, 3514, 3515, 3516, 3517, 3518, 3519**

**I62** .......... Composite Moisture Stability Chart
**3525**

**I64** .......... Significant Weather Prognostics
**3520, 3521, 3522, 3523, 3524**

# AIM: Aeronautical Information Manual

**J01** ......... Air Navigation Radio Aids
**3598-1, 3598-2, 3598-3, 3598-4, 3759**

**J03** ......... Airport Lighting Aids
**3760, 3761, 3762, 3763, 3764, 3765, 3766, 3767, 3768, 3769, 3770, 3771, 3772**

**J05** ......... Airport Marking Aids and Signs
**3773, 3774, 3775, 3776, 3777, 3778**

**J08** ......... Controlled Airspace
**3599, 3600, 3779, 3780, 3781, 3782**

**J09** ......... Special Use Airspace
**3601, 3602, 3783, 3784, 3785, 3786**

**J10** ........ Other Airspace Areas
**3603, 3787, 3788, 3789**

**J11** ......... Service Available to Pilots
**3604, 3605, 3606, 3607, 3608, 3609, 3610, 3611, 3612, 3790, 3791, 3792, 3793, 3794, 3795, 3796, 3797, 3798, 3799, 3800, 3801, 3802, 3803**

**J12** ......... Radio Communications Phraseology and Techniques
**3613, 3614, 3615, 3804**

**J13** ......... Airport Operations
**3805, 3806, 3807, 3808, 3809, 3810, 3811, 3812, 3951, 3952, 3953, 3954, 3955**

**J14** ......... ATC Clearance/Separations
**3813, 3814**

**J15** ......... Preflight
**3815, 3816, 3817, 3818**

**J22** ......... Emergency Services Available to Pilots
**3819, 3820, 3821, 3822**

**J25** ......... Meteorology
**3616, 3617, 3823**

**J27** ......... Wake Turbulence
**3824, 3825, 3826, 3827, 3828, 3829, 3830**

**J28** ......... Bird Hazards, and Flight Over National Refuges, Parks, and Forests
**3618, 3831**

**J31** ......... Fitness for Flight
**3832, 3833, 3834, 3835, 3836, 3844, 3845, 3846, 3847, 3848, 3849, 3850, 3851, 3852, 3853**

**J33** ......... Pilot Controller Glossary
**3837**

**J34** ......... Airport/Facility Directory
**3619, 3838, 3839, 3840, 3841, 3842, 3843**

**J37** ......... Sectional Chart
**3620-1, 3620-2, 3621-1, 3621-2, 3622, 3623, 3624, 3625, 3626, 3627, 3628, 3629, 3630, 3631, 3632, 3633, 3634, 3635, 3636, 3637, 3638, 3639, 3640, 3641, 3642, 3643, 3644, 3645, 3646**

## Additional Advisory Circulars

**L05** ......... AC 60-22, Aeronautical Decision Making
**3931, 3932, 3933, 3934, 3935, 3936, 3937, 3938, 3939, 3940**

**M52** ........ AC 00-2, Advisory Circular Checklist
**3709, 3854, 3855, 3856**

## Soaring Flight Manual—Jeppesen Sanderson, Inc.

**N20** ......... Sailplane Aerodynamics
**3340**

**N21** ......... Performance Considerations
**3341, 3342, 3859, 3860, 3861, 3862, 3863, 3864, 3865, 3866, 3867, 3868**

**N22** ......... Flight Instruments
**3343, 3344**

**N23** ......... Weather for Soaring
**3647**

**N27** ......... Computations for Soaring
**3345, 3346, 3347, 3348, 3349, 3648, 3649**

**N30** ......... Aerotow Launch Procedures
**3869, 3870, 3871, 3872, 3873, 3874, 3875, 3876, 3877, 3878, 3879**

**N31** ......... Ground Launch Procedures
**3857, 3858**

**N32** ......... Basic Flight Maneuvers and Traffic
**3880, 3881, 3882, 3883**

**N34** ......... Cross-Country Soaring
**3350, 3650, 3884**

# Flight Instructor Manual—Balloon Federation of America

**O10** ........ Flight Instruction Aids
**3905**

# Balloon Digest—Balloon Federation of America

**O150** ...... Balloon–Theory and Practice
**3367**

**O155** ...... Structure of the Modern Balloon
**3351**

**O170** ...... Propane and Fuel Management
**3352, 3353, 3354**

# Balloon Ground School—Balloon Publishing Company

**O220** ...... Balloon Operations
**3355, 3356, 3357, 3358, 3359, 3360, 3361, 3362, 3363, 3885, 3886, 3887, 3888, 3889, 3890, 3891, 3892, 3893, 3894, 3895, 3896, 3897, 3898, 3899, 3900, 3902, 3903, 3904, 3906, 3907**

# How to Fly a Balloon—Balloon Publishing Company

**O263** ...... Maneuvering
**3910**

**O265** ...... Landings
**3901**

# Powerline Excerpts—Balloon Federation of America

**O30** ........ Excerpts
    **3364, 3365, 3366, 3908, 3909**

# Goodyear Airship Operations Manual

**P01** ......... Buoyancy
    **3368, 3369, 3370, 3371**

**P03** ......... Free Ballooning
    **3911**

**P04** ......... Aerostatics
    **3372, 3373, 3374, 3375, 3376, 3377, 3378**

**P11** ........ Operating Instructions
    **3379, 3380, 3912, 3913, 3914, 3915**

**NOTE:** AC 00-2, Advisory Circular Checklist, transmits the status of all FAA advisory circulars (ACs), as well as FAA internal publications and miscellaneous flight information such as Aeronautical Information Manual, Airport/Facility Directory, knowledge test guides, practical test standards, and other material directly related to a certificate or rating. To obtain a free copy of AC 00-2, send your request to:

Department of Transportation
Utilization and Storage Section
M-443.2
Washington, DC 20590